STOPPING THE PANZERS
The Untold Story of D-Day

Marc Milner

University Press of Kansas

Published by the University Press of Kansas (Lawrence, Kansas
66045), which was organized by the Kansas Board of Regents and
is operated and funded by Emporia State University, Fort Hays State
University, Kansas State University, Pittsburg State University, the
University of Kansas, and Wichita State University

Library of Congress Cataloging-in-Publication Data
Milner, Marc.
Stopping the panzers : the untold story of D-Day / Marc Milner.
    pages   cm. — (Modern war studies)
Includes bibliographical references and index.
ISBN 978-0-7006-2003-6 (cloth : alk. paper)
1. Operation Overlord. 2. World War, 1939–1945—Campaigns—
France—Normandy. 3. World War, 1939–1945—Tank warfare.
I. Title. II. Title: Untold story of D-Day.
D756.5.N6M495 2014
940.54'21421—dc23
2014029772

British Library Cataloguing-in-Publication Data is available.

Printed in the United States

10 9 8 7 6 5 4 3 2 1

The paper used in this publication is recycled and contains 30
percent postconsumer waste. It is acid free and meets the minimum
requirements of the American National Standard for Permanence of
Paper for Printed Library Materials Z39.48-1992.

Once upon a time there was a war, but so long ago and so shouldered out of the way by other wars and other kinds of wars that even people who were there are apt to forget.

John Steinbeck, *Once There Was a War*, 1958

CONTENTS

MAPS

ABBREVIATIONS

AGRA   army group, Royal Artillery
AHEC   Army Heritage and Education Center
APCBS   armor-piercing, capped ballistic shell
AVRE   armored vehicle, Royal Engineers
CCRA   corps commander, Royal Artillery
CSR   Canadian Scottish Regiment
CinC   commander in chief
COSSAC   chief of staff to the supreme Allied commander and/or his
           staff
CRA   commander, Royal Artillery (division level)
DD   duplex drive, swimming Sherman tanks
DF   defensive fire
DHH   Directorate of History and Heritage, Ottawa
DUKW   amphibious truck
FOO   forward observation officer
FOB   forward officer, bombardment (naval)
FUSAG   1st US Army Group
GR   grenadier regiment
IJP   Initial Joint Plan
JIC   Joint Intelligence Committee
KSLI   King's Shropshire Light Infantry
LAC   Library and Archives of Canada
LCA   landing craft, assault
LCMSDS   Laurier Centre for Military Strategic and Disarmament
           Studies
LCT   landing craft, tank
M7   105mm self-propelled gun

M10	self-propelled antitank gun
NNSH	North Nova Scotia Highlanders
NSR	North Shore (New Brunswick) Regiment
OKW	Oberkommando der Wehrmacht
PIAT	projectile, infantry antitank
PR	panzer regiment
PG	panzer grenadier
PGR	panzer grenadier regiment
PGLR	panzer grenadier Lehr regiment
POW	prisoner of war
RA	Royal Artillery
RAF	Royal Air Force
RCA	Royal Canadian Artillery
RCAF	Royal Canadian Air Force
RCT	regimental combat team
RM	Royal Marines
RMAS	Royal Marine Assault Squadron
RWR	Royal Winnipeg Rifles
SHAEF	Supreme Headquarters, Allied Expeditionary Force
SOS	prearranged emergency close fire support
SPs	self-propelled guns
SS	Schutzen Staffel, Nazi military force
TNA	The National Archives, Kew, England
WN	Widerstandsnest (strongpoint)
WO	War Office, UK

ACKNOWLEDGMENTS

This book has been decades in the making. Indeed, as the son of a D-Day vet who fought in these epic engagements, I have long been aware of the landings and the initial beachhead battles. The debates and discussions with my father over the who, what, when, where, and how of Normandy began early and only ended with his death in 2006. My discovery (only after enrolling) that the University of New Brunswick had a program in military history simply stoked that interest. So, too, did the mentoring of another Normandy vet, Professor Dominick S. Graham. The rest, as they say, is history.

Despite my thirty-five-year distraction as a naval historian, Normandy was never off the radar. Since coming back to UNB in 1986, most of what I have taught in the classroom and supervised at the graduate level has been "army" history. Given UNB's proximity to the Canadian army's corps schools at CFB Gagetown, army history was—and remains—a natural focus for our program. You can, quite literally, do military history here to the sound of guns firing. Heated discourses on tactics and doctrine, weapons templates, beaten zones, command thresholds, "in support or under command," and C3I issues still dominate casual discussion in the hallway. Not surprisingly, then, most of the sixty-plus master's and doctoral theses I have supervised over the years have been on army topics. Among these, several graduate students require special mention for feeding the Normandy passion: David Wilson, who worked on armored doctrine, Dan Malone for his work on naval fire support, Mike Sullivan for his look at combat motivation in the 12th SS, Arthur Gulachsen for taking a closer look at casualties in the 12th SS, and Larry Zaporzan for his MA on Radley-Walters. John Rickard's PhD on General Andy McNaughton changed my thinking (and probably that of many others) about that much-maligned Canadian general. Chris Kretschmar, an MA student who actually did a thesis on naval history, worked for me on a number of occasions as a research assistant and very kindly ferreted out the information of the personnel strength of 12th SS in the spring of 1944.

Battlefield touring gave this project its impetus. My first visit to Normandy was in 1993 with my father and Toby Graham. I knew by then, based on a 1984 professional development tour of the Gothic Line battlefield in northern Italy that Toby and I ran for CFB Halifax, that no account of battles makes sense until you have seen the ground. So I jumped at the chance in 1997 when Terry Copp asked me to start leading tours of northwest Europe and Italy for what was then the Canadian Battle of Normandy Foundation (now the Canadian Battlefields Foundation). I am grateful to Terry for that opportunity, and for insisting that generations of young Canadian students, and historians, study the ground as the primary document in any account of what happened. Indeed, having studied and taught the Normandy campaign for years, my first contact with the ground in a systematic fashion convinced me that what I thought I knew was either wrong or woefully incomplete. I am grateful to the students and serving Canadian Forces personnel of numerous tours over the last two decades for the opportunity to guide them around and, in many memorable cases, "rewrite" history on the spot with the aid of maps, aerial photos, war diaries, memoirs, regimental accounts, and the ground itself (and, in many cases coming away with a head shake, muttering, "Well, that just does not work out!").

Regrettably, I got to aging veterans of this campaign twenty years too late. By the time I shifted a little energy to my father's unit, 13th Field Regiment, RCA, it had stopped having reunions, and many of the vets had passed on. In 2001 and 2002, Tom Greenless, a survey officer with 13th RCA, exchanged a few letters, as did Bud Lund, and Tom sent a transcript of interviews done with his regiment's vets. I tracked down one battery commander, Major R. K. MacKenzie, in Toronto. Robert Spencer, PhD, a veteran of 15th Field Regiment, RCA, the author of his regiment's monumental history, and a distinguished historian, carefully explained how an artillery regiment worked in the field. Remarkably, Freddie Clifford, 13th RCA's commanding officer at this stage of the war, was still alive and well in his nineties when I started this project. He allowed me a couple of hours over a beer in the Ottawa army mess in April 2002. I am grateful to all of them and to countless other veterans whom I talked to over the years (including British vets in Normandy) for sharing their stories and their insights.

Two other veterans deserve special mention. Ken Newell, who served with 3rd Anti-Tank Regiment, RCA, shared his memories and memorabilia. This helped enormously with sorting out that regiment's contribution. I was also in regular contact with the brigade major (essentially the staff officer operations) of 9th Canadian Infantry Brigade from this period, the late David Dickson. Still sharp as a tack well into his nineties, David was no mean critic. He commanded a company of the North Nova Scotia Highlanders during the Rhine crossing in 1945 and retired as the chief justice of the New Brunswick Supreme Court. His comments on and endorsement of this manuscript mean a great deal to me, and I am grateful for his interest and support.

To a considerable extent the lack of veterans to interview has been overcome by several sources. One is the remarkable collection of interviews done by the late Jean Portugal, transcribed and published as *We Were There* in five volumes by the Royal Canadian Military Institute in Toronto. Portugal's work is a priceless resource for historians and an invaluable legacy to Canada. The second, equally crucial source of first-person accounts is the work compiled by Doug Hope of Toronto. Doug is a passionate amateur historian who has been working on the failure of Canadian artillery on 7 June for nearly two decades. Over that time he recorded interviews with a great many veterans of 14th Field Regiment and other units of the vanguard of 9th Canadian Infantry Brigade on 7 June. His pointed questioning and relentless pursuit of the problems resulted in a unique group of recollections, which he shared unreservedly with me. This would be a much poorer book without Doug Hope's enormous curiosity, his zeal for record keeping, and his passion for wrestling with the material in conference papers. I cannot thank him enough for his trust and generosity.

The third key source of personal accounts is Walter Keith of Calgary. If archives are like a "pull" logistic system, where you have to ask for specific information and you only get what you ask for, Walter would be a "push" system: the stuff just keeps coming, and it's all good. Walter did not fight in these battles, but he joined the Regina Rifle Regiment in the fall of 1944, he knew many who did, and he kept in touch. Moreover, as a retired geologist, Walter has a trained eye for information and an urge to compile it. Then, like most good academics, he knows it needs to be shared. I have a stack of handwritten notes, photocopies of citations for bravery, excerpts from war diaries, and other miscellany that Walter pushed my way. He also very kindly read an early draft of the book, saved me from many egregious errors, and then sent more information to fill in the gaps. The Reginas, and the little army it served, owe a great debt to Walter Keith for keeping the memory alive: my debt is no less.

The work of many professional and amateur historians has recorded the experiences of the German side of this battle. Much of this reflects popular interest in things Nazi and panzer, but it has served to record first-person accounts. One record of German experience that does not fit this mold, but has contributed enormously to this project, is the publication of *Kurt Meyer on Trial [A Documentary Record].* Edited by Whitney Lackenbauer and Chris Madsen, this tome reproduces the transcript of the Meyer war crimes trial and is one of the few sources that provides almost contemporary first-person accounts from the German side. I am enormously grateful to Whitney and Chris for their efforts in compiling and publishing the volume.

I am especially grateful to colleagues in Canada, the United States, and Great Britain who have encouraged and supported this project. David Charters, Steve Harris, and Lee Windsor all read an early draft and offered both suggestions for improvement and encouragement. Rob Citino and Harold Winton did the same with a later draft and supported publication when that was required. The late Eugene Feit and the New York Military Affairs Symposium heard a paper on this subject during the preliminary stages in 2006 and offered helpful suggestions, and Bruce Vandervoort was kind enough to publish the revised paper as an article in the *Journal of Military History* in 2010. From all this the book grew. Steve Bourque, Stephen Zolaga, Marcus Faulkner, Robert von Maier, Roger Sarty, Andrew Wheale, Kathy Barbier, and many others offered help and encouragement along the way. Andrew Lambert read some of the early chapters and helped me try to find a British publisher. Thanks to Dennis Showalter for putting me in touch with a New York literary agent (which did not work out, but that's another story!), and to John Ferris, who read the sections on Fortitude South and offered insight, sources, and encouragement. I want to say a particular thanks to Robin Brass, one of Canada's finest publishers, for his early expression of interest in the manuscript, and

I am grateful for his encouragement. He also loaned me his copy of General Sir Charles Loewen's privately published memoirs, for which I am especially thankful. Thanks to Cindy Brown for helping with the photos and the final production, and to my son Matthew Milner and my wife, Barbara, for reading several draft chapters.

Research for this book has been undertaken as part of a much larger project, for the moment titled "Normandy and the Battle for History," which has been under way for more than a decade. This has allowed me to visit some archives that historians of the Normandy campaign would not normally use. I would especially like to thank the staff at the following: the Library and Archives of Canada (LAC), Ottawa; the University of Toronto Archives, Toronto; the Directorate of History and Heritage, National Defence Headquarters, Ottawa; the Public Archives of Nova Scotia, Halifax; the First Division Museum, Cantigny, Illinois; the National World War II Museum, New Orleans, Louisiana; the George Marshall Research Library, Lexington, Virginia; the Howard Gottlieb Archives, Boston University; the National Archives, Kew, England; Churchill College Archives, Cambridge; The Liddell-Hart Centre, Kings College, London; and the Imperial War Museum, London.

Considerable effort went into finding documentary photos for the book. I would like to thank my friend and colleague Brent Wilson for dealing with the LAC; my former graduate student Colonel Doug Mastriano for searching through the holdings of the US Army Heritage and Educational Center, Carlisle, Pennsylvania, and for employing his expertise as an intelligence officer to confirm the time of an aerial photo; Mike McNorgan for his efforts to find a photo of Gordon Henry and a good Firefly for the cover; James Hoyle of British Pathé for his prompt and courteous service; Dr. Jean-Pierre Benamou, the doyen of Normandy history and commemoration in France, for his help with photos; Delores Hatch for sharing her photos of the Reginas; Gerry Wood and Fred Jeanne of the Royal Winnipeg Rifles museum for help with photos; and Mike Bechthold and the Laurier Centre for Military Strategic and Disarmament Studies for sharing their remarkable collection of photographs.

But Mike Bechthold deserves credit for more than just sending along photos. Mike has done an extensive workup on the battle for Putot, and so the original idea for this book was joint authorship. The pressures of a new family and completing his dissertation prevented Mike from participating in the project. However, he shared his work on Putot, responded promptly to my seemingly endless e-mail appeals for more photos, and drew all the maps for the book. He has been a source of steady support and encouragement, and I am deeply grateful for his skill as a mapmaker, his ready response to photo requests, his insights as a historian, and his professionalism and friendship.

The staff at the University Press of Kansas made the whole publishing process a pleasant one. Sara Henderson White's persistence over photo permissions kept me on my toes and kept me honest, while Mike Kehoe and the people in marketing and sales did a great job and showed commendable forbearance in dealing with me. Kathleen Rocheleau compiled the index, for which I am eternally grateful. Kelly Chrisman Jacques, the production editor, handled my Luddite tendencies with the patience of Job, which I very much appreciate. Finally I am especially grateful to Mike Briggs, the editor in chief, for supporting the book from the outset. I hope and trust that his faith has not been misplaced. All of these folks, and no doubt many more whom I have missed and to whom I apologize for the oversight, have helped make *Stopping the Panzers* a reality. Any errors or omissions that remain are mine.

Finally, as always, thanks to Bobbi for suffering through long days on Normandy battlefields, and the agony and distraction of another book. Thanks Bud.

INTRODUCTION

What passing-bells for those who die as cattle?
Only the monstrous anger of the guns.
  Wilfred Owen, "Anthem for Doomed Youth"

BY THE TIME Lieutenant Gordie Henry led his troop of London, Ontario's First Hussars into position east of Bretteville L'Orgueilleuse, the battle for the Normandy beachhead was in its fourth day. The village itself and the magnificent church of St. Germaine were already crumbling under the weight of German shells. Wrecked enemy tanks, including a half dozen of the vaunted Panthers, smoldered in the fields nearby amid the dead panzer grenadiers.

The First Hussars, supported by two troops of Shermans from the Fort Garry Horse of Winnipeg, had shifted to 7th Canadian Infantry Brigade's eastern perimeter to help tackle an imminent attack. Farther east along the crucial Caen-Bayeux highway, sheltered by the verdant foliage of the Mue River valley, elements of the 12th SS Hitler Youth Panzer Division were already in place, ready to assault the Regina Rifles' forward position at Norrey. For a few moments around noon on 9 June 1944, things were ominously quiet on this sector of the Canadian front.

Gordie Henry's tank, nicknamed the "Comtesse de Feu," was a Firefly, a British adaptation of the basic American model M4 with the new 17-pounder high-velocity gun jammed tightly into the turret. It fired a 76.2mm (3-inch) armor-piercing, capped ballistic shell (APCBS) at 1,204 meters per second, capable of cutting through 131 millimeters of plate armor at 900 meters. The 17-pounder was the most powerful antitank gun in the arsenal of the Western Allies, and Normandy was its battle debut.

But it had been rushed into service and was a fickle and problematic weapon. The jury-rigged fit in the cramped Sherman turret was far from ideal and made it tough to load. The enormous blast from the gun's muzzle slapped the ground like a thunderbolt and threw up a huge

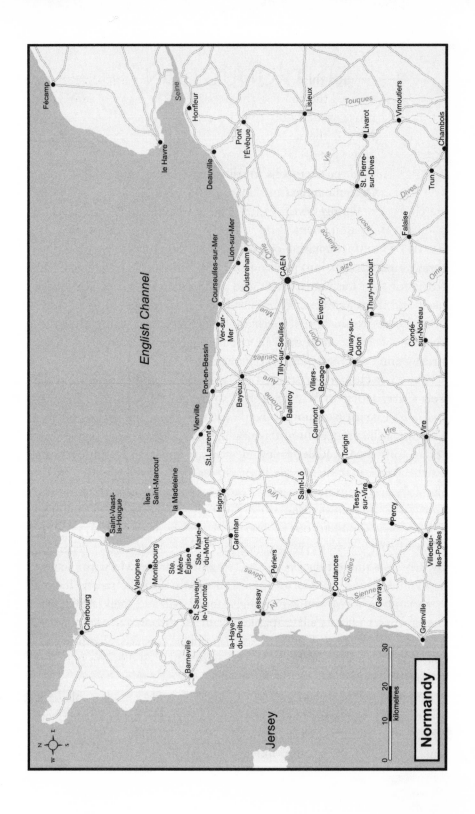

Normandy

cloud of smoke and dust. This, coupled with the tremendous speed of the shell, prevented the gunner from seeing if he had hit anything. And not all the smoke vented out the muzzle. The backdraft from opening the breech to load the next round filled the tank with acrid smoke. Normally Fireflys got off one good shot before the 17-pounder's smoke totally obscured the enemy—and drew heavy retaliatory fire.

Allied tank commanders typically fought with their heads out of the hatch, but for Firefly commanders like Gordie Henry, that risk was a fundamental requirement. Not only was it necessary to vent the tank, but he had to track the shot. Everything depended on Henry's ability to see through the murk to guide the gunner, and on his crew's ability to fire fast and accurately enough to kill the Germans before they killed them. If Henry and his crew knew all this by 9 June, they had learned fast. Their introduction to the 17-pounder had been on a range tank in Westmorland two months before. They never fired the main armament of the "Comtesse de Feu" prior to D-Day, and it is not clear how often—or even if—they had fired it since landing three days earlier. It was all new.

On this day, everything worked fine, a tribute to skill and training. Henry and his troop, plus tanks from the Fort Garry Horse under Captain C. D. A. Tweedale, had barely settled into their position north of the rail line at Bretteville when the 12th SS attack on Norrey began. The Germans had to cover about 400 meters of flat, gently rising open field to reach the Reginas' C Company positions. They had been trying to throw them out of Norrey for three days, and all previous attempts had ended in bloody failure. This one would be no different. Anglo-Canadian artillery poured a murderous fire into the valley of the Mue, stripping away German infantry. All that finally emerged from the smoke were a dozen Panther tanks. The Panthers crawled from the low ground to Henry's left and were soon moving across an open field right before his eyes. The Canadian tanks had arrived at just the right time. As the twelve Shermans lined up along the railway line southeast of Bretteville, the closest Panthers were running across their front less than 1,000 meters away.

"Seventeen-pounder! Traverse left! Steady!" Henry barked through his microphone. His gunner, Trooper Archie Chapman, swung the turret slightly, aligned his sights on a tank 900 yards away, and then reported: "ON! 900. Tank!" Once the target and range were confirmed, Henry ordered "Fire!" and Chapman squeezed the trigger on the 17-pounder's electronic firing mechanism. Nearby, Tweedale and his gunner, Trooper W. L. Bennett, went through the same sequence. Who fired first we will never know.

At 1,204 meters per second the APCBS shell reached its target almost instantaneously. The first to feel its impact was a Panther of the 3rd Company, 1st Battalion, 12th SS Panzer Regiment, commanded by SS Sergeant Alois Morawetz. Morawetz was on the right flank of the German formation, just a few yards from the rail line, and was charging hard for Norrey with his flank exposed. The forty to fifty millimeters of side armor of his Panther was no match for a 17-pounder armor-piercing shell. The Canadians' first round hit the front of Morawetz's tank, seriously wounding the gunner and bringing the tank to a halt. Morawetz heard the bang and felt his Panther sway to a stop: he thought they had struck a mine.

It took a moment for Morawetz to react to the hit. When he finally glanced out to the left through his hatch periscope to see if anyone else from his section had struck a mine, he watched the turret of the Panther on his left, probably the section leader Stagge, fly off in a shattering explosion. Morawetz scrambled out and briefly collapsed on the Panther's engine compartment: he awoke moments later with flame shooting out of the turret hatch like a blowtorch. By then he noticed that the third tank in the German formation was on fire.

It took only seconds for Henry and his gunners to light up the third Panther, and from there on it was largely their show. Their first round stopped the tank, the second went through the turret, right under the seat of the tank's commander, Willi Fischer. He scrambled out as the Panther began to blaze. By then Henry had already switched his attention to Sergeant Hermanni's tank, which Chapman struck with his first round and set alight. In just a few minutes, Henry and his crew had destroyed four Panthers with five shots, but they were not quite finished.

Most of the Shermans banging away at the Panthers had the standard 75mm gun. Reliable, fast, and accurate, the 75mm guns peppered the Germans with a barrage of shells that could not kill but could stun crews, shear off a track, or—as they soon learned—shatter the Panther's vulnerable hydraulic system and set it on fire. They added to the din and to the shower of explosions engulfing the Panthers.

By the time Henry and Chapman settled on a fifth Panther, the leader of 3rd Company's second section farther back in the field, moving targets were harder to see. As a result, the shell from Henry's 17-pounder struck his fifth Panther just as one from another Firefly hit the same tank. No matter, Henry was already searching for another target, and Trooper Chapman was just laying on a sixth Panther when it was destroyed by a 17-pounder shell from the Firefly of Henry's troop sergeant, Art Boyle.

In the end, seven Panthers were destroyed by the First Hussars and the Fort Garry Horse on 9 June 1944. At the time Henry and his crew were credited with five, Tweedale with two, and the other Garrys with one. It is not clear if Boyle received any credit for his—that would have made eight in all. The math was wrong, of course, but the outcome was unquestionable: seven Panthers were destroyed in an action that lasted just four minutes. The attack on Norrey by the Panthers of 12th SS was broken. Survivors from the blazing tanks scurried back to the shelter of the railway underpass at la Villeneuve under a torrent of Anglo-Canadian small arms and artillery fire. Max Wunsche, something of a poster child for the SS and the commander of the 12th SS Panzer Regiment, watched the action and saw his Panthers burn. Later he wrote that he "could have cried for rage and sorrow."[1] No Canadian casualties were reported.

In the summer of 1944 several Canadian newspapers carried brief accounts of Henry's remarkable accomplishment, and in 1945 he was finally awarded a French decoration, the Croix de Guerre "with Vermillion Star." No Canadian decoration was ever awarded for his remarkable feat of arms. The commanding officer of 2nd Canadian Armoured Brigade, Brigadier R. A. Wyman, was notorious for not awarding medals to his troops for doing their job: destroying German tanks was what Henry and his colleagues were supposed to do. Even the First Hussars Museum in London, Ontario, has no commemoration of Henry's action on 9 June, and no photo of Henry other than a grainy image of the troop commanders of C Squadron has ever emerged. Not surprisingly, Henry remains completely unknown in the wider literature of the Normandy campaign. Had he been British or American, Gordon Henry would be one of the iconic figures of the Overlord story.

The same might be said of the accomplishments of 3rd Canadian Infantry Division in those first fateful days following the landings. In the laconic language of the Canadian army official history, the task of the Canadian division was to seize its D-Day objectives and hold them against counterattack. There was nothing special in that. Indeed, every Allied division that landed on 6 June 1944 was supposed to do the same: take the objective and hold it.

In the event, 3rd Canadian Infantry Division was the first of the five divisions in the amphibious assault to reach and secure its D-Day objective. Its task, as historians have understood it, was to sever the crucial Caen-Bayeux highway and secure the vulnerable western flank of I British Corps until a proper junction with 50th British Division and XXX British Corps, landing north of Bayeux, could be achieved. The British had the important jobs on either flank, the capture of Caen and Bayeux. The Canadians simply filled the space in between. In general, these unremarkable Canadian objectives were accomplished. One arm of the Canadian advance, 9th Brigade, failed to take its objective of Carpiquet on D+1 and was driven back by the Germans. But the positions taken and held on 7 June by 7th Canadian Infantry Brigade astride the highway and rail line west of Caen at Bretteville, Norrey, and Putot constituted ultimate success.

In the days that followed (8–10 June), the Canadians' advance into France apparently stalled. They never did get to the high ground around Point 112 southwest of Caen, as their orders suggested they might. And, as one recent British historian lamented (not the first to do so), 3rd Canadian Division failed to take Caen from the west when it had a chance.[2] Instead, Canadian hesitancy and tactical ineptitude and superb German defending apparently checked the Canadian advance in the aftermath of D-Day.

In the literature on the Normandy campaign, Canadian failure to get forward between 7 and 10 June is simply part of a larger narrative of the failure of I British Corps in front of Caen. In this sector of the Overlord front, hasty German counterattacks designed to stop the Allies so they could be driven back into the sea proved to be entirely successful. In particular, the skillful and ruthless 12th SS quickly cowed the timid Canadians—and their equally unimaginative and battle-shy British compatriots—into a defensive posture. Indeed, in American popular culture surrounding the Normandy campaign, the ineffectiveness—in fact idleness—of the Anglo-Canadians has become an article of faith. Steven Spielberg even built it into his D-Day Hollywood epic, *Saving Private Ryan.*

And while the Anglo-Canadians were bungling their opportunities ashore in the early phase of Operation Overlord, the German forces in the west were being held at bay by a deception operation fronted by American general George S. Patton. Patton was the notional commander of the entirely fictitious "1st US Army Group" based in the southeast of England. This group's task was to convince the Germans that the real landings would come in the Pas de Calais region. This was accomplished, so historians tell us, largely because Patton was the Allied general whom the Germans "feared" most.

The problem with this popular view of the early phase of Operation Overlord is that it is simply wrong, at virtually every level. In fact, changes in German dispositions rendered the I British Corps plan for the Caen sector on D-Day out of date weeks before the landings went in, and things only got worse as D-Day neared. As early as April it was clear that 3rd British Division probably lacked the combat power to capture the city by a coup de main on D-Day itself, a development that was confirmed in late May. British caution around Caen in the days immediately following the landing had a great deal to do with the presence of German armor, on a huge scale, in the I Corps sector. As for 3rd Canadian Division, its job was never generic, it never had the option to take Caen from the west, and the option of pushing 2nd Canadian Armoured Brigade onto the slopes of Point 112—where thousands of British soldiers would later perish in Operation Epsom—was never more than a staff officer's dream. The Canadian task in Operation Overlord was clear to the chief of staff to the supreme Allied commander (COSSAC), to Supreme Headquarters, Allied Expeditionary Force (SHAEF), and to 21st Army Group planners, and to the senior officers of 3rd Canadian Division if not to subsequent historians. The Canadians were to take and hold the only ground on which planners, both Allied and German, believed that an attack on the Allied landings in Normandy could be decisive. Their job was to stop the panzers.

A similar task befell the rump of First Canadian Army, the formation that until late 1943 was designated to lead the British Commonwealth onto the beaches of France. Again, it seems that everyone at the time, including the Germans, knew this. As a result, it was possibly First Canadian Army, and certainly not Patton, that was the beating heart of the Allied deception operation code-named Fortitude South until the initial beachhead battles were over. It, too, would stop the panzers in its own way at a critical moment of the first week of Overlord.

By the time the initial beach battles ended on 10 June 1944, 3rd Canadian Division was indeed stalled on its objective, just as historians have claimed. It was exhausted, battered, and down 3,000 men. But the Canadians were utterly unshaken, and they were surrounded by wreckage from three panzer divisions, one of them the most powerful panzer division in the west, filled with the elite of the Hitler Youth. When it was all over, it was the Canadians who held the ground that the Germans needed in order to defeat Overlord.

This book tells that untold story.

Canada's role in Normandy has been a sidebar to the history of the campaign from the outset. Canadians know this very well. My first inkling of neglect of the Canadian role came at a tender age in 1962, after watching the Hollywood version of Cornelius Ryan's epic *The Longest Day*. My father was the only D-Day vet in our neighborhood, and he volunteered to take his sons and a gaggle of boys to see the film at the Vogue theater. Three hours later we emerged bug-eyed and chattering, ready to turn a nearby vacant lot into a network of trenches and pilfered barbed wire so we could reenact the whole movie. I do, however, vividly remember my father's reaction because it was in such contrast to ours. I recall him standing on the sidewalk muttering, "We were there, why didn't they show us?" over and over again.[3]

Ryan had, of course, interviewed Canadians for his book. In many ways their tales were just more of the same, variations of the acts of heroism and horror common to all participants. But it was British and American moviegoers, not Canadians, who would make the film a commercial and critical success. Nothing has changed since then, for either filmmakers or book publishers. The Canadian market is too small, and it is easier to simply write the Canadians out of the story—as they were for the Hollywood film *The Great Escape* (1963).[4] No one except Canadians cares anyway. As this is written, the blogosphere is full of complaints about Ben Affleck's Academy Award–winning film *Argo*, which tells the story of how the CIA masterminded and ran the Iran hostage escape in 1979. Jimmy Carter, who was the US president at the time, commented after seeing the film that Affleck had it all wrong. The CIA had little to do with the affair, while 90 percent of the work—and the risk—was Canadian. His comments were irrelevant. Affleck admitted to turning the tale around to make it marketable: it is all about selling the story to the only audience that matters.

In fairness, the neglect of Canada's role in the early beachhead battles of Normandy is not unique. The history of the Second World War is replete with "missing" lesser players: neither the Australians in the South Pacific nor the Indian army in the Western Desert appear much in Anglo-American literature. But the Canadian case in Normandy also owes a great deal to shortcomings in Canada's own storytelling. This is particularly true of the ultimate purposes of the Canadian assault on D-Day and the battles ashore between 7 and 10 June. In fact, it seems that Colonel Charles Stacey and his team of Canadian army official historians never knew the ultimate purpose of the Canadian assault. They were not alone. Like most of the initial historians of Operation Overlord, Stacey's team, despite their status as official historians of one of the major combatants, never had access to all the necessary documents. Nor were they much interested in the early defensive battles. Perhaps that was because of the delicate nature of the issues discussed later in this book. It is not clear, for example, that they were at liberty to probe too deeply into what happened to the role of First Canadian Army and its commanding officer, General Andrew McNaughton, in the original plans for Overlord, or into the artillery failure that seriously marred the first major battle on D+1.

Rather, Stacey and his staff were absorbed in the "failure to move forward" paradigm that dominated the Normandy story from July 1944 onward. For Stacey, as for many of the Canadian army's senior officers, the efforts of 3rd Canadian Division after the initial landings were disappointing, and the official history reflects that sentiment. The Canadians did not advance much beyond their original D-Day objectives for a month. British, American, and German historians were content with this view of the Canadians as unimaginative, cautious, and tactically inept because it fit well with their own agendas, both national and interpretive.

The Normandy campaign nonetheless meant a great deal to Canadians at the time. This is evident by the fact that the Canadian Army Historical Section, led by Stacey, published an account of the Normandy campaign within two years of the event. The booklet, *Canada's Battle in Normandy 6 June–1 September 1944*, appeared in 1946,[5] and was one of only three brief books published by Stacey's section in the Canadian Army at War series before the official summary, *The Canadian Army 1939–1945*, emerged in 1948.[6] Both of these—the booklet on Normandy and the summary—were based on a series of historical narratives (now available online) developed as events unfolded. It is significant that these early works were written with only a cursory knowledge of the actual Overlord planning, scant access (if any) to higher-level documents, and little knowledge of what the Germans were up to.

Not surprisingly, both accounts are primarily narrative and descriptive, and both accounts of the 7–10 June period are quite brief. If Stacey and his team were aware of the contretemps in 1943 over the fate of First Canadian Army in the overall Overlord plan, or the ultimate objectives of the Canadian landings, none of that emerged in these early works. *Canada's Battle in Normandy* states emphatically that Second British Army was designated to lead the assault "at an early date . . . even before exercise Spartan" in April 1943.[7] This is strictly true, although it misses the period in late 1943 when First US Army replaced Second British, leaving First Canadian Army as the lead British Commonwealth formation. *The Canadian Army* comes closer to the truth on this. First Canadian Army's task was exploitation, but "there was some discussion of the possibility of the Canadian Army Headquarters taking part in the assault, with its own divisions under command." With General Bernard Law Montgomery's return in January 1944, however, First Canadian Army reverted to its exploitation role.[8]

In both of these early books, Canada's role once ashore was unspectacular. The British on either side had the key tasks of capturing Caen and Bayeux. The Canadians—in the words of *Canada's Battle in Normandy*—held "the Army's central sector between the two places."[9]

The Canadian Army summation of the ultimate task of the Canadians in the D-Day plan was not much better: the Canadians were simply the connecting tissue between the main thrusts on the British front.[10]

It is likely that Stacey had seen the key components—but not all—of the final Overlord plan and the operational order for 3rd Canadian Division before *The Canadian Army* appeared in 1948. Neither would have clarified things much for him without some wider context. Certainly the cryptic instruction in the operational order to "defeat the counterattack" would have been no cause for excitement: that's what everyone was supposed to do. But Stacey and his team of Canadian army historians had no access to British Cabinet Office planning documents, special intelligence—especially Ultra information—and Operation Fortitude, or it seems even 21st Army Group intelligence documents, none to key COSSAC planning material, and little to captured German documents at this preliminary stage.

By the time serious work began on the major Canadian official history of operations in Europe, Stacey's army historians had better access. Major T. M. Hunter's masterful and highly informative narrative, "Preliminary Planning for Operation 'OVERLORD': Some Aspects of the Preparations for an Allied Re-entry to North-West Europe, 1940–1944," Army Headquarters Report No. 42, completed in March 1952, draws on Overlord, Combined Chiefs of Staff, and some COSSAC and 21st Army Group planning documents. Much of the discussion in Hunter's 210-page, single-spaced report focuses on the larger issues, such as sorting out Round-Up and Sledgehammer (two previous plans for landings in France) from the final Overlord plan. Hunter's discussion is driven by debates at formal conferences at Washington, Quebec, and Tehran in 1943, and it is informed by notes from selected British Cabinet Office documents provided by Canadian army liaison staff in London. In his final description of the Overlord plan, Hunter drew heavily on Lieutenant Colonel H. A. Pollock's Cabinet Office narrative, "Invasion of Northwest Europe 1944," a 140-page document completed in 1949, and on discussions with Pollock himself.[11] Significantly, Pollock's narrative of the planning for Overlord contains no references at all to Canada, Canadians, or the Canadian army: it is entirely an Anglo-American story. It was likely that this was no oversight but rather part of a deliberate British policy of subsuming the Canadian story under the larger "British" umbrella. And although Hunter clearly saw some COSSAC files, there are no signs in his narrative of the key staff appreciations from 1943 or of the detailed COSSAC planning documents anticipating when and where the panzers were likely to attack. It remains unclear what Hunter really knew and, perhaps just as important, what he felt he could say.

In the meantime, the very cursory and unassuming versions of the Canadian role described in the two summaries published in 1946 and 1948 held sway. As for color, Ross Munro, a reporter with the Canadian Press who landed on D-Day with the Canadians, provided that in his popular account of the northwest Europe campaign, *From Gauntlet to Overlord* (1946). Munro described 3rd Canadian Division—suggestively—as virtually a "pocket corps" with all the attached troops, but without much context and comparison this was a hollow claim. For Munro the Canadian task was straightforward: "The Canadians were to thrust inland to the Caen-Bayeux highway and hold the slopes astride the road."[12] So at best, then, the Canadians were to hold the road and presumably deny it as a lateral route for German movements.

More might have been expected from Milton Shulman's classic work *Defeat in the West* (1947).[13] Shulman was a Canadian army intelligence officer during the war who joined First Canadian Army shortly before D-Day and stayed with it to the end. His job was tracking the Wehrmacht order of battle, and as a serving intelligence officer he interviewed many senior German officers in 1945. As a result, *Defeat in the West*, which deals with the whole campaign in northwest Europe, is a gold mine of first-person accounts and insight from the German perspective. His nine-page "Chapter XV: The First Days," dealing with the initial beachhead battles against 1st SS Panzer Corps, still rewards reading. But only once in that chapter does Shulman say who the panzers were fighting against, and it is not the Canadians but the British. That lone reference to early battles is to the struggle around Tilley-sur-Seulles on 10 June, which cost Panzer Lehr about a hundred tanks.[14]

The Normandy story was so vast, so fascinating, so complex, and, in view of the very public spat going on in the international media over Montgomery's role, so political that in the immediate postwar years, no one other than Canadians was interested in the Canadian role. This was certainly the case with Chester Wilmot, who was busy preparing his seminal work *The Struggle for Europe* (1952) during this period. As a correspondent Wilmot was also a witness to the events he described, and he had a long association with the British army during the war. Much of what he knew he learned firsthand or was fed by friends who knew what he was writing. While preparing his book, Wilmot actively corresponded with British officers of all ranks and sought background information on Anglo-American operations. For his account of the Canadians, however, Wilmot was content to rely almost entirely on material sent to him by Stacey's Army Historical Section, including preliminary narratives and drafts of the first histories.[15]

As a result, *The Struggle for Europe* adds color but little insight into the Canadian role. Echoing Stacey, Wilmot's account of Canadians simply finds them in between two British formations that were trying to capture key urban areas. In the process, the Canadians are rather inadvertently attacked by 12th SS Panzer. The latter, apparently, was trying to exploit the gap between 3rd Canadian and 3rd British and "was distracted to the west by a Canadian advance."[16] In this view, it was the *advancing* Canadians who drew the panzers to themselves. What followed over the next two days was a Canadian defense of Putot and Bretteville forced on them by 12th SS, while the Germans held the front "against repeated probing attacks by the British and Canadians." Like many subsequent "British" and American historians (Wilmot was actually an Australian), much of Wilmot's explanation of German responses to the Allied landings centers on how the Germans reacted to the actions of the dominant Allies, and especially the key urban centers of Caen and Bayeux. According to Wilmot, 21st Panzer focused on fighting *British* 3rd Division—not strictly true—while 12th SS was apparently in search of the *British* left flank west of Caen. Meanwhile, Panzer Lehr moved to stop the *British* near Tilley-sur-Seulles, in an attempt to retake Bayeux.[17] Thus, for Wilmot as well, the Canadians were simply the "connective tissue" between places and stories that matter.

Subsequent Canadian, American, and British official histories add nothing to the role of the Canadians (except details) and do much to diminish it. The first substantive official history to appear was Gordon Harrison's *Cross-Channel Attack* (1951), part of the massive United States Army in World War II series—the so-called Green Series for its canvas covers. It was not Harrison's task to provide detailed coverage of action on the Anglo-Canadian front, but events there were naturally mentioned. His comments were brief: "British troops were to take Bayeux and Caen on D-Day, and then push the bridgehead south and southeast." Harrison made no specific mention of the Canadian role on D-Day or subsequently. For Harrison, the operational plan allowed for no exploitation of "the favourable tank terrain at any phase of the operation for a direct thrust southeast towards Paris." True, but it did allow for defending the beachhead against panzer attack. Later on, Harrison noted that three panzer divisions were assembled around Caen, but the Canadians played no evident role in stopping them. His only comment on the battle between the Canadians and 12th SS on 7 June is in footnote 20 on page 348. Referring to a Hitler Youth "reconnaissance battalion" operating northwest of Caen, Harrison says: "Apparently this reconnaissance unit tangled with the 3rd Canadian Division near Authie and an engagement resulted heavy enough to give the Canadians the impression of an enemy counterattack." His authority for this was British Cabinet Office files and the war diary of Seventh German Army. The latter was "emphatic on the point that no attack by I SS Panzer Corps took place on 7 June."[18]

Harrison's volume, and indeed all the volumes of the Green Series relevant to Canadian operations, circulated in draft form to Stacey's Army Historical Section in Ottawa. What Stacey and his historians thought of Harrison's comments we will never know. The drafts, with minor annotations in the margins (some from senior Canadian generals), were shredded in 1983 by a junior historian at what was then the Directorate of History, National Defence Headquarters, Ottawa. I know this with certainty because I shredded them. My protests that the destruction was outrageous were met by reminders that I was still on probation and any attempt to remove the documents would be punished under the Official Secrets Act.[19]

But we do know that Harrison's volume had an impact on Stacey's later account. Until it appeared, he had little idea, for example, that 21st Panzer's counterattack on 6 June reached the sea.[20] Beyond that, Stacey was uninterested in 21st Panzer, probably because research by his German-language expert, Captain A. G. Steiger, failed to discover its presence in the Canadian sector. By the end of 1951, Steiger had produced two lengthy reports for Stacey on German forces in Normandy, one dealing with the pre–D-Day situation and the other with events from 6 June to 22 August. It is significant that the position, movements, and role of 21st Panzer on the Canadian front are almost completely ignored.[21] Steiger based his reports largely on captured German records held in Washington, and on the interviews and reports prepared by German officers for the US Army Center of Military History. The latter project focused largely, but not exclusively, on what the Germans did in front of US troops. Although it remains a remarkably useful compendium, it was not shaped to answer everyone's potential questions, and the reports, subsequently published, do not present a balanced view of the war.[22] Perhaps not surprisingly, then, Steiger knew little of what 21st Panzer did in the early beachhead battles and also failed completely to uncover Panzer Lehr's presence in front of the Canadians on 8 June. In fact, he went on to admit in his narrative that he had no idea whatsoever of what the Germans were doing on the Canadian front between 9 and 11 June.

Based on Steiger's work, Stacey's primary focus for the first days ashore was therefore the battle with 12th SS.[23] As a result, Stacey's final word on these battles, which appeared in *The Victory Campaign: The Operations in North-West Europe, 1944–1945* (1960), the third volume of the Canadian army official history, was cursory, ill-informed, and rather dismissive. This work is largely to blame for the similar attitude shown by subsequent historians to the early phase of Canada's battles ashore. Even Stacey's account of D-Day ends with disappointment. It was a remarkable accomplishment, and he lauded the men and their commitment. But Stacey lamented that the Allies were slow to exploit their success, and he accepted German criticism that Allied infantrymen were too "hesitant and careful."[24] His accounts of the beachhead battles echo that tone. Stacey devoted seven pages to 9th Brigade's battle on 7 June: four and a half setting it up, and most of two analyzing why the brigade "had been caught off balance and defeated in detail."[25] In Stacey's view, the Canadians fought with "courage and spirit, but somewhat clumsily" against "an unusually efficient German force *of about its own strength* [my emphasis], and had come off second best." The result was a "severe local reverse" that—in words that damned the whole of 3rd Canadian Division's efforts for generations—"helped to ensure that Caen remained in German hands."[26] In fact, Stacey's account of the advance of the vanguard of 9th Brigade on 7 June is an eighteen-line paragraph, and six of those lines are devoted to brigade consolidation at the end of the day. His entire description of the struggle for Authie consists of eleven words: the vanguard "fought hard but were overrun: only a few men got away."[27]

Stacey's account of 7th Brigade's battle at Putot, Bretteville, and Norrey from 8 to 10 June is more detailed, but he set the tone of those three days right off by describing the battle as "a series of violent *local* [my emphasis] counter-attacks." And he ends with an emphatic statement, echoing Harrison and the Seventh German Army war diary, that "the large armoured counter-offensive planned on D-Day (discussed on p. 123) had never come to pass." In the strictest sense, all this is true: most of 12th SS's counterattacks were designed to clear the start line for the 1st SS Panzer Corps attack, so they were technically local. But Stacey was unaware that the larger panzer corps attack remained a consistent German objective until 10 June, unaware that Panzer Lehr and about one-third of 21st Panzer were present on the Canadian front during this period, and unaware that Canadian fighting helped thwart the German's plans.

Stacey was also apparently totally unaware that II Canadian Corps played a key role in Operation Fortitude South, the deception scheme to both retain Fifteenth German Army in the Pas de Calais and deflect panzer reserves from the Normandy front following the landings. His accounts of II Corps training in April and May 1944 are described as preparation for crossing the tidal estuaries of the Seine and the Scheldt Rivers as part of the general advance of First Canadian Army along the coast of Europe.[28] It would seem that none of Stacey's historians were aware of the Normandy deception operation.

In the end, Stacey never discussed the 3rd Canadian Division operational order at length, and of course he had not seen all the COSSAC and 21st Army Group planning documents that set the context for the Canadian role. In addition, his knowledge of the German side of the beachhead battles was, as noted, extremely limited. His accounts of Normandy (the 1947 booklet, the 1949 summary history, and the 1960 official history volume) were primarily interested in attempts by the Canadians to push forward. As my colleague Lee Windsor reminded me, the whole postwar generation of historians was focused on movement as the basic measure of success: failure to gain ground meant failure. After all, Montgomery set movement as the standard metric: no battle of attrition in Normandy. And so Stacey describes battles with 12th SS as attempts to stop the Canadians from advancing, not as part of the failure of a larger German scheme.[29] Other historians do the same. In this paradigm, the disastrous Canadian attack on 11 June at le Mesnil-Patry represents the ultimate failure of the army in this early phase—indeed, the culmination of a general failure to get forward.

The British official history of the Normandy campaign, the first volume of Major L. F. Ellis's *Victory in the West*, published two years after *The Victory Campaign*, did nothing to illuminate the Canadian role in the opening phase of Overlord. Ellis's writing is more descriptive than analytical, but it supports the view that the initial beachhead phase was all about movement, about country to be seized.[30] Ellis does say that on 7 June the Canadians "bore the brunt of a strong counter-attack by the 12th SS Panzer Division." This he described as the "second armoured division to be opposed to the *British advance* [my emphasis]."[31] His choice of words reflects two critical elements of Ellis's wider interpretation, and indeed the larger theme of all British accounts of the Normandy campaign since 1944: the Canadians are British, and the British are advancing. The absorption of the Canadians into the British fold is often assumed: Canada was part of the Commonwealth family, after all. But in the struggle for legacy—and for influence in the postwar world—it was vital that "British" power be seen as a unified force, not a fractured and decaying amalgam of empire, dominions, and associated lesser countries.[32] The strength of this British policy is evident in Ellis's foreword, in which he lists the countries that contributed to victory in Normandy: Britain, the United States, France, Poland, Belgium, the Netherlands, and Czechoslovakia. Canada is not on the list, so presumably there is nothing uniquely Canadian about Canada's role in the D-Day plan.[33]

With Canadian historians so ill-informed and laconic, and Canada's efforts subsumed under the British in British official histories, it was too much to expect later historians of the campaign to probe deeper into Canada's role in the Overlord plan. Indeed, as a rule, Anglo-American historians are not intellectually curious about Canada's often important role in the Second World War, on land, on sea, and in the air. Few—if any—non-Canadians working on the Normandy campaign have ever even looked at Stacey's final volume of official history, *Arms, Men and Government* (1971).[34] It was there where he wrestled, obliquely to be sure, with the sacking of Andy McNaughton, the collapse of the central role of "McNaughton's Dagger" in the Overlord plan. In fairness, the discussion is set entirely in the context of McNaughton's fitness to command. Again, there is no evidence even by this stage that Stacey saw the COSSAC planning documents of late 1943 that gave First Canadian Army a major role in the Overlord assault. His one reference to the impact of the redirection of Canadian formations to Italy in the fall of 1943 was a reference to the fact that First Canadian would now likely become an Anglo-Canadian army for Overlord planning purposes.[35]

The first full-scale, intensely researched account of the Canadians in Normandy appeared in 1984 with the publication of Reg Roy's *1944: The Canadians in Normandy*.[36] A combat veteran of the Italian campaign, Roy had joined Stacey's staff around 1950 and had completely reworked the account of the Normandy campaign. It was Roy's compressed work that appeared in *The Victory Campaign*, and he finally got permission to publish his complete work—revised and updated—by the early 1980s. Roy added great detail to the story, but his narrative style did nothing to shift the odor of failure from the initial Canadian battles. As a result, Roy's *1944* seems to have had little international impact. Anglo-American historians were quite content with the negative tone of Stacey's operational history of the northwest Europe campaign, and it was their books—not Roy's—that garnered the limelight on the fortieth anniversary of D-Day. Max Hastings's old standby, *Overlord* (1984), is a case in point. When interviewed by Peter Gzowski on the CBC radio program *Morning Side* in 1984 during his international book tour, Hastings said he was hard on the Canadians because he was simply repeating the criticism in the Canadian official history. Canadians, it seems, fought hard but not well. In his book Hastings described the Canadians' battle with 12th SS as wild and confused, apparently because the Canadians were basically brawlers. He says emphatically of these battles, "While the Germans co-ordinated armour, infantry and artillery superbly, the Canadians did not."[37] The only "Canadian" Hastings quoted extensively in his book was Corporal Dick Raymond of the Cameron Highlanders of Ottawa. In fact, Raymond was an American farmer from upstate New York who joined the Canadian army in 1942. Raymond thought the Canadians "went at it like hockey players." That seemed to fit the paradigm.

The notion that the Canadian army in Normandy was a combination of "lions led by donkeys"—or perhaps more appropriately "hockey players led by donkeys"—was reaffirmed for a new generation in 1991 by John English's extensively researched and powerfully argued book *The Canadian Army and the Normandy Campaign: A Study of Failure in High Command*. Like Stacey, English never looked closely at Canadian combat performance at the battalion level. Rather, his critique evolved from the discontent evident among grousing senior officers who were not happy with the way the war was run. His book's subtitle summarizes the point: Canadian "failure"—and the campaign was apparently a litany of failures—started at the top, with the army's senior generals. English agreed with Stacey's conclusion (presumably derived from his discussions with senior Canadian officers) that the Canadian army overseas "got rather less than it might have" from its training. This was because of "a proportion of regimental officers whose attitude toward training was casual and haphazard rather than urgent and scientific." English pushes responsibility for that problem back up the chain of command. Canadian shortfalls in Normandy, English stated, stemmed from the Canadian high command, which "did not know how to train them properly."[38] His critique of senior Canadian generals very much echoes that of both Alan Brooke and especially Montgomery.

The result of all this is much ill-informed and gratuitous criticism of the Canadian effort in the first beachhead battles. The historian of 12th SS, Hubert Meyer (the former chief of staff of the division), chastised the Canadians for failing to seize the initiative and for not surging onto Point 112, north of Evrecy, on 7 June. The Germans would have done this, Meyer asserts. Perhaps. But the German army was no font of wisdom on large-scale amphibious assaults: Who would have filled in behind the Canadians if they had charged madly off to Point 112? As things turned out, 3rd Canadian Division's flanks were in the air throughout this period even at Putot, Bretteville, and Norrey. Perhaps the most bizarre dismissal of the Canadian effort between D-Day and 10 June was that of British historian Stephen Badsey, whose reappraisal of the first week of battle in a collection of essays asserts, rightly enough, that "it was in its first week that the battle [of Normandy] was won and lost." His entire assessment of the Canadian role during the critical period then consists of one grotesquely ill-informed sentence: "For D Plus 1 and the following days, attention has mostly been paid to 12th SS Panzer Division's *prevention* of 3rd Canadian Infantry Division *reaching Caen from the west* [my emphasis], while 21st Panzer Division blocked the British advance from the east."[39] Clearly, neither Meyer nor Badsey read the Canadian operational order.

Russell Hart, who echoed both Hastings and, more important, English in his important book *Clash of Arms: How the Allies Won in Normandy* (2001), is worth quoting at some length because his description of the early Canadian battles so nicely encapsulates conventional wisdom about the Canadians and those crucial first few days west of Caen:

> After D-Day, however, the British advance quickly stalled as powerful enemy reserves massed at Caen in an effort to drive the Anglo-Canadians back into the sea. In the process, these Allied forces suffered a number of local reverses, the Canadians especially so. The most serious of these occurred on 7 June as the Canadian 3d Division pushed boldly inland toward its D-Day objective of the Carpiquet airfield, despite the known movement of powerful German armored reserves toward Caen. The Canadian spearhead was ambushed and outfought by the vanguard of the 12th SS Panzer Division Hitlerjugend and thrown back in confusion. Further local Canadian reverses followed as German armor conducted an aggressive defense, probing for weak spots in the Allied lines that they might subsequently exploit in a planned, general offensive. On 8 June SS troops defeated the Royal Winnipeg Rifles and retook Putot.[40]

This passage is a complex mixture of simple errors of fact, a muddled story line, and a predisposition to see the Anglo-Canadians as bungling incompetents. But it fits well with the sharply negative tone of Hart's chapter titled "Canada 1939–1944: The Politics of Neglect," which concludes that the Canadian army was so poorly prepared for modern war that "SHAEF wisely assigned First Canadian Army the subsidiary role of landing only after the Allies had established a successful bridge-head."[41] In fact, of course, First Canadian Army had been preparing for just that follow-on, breakout role for over a year, and SHAEF had little to do with it. Not surprisingly, popular accounts simply pick up the tone set by these more authoritative accounts.[42]

In recent years Canadian historians have "counterattacked" this "hockey players led by donkeys" school. In particular, the work of Terry Copp has shown that Canadians fought very effectively indeed, at least as well as anyone else. His *Fields of Fire* (2003) tackled the whole Normandy campaign and shed much new light on issues from tactics to operations and strategy. In fact, Copp contributed three crucial elements to the debate over Allied performance in Normandy. He operated on the assumption that the official histories were not proper, academically rigorous histories at all. They were either incomplete, wrong, or too didactic and, even in Stacey's case, compromised by the requirement to obtain approval to be published from a General Staff composed of the men who made the history he wrote.[43] Copp also flatly rejected the staff college approach to military history evident in books like English's and sought to understand people and events in their historical context. Based on those assumptions, Copp believed that it was necessary for historians to go back to basics, back to the surviving documents, and back to the veterans to create a new narrative. Finally, a crucial element of Copp's process was the use of the ground itself as a key document.[44] Over the last twenty-five years, Copp has revolutionized how Canadian historians do military history, especially the way they employ close analysis of the battlefield itself in their research. His work has been far-reaching and has profoundly affected generations of historians.

However, Copp, like most other historians of Normandy, had much to cover and was not primarily focused on the early defensive battles. He did not assume that they were failures or that the Canadians fought badly. Indeed, like the Canadians who fought these battles, Copp is sharply critical of 12th SS. But Copp did not explore these battles in detail. Mark Zuehlke's *Holding Juno*[45] (2005) provides the best narrative of events between 7 and 10 June, and it is filled with gripping anecdotes. But Zuehlke, too, had little idea of the larger context of the Canadian effort from 7 to 10 June and simply set his account within the existing Normandy narrative.

Fortunately, much of the German side has now been well mapped in Brigadier Michael Reynolds's *Steel Inferno: 1 SS Panzer Corps in Normandy* (1997). In fact, the Canadians fought the SS so consistently throughout the Normandy campaign that Reynolds's book is a kind of semiofficial history of the other side of the Canadian story. Reynolds, too, is critical of German combat effectiveness in the early beachhead battles and is much kinder to the Canadians. It was Reynolds, after all, who asserted that the Canadian defense of Bretteville and Norrey "must surely go down as one of the finest small unit actions of WW II."[46] Clearly, some part of Canadian training, motivation, and leadership worked well.

This work therefore builds on much that is new and exciting in the literature on Normandy, and especially the work of Copp and his efforts with the Canadian Battlefields Foundation. Indeed, the opportunity to work on behalf of the latter and guide students around Normandy for many years provided much of the genesis of this book. I have seen, driven over, and walked the ground often enough to be very familiar with it. That experience opened my eyes to the fact that trying to reconcile most history books with the actual battlefield results in a lingering mistrust of accounts derived solely from archival sources.

This project began as a simple attempt to find out what my father's unit, 13th Field Regiment, Royal Canadian Artillery (RCA), did in those first days ashore. He was a veteran of the battles described here, and he remembered them as the most harrowing days of his eleven-month war. By the time I started serious research on this subject, most of the key actors in this story were long dead, although astonishingly 13th RCA's commanding officer, Colonel Freddie Clifford, was alive and well when I interviewed him in 2002. Clifford's regiment kept good records from the outset, but nothing survives from the other RCA regiments involved (12th, 14th, and 19th RCA) except their basic war diaries. Curiously, I soon discovered that the war diary of the division's artillery commander for the first two weeks ashore was a complete fudge (it was not written until thirteen months later), and that no one from 14th RCA seemed to remember what happened on 7 June. Then my graduate student Dan Malone passed me a copy of the Canadian artillery operational order for Overlord, with its remarkable layout of the division covering position, and Doug Hope began to share his findings on the gunnery problems with 14th RCA on 7 June during the advance of 9th Brigade. More discovery and questions followed from there. Why were Canadian field artillery regiments all equipped with American self-propelled guns (SPs), apparently drawn from American stocks in the United Kingdom? (And the corollary to that question, Why was Canadian assault artillery completely and exclusively equipped with American SPs while the US Army's assault artillery on D-Day was primarily towed?) Why was so much artillery assigned to the Canadians and massed behind their front? Why did the guns fail on 7 June? Was the ground on either side of the Mue River seen as crucial counterattack country by Overlord planners? What did the original COSSAC appreciations say? How were they changed as a result of Montgomery's return? And what did the Germans plan—and do?

The process of answering these and many more questions simply piled revelation upon revelation. It is clear that historians have been content with a rather superficial analysis of the pre–D-Day plans, little more than a description of the Initial Joint Plan of 1 February 1944. That the dominant paradigm for understanding the initial phase of the Normandy landings was set decades ago and has endured virtually unchallenged. That much of what has been written is narrative and descriptive, not reflective and analytical. That the diminution of the Canadian role in the early phase of the campaign stems in part from shortcomings in Canadian accounts. That these shortcomings resulted from an inability to access and use all the necessary sources, from a focus on movement as the ultimate measure of success, and perhaps from a reluctance to probe too deeply into the breakup of First Canadian Army in the fall of 1943. For it is clear that a cabal of gunners from the Canadian Corps of the Great War nearly succeeded in having First Canadian Army lead the charge onto the beaches of France in 1944. And finally, that politics—domestic Canadian, interservice, and international—conspired to reduce Canada's role, and to some extent even reduce the recounting of what was accomplished.

Popular notions of Anglo-Canadian incompetence and idleness in Normandy persist. They will, no doubt, die hard—if at all. Given what Ben Affleck did with the truth in a film that won the Best Picture Academy Award in 2013, it is difficult to be optimistic. In that sense it was probably best that my father never saw Steven Spielberg's Hollywood blockbuster *Saving Private Ryan* (1998). Two elements of that film would have angered him greatly. The first was the gratuitous criticism offered by the Ranger Captain Miller, played by Tom Hanks. When asked by US airborne pathfinder Lieutenant Fred Hamilton (Ted Danson) how things were going, Miller responded, "Monty's taking his time moving on Caen: we can't pull out 'til he's ready." Even more curious is Hamilton's response. After saying that Monty was overrated, Hamilton says, "You gotta take Caen so you can take St. Lô." It is hard to know what to say about that one. The notion that the British were responsible for delays in Americans getting forward is an old canard in American popular perception of both the war in general and Normandy in particular.

This would have been bad enough, but the second overt bit of license taken by Spielberg would have sent Gunner William "Bill" Milner over the edge. Having slagged the British (and Canadians) for being slow to take Caen, Spielberg then moves heavy German armor west to fight his heroes. Some assault guns or antiquated French tanks bearing Iron Crosses would have added verisimilitude to Spielberg's story at this stage. Instead, he conjured up Tigers. When this scene appeared during a private screening of the film for my students, the audience broke out in muted, derisive laughter: not a common response to Spielberg's epic. The appropriation of the panzer threat, which those idle Anglo-Canadians were wrestling with at that very moment of the campaign, and the gratuitous criticism about the Anglo-Canadians being slow speak to the politics of history and the struggle for legacy. My father respected any man (on either side) who fought in Normandy, and he would not have traded the openness of the plain around Caen for the lethal embrace of the bocage. But he knew where the tanks were, and he would have been apoplectic with anger with Spielberg's historical license. Film is art, make no mistake. But film that takes on historical themes becomes the truth for the masses. And so it is for Normandy, from Cornelius Ryan to Steven Spielberg.

The Canadian moment in the early phase of Operation Overlord was brief but vital. Third Canadian Division did not storm Juno Beach simply to hold the space between British formations, it did not fail to take Caen when it had a chance, and it was certainly not forced into a tenacious defense because of the scale and quality of German counterattacks. The Canadians came to Normandy on 6 June 1944 to kill those counterattacks: to kill panzers. Over four intense days of brutal, close fighting, they did just that. When those initial battles were over, 3rd Canadian Division was indeed a spent force: fought-out, down 3,000 men, and exhausted. But it had stopped the panzers. It is time someone noticed.

I

All Roads Lead to Courseulles

We're going to see this through, you and I . . .
General B. L. Montgomery,
to 3rd Canadian Division, February 1944

ON 28 FEBRUARY 1944 General Bernard Law Montgomery, the ground force commander of Operation Overlord, visited the 3rd Canadian Infantry Division at Bournemouth. After the usual demonstrations arranged for "distinguished visitors," including presenting trophies to the winners of the Canadian army hockey championship, Montgomery rallied the division's gunners around his jeep. "*My* Canadians," he called them. He knew of their Great War reputation for combat effectiveness, but his personal affection for Canadian soldiers began during his time commanding Home Forces two years earlier. In 1942 he described the Canadians as "probably the best material in any armies of the Empire . . . fit and tough."[1] Monty's recent experience commanding Canadians in Italy confirmed that view. The success of Overlord now depended heavily on the gunners who rallied around his jeep on that cool winter afternoon, but not because they were all Canadians. In fact, barely half of them were. But artillery was the key to British Commonwealth battlefield doctrine, and 3rd Canadian Division had more than 8,000 gunners in its complement for the coming assault on France.

By 1944 the "Victor of Alamein" was a living legend. Described by one of his peers as "An efficient little shit!" Monty knew how to train troops, and he was well known as an efficient planner. His arrogance and self-serving attitude would later alienate him bitterly from his American colleagues and from most American historians. However, his appointment as Overlord ground force commander at the end of 1943 was welcomed by most, including the staff of First US Army. They knew that whatever else happened, the planning and the staff work for Overlord would be first-rate. As the First US Army history observed,

"The Canadians went at it like hockey players" because many of them were:
General B. L. Montgomery greets players from the Cameron Highlanders of
Ottawa during his visit to 3rd Canadian Division, February 1944.
(LAC e011108372)

Montgomery brought "the aura of success to Overlord." The Americans also knew that Monty would leave them alone to fight their own way—although not without the occasional suggestion on how things might be done differently.[2]

The diminutive British general also knew how to cultivate a rapport with his troops. When asked after the war who they served under, most Canadian veterans of Italy or northwest Europe would say unhesitatingly, "Monty." While most Canadian generals were dour and uninspiring, Montgomery knew how to foster a following. On one occasion when driving through Canadian lines in Italy in 1943, Montgomery was confronted by a naked soldier wearing a top hat who threw him a smart salute as his car rolled by. Without batting an eye, Montgomery returned the salute. Later he circulated an order that "top hats will not be worn in 8th Army."[3] The Canadian rank and file ate this up, not least because everyone suspected that a Canadian general would have put the man on charge.

On that wintry late February day in 1944, just weeks before the greatest moment in the war in the west, Monty had "his" Canadians enthralled. "We are going to see this through, you and I," he said to the men assembled around him, taking them into his confidence as was his usual practice and making the job ahead a joint effort. "I have never seen so many gunners together at one time before. To see so many is good, as it is the gunners who win battles."[4]

Montgomery's faith in gunners was sincere. Since the Great War the British army had possessed one combat arm that was unsurpassed: its artillery. Many Americans found British artillerymen "stodgy" and conservative, and the British army itself "addicted" to artillery. But the British had learned the hard way in the First World War, and in the early years of the Second, that they could not match German skill at mobile warfare. What they had learned from fighting the Germans on the Somme, at Arras, and at Ypres in 1917–1918, and again in the Western Desert from 1941 to 1943, was that you could kill them in large numbers—and destroy their vaunted counterattacks—with well-controlled and powerful artillery. Monty's great victory at Alamein fifteen months earlier was built around concentrated artillery, that and dogged fighting by the infantry. Normandy would be the same.

Since the previous summer, the gunners of 3rd Canadian Infantry Division had worked hard to develop and perfect the methods crucial to the success of Operation Overlord. They had also grown in number. A British Commonwealth infantry division's order of battle normally included three field regiments of artillery totaling seventy-two guns. A fourth—another twenty-four guns—was added to 3rd Canadian Division in the late summer of 1943, and by February 1944 two British field regiments and a medium regiment (sixteen 4.5-inch guns) had joined. The final addition to the artillery of the Canadian division for the beachhead battles was the I British Corps antitank reserve, 62nd Anti-Tank Regiment, Royal Artillery (RA), with its forty-eight 17-pounder guns. No other Allied formation in Operation Overlord controlled comparable firepower. For the assault on Normandy, 3rd Canadian Division had nearly as many gunners on its order of battle as it had infantry.

Montgomery did not mince his words about the task ahead. The Canadians were in the assault wave; they would have to cross fire-swept beaches, fight their way inland, and then fight off the German panzer counterattack in order to secure the lodgment. Casualties, he warned, would be high. The Germans would hit them with everything they had; there was no going back once they got ashore, and in the early days there would be virtually no one except support echelons behind them. Monty was certain of success, but the initial battles promised to be grim affairs. Gunner Bill Milner of 13th Field Regiment, Royal Canadian Artillery, recalled many years later that Montgomery told them he would accept 75 percent casualties to make the lodgment secure. Monty's Canadians knew what they had to do, and they knew that Montgomery and his staff were working hard to ensure success without the fearful butcher's bill.

Historians tend to focus on the planning and execution of the actual assault landings on 6 June 1944 and assume that what followed afterward would be shaped largely by the fortunes of war. "It had always been impossible to imagine D plus 1," the history of 3rd British Infantry Division observed in 1947. "Try as you would during the days of preparation, you could never project your mind beyond the great assault."[5] Many Canadians who landed that day would agree. But for the Canadians, the days immediately following D-Day were scripted well in advance. Certainly, the senior officers of 3rd Canadian Division understood that their task was to defeat the panzer threat to Overlord itself. The road to that onerous responsibility began in the spring of 1943 and culminated in the operational order received from I British Corps on 5 May 1944, one month to the day before the scheduled landings in France.

The initial task of planning what became Operation Overlord fell to British brigadier Freddie Morgan, the chief of staff to the supreme Allied commander. Morgan, a garrulous and overweening gunner with little combat or command experience, and his small staff of British and American officers, along with a number of Canadians, began work in earnest on 5 March 1943. COSSAC's problems were many and his resources few. Morgan was the chief of staff to a commander who did not yet exist, planning an operation that the Americans thought the British were trying to dodge, and doing so without command of any forces: no divisions, no armor, and, most important of all, no landing craft. Nonetheless, through March and April, Morgan and his staff worked on a five-division assault along the beaches of lower Normandy, between the Seine and the Vire Rivers. A broad front, Morgan knew, was crucial to prevent a small landing from being isolated and destroyed. Lack of resources, however, soon trimmed these ambitions. In May 1943 COSSAC was ordered to scale back his intended five-division assault to just three and to present a coherent plan to the Anglo-American Combined Chiefs of Staff by the summer.

On 15 July 1943 the preliminary COSSAC plan was presented to the British Chiefs of Staff. It called for a landing by three divisions, reinforced on D-Day by one additional infantry brigade and three armored brigades, northwest of Caen in lower Normandy. Its objective was to seize "a bridgehead on the general line all inclusive GRANDCAMP, BAYEUX, CAEN, to land two assault divisions (one British and one Canadian) on the Eastern beaches and one assault division (U.S.) on the Western beaches of the Caen sector."6 The assault was to be conducted by Second British Army, with both American and Canadian armies as follow-on formations. By D+14, the day Morgan hoped to capture Cherbourg, there would be six British, five Canadian, and seven American divisions ashore. The Canadians and British were to exploit south and southeast, taking Caen, clearing areas for airfields, and then First Canadian Army was to lead the breakout toward the Seine. Meanwhile, the Americans would drive into Brittany to secure the ports needed to support the larger campaign into Germany that would follow, probably in 1945. Despite significant changes to the scale of the Overlord plan in early 1944, this remained the general outline of the Normandy campaign.

The core of COSSAC's initial lodgment was the Sommervieu-Bazenville ridge, a broad, flat crest of open farmland running northeast from Bayeux toward Courseulles-sur-mer. Control of the ridge would secure the landing beaches from direct enemy observation, while the Seulles River along its southern edge provided a defensible line and a tank obstacle. Airborne landings (and later commandos) at Colleville-sur-mer and Ouistreham would secure the flanks. The immediate objective of the assault was Bayeux, followed by a quick dash east on D+1 or D+2 to seize Caen. All of this was predicated on the poor state of beach defenses in 1943, on the low level of German troop strength in Normandy, and on the presence in France of no more than twelve first-quality German divisions.

The British Chiefs of Staff accepted Morgan's plan, and it was put before the Combined Chiefs of Staff at Quebec in August 1943 during the Quadrant Conference. They, too, accepted COSSAC's scheme and agreed on 1 May 1944 as the tentative date for D-Day.[7] Thus, by the end of the summer of 1943, a basic plan, the landing area, and a date had been chosen for Overlord.

Canadians were fully engaged in Overlord from the outset. Like the British, they, too, had left France unceremoniously in June 1940, after 1st Canadian Division's ill-fated and mercifully brief sojourn ashore in Brittany. And they had been back in force again in August 1942, only to be repulsed in bloody fashion at Dieppe. In the meantime, while British Commonwealth and empire armies fought in North Africa and the Far East, the Canadians garrisoned Britain. Their consolation from 1942 onward—in theory at least—was that the Canadian army formed the spearhead of the plan to return to France.

By the summer of 1943, First Canadian Army comprised three infantry divisions, two armored divisions, and two armored brigades organized into two corps. Their focus was northwest Europe, and their purpose was to do what their fathers and uncles had done a generation earlier: fight the main body of the German army in the decisive theater of the war in the west. Indeed, many of the Canadian senior officers, like General Andrew McNaughton, who commanded First Canadian Army, had earned their spurs in the Great War. A skilled gunner and scientist, and well loved by his men, Andy McNaughton had been the brilliant counterbattery officer of the Canadian Corps during the Hundred Days campaign of 1918. During the interwar period McNaughton had become chief of the Canadian General Staff, then retired to assume the founding presidency of the National Research Council of Canada. A friend and confidant of the Canadian prime minister, W. L. Mackenzie King, McNaughton was recalled to active service in 1939.

It was McNaughton who led elements of 1st Canadian Division to Brittany in late June 1940, as the British scrambled to build a second expeditionary force to check the German wave sweeping through France. His unceremonious return was softened by a kind letter from then lieutenant general Alan Brooke, who had commanded the failed second British Expeditionary Force. Brooke and McNaughton knew

General Andrew Latta McNaughton. Portrait by the famous Ottawa photographer Karsh. (LAC PA-164285)

each other well. Brooke had served on the Canadian Corps counter-battery staff under McNaughton in 1917–1918. Both had taken credit for some key developments in artillery, and they remained uneasy partners in the new war against Germany. Now it was McNaughton's turn to serve under Brooke. When Brooke assumed command of British Home Forces in the summer of 1940, McNaughton commanded VII British Corps, which, when 2nd Canadian Infantry Division arrived later in 1940, became the new Canadian Corps. By early 1942 there were enough Canadian formations in England to form a second Canadian Corps, and McNaughton took command of First Canadian Army. Under his leadership the Canadians became known as "McNaughton's Dagger," the sharp point of the British Commonwealth and empire pointed at Berlin. Canadians assumed, not least because they had been told often enough and it was repeated often enough in the media, that they would lead the return to France.

Others believed that, too. McNaughton's face graced the cover of *Time* magazine on 10 August 1942 as part of feature coverage of the looming "second front"—the anticipated Allied descent on the French coast. *Time* devoted two full pages to the role McNaughton's Canadians would play. His army was modern, scientific, and accomplished; its heritage was unsurpassed. "The Canadians of World War I seemed to shine out of the blood and muck, the dreary panorama of trench warfare," *Time*'s editors wrote. "They seemed to kill and die with a special dash and lavishness." Indeed, the editors waxed on, in a war in which "glory had almost lost its meaning, when the word was a travesty upon the heaping millions of dead, the Canadians in France kept the sheen of glory." It was unclear where and when the return to France would happen, the editors observed, "but the news that the Canadians will be in the vanguard of invasion is freshening and heartening to a world which needs good news."[8] Eight days later the Canadians did return to France, leaving more than a thousand dead on the beaches of Dieppe. That simply added another reason to focus on getting back to France.

How much of this buzz over First Canadian Army was hype and how much was believable is hard to say. McNaughton surrounded himself with an extensive public relations apparatus, and in the long years of waiting the key message it spread in England was hope. The

A major problem for the British in the fall of 1943: General A. L. McNaughton, on the cover of *Time* magazine, August 1942. (Press clippings, McNaughton Papers, DHH)

army preparing for the return to France was modern, agile, mechanized, and tough. McNaughton's public relations staff also dealt in expectation, the expectation that when the return to France came, Canadians would be in the lead. It helped in selling the message that McNaughton himself was a man of remarkable accomplishment, with a powerful intellect and powerful friends. The Canadian prime minister, Mackenzie King, was an admirer. When McNaughton returned to Ottawa for a visit in February 1942, King met him at the train station. Later that month in Washington, McNaughton had a long chat with General George C. Marshall, the chief of the American General Staff. That was followed by an hour with President Franklin Roosevelt. McNaughton traveled comfortably in senior British circles, too, including weekends at Chequers with Winston Churchill, and was occasionally touted in the London newspapers as a candidate for a British cabinet post.[9] For all these reasons, and because of the troubled legacy of their shared Great War experience, McNaughton was a difficult subordinate for Brooke to manage. However, until mid-1943 even Brooke endorsed the key role that First Canadian Army would play in the anticipated landings in France.

By the summer of 1943 the belief that the Canadians would be central to the launching of the second front remained strong, and it was not misplaced. As Freddie Morgan later observed:

> A high proportion of the troops forming the expeditionary force was in fact, we knew from the start, to be Canadian. By special arrangement therefore with General Andy McNaughton, a Canadian observer was attached to the COSSAC staff in the person of Major General Guy Turner, both these [McNaughton and Turner] being old friends of mine since the days when I had served in the Canadian Army in France from 1915 to 1917. Further than this, taking advantage of our old friendship, I asked General McNaughton for help in filling certain of the vacancies on the COSSAC staff.[10]

From the outset, Overlord was to be a joint American-British-Canadian operation in about equal measure. The initial COSSAC plan called for a three-division landing under Second British Army as the lead formation. One of the initial assault divisions was to be Canadian, and II Canadian Corps was to be the first British Commonwealth corps headquarters to land. Canadians knew of this even before the initial COSSAC plan was completed. In April 1943, just a few weeks after Morgan formally took on the COSSAC role, the commanding officer of 3rd Canadian Division, Major General Rod Keller, and his commander, Royal Artillery (CRA), Brigadier Stanley Todd, were summoned to London for a meeting in the War Office. "At once, we knew this was to be no ordinary meeting," Todd recalled many years later, "because of those present—the Prime Minister, the Chief of the General Staff, the First Lord of the Admiralty and a number of others, all high ranking officers of the three services." It was then that Keller and Todd were told that 3rd Canadian Division had been chosen as one of the assault divisions for the attack on France.[11] The general schedule of activities was outlined, with training to be completed by 31 January 1944, followed by final planning, sea exercises, and rehearsals.

Third Canadian Division's CRA, Brigadier Stanley Todd, was considered a superb choice to coordinate the firepower that lay at the heart of the Anglo-Canadian assault. Born in Ottawa, Todd finished his secondary education in England and enlisted in the Royal Artillery in 1916. He served with distinction in Egypt and Palestine under General Allenby before being invalided out of service in 1919. Back in Canada, Todd immediately joined the militia (the army reserve force) and was soon in the 1st Field Brigade, Canadian Artillery. Undeterred by the lack of funds and training opportunities in the interwar reserves, Todd continued to train and experiment with indirect firepower. By 1939 he was a lieutenant colonel, but he took a demotion to go overseas as a battery commander with 5th Field Regiment, RCA, in July 1940. Montgomery's senior gunner, Major General Meade Dennis, later described Todd as one of the most innovative artillery commanders of the Second World War. "In Normandy," Dennis recalled, "Canadian gunners set a standard for the rest of the seaborne artillery."[12]

In the event, Todd was not alone. He operated in an environment dominated by skilled gunners. Andy McNaughton was among the best on the western front in the Great War, particularly in counterbombardment methods. Morgan and Alan Brooke were both gunners—and

Brigadier P. S. A. Todd, RCA, the quiet and competent Canadian militia gunner who commanded the most powerful concentration of artillery in the Allied assault. (DHH 112.3P1 D1359)

both very familiar with the technical competence and innovative nature of Canadian artillerymen. Even Todd's corps commander, Lieutenant General Harry Crerar, had served with distinction on the gunnery staff of the Canadian Corps in the Great War. In British doctrine much depended on artillery, and in the Overlord plan much of that responsibility fell on the staff and gunners of 3rd Canadian Division.

There was much to be done, and work began immediately. The task of organizing this fell to the newly created 21st Army Group commanded by General Sir Bernard Paget—recently commander in chief (CinC) Home Forces. His chief of staff, then brigadier Charles Loewen (a Canadian serving in the British army), later described Paget as "stern and unbending . . . straight as a die," and a man who "consistently put his country's interests ahead of his own."[13] In the summer of 1943, Paget's 21st Army Group consisted of First Canadian and Second British Armies. The latter, designated the lead formation in the Overlord plan, was the least well developed and trained of Paget's two army staffs, but it assumed responsibility for working out the details of the assault. The actual mechanics of the operation were passed, in turn, to 3rd and 49th British Divisions of Second British Army, and 3rd Canadian Division of First Canadian Army. In a series of exercises through the summer and fall of 1943, Canadian and British units focused on how to land the first wave, how to get reserve brigades ashore, and how to sequence follow-on units over the assault beaches, and helping the navy work out the procedure, method, and timing of their jobs.

Considerable effort was also focused on fire support for the initial assault and getting guns over the beach into action quickly to defeat the expected counterattacks. This included firing artillery from landing craft during the approach, later known as "drenching fire." The idea was worked out by the I Canadian Corps commander, Lieutenant General Harry Crerar, who started by tying 3rd Division's 25-pounder field guns to the decks of their landing craft. Drenching fire was tried successfully in Exercise Pirate in Studland Bay on 16–19 October, when 7th Canadian Infantry Brigade landed with the full panoply of naval, air, and army fire support.

Lashing towed artillery to the deck of a landing craft proved the concept of drenching fire, but it was also important to get the guns ashore and into action quickly. Towed artillery could not do both. Drenching fire required that the guns be pointed forward, which made rapid deployment ashore virtually impossible. The solution was self-propelled artillery. Fortunately, self-propelled artillery was already at the heart of British amphibious doctrine.

British (and COSSAC) planners understood by 1943 that large-scale amphibious assaults had to culminate in the establishment of "a defensive perimeter to allow follow-on forces to assemble behind" and had to be "strongly consolidated against counter-attack." Trying to wrestle towed artillery across a defended beach could not ensure that the defensive perimeter could be established. A British Home Forces G-3 planning document from May 1943 on the problems of invading northwest Europe stated emphatically that the Germans would defeat any invasion on the coast "with reserve divisions, which are usually armoured divisions." To get ashore safely and quickly and to deal with the panzer counterattack, Home Forces planners recommended that "all field artillery and some anti-tank artillery" be self-propelled.[14] Landings in Sicily in July and Salerno in September, during both of which American forces were nearly driven back into the sea by panzer attacks, confirmed the importance of a well-established covering position supported by overwhelming firepower.

So, following Exercise Pirate in October 1943, all of 3rd Canadian Division's artillery regiments—three from its own order of battle plus 19th RCA assigned for the landings—converted to the American M7 self-propelled 105mm gun, the "Priest" (named for its pulpit-like machine gun position). By November, 13th RCA was in Studland Bay with its new Priests working out the mechanics of drenching fire from landing craft.[15] Eventually, all British Commonwealth field artillery regiments designated for the initial Overlord assault were converted to SPs, either the M7 for 3rd Canadian and 3rd British Divisions or, in the case of British 50th Division, the new Canadian-designed and Canadian-built Sexton 25-pounder.

The shift to American SPs was not a simple matter. Anglo-Canadian gunnery calculations were based on degrees and minutes: American artillery used the metric system and graded their sights in mills. Ninety degrees in the British system worked out to 1,600 mills on an American gun, and the range setting was in meters, not yards. "With 4 men to a Detachment," Todd later recalled, "that meant 400 men to retrain on laying and aiming guns." It also meant that all the drill manuals had to be converted to metric, including all the tables to calculate wind, weather, and barometric pressure, and forward observers had to be retrained. Even the drivers of gun tractors now had to learn to drive a tracked vehicle. In fact, everything had to be redone: 3,000 artillerymen of the division's own three regiments, plus those of 19th Field, all of whom were in a high state of readiness in the fall of 1943, now had to go back to basics.[16]

While Canadian and British units worked out the mechanics of the assault and the battle to follow, COSSAC and 21st Army Group staffs worked on the plans. The first appreciations of what the COSSAC three-division assault might look like were done by 21st Army Group. By 1 September the preliminary assignments were worked out. In the meantime, the Canadians planned possible alternative amphibious assaults on the Pas de Calais or in the approaches to Antwerp—both to be executed in the event of a sudden German collapse as had happened in 1918.[17] There appears to be no suggestion yet, in the summer of 1943, that these alternate schemes were part of an emerging deception operation in support of the Normandy landings, although in time that's what they became.

An understanding of how the assault on Normandy was to unfold therefore emerged by the end of August. Third British Division was to land along the coast between Courseulles and Bernieres-sur-mer and hold itself ready to dash to Caen. To the west, 3rd Canadian Division was to land in the middle of the assault between St.-Come-de-Fresne and Ver-sur-mer, secure a covering position between the line of the Seulles River and the Caen-Bayeux highway, and possibly take Bayeux (if the Americans did not do so). The US division was to land farthest west, probably around Arromanches, and possibly take Bayeux. Details of the American role were not yet clear because the US Army was not yet fully part of the planning process, and no US Army formations had been designated. Commandos and Rangers might land at Ouistreham at the mouth of the Orne River or Port-en-Bessin, while airborne troops dropped on both Caen and Bayeux.

The core of the landing zone in both the COSSAC and 21st Army Group plans in the summer of 1943 was the Sommervieu-Bazenville ridge. From there either Caen or Bayeux (preferably both) would have to be secured early. The plan for the "covering position" south of the ridge called for a penetration to a depth of ten kilometers inland, which pushed the forward edge of the lodgment well beyond the natural obstacle of the Seulles River to Esquay-sur-Seulles, Vaux-sur-Seulles, and Brecy. The 21st Army Group estimation of 1 September observed that this covering position west of Caen was "generally speaking devoid of natural anti-tank localities and highly suitable for the employment of armoured divisions." The only way to secure the open area effectively at this stage was with extensive minefields.[18]

Not surprisingly, COSSAC was also working on potential threats to the landings and the likely German response. The first COSSAC appreciation was submitted by the Intelligence Branch on 4 September 1943 and formed the core of COSSAC's "Memorandum on Possible Course of Action Open to German Reserves on D-Day or D Plus 1."[19] At this early stage German troop density in Normandy was low and beach defenses rudimentary. Getting ashore was not the dominant issue; defeating the counterattack was key. Only the four or five mobile divisions then in France and Belgium posed an immediate threat. In September 1943 COSSAC planners expected to face one panzer division (known to the planners as Division Y) garrisoned around St. Lô and a mechanized division (X) at Lisieux, along with one or more infantry divisions in lower Normandy, and another panzer division within one to two days' march at Laval (outside Paris). For planning purposes at this stage, movement of these forces was considered a normal operational road move without serious disruption from air attack or transportation disruption—elements that would later be crucial components of the Overlord plan.

The memorandum of 4 September proposed three options for German action on D+1 or D+2. Option A was a direct attack from their billets by the panzer and mechanized divisions on D-Day: Panzer Division Y striking from St. Lô to the sea north of Bayeux, and Mechanized Division X concentrating west of Caen and striking toward the coast across the open ground on either side of the Mue River (i.e., toward Crepon, Creully, Courseulles, and Douvres). Option B called for the Panzer, mechanized, and infantry divisions to concentrate south of the Caen-Bayeux highway and then attack en masse northward toward the landing beaches.

A variation of the second scenario, option C in the Intelligence Branch estimation, called for a slight delay in the German counterattack until a second panzer division arrived on D+2 or D+3. With four divisions available, COSSAC planners expected the Germans to line up on the Caen-Bayeux highway and attack with three divisions up, with the armor weighted on the right around the Mue River. Mechanized

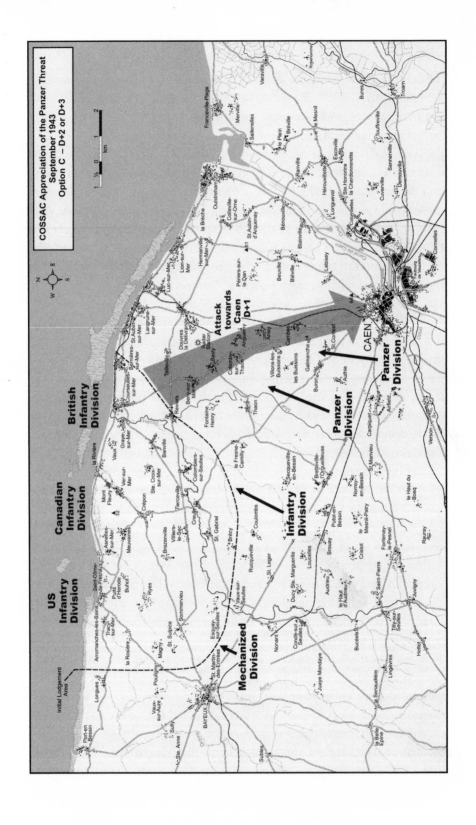

COSSAC Appreciation of the Panzer Threat
September 1943
Option C – D+2 or D+3

Initial Lodgement Area

US Infantry Division

Canadian Infantry Division

British Infantry Division

Mechanized Division

Infantry Division

Panzer Division

Panzer Division

Attack towards Caen D+1

CAEN

BAYEUX

Port-en-Bessin

Arromanches-les-Bains

Longues

Ste. Anne

la Belle Épine

la Senaudière

Hottot

Tilly-sur-Seulles

Langevres

Bucelels

Vavigny

Saint-Pierre

Raurary

le Haut du Bosq

Fontenay-le-Pesnel

Cristot

le Mesnil-Patry

Fontenay-le-Pesnel

Putot-en-Bessin

St. Manvieu

Carpiquet

Airfield

Verson

Aubie

St. Contest

Buron

Galmanche

Cambes

les Buissons

Villons-les-Buissons

Anisy

Anguerny

Basly

Colomby-sur-Thaon

Thaon

Cainet

le Fresne-Camilly

Fontaine Henry

Reviers

Berry-sur-Mer

Tailleville

Douvres la Délivrande

Radar Station

Bernières-St-Aubin sur-Mer

Langrune-sur-Mer

St-Aubin-sur-Mer

Coursseulles-sur-Mer

Graye-sur-Mer

la Rivière

Ver-sur-Mer

Mont Fleury

Crépon

Asnelles-sur-Mer

Meuvaines

Brazenville

Villiers-le-Sec

St. Gabriel

Brécy

Rucqueville

Coulombs

St. Léger

Loucelles

Norrey-en-Bessin

Secqueville-en-Bessin

Bretteville-l'Orgueilleuse

Brouay

Audrieu

le Haut d'Audrieu

Vaux-sur-Seulles

Ducy Ste. Marguerite

Condé-sur-Seulles

Nonant

Juaye Mondaye

St. Martin-des-Entrées

Esquay-sur-Seulles

Sommervieu

St Sulpice

Magny

Poulongy

Vaux-sur-Aure

Sully

Suibes

Ste. Croix-sur-Mer

Colombiers-sur-Seulles

Creully

Tiercerville

Bainville

Vaux

St Martin

Ryes

Buhot

Puits d'Hérode

Tracy-sur-Mer

Saint-Côme de-Fresnê

la Rosière

Lion-sur-Mer

Luc-sur-Mer

la Brèche

Hermanville-sur-Mer

Colleville-sur-Orne

Ouistreham

St-Aubin d'Arquenay

Périers-sur-le-Dan

Beuville

Biéville

Lebisey

Bénouville

Blainville

Hérouvillette

Ranville

le Plein

Sallenelles

Franceville-Plage

Merville

Merville

le Mesnil

Varaville

Breville

Ste. Honorine

la Chardonnerette

Cuverville

Démouville

Sannerville

Touffreville

Bures

Troarn

Escoville

Longueval

Colombelles

Faubourg de Vaucelles

Cormelles

Canal de Caen

km

Division X was to attack on the left flank, west of Conde-sur-Seulles, while the infantry division attacked between the Seulles and the Mue Rivers. The panzer divisions were to attack down the east side of the Mue River, led by Panzer Division Y, with the second panzer division echeloned to the right rear, "ready to add impetus to the attack of Pz Div 'Y' on D+1 and to take advantage of any success gained."

The ground selected for the panzer divisions in option C gave them a straight run to the sea over open ground to the area east of Courseulles. Success here would cut off and destroy the British division slated to dash into Caen on D+1 and recapture its landing beaches between Courseulles and Bernieres. However, option C did not immediately put the Germans into the Allied landing zones west of the Seulles River. And so COSSAC planners conceived of the panzer counterattack in two phases: clearing ground up to the Seulles River and the coast between Courseulles and Bernieres on D+1/2, and then an assault across the Seulles into the eastern flank of the landing beaches on D+2/3. Option C was remarkably close to the scheme adopted by the Germans after 6 June 1944, especially the 1st SS Panzer Corps attempts from 8 to 10 June.

COSSAC's initial appreciation of German responses was tested in late September in a war game and modified. The new Overlord "plan" by early October 1943 called for airborne landings on the Aure River crossings west of Bayeux and directly on Caen itself, as well as airborne and commando landings at Ouistreham in the east and Colleville-sur-mer in the west. This was as far as COSSAC planners could go with the resources allocated to them. Three seaborne divisions were still to land north of Bayeux, and so it was expected that the Germans would fight tenaciously to hold both it and the line of the Seulles River. Holding Bayeux was now believed to be the key to German defeat of the landings. The road network coming into Bayeux from all directions would be used to assemble panzer forces for a counterattack down the Sommervieu-Bazenville ridge toward Crepon, into the heart of the assault beaches, on D-Day—and into the positions held by 3rd Canadian Division in the COSSAC plan.

In the COSSAC "game" played in late September 1943, the Bayeux-based panzer attack failed on D-Day. It was then relaunched on D+1 as earlier planned, on the plains to either side of the Mue River.

In this scenario, newly arrived panzer forces concentrated along the Caen-Bayeux highway near Putot and Bretteville l'Orgueilleuse for an attack down the west side of the Mue toward Banville, Ste.-Croix-sur-mer, Courseulles, and Crepon. As the Germans struggled to contain the assault, "Anglo-American" forces (actually American-Canadian) pushed hard toward Bayeux as one division (3rd British in the 21st Army Group plan) and made a dash to link up with the airborne forces in Caen. The result on D+1 was an encounter battle northwest of Caen between the reconnaissance elements of two panzer divisions and a British infantry division, which the British division wins and is able to push through to Caen. Bayeux falls to the Allies on D+2, and by D+3 the Germans have resorted to trying to recapture Caen using infantry divisions to envelop it from the northwest.[20]

The COSSAC war game of September 1943 resulted in a "New D-Day Scenario" by early October. It was now anticipated that Bayeux would fall quickly to the Allies followed by the same mad dash to Caen on D+1 by 3rd British Division. In this scenario the Allies anticipated that the Germans would fight hard to hold the line of the Seulles River while they concentrated their armor around Ste.-Croix-Grand-Tonne on the Caen-Bayeux highway. The panzers' task was to strike toward the open ground northeast of Bayeux, to the Sommervieu-Bazenville ridge, from where their panzers could roam unimpeded to the sea and crush the landings.[21]

This key piece of ground on the Sommervieu-Bazenville ridge was assigned to 3rd Canadian Division in the 21st Army Group plans, so from the outset the Canadian task was to stop the panzers. This was to be done by holding a covering position south of the Sommervieu-Bazenville ridge and just short of the Caen-Bayeux highway east of Bayeux from St. Martin les Entress through Vaux-sur-Seulles to Brecy, and—presumably—by taking Bayeux itself.[22]

These early COSSAC estimates of German responses focused on two crucial pieces of ground: the area west of Caen on either side of the Mue River, or the Sommervieu-Bazenville ridge northeast of Bayeux. Both thrusts culminated at the mouth of the Seulles, at Courseulles-sur-mer. However, COSSAC planners were convinced that the ground west and north of Caen was the key terrain in any panzer counterattack on Overlord. This was evident in a major assessment of the role of terrain submitted by the G-2 of the Intelligence Branch to the headquarters of First US Army on 22 October 1943, a follow-up memo on the subject a month later, and a further memo on terrain in January 1944.

The COSSAC terrain assessment of October was written as a German staff appreciation of the role of ground in defeating an Allied landing. "If it is desired to drive the enemy into the sea on D-Day," the appreciation observed, "SOMERVIEU ridge EAST of BAYEUX and BRAZENVILLE [*sic*] ridge, still further EAST, stand out as logical places for a counter attack with Panzer formations." If, however, the Allies advanced quickly across the Seulles River, or the German commander wanted to assemble more forces before dealing the death blow to the landings, "then CAEN and the flat, high ground north-west of it stand out as important places for counter-attack." Appendix A of this appreciation was even more emphatic: "The country northwest of CAEN is supremely suited to tank action, it is therefore in this area that the panzer battle should be staged in order that the landing forces may be driven back into the sea."[23]

By the late fall of 1943, COSSAC planners operated on the assumption that the Germans would attack immediately with units and formations already in place, rather than wait until overwhelming force arrived. This was based on the "Comparison of Neptune and recent landings in Italy," completed by G-2 Intelligence on 21 November. It concluded, "German policy against seaborne landings is one of immediate counterattack. . . . As soon as reinforcements are available, full scale counter attacks will be launched." Further comparisons with Italy done in early 1944 confirmed this view, especially the German reaction at Gela, Sicily, in July 1943, when Tiger tanks nearly threw the Americans into the sea. "The German action at Gela is exactly what one would expect in France," Major General P. G. Whiteford, G-2 Intelligence on the COSSAC staff, wrote on 13 January. "The Germans will not risk delaying their counterattacks." Whiteford and his staff concluded that the Germans now knew that they had to beat the Allies on the beach or risk defeat.[24]

As the COSSAC and other planners worked through the likely German responses to a landing in lower Normandy in the fall of 1943, politics intruded into the planning for Overlord. As Morgan warned his Canadian friends, 1944 was an election year in the United States, and all planning for Overlord was contingent upon American sensibilities.[25] These came to the fore during the Quadrant Conference of August 1943 in Quebec, when the US Chiefs of Staff and President Roosevelt finally drew a firm commitment from the British that Overlord would go in the spring of 1944. It was also agreed at Quebec that the assault would be led by the Americans. When First US Army under Lieutenant General Omar Bradley was established in England in early October under 21st Army Group, it would become the lead formation of the three-division COSSAC assault plan. By then US V Corps was already working on detailed planning (as I British Corps had been since the summer). With 3rd Canadian and 3rd British Divisions already assigned to the initial assault wave, the final missing American piece was filled in in November when 1st US Infantry Division returned from Italy.

The insertion of Americans into a leading role in Overlord did not, for the moment, reduce the high-profile role of First Canadian Army. Through 1942 and early 1943, First Canadian Army was primed as the Normandy "breakout" force. Exercise Spartan, run in March 1943, tested the concept of a breakout force, and in the public relations run-up McNaughton had characterized it as "a dress rehearsal for full scale invasion on the continent."[26] McNaughton also considered Spartan a test of the battle worthiness of his key staff officers. It was, in McNaughton's words, a test of both the "physical condition and endurance of the troops" and "the ability of commanders and staffs to administer, handle and fight their formations and units."[27] The chief of the Imperial General Staff, General Alan Brooke, had similar aims in Exercise Spartan. He designed the exercise to test two things: the Canadian ability to break out of a beachhead and conduct mobile warfare, and McNaughton's ability to command the breakout force. As John Rickard concluded in the only serious study of Spartan, "McNaughton did not have to exhibit Napoleonic brilliance, but he did have to pull off a solid, workmanlike performance." What McNaughton really had to do, Rickard concludes, was impress Brooke.[28]

McNaughton's three-corps First Canadian Army, composed of I Canadian Corps, II Canadian Corps headquarters commanding an armored corps of two divisions, and XII British Corps, was to break out of a beachhead along the Channel coast, sweep through a two-corps "German Sixth Army" west of London, and initiate a war of movement north to the Fens. Exercise Spartan went well, until McNaughton attempted to totally unhinge the defenders by sending his armored corps on a wide sweeping maneuver. The armored corps headquarters was short of signals staff on its first exercise and had no experience commanding armor. McNaughton was well aware of this when he included them: it was a training exercise, after all. But Lieutenant General E. W. Sansom bungled II Corps' movement and was only just recovering when the exercise was halted. Otherwise, for the most part First Canadian Army had done well.[29]

Certainly this was the view of CinC Home Forces at the time, General Paget, and his report on Exercise Spartan said as much. Most observers agreed that McNaughton had done well, but several of his subordinate commanders had not. Paget was sharply critical of Sansom's performance in command of the armored corps and urged McNaughton to fire him. McNaughton refused, and by July the two old friends had fallen out over the issue.

While General Sir Bernard Paget gave McNaughton a passing grade on Exercise Spartan, Brooke expressed strong displeasure with his "failure" as an army commander during the exercise. Paget "has no idea how bad Andy McNaughton really is," Brooke recorded in his personal notes.[30] McNaughton's greatest shortcoming as an army commander was his failure to either train his subordinates or fire the failures. Either way, the larger problem was McNaughton. By June word reached Ottawa of rumors circulating in British circles that McNaughton had done poorly in Spartan. Lester Pearson, on the staff at the Canadian legation in Washington, was so upset by these rumors that he secured a copy of the umpire's report. "On reading it," he recorded in his diary in late June, "there seemed to be no serious reflections on McNaughton of any kind." He immediately phoned Ottawa "to stop at once any silly stories that might be going around."[31] It was already much too late.

Domestic politics in all three Western democracies now conspired to undermine the role of Canadians in the final Overlord scheme. It started at home. While McNaughton's Dagger assembled in England, preparing for its great moment on the plains of northern France, the

Canadian electorate grew angry and unsettled over Canada's small role in the actual fighting. As the high tide of fascism began to recede in late 1942, the Canadian defense minister, Colonel J. L. Ralston, warned his cabinet colleagues that the war might end abruptly, as it had in 1918. Should that happen, he lamented at a cabinet meeting in December, then "Canada would have to hang its head in shame" because its army had not been in the fight.[32] As Ralston opined, even the Americans were engaged in ground combat. Canada had been at war for more than three years, and apart from disasters at Dieppe and Hong Kong, the army was still idle. Ralston—a distinguished Great War battalion commander—was aware that the army's idleness was well in keeping with his government's plans. Until that point Prime Minister Mackenzie King had worked hard to keep the army inactive for fear that a high casualty bill would prompt a return to demands for conscription and lead to rioting in Quebec. McNaughton was also sensitive to those concerns, and it seems the plan to hold Canada's army for the final show suited both the government and McNaughton well until 1943.

But popular unrest with King's government mounted through early 1943, and with some key elections looming in the summer, King and Ralston pushed to get 1st Canadian Division into the Sicilian landings in July. This was arranged, in great haste, late in the Operation Husky planning stages despite the reservations of senior British commanders and reluctance of British politicians. But everyone understood that the Canadians needed combat experience, and that King's government needed to placate an angry electorate. The intent, at this stage, was to bring 1st Canadian Division back to the United Kingdom in time for any landing in France.

By the time 1st Canadian Division waded ashore at Pachino, the pressure on Mackenzie King's government in Ottawa was intense, and it was already lobbying for the deployment of another division and a corps headquarters to the Italian theater. In theory, these units too might fight in Italy and come back to the United Kingdom for the spring of 1944, and by then senior Canadian generals would have much-needed combat experience handling divisions and a corps.[33] Although the Canadian government made the best of its new—limited—role in Italy, the hoped-for boost to morale at home was botched in July when the initial Anglo-American news releases for Operation Husky failed (despite arrangements to the contrary) to mention the Canadian role. In the event, Canadians had little interest in Sicily, and the campaign was short. Moreover, getting one division into a global war impressed no one. Even Australian liaison officers were overheard in the stalls of an Ottawa washroom in late July snorting derisively in sotto voce over Canada's "boasting and bragging about one Division."[34]

By the time of the Quebec Conference in August, the campaign in Sicily was long over, and the Canadian army was idle again. King also now had the measure of public discontent. In early August his government lost four federal by-elections, and his party, the Liberals, was booted from power in Ontario. Most of King's cabinet blamed McNaughton's policy of keeping First Canadian Army intact as a single, unified national unit as the reason their government was unpopular. The Canadian army was not doing what the Canadian electorate expected it to do: fight. Blame for the faltering popularity of King's government now fell squarely on General McNaughton, whom Colonel Ralston also intensely disliked. Now, for domestic political reasons, King needed the army in the fight, and he needed newspaper stories about Canadians in combat.[35] To do that, it seemed that Andy McNaughton had to go.

The British wanted McNaughton gone, too, and the First Canadian Army dispersed, for their own reasons. After Exercise Spartan, Alan Brooke was convinced that the Canadians lacked the general officers and staff ability to command a field army, and that Andy McNaughton was not the man to fix the problem. Sending Canadian generals and their higher formations to Italy to cut their teeth might solve that problem—and others besides. Ralston, the Canadian defense minister, had already broached the idea of an increased Canadian role in any campaign on the Italian mainland with senior British officers during a visit to London in July. At the Quebec Conference the next month, Ralston made the pitch directly to General Brooke. The Canadian government now wanted another division and a corps headquarters sent to the Mediterranean for the forthcoming campaign in Italy. Brooke warned Ralston that there could be no guarantees that forces on this scale would get back to the United Kingdom in time for a landing in France in the spring of 1944. In fact, he warned that if a Canadian corps was sent to Italy, "it would be advisable to abandon [the] idea of [a] Canadian army."[36]

The real problem for the British was not the Canadians but the Americans. As McNaughton confided to a member of his staff in May, when 1st Canadian Division replaced 3rd British Division for the landings in Sicily, it remained essential to keep British formations in the United Kingdom to balance the rising tide of American strength. Moreover, the British had been chided by both the American and the German press for fighting the war on the back of the empire—again. Sending more Canadians out to the Mediterranean threatened to reduce "British" forces at home and add to the Commonwealth presence in Italy.

However, by the late summer of 1943, British problems were much bigger than that. At Quebec it was agreed that the new lead formation for Operation Overlord would be First US Army rather than Second British Army. With the Americans now in the lead and First Canadian Army trained as the breakout force, Second British Army would not arrive in Normandy until some unspecified later date. In short, the British role would not even be secondary to the Americans: the British would be the "also-rans" of Operation Overlord, leaving the Canadians to receive the accolades for what was to be the critical moment of the war in the west. This was, in fact, the COSSAC plan until a final revision was issued on 27 December 1943, just prior to Montgomery's major alteration of the Overlord scheme.

By the fall of 1943, much remained to be resolved, and the pressure to do so rested heavily on General Alan Brooke. "I very much sympathize with you in the return of the Beaver," Field Marshall Sir John Dill, the British representative to the Combined Chiefs of Staff in Washington, wrote to Brooke in a personal letter of 16 October, "& in your many other difficulties." "The Beaver" Dill referred to was Lord Beaverbrook, the Canadian press baron, erstwhile minister of aircraft production, by 1943 Lord Privy Seal, and throughout the war one of Churchill's intimate circle. It was the Beaver, as Sir Max Aitken, who organized the press campaign of the Great War that lauded the Canadians, and other colonial troops, as the backbone of the British army and the keys to Allied victory in 1918. Just how much he was a part of the selling of McNaughton's Dagger as the leading force in the Allied return to France remains unclear. But he was a nettlesome force in Brooke's attempts to manage Churchill and the war, as Dill's unguarded comments suggest. More ominously, Dill also warned that "our difficulties with the Americans are going to increase rather than diminish with the growing strength & a Presidential election approaching." This was the real issue, and pressure was mounting to have the American chief of staff, George Marshall, appointed as Allied supreme commander as a reflection of that growing American importance.[37]

Fortunately for Brooke, the increasing Canadian commitment to Italy undermined the viability of First Canadian Army and gave the British the "out" they needed to push the Canadians aside. It was soon confirmed, as Brooke had warned, that the I Canadian Corps headquarters and 5th Canadian Armoured Division could go to Italy, but they could not be brought back in time for a spring landing in France. The faint hope of maintaining a major Canadian role in Overlord remained only if the landing was set back to September 1944. In truth, time was short. All the British formations coming home from the Mediterranean for Overlord were either back or on their way by the end of 1943.[38] By then, I Canadian Corps had just become operational, and 5th Canadian Armoured Division had yet to fight its first battle. Mackenzie King's government, now desperate to get into the fight on a larger scale, offered no objection to the implications of the Italian commitment to the fate of First Canadian Army and Canada's role in the forthcoming invasion of France. Perhaps this was because through the fall of 1943 the fiction of a First Canadian Army composed of II Canadian Corps and one British corps as a key component of Overlord was maintained.[39] In the fall of 1943 the only way to fix this problem, and get the British back into a central role in Overlord, was to get rid of McNaughton.

This was accomplished in November.

Through the fall Brooke remained adamant that McNaughton was not fit to command in the field, and he made that clear to the Canadian government. By then Paget, now commander of 21st Army Group, had had a change of heart about McNaughton's performance in Exercise Spartan and supported Brooke's position. McNaughton later claimed that Paget "was under orders" to do so.[40] Perhaps, as Charles Loewen observed, Paget was a man who "consistently put his country's interests ahead of his own."[41] Rickard claims the falling-out was over

McNaughton's refusal to fire Lieutenant General Sansom. It mattered little. On 12 November, while in London, Ralston—against his own judgment—made one final appeal to Brooke on behalf of his government to retain McNaughton in command of First Canadian Army. The pressure to do so came from Prime Minister King. There would be, King reminded Ralston, an "appalling series of consequences" if McNaughton's dismissal was made public. Brooke refused to budge: McNaughton had to go. The next day Ralston, General Ken Stuart (formerly chief of the General Staff in Ottawa and recently appointed chief of staff, Canadian Military Headquarters, London), and Paget met with McNaughton and broke the news. Paget's about-face and King's personal appeal to go quietly took the fight out of McNaughton. On 7 December, following a medical exam, McNaughton announced that he needed leave. Rickard concludes that he was simply exhausted by the intrigue and wanted out.

McNaughton's looming departure left what was now COSSAC's proposed "First Anglo-Canadian Army" in an even more perilous state: an army without a designated commanding officer. To keep First Canadian Army in the mix, McNaughton wanted his successor named immediately. But no one in the British senior staff was any happier with the likely candidate, General H. D. "Harry" Crerar. A plodding, colorless gunner who Brooke also knew from the artillery staff of the Canadian Corps in 1918, as chief of the Canadian General Staff, Crerar was the architect of First Canadian Army, and he exhibited barely restrained enthusiasm to command it in battle. Crerar had handled I Canadian Corps well in Exercise Spartan, and Brooke liked him. Montgomery did not, and he later described Crerar as a "good plain cook." Unfortunately, Crerar had no recent combat experience and none in command of higher formations in action. So in late 1943 Crerar was sent out to Italy to get experience. In theory he, too, would come back for Overlord. If Montgomery had had his way, Crerar would have stayed in Italy for the balance of the war.[42]

The result of all this was that the remnants of First Canadian Army in Britain were in disarray by the end of 1943 and hardly able to assume a key role in Overlord. Canadian hopes that the British would parachute in a capable senior British officer to command First Canadian Army were pure fancy. The British had their own reasons for

Three key players in the fate of First Canadian Army meet in May 1944: General B. L. Montgomery, Prime Minister William Lyon Mackenzie King of Canada, and General H. D. G. Crerar, just back from Italy and now in command of First Canadian Army. (LAC 32883 MMD)

wanting a prominent role in Overlord, now that it was really going to happen. On 26 December 1943 McNaughton handed over command of First Canadian Army to General Stuart, who took over temporarily until Crerar returned from Italy. McNaughton had warned Ralston on Christmas Day that Stuart's appointment as a caretaker would be seen as "a clear indication that the dispersion of the remains of the Canadian Army is in fact to be proceeded with."[43]

Under these circumstances, First Canadian Army could never have been a lead formation in Operation Overlord. However, its long-touted role as a "dagger pointed at Berlin" would later contribute to Operation Fortitude, the deception operation that sought to convince the Germans that the main Allied landing would be in the Pas de Calais. This was part of the much larger Overlord deception covering operation, Bodyguard, which was approved on Christmas Eve 1943. It says a great deal about the expectations of the Canadian role in any forthcoming landing in France to note that the Germans commented publicly on McNaughton's removal from command of First Canadian Army. In the Great War the Germans learned to anticipate a major offensive by locating the Canadian troops. For years now they had been in Britain, although a few had recently turned up in Italy. On 29 December, three days after McNaughton resigned, the German international radio service broadcast the news. "During the past few years," the newscaster reported, "ever since there has been talk about a Second Front, McNaughton was put down as the favourite for the post of Commander in Chief of the invasion forces." Now that General Dwight D. Eisenhower had been announced as the commander, apparently McNaughton had no desire to "command Canadian troops under an American superior" and have them slaughtered by a foreign general, as had happened so often under the British.[44] If the Germans actually believed that, and that First Canadian Army remained a key component of planning for the Second Front, then the Canadian role in strategic deception that followed was more important than historians suspect. Events in the spring of 1944 would seem to support that view.

While the Canadian army's major role in Overlord collapsed in December 1943, what was salvaged was the participation of 3rd Canadian Division. Early in the month it was transferred to I British Corps for training purposes, and on 19 December it was formally placed under command of the British corps for Operation Overlord. The final COSSAC plan, issued on 29 December, retained it as part of an unspecified "British-Canadian" composite army.[45]

If the Canadians' mood over their declining role in Overlord was somber by December, that of COSSAC and 21st Army Group planners was gloomy, too. D-Day was barely six months away, and the prospect of the Germans crushing the tiny three-division landings of the COSSAC plan had driven Morgan's planners "to frank defeatism" by late 1943.[46] Steel-reinforced concrete gun positions, trenches, wire, and minefields were being installed on the coast of France at a frantic pace. And in December the "Desert Fox," General Erwin Rommel, was appointed amid much fanfare to command the coast defenses of western Europe. Everyone expected Rommel, the "wunderkind" of the

Nazi generals, to work miracles before the winter storms gave way to good invasion weather.

The Allies also brought their A-team home in late 1943 to oversee the forthcoming invasion of France, a development that would have led to a subordinate role for First Canadian Army in any event. On 23 December 1943 General Montgomery, then in command of the British Eighth Army in Italy, was appointed Overlord ground force commander. Bringing home the Victor of Alamein to lead the assault on France was proof of the importance that the British government attached to the culminating act of a long and bloody war. Four days after getting the news, Montgomery flew to Tunisia to discuss Overlord with its newly designated supreme commander, General Dwight D. Eisenhower. Montgomery had already concluded that the COSSAC plan would not do; it was too small, too prone to being overwhelmed. Ike had already reached the same conclusion. By the time Montgomery arrived in London and had his first meeting with COSSAC planners, it was clear that the landings had to span a much wider area. After several days of debate and reconsideration, Montgomery ordered planning to start for a five-division assault between the Orne and the Vire Rivers.

The idea of a five-division assault was not original; it had been the basis of Morgan's planning in the spring of 1943 until he was ordered to cut back to three. Now Montgomery made the idea his. He spent the first weeks of January revising the Overlord plan and putting his stamp on it and much else besides. This included building a staff he trusted, typically his "own" people. Many of 21st Army Group staff assembled under Paget as well as Morgan's COSSAC staff left for other jobs, and many more were pushed aside. Eventually even COSSAC himself, Lieutenant General Freddie Morgan, a bitter personal enemy of Montgomery and·one of his most relentless critics, had to go. Monty brought his favorites back from Italy to help run the operation. These included Lieutenant General Sir Miles Dempsey to command Second British Army.

On 21 January 1944 the tentative new plan was discussed at what was now the Supreme Headquarters, Allied Expeditionary Force at Norfolk House, in London. Montgomery made the case for a five-division assault spanning lower Normandy from the Orne to the Vire Rivers, with supporting airborne landings to secure either flank. The increase in the scope and scale of the assault would delay the landings from early May until later in the month or perhaps early June. Morgan protested that abandoning COSSAC's proposed airdrop on Caen ensured that it would not be captured on D-Day, but his objections were ignored. The new plan also altered the assessments of how the enemy might respond. All of this had major implications for the landings and for the role of 3rd Canadian Division.

While Montgomery's staff worked on the new Initial Joint Plan (IJP), on 31 January 1944 COSSAC issued its last appreciation of likely enemy responses to the expanded Overlord scheme. Morgan's estimates of where the panzers would go remained largely unchanged from the previous fall. The panzer division known to be at Lisieux (at this stage 10th SS Panzer "Frundsberg" Division) would likely bypass Caen (unless ordered to attack Allied airborne troops landing there) and then do one of two things, both focused on the Mue River. It would either attack down the east side of the Mue toward Douvres and seize the high ground northwest of Caen, or attack west of the Mue toward Crepon, Banville, Bazenville, and Courseulles. The scenario for D+2 was for the Germans to secure the Bayeux pivot "by sheer weight," then radiate attacks with three divisions on the assault beaches from Port-en-Bessin to Courseulles-sur-mer along the Sommervieu-Bazenville ridge.[47] For COSSAC, at least, the expanded landing zone did not change the fundamentals of geography or the German response: rapid panzer thrusts at the heart of the landings across good tank country.

On 1 February 1944 the new IJP was issued, and the whole operation was now firmly in the hands of SHAEF. The IJP called for a landing by two armies, side by side, with First US Army west of Bayeux and Second British Army to the east. First Canadian Army was now a follow-on formation. This changed the air support plan. Faced with the option of remaining with First Canadian Army or continuing its high-profile role in providing air support for the leading wave, No. 84 Group (Royal Canadian Air Force [RCAF]) opted to support Second British Army. As the director of air staff at the RCAF's overseas headquarters concluded, "The fact that the Canadian Army has not been picked to launch the first assault is no good reason why the RCAF should relinquish its honoured place."[48] No. 83 Group, all Royal Air Force (RAF) squadrons, would now work with First Canadian Army.

Under the IJP, airborne landings secured the flanks of both armies, but details of these remained unclear. The new plan called for the capture of Bayeux by a division of XXX British Corps, which would land on the beaches previously designated by COSSAC for the Canadians just north of the Sommervieu-Bazenville ridge. The two divisions of I British Corps, 3rd British and 3rd Canadian, which had been working on their role since the summer of 1943, now shifted east. The Canadians would land between Courseulles and St. Aubin (the original 3rd British Division beach), with 3rd British landing between Langrune and Ouistreham, at the mouth of the Orne River.

The IJP called for Caen and the canal and river lines running through it to the sea to be taken and held on D-Day. This would provide a solid defense along the river and canal from Ouistreham right through the dense urban area of the city to the western outskirts of Caen. Taking these objectives would completely deny the German panzer division at Lisieux easy access to the open ground north of the city, which had been the focus of some COSSAC concern.[49] While the river and canal to the north of the city were taken by paratroops and glider infantry, capturing Caen itself on D-Day would be the task of 3rd British Division landing on Sword Beach. To complete this defense against panzer attack, it only remained to secure the plains to the west of Caen on either side of the Mue River, the primary focus of COSSAC estimations of likely panzer counterattacks. This would now be the job of 3rd Canadian Division.

Montgomery's IJP accepted the idea that the Germans would immediately attack the landings with mechanized and panzer formations, and on a scale that dwarfed COSSAC estimates from 1943. Not only were the beaches now heavily defended, and increasingly strengthened by concrete, wire, and guns, but Monty's intelligence staff expected at least seven mechanized or panzer divisions to arrive in the assault area by D+4 and to be ready for battle by D+5.[50] No one could be sure how this would play out. The only certainty for 21st Army Group by mid-February 1944 was that the armored division garrisoned in the Lisieux area would likely be on the beaches north of Caen, somehow, within eight hours of the landings.

What the Germans would do with the rest of their counterattack divisions was now obscured by the increased breadth of the invasion front.

There seemed many possibilities. COSSAC staff always assumed that the ground west of Bayeux was unsuitable for large-scale mechanized forces, but the new direct threat to Cherbourg from a landing west of the Vire by an American division muddied the waters. In particular, La Haye du Puits, the crucial road junction controlling routes up the west coast of the Cotentin Peninsula, was now identified as a potential major target of German mobile reserves. That threat came from 21st Panzer Division at Rennes, just to the south. But where would the rest go?

The notion that German panzer divisions would move into the Cotentin survived until a few weeks prior to the landings, but it was not given much weight because the ground was simply unsuitable for a large-scale mechanized assault. As Major General N. R. Bull, the American G-3 at SHAEF, explained in a memo to SHAEF on 24 February 1944, the real problem was that they just did not know what the Germans would do. As he saw it, the Germans had two choices: try to deny the Allies the port of Cherbourg or attack "the main threat" in the Caen-Bayeux area.[51] In the event, they did both but used different forces for each task: moving infantry divisions into the base of the Cotentin and shifting armor east toward Caen.[52]

While SHAEF planners remained uncertain during the winter of 1944 over just where the main German counterattack on the landings might occur, there was little doubt that threat of a major panzer attack in the Caen area dominated Montgomery's thoughts. When asked by airmen in late March 1944 to push forward the timetable for capture of ground around Caen for airfields, Montgomery refused to budge. According to a report on the meeting, "He had in mind the possibility that the enemy might concentrate their forces on this flank."[53]

What this all meant for 3rd Canadian Infantry Division was clear enough. The Canadians were training to hold the key ground west of Caen on either side of the Mue River, and they were going to do it with overwhelming firepower. By February 1943, when Montgomery called the gunners of 3rd Canadian Division around his jeep, there were 8,000 of them manning nearly 200 artillery pieces for the beachhead battles. These included 144 field guns, eighteen mediums, and thirty-two 95mm howitzers. The Canadians also controlled all forty-eight of I British Corps' powerful 17-pounder antitank guns (half of them self-propelled), in addition to 3rd Canadian Division's own antitank regiment (3rd Anti-Tank, RCA) and, of course, the antitank guns of the infantry battalions.

The task of 3rd Canadian Division on D-Day and in the beachhead battles was confirmed on 4 March, when I British Corps issued its "Operational Instruction No 1." The Canadian division was "to establish itself with two bdes [brigades] up on the general line PUTOT EN BESSIN 9072–CARPIQUET 9769 as soon as possible on D-Day." This position, astride the Caen-Bayeux road and rail links, stands at the head of the two broad plains that run on either side of the Mue River to the sea. According to the I British Corps instruction, the Canadians' objective covered "the probable areas for enemy counter attacks."

The language of the I Corps operational instruction of 4 March is deliberate and spare but clear. Nowhere else in the document is there a generic guesstimate of the area for likely enemy counterattacks. The task of 3rd British Division, for example, was to capture Caen and secure the crossings over the Caen canal and the Orne River. It was warned that, "The enemy *may* develop counter attacks" through the city, to the north at the canal and river crossing, and in the open ground to the west of Caen in an attempt to drive them out of the city.[54] The I Corps operational instruction of 4 March 1944 therefore put the Canadians on the key ground that intelligence staff had long identified for a decisive counterattack against the Overlord operation.

Meanwhile, I British Corps' "Operational Instruction No. 1" of 4 March 1944 evolved into "I Corps Operational Order for OVERLORD," which was issued on 5 May 1944. The tasks assigned to 3rd British Division had undergone a subtle change (for reasons discussed in the next chapter). Capturing Caen on D-Day remained its primary objective, but the order guarded against failure by digressing at some length on what to do if Caen could not be taken quickly. If Caen did not fall on D-Day, or by efforts shortly afterward (conducted in consultation with corps headquarters with follow-on forces assigned to the task), 3rd British Division was to "contain it," secure the eastern flank of the landings, and "stay mobile."[55] In this scenario, the actual work of capturing Caen would fall to two reserve formations, 51st Highland Division and 4th Armoured Brigade, both slated to land on D+1.[56]

The task assigned to 3rd Canadian Infantry Division in the final operational order of 5 May is also a little more nuanced. The Canadians were to advance to their brigade fortress positions on the Caen-Bayeux highway on either side of the Mue River and guard the "probable alternative areas [i.e., east *or* west of the Mue River] of enemy counter attack." Historians have observed that the Canadians' orders for Overlord allowed for exploitation to the valley of the Odon River against light opposition, or even sending 2nd Canadian Armoured Brigade and some infantry to hold the heights of Point 112 on the other side of the Odon, if the German response to the landings was unexpectedly slow. This was true. And Montgomery made much fuss about driving deep with armored formations and upsetting the enemy's rhythm. But the operational order issued to 3rd Canadian Division on 5 May 1944 was quite clear: it was to ensure that "the firm base [at Putot-Carpiquet] will be retained," and it was to stop the "*probable*" enemy counterattack.

So on the eve of D-Day the Canadians knew what they had to do on D+1 and the days that followed. Montgomery knew it in February when he spoke to the gunners of 3rd Canadian Division—both Canadians and British. It was indeed good to see so many gunners. The Allies were going to need them.

2

Prelude to Battle

Now all the youth of England are on fire.
And silken dalliance in the wardrobe lies;
Now thrive the armourers, and honour's thought
Reigns solely in the breast of every man.
William Shakespeare, *Henry V*, II, 1

ON 15 MAY 1944 the last great briefing for Operation Overlord took place in a simple lecture room at St. Paul's School, London. The proper chairs across the front of the room were reserved for King George, Winston Churchill, and the British Chiefs of Staff. Behind them, on hard benches stretching to the back, were ranks of generals, admirals, air marshals, and lesser mortals in descending order. Dwight Eisenhower later wrote that Hitler missed his chance that day to kill the entire senior command of the Western Alliance with a single bomb.

Everything was now in place for the great assault on France—or so it seemed. Even as the audience assembled for the briefing at St. Paul's, the final operational orders for D-Day were being issued to the assault divisions and brigades. The basic plan, the order of battle, the tables of loading, allocation of objectives, calls signs, landing schedules—everything needed to get the great machine moving—was now fixed. "This is probably the largest and most complicated operation ever undertaken," Admiral Sir Bertram Ramsey, Royal Navy, observed in the introduction to naval orders for Operation Neptune, the assault phase of Overlord. The final "Operational Plan No. 2-44" for the Western Task Force, which landed First US Army, was issued on 21 April. It was a full two inches thick, double-sided on foolscap paper.[1]

Once the larger plans were complete, Operational Orders for 21st Army Group, with their extensive appendixes, tables, traces, and schedules, poured forth from various commands and formations in cascades of paper over the next few weeks: army to corps, corps to divisions, and by mid-May divisions to brigades. By the time General Eisenhower called the briefing to order in St. Paul's School, the staff work of modern warfare was largely complete. In that sense at least, by 15 May 1944 the die had been cast. Eisenhower now had only two options: postpone the assault (the plan for that contingency was ready, too) or cancel it. Otherwise, it was too late to tinker with the basics of the plan.

On that fateful day in May, General Eisenhower as supreme Allied commander spoke first, but much of the attention—especially that of historians since—was on what General Bernard Law Montgomery had to say. What happened on the beaches and in Normandy over the days and weeks to follow was his responsibility. His comments were part information, part inspiration. At the very least, subordinates needed to know their commander's intent, and those familiar with only their parts of the plan now needed some sense of the larger picture.

In keeping with the public relations mood of the moment, Montgomery chose to personalize the forthcoming battle in France by focusing on his old nemesis, General Erwin Rommel. The duel between Montgomery and Rommel, the subject of much contemporary media hype, had begun two years earlier in the Western Desert. Rommel had outfoxed every British commander until Montgomery arrived to take command in August 1942. After that, Monty and his Eighth Army chased Rommel across Africa, out of Sicily, and up the boot of Italy. Now the Desert Fox commanded the defenses of Normandy. Montgomery knew him well. He warned that Rommel would try to "Dunkerque" the landings. Impetuous and well aware of Allied strengths, since December Rommel had worked diligently to thicken the beach defenses. But that was not what mattered. More important, Monty confided, Rommel had adjusted German armored reserves in order to hit the landing beaches quickly and hard. So it was vital to get well established inland as soon as possible to withstand the initial counterattacks. If those failed to dislodge the Allies, Rommel would cordon off the assault while building up reserves for a massive blow later.

For Montgomery, the key to Allied success was control of three nodal points: Carentan, Bayeux, and Caen. Rommel's obsession, he contended, would be Bayeux, which "splits our frontal landings in half." But Monty's ultimate objective was much more ambitious than

Field Marshal Erwin Rommel, right, inspects the crew of a "Wespe," 105mm self-propelled artillery of 21st Panzer Division, 18 May 1944. (Bundesarchive Bild 101 I-300-1865-05)

merely securing Bayeux. "Once we can get control of the main enemy lateral Grandville-Vire-Argentan-Falaise-Caen, and the area enclosed in it is firmly in our possession, then we will have the lodgment area we want and can begin to expand."[2] The capture of Cherbourg, as a key port for further development of the assault on France, remained the initial strategic target. This was to be followed by expansion of the lodgment to include ports on the Biscay coast and occupation of the area between the Seine and the Loire valleys west of Paris by D+90.

The greatest threat to Montgomery's plans, even to his modest minimum for D-Day, was German panzers and the fear that Rommel would immediately hurl them at the landings. The Germans had done this twice before and were almost successful each time. At Gela, Sicily, in July 1943, Tigers of the Hermann Goering Division had nearly thrown the American landings into the sea. Two months later at Salerno, the Americans were again driven to the brink of evacuation by savage counterattacks by German mechanized forces. Amphibious assaults were notoriously precarious undertakings. Armies landing over open beaches fought without their full panoply of weapons and supporting elements, and their position invariably lacked operational depth in the initial stages. Much depended on fire support from the sea and air, on specialized equipment, and on ad hoc arrangements with airborne or engineer assault formations. A quick descent and rapid consolidation, especially when attacking beaches defended by Germans, were the keys.

The Allied plan, long familiar now and explained in some detail by Montgomery on 15 May, can be summarized briefly. The First US Army was to land west of Bayeux astride the Vire River estuary. Its western flank was to be secured by two US airborne divisions, the 101st and 82nd, dropping west of the Vire River. They would destroy several major coastal gun batteries and help secure beach exits for 4th US Infantry Division, which was also to land west of the Vire along a strip of dunes dubbed Utah Beach. These assaults would secure a vital Allied lodgment on the Cotentin Peninsula as a preliminary to the capture of Cherbourg.

On the east side of the flooded valley of the Vire, US Rangers were to assault the gun position at Pointe du Hoc, while the main American landing was made by 1st US Division and elements of 29th US Division. They drew the toughest beach of all, Omaha. A long arc of sandy beach, Omaha is overlooked its entire length by a steep bluff. The bluff came to the water's edge in the west at Vierville but was set back behind a dune system in the east at St. Laurent. This line of bluffs was broken at intervals by deep valleys—"draws" in American terminology—carrying roads inland. When Rommel first saw Omaha in early 1944, little had been done to guard it against assault. But he knew immediately that the Allies would land there and so ordered an intense program of work. In particular, the draws were barricaded, and heavily fortified points along a network of trenches, wire entanglements, minefields, and numerous steel-reinforced concrete emplacements were constructed. Omaha was, without a doubt, the most difficult natural obstacle faced by any assault division on D-Day, and it was made infinitely more difficult by last-minute changes in the German defenses and major shortcomings in the American plan.

A twenty-kilometer gap of rugged headlands separated Omaha Beach from the most westerly British assault area, Gold, northeast of

Bayeux. This was the beach slated for the Canadians in the original COSSAC attack plan of 1943. It was here that 50th British Division, the leading element of XXX British Corps, was to land on a low, open strand between the seaside villages of le Hamel in the west and La Riviere in the east. The beach gave immediate access to the broad and largely open Sommervieu-Bazenville ridge, which was guarded along its southern and eastern limits by the valley of the Seulles River. Gold allowed the crucial small ports of Arromanches and Port-en-Bessin to be enveloped from the rear and provided direct access to the road hub of Bayeux, the ultimate target of 50th Division's assault.

A short interval of sandy dune lay between Gold and the beaches of I British Corps north of Caen. The most westerly of I Corps' formations, 3rd Canadian Division, was assigned Juno Beach. Juno was characterized by seafront villages along a low waterline, with open farmland rising in a gentle plain behind. Courseulles-sur-mer, at the mouth of the Seulles River, had a snug little harbor accessible at high tide that was guarded by a series of large concrete emplacements right on the waterline. The strongpoint at Courseulles made it the toughest beach after Omaha. Bernieres-sur-mer, in the middle of Juno Beach, was heavily defended by machine gun positions and lighter antitank guns at the waterline. At the eastern edge of the Canadian landing zone was the village of St. Aubin-sur-mer. The village itself, characterized by three- and four-story brick and stone buildings, towered over the seawall like a medieval castle. An extensive and a powerful strongpoint on the headland of Cap Romain to the west controlled the shoreline on either side like a tower on a castle wall. So the force attacking St. Aubin would land to its west, over more open beaches astride Gap N7, and capture the village and strongpoint from the rear.

Much of Juno sheltered behind a long reef just offshore, which complicated landing schedules and on D-Day the landings themselves. So, too, did the massive radar station at Douvres, four kilometers inland of St. Aubin, and the regimental and artillery headquarters complexes around Tailleville. This was the only area in the Canadian sector where the second line of German beach defenses was fully developed, and it would have a serious impact on the course of events.

Royal Marine Commandos landing with the Canadians were tasked with clearing the largely unbroken line of seaside villages between Juno and 3rd British Division's Sword Beach west of the Orne River. Sword veterans would contend, with some justification, that it was the nastiest beach after Omaha. It, too, was heavily defended right to the water-line. The landing here was also complicated by the fact that the gap in the offshore reef necessitated landing on a one-brigade front. Finally, and perhaps more important, the second (inland) line of fixed defenses behind Sword Beach was complete and fully manned by 6 June. These factors would profoundly upset the D-Day timetable.

Finally, the high ground east of the Orne River and Caen canal was the objective of 6th British Airborne Division and several glider-borne air landing brigades. They secured the eastern flank of the landings, denying the enemy easy oversight of the beaches and anchorages just offshore, and secured Allied control of the bridges over the Orne River and Caen canal. It was also necessary to eliminate the coast battery at Merville that threatened the assault area.

In total the Overlord front extended over eighty kilometers. It was to be taken by an assault force of more than 150,000 troops landing on the first day. Their task was to get ashore, secure their objectives, de-feat local counterattacks, try to link up as soon as possible, defeat the anticipated major counterattack around D+5 or D+6, and then push on with the Normandy campaign. Overlord was the most complex op-eration undertaken by the Allies in the Second World War. By the time Montgomery rose to speak in St. Paul's School on 15 May, the whole elaborate plan was largely cast in stone.

Montgomery left those assembled for the briefing energized and op-timistic about the coming assault. If he harbored doubts, he did not share them. His talk is better remembered for his suggestion that he wanted to get ashore and "crack about south of Caen with tanks." Eisenhower was not so sure things were going to be that easy. Later, on the eve of the landings, he drafted a message taking full responsibility for the failure of the assault and kept it safe in case he had to use it. This has been taken by subsequent writers as reflective of a general anxiety about the attack, about the marginal nature of the weather in which it was launched, and about the complexity and uncertainty of the whole affair.

But Eisenhower's doubts may also have reflected his knowledge that conditions in lower Normandy, conditions upon which the Allies had developed their plans, were changing rapidly even as the final preparations for Overlord were made. In fact, the Germans increased their strength in lower Normandy by 50 percent during May 1944 and moved some of their first-class divisions directly into the assault area. In a twinkling, the landings at Omaha Beach looked perilous, and 3rd British Infantry Division no longer had the combat power to capture Caen on D-Day. Indeed, if intelligence at the end of May was right, I British Corps faced annihilation by panzer forces. In these circumstances, Eisenhower's anxiety seems entirely understandable. They also made the Canadian role west of Caen even more crucial.

Operational orders for Overlord allotted 3rd Canadian Division additional resources in order to defend the crucial ground west of Caen against panzer attacks. Among these was 19th RCA, assigned from First Canadian Army and nominally attached to 4th Army Group, Royal Artillery (AGRA), a corps of army-level asset. It had been training with 3rd Canadian since the fall of 1943 and was slated to land alongside 12th, 13th, and 14th Field Regiments, RCA, on the morning of 6 June. They were not, however, the first self-propelled artillery scheduled to land on the Canadian beaches. That task fell to two batteries (thirty-two guns in all) of the 2nd Royal Marine Assault Squadron (RMAS) equipped with 95mm howitzers mounted in Centaur tanks. These guns could, and did, provide both direct and indirect fire support during that critical initial stage of the landings. The two British regiments of towed 25-pounders, added to the Canadian order of battle in February 1944, were to arrive in the days following D-Day to help with the beachhead battles. Sixth Field Regiment, RA, from 4th AGRA would land on D+2, and 191st RA, lately of 2nd Canadian AGRA, on D+3. Thus, only by D+3 would the number of field guns deployed on the Canadian front reach 144, the day after the sixteen 4.5-inch guns of the 79th Medium Regiment, RA, came ashore.

Finally, all forty-eight guns of the I British Corps antitank reserve, the 62nd Anti-Tank, RA, were assigned to 3rd Canadian for the early stages of the Normandy operation. They were all to land on D-Day, along with the division's own 3rd Anti-Tank Regiment, RCA. When 62nd Anti-Tank, RA was assigned to the Canadians in February, its two towed batteries were already equipped with 17-pounders, while the other two were equipped with M10s with the 3-inch American gun.

That month 62nd Anti-Tank received top priority in 21st Army Group for conversion of its M10 batteries to the new "Achilles" self-propelled gun: 17-pounders mounted on an M10 chassis.[3] It is significant that the operational order placed all these guns under control of Brigadier P. S. A. Todd, the CRA of 3rd Canadian Division, for the initial beach-head battles.

The unprecedented allocation of artillery for the beachhead battles made 3rd Canadian Division the most powerful Allied formation in the assault. All Allied divisions landing on D-Day received some level of special equipment, but none had more guns than the Canadians. The other assault division of I British Corps, 3rd British, landed with its own three regiments (all converted to M7s) and added two towed field regiments on D+1, which were to be allocated to support 6th Airborne across the Orne. Fiftieth British Division landing on Gold as the lead element of XXX British Corps brought five field regiments ashore (all equipped with the new Canadian-built 25-pounder Sexton SPs) and one (American) medium battery.[4] Artillery assigned to American divisions was normally much less than that of Anglo-Canadian formations: typically thirty-six field pieces per division, plus the cannon companies of the infantry regiments. For the D-Day assault this was augmented as well by assigning additional artillery battalions to the attacking divisions. Virtually all American field artillery, including most of those landing in the assault, were towed.

To handle his guns, Brigadier Todd organized them into two "field artillery groups" and planned to deploy them on either side of the Mue River. The 14th Field Group consisted of 14th and 19th RCA along with 191st and 79th (Medium) RA, and 3rd Battery of 2nd RMAS. This group's D-Day task was to support the advance of 9th Canadian Infantry Brigade to the fortress planned for the Carpiquet area. Then it was to settle into gun area "Dorothy," three grid squares on the east side of the Mue behind Authie-Buron. The 12th Field Group, composed of 12th and 13th RCA, 6th RA, and 4th Battery from 2nd RMAS, deployed on the other side of the Mue around the little hamlet of Bray in gun area "Nora." They back-stopped the 7th Canadian Infantry Brigade fortress at Bretteville and Putot. The howitzers of 2nd RMAS had a countermortar role. So the Canadians, in the center of the British assault, commanded an exceptional level of artillery resources on the

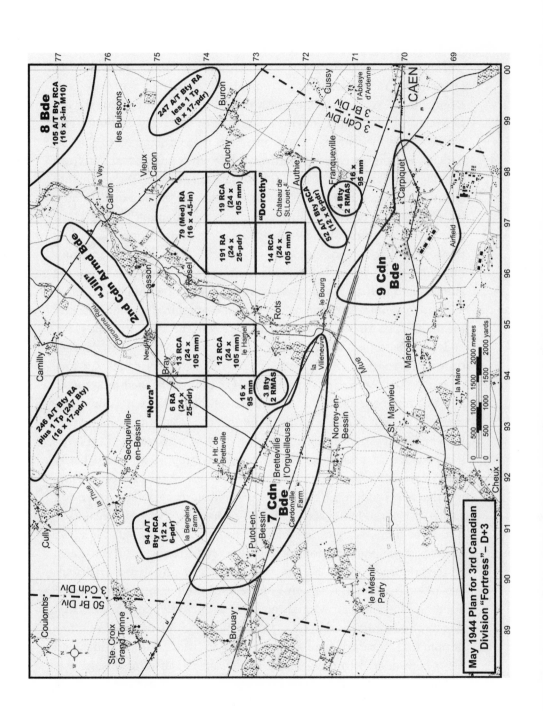

May 1944 Plan for 3rd Canadian
Division "Fortress" – D+3

ground, which planners had long identified as crucial to the successful defense, or defeat, of Overlord itself.

The antitank gun plan for the division was the responsibility of Lieutenant Colonel J. P. Phin, commanding officer of 3rd Anti-Tank Regiment, RCA. It was Phin's task to coordinate and control the deployment of his own regiment, as well as the infantry anti-tank gun platoons and the I British Corps anti-tank reserve assigned to the Canadians for the beachhead battles. While Phin scurried about from meeting to meeting, 3rd Anti-Tank was equally busy with last-minute training, reorganization, and new equipment. At the end of February, the regiment's 6-pounder batteries went to the ranges at Beachy Head to zero their guns on the new discarding sabot ammunition. According to the war diary, "Shooting was very good." With the new ammunition there was no need to lead the target: the shot went so fast that the gunners had only to lay the crosshairs on anything within 2,500 yards and shoot. In mid-April the regiment also reorganized its four batteries for the assault. All of the 6-pounders were concentrated into 4th, 52nd, and 94th Batteries, while the regiment's twelve M10s were concentrated into 105th Battery specifically to support 9th Brigade's advance inland. In late April, 3rd Anti-Tank, RCA also exchanged its wheeled gun tractors for tracked Universal Carriers (better known as Bren gun carriers) to help ensure that the 6-pounders got off the beach. Trials loading Bren carriers and their guns on landing craft, tanks (LCTs) began on 20 April, and by 22 April the regiment reported "results better than expected."[5] Unfortunately, that would not be the case on D-Day.

Brigadier Todd and his gunners worked hard over the winter and spring of 1944 to hone their skills and ensure that this massive concentration of firepower was flexible and responsive. "In England, as we developed the planning for Normandy," Todd recalled, "I was given all the privileges I could ask for. I was allowed to go to any of the artillery ranges I wanted. I was given unrestricted limits on ammunition." Todd and his gunners worked out how to call down all the fire from this huge concentration of guns on a single grid reference in a matter of minutes. "We developed a thing called an 'Uncle Target' which had never been done before the war. If an OP officer called for this, he was calling for every Field or Medium gun in the Division to shoot at the target." In the case of 3rd Canadian Division this meant 144 field guns

A 6-pounder of 3rd Anti-Tank, RCA, deployed for action on exercise, April 1944. Antitank guns were normally deployed in sections of two guns, which photographers were forbidden to photograph. (LAC e011083974)

and sixteen 4.5-inch. "This took a lot of drill and a lot of practice," Todd explained, but they made it work.[6]

Much of the key gunnery preparation was done on the small artillery range at Alfriston, a picturesque village on the Cuckmere River in east Sussex. The range had space for only one regiment at a time. So Todd turned things around and got permission to "use the Alfriston range as a target area and deployed the 6 regiments [of field artillery] in the most suitable areas some 3,000 yards away throughout the English countryside. Imagine the little English villages with civilians going shopping and hearing as many as 100 guns firing live shells right over their heads."[7] By all accounts only one shell fell short, landing in a farmyard near Alfriston and killing a pig.

Through April and May the reequipping and training of the assault force continued unabated. New equipment was constantly being issued and tested, then it had to be waterproofed and marshaled into assembly areas. British units operating Churchill tanks discovered in April that many of their vehicles were approaching the Churchill's very short track and transmission life of 200 miles. They would need over-hauling or replacement before the landings. They also discovered that the Churchill, unlike the Sherman, could crush every beach obstacle in Normandy except the massive "Belgian Gates." Other units, like reg-iments of the 2nd Canadian Armoured Brigade, traded in their Cana-dian Ram Mk II tanks for new American-built Shermans. This meant new guns, too, including the Sherman's standard short-barrel 75mm gun and the new 17-pounder gun of the Sherman Mk Vc "Firefly," designed to level the playing field when fighting the Germans.

As with the adoption of the M7 Priest by the artillery regiments the previous fall, the introduction of new tanks and new guns required a round of training programs for the men of Canadian armored regi-ments. All this was done in great haste in April and May 1944. Shift-ing to the standard Sherman with its 75mm gun was manageable. The drive train was comparable to the Canadian Ram, and the 75mm gun could be fired on the ranges of southern England. But the 17-pounder on the Firefly was a major problem because not enough Sherman Mk Vc's were available before May, and there were no ranges in the south able to handle the gun. The Fort Garry Horse of Winnipeg converted from Canadian-built Ram tanks in December 1943 and were the first to get Fireflys in February. The other regiments of 2nd Canadian Ar-moured Brigade (which was landing in support of 3rd Canadian Di-vision), the 1st Hussars of Ontario and the Sherbrooke Fusiliers from Quebec, did not convert to Shermans until mid-April.[8]

As a result, all twenty-nine Firefly crews (tank commander, gun-ner, and loader) of 2nd Canadian Armoured Brigade, one for each three-tank troop, traveled to the Warcop ranges in Westmorland in early April for a two-day gun camp. On 6 April each gunner fired five high-explosive rounds, and the next day the whole crew took turns fir-ing a total of forty-nine rounds of armor-piercing ammunition. It says a great deal about the newness of the 17-pounder that maintenance was a crucial part of the Warcop program. After every twenty rounds the crews had to stop and take twenty minutes to check every screw and bolt on the gun and do "a general overhaul of the gun" before re-suming. The whole experience was nonetheless positive, and Canadian

Better late than never: new Shermans of the Sherbrooke Fusiliers being serviced, May 1944. Note the Canadian pattern steel tracks. (LAC e011083970)

tank gunners were very good. The Sherbrooke Fusiliers reported that their crews "were generally on [target] on the second shot" and were "quite enthusiastic and greatly impressed with this new weapon."[9]

In the weeks that followed the Warcop exercise, the new Shermans arrived in 2nd Canadian Armoured Brigade lines in batches, and the final Rams were turned in. The last Shermans were not taken on strength by the Sherbrookes until 15 May. Whether these late arrivals were ever taken onto the ranges by their crews remains unclear. The 1st Hussars seem to have had one chance to fire their new 75mm guns. There is no indication that the Firefly crews with their 17-pounder guns were so fortunate. Lieutenant G. A. Henry of the 1st Hussars eventually got one of the new Fireflys in May. His crew had attended the Warcop gun camp, but he probably never fired their own tank's gun before landing in Normandy. The focus in May was on general readiness and preparation for landing. Once the tanks were "run in" for 160 kilometers, they were waterproofed and put in storage.[10] This much at least was done with Henry's "Comtesse de Feu," then it was two weeks before he got into his tank again to back it onto the LCT that would carry them to France.

Fortunately, infantry training in 3rd Canadian Division was a little more basic, and it had been under way for their assault role since the previous summer. Training at the Combined Operations base in Inverary, Scotland, was conducted with the same naval forces that would, on D-Day, land the units on the coast of France. Final training over the fall and winter of 1943–1944 included working closely with units the infantry would have to fight alongside. The North Shore (New Brunswick) Regiment, for example, trained with 12th Field Regiment, RCA, tanks of the Fort Garry Horse from 2nd Armoured Brigade, heavy machine guns and mortars of the Cameron Highlanders of Ottawa, and the engineers and ambulance troops that would support their 8th Brigade in action. The training was progressive, moving from less complex skills to increasing complexity and more units involved, and it was intense. The men were exceptionally fit, motivated, tough, and well trained. A Company of the North Shores won the award for the best company in 3rd Division following a grueling "efficiency competition" in January 1944. After the competition finished in the darkness of a cold English winter evening, the company marched twenty-five miles in quick time to get home for a dance. Everyone in 3rd Division knew what their task was: they had to get ashore and stay there.

Serious planning for the assault began in March 1944, when maps, terrain models, and aerial photos, none of them using their real place-names, became available. Based on these, battalion commanders, in consultation with their supporting units, developed specific plans for their own tasks on D-Day. In early April the infantry moved into concentration areas along the Channel coast, sending all their surplus clothes and personal effects to long-term storage. A number of final exercises followed to ensure that men could get on and off landing craft efficiently, that the navy could coordinate operations, and that men, tanks, and their supporting weapons were able to get inland quickly. By mid-May the camps were sealed, encircled by barbed wire, and patrolled by armed American guards; no one got in or out. On 18 May, three days after Monty's briefing at St. Paul's School, battalion com-

manders took all their company commanders aside and told them they
were going to France. New maps and aerial photos, with real place-
names applied, were handed out and studied. The infantry was ready
to go.

Through all this, the training for the assault and for the advance
from the beach continued. In early April, while the 17-pounder crews
were at Warcop, the Sherbrooke Fusiliers moved into West Walk Camp
South, near Wickham, alongside the North Nova Scotia Highlanders.
The combination was no accident. The Sherbrookes were to support
the Novas in the vanguard of 9th Canadian Infantry Brigade during
the advance from the beach to the final brigade objective of Carpiquet.
Their task was to cross beaches won by 8th Brigade, advance twenty
kilometers, and establish the brigade fortress: exactly what the Overlord plan called for them to do on the afternoon of D-Day. On 14 April
they practiced that task on Wepham Downs, in a live fire exercise called
Operation Pedal II. The Novas rode on the backs of the Sherbrookes'
tanks across the downs, as supporting artillery fire roared overhead.
That fire should have come from 14th and 19th RCA, the regiments of
M7 SPs designated for the task, but they were not there. The gunners
of 14th Field Group, RCA, and the other assault artillery regiments of
3rd Canadian Division were off on Exercise Trousers, working through
the final details of drenching fire during the run-in. In their place, one
of 3rd Canadian Division's towed 25-pounder regiments, 6th RA, provided the fire support and the forward observation officers (FOOs) for
Exercise Pedal II.[11] The exercise assumed that resistance against the
vanguard would come from one enemy battalion: no one in 9th Brigade expected to meet panzers until late the next day (D+1), after the
brigade was dug in on the objective. The exercise went well.

Exercise Fabius in late April settled the last issues of combat loading
and the final rehearsals for the assault force. But much remained to be
done, and the days were filled with discussion, trials, and adjustments
of how to pack everything required into the various waves of landing
craft, and just when reserves and rear echelon personnel would land.
Historians who speculate on why last-minute adjustments were not
made to suit the changing intelligence on German defenses would do
well to read through the operational orders and the war diaries of units
preparing for the assault. The days were full, and the final details of

Lieutenant J. H. Couper, Cameron Highlanders of Ottawa (left), and Major
C. F. Kennedy, NNSH, pose for the cameraman during Exercise Pedal II,
April 1944. Couper died in action on 7 June, bringing his Vickers guns
forward to support the Novas in Authie. (LAC e32131)

who and what were going where and when were not settled until mid-
May. Permission to stack fully assembled 105mm rounds in the open
around the M7s in the LCTs (100 to 150 rounds per gun) was only received at the last minute. With the back deck of each M7 stacked three
to four feet high with mines, mortar rounds, and small arms ammunition, sitting on top of a "porpoise" to be dragged ashore packed with
ammunition, and nearly a thousand rounds of ready-to-fire 105mm
rounds stacked in the well deck, the LCTs carrying the artillery regiments were a safety officer's nightmare.

The discovery in April that the Germans had extended beach defenses
down to the low-water mark occasioned hurried changes to the Allied
plan and provides a good example of just how little flexibility was left
to Overlord planners by then. According to Brigadier Todd, "We had

Storm on the Calvados coast, probably along Omaha Beach, spring 1944. Note the obstacles below the waterline. (AHEC)

everything ready about 23 April. Then the Germans conceived the idea of putting all those obstacles under the water." To overcome them it was decided to attack at low water, and so all the landing tables had to be changed. As Todd recalled, "What we'd done over three months had to be redone in four weeks!"[12] Final operational orders for the Canadian brigades were not issued until the third week of May.[13]

In the meantime, the rump of "McNaughton's Dagger," First Canadian Army, fulfilled its vital role in the deception operation that ultimately made Overlord a success. The critical part of the scheme, code-named Operation Fortitude South, played to German fears that the primary Allied assault would come in the Pas de Calais or in the Scheldt estuary. The intent was to reinforce those fears by "massing" an invasion army in southeast England and thereby force the Germans to concentrate the bulk of their troops behind Calais. The core of Fortitude South was the fictional 1st US Army Group (FUSAG). It was composed of First Canadian Army and Third US Army, each composed of two corps. First Canadian Army was, of course, an operational formation that, in the FUSAG ruse, commanded one Canadian and one

American corps. Third US Army was still forming. Behind them both, the Germans were led to believe, were no fewer than sixty additional Allied divisions ready for action. The deception was enormously successful, holding German Fifteenth Army in place not only during the critical initial phase of Overlord but eventually through June and July as well.

Historians typically observe that one of the keys to the success of Fortitude South in holding Fifteenth Army in place prior to D-Day was that FUSAG was "commanded" by General George S. Patton, the commander whom, in Anthony Beevor's recent assessment, "the Germans feared the most."[14] Carlo D'Este, in his massive biography of Patton, *A Genius for War*, asserts that the Germans "were permitted to learn" that Patton was to command FUSAG, but he does not say when this occurred and offers no proof.[15] The British official history of strategic deception, written by Sir Michael Howard, makes a similar, equally unspecific and unsupported claim.[16] They, and scores of other historians before and since, seem to have muddled the time line. According to the classified in-house history of Operation Fortitude, completed immediately after the war by Roger Hesketh (published in 2000), Patton played no specific role in Fortitude South until the end of May at the earliest and probably not until 12 June. The Germans were told, through agents, in January 1944 that FUSAG was commanded by US general Omar Bradley. By the end of March the enemy assumed that Patton would command one of the US armies assembling in the United Kingdom. It is generally assumed that they knew he commanded US Third Army, then supposedly concentrating in East Anglia (north of the Thames, it was actually in the west midlands). But no confirming information was fed to the enemy as part of the deception operation, and even D'Este observes that "Patton's appointment as Third Army commander was deliberately kept a secret."[17] What historians fail to mention is that the Germans were also anxious to know where the Canadians were and under whose command they served.[18]

Fortitude South began in earnest in late April 1944 with the apparent concentration of FUSAG in southeast England.[19] What followed was a very carefully choreographed burlesque, with just enough revealed (or allowed to be discovered) to fire the imagination of the audience and lead them in the direction they already wanted to go. The first critical revelation about FUSAG and the "looming" assault on the Pas de Calais was made when agents controlled by MI5 began to feed information to the Germans about the concentration of FUSAG in the south and southeast of England. The Germans were allowed to believe that FUSAG was entirely US-Canadian, with an American corps in First Canadian Army, and that many more divisions, including three Canadian, were not yet assigned but were ready for operations.[20]

The second revelation passed to German intelligence by agents at the end of April 1944 was the concentration of First Canadian Army along the Channel coast opposite Calais. In fact, the "movements" of Canadian units and First Canadian Army formations were among the major cards played by MI5 as part of Fortitude South in the weeks just prior to D-Day. The shift of II Canadian Corps from Sussex to Kent in late April was one of the few actual movements of Allied formations undertaken as part of the Overlord deception. Significantly, the move was not leaked to the Germans, and their plot of Allied formations in England on 15 May still showed it in Sussex. They would be allowed to discover the presence of Canadians in Kent on their own through signal traffic, and then have that confirmed later by agent reports. From 24 April until 14 June, the Canadians also played a key role in Exercise Quicksilver, a wireless deception scheme designed to mimic radio traffic within FUSAG. As part of this ruse the headquarters of the American corps in First Canadian Army, VIII US Corps, was notionally established at Folkestone, just south of II Canadian Corps' real headquarters at Dover, and a US army communications team was deployed there to simulate the corps' radio traffic. Similar communications teams were established for each of VIII Corps' divisions "concentrated" in Kent: Heathfield (79th), Elham (83rd), and Tenterden (28th).[21] While First Canadian Army ran this part of the exercise, a similar group of radio and wireless operators were deployed through Essex, north of the Thames, to mimic US Third Army, which was still forming on the other side of England.[22]

Second Canadian Corps also ran a series of amphibious exercises in the Trent and Medway Rivers though late May, and on 1 June in Exercise Rattle began to mimic the radio traffic of 7th, 8th, and 9th Canadian Infantry Brigades, the very brigades that had been training since July 1943 to invade France.[23] Meanwhile, the notional movement of

VIII British Corps and the movement of some smaller Canadian units were fed to the Germans through controlled agents. So, too, was the actual movement of a British corps from Yorkshire to the south coast. Apart from II Canadian Corps, this British corps was the only other formation to relocate as part of the deception play at this stage.

The movements, radio deception scheme, and release of information by double agents were all part of the very careful subterfuge. The moves of formations, many of them involving First Canadian Army in some fashion, were those that Roger Hesketh claimed "had to be shown" to the enemy in order to sustain the deception that the Pas de Calais was the main target.[24] These were supported, in turn, by a very public visit to Dover on 23 May by Montgomery, Crerar, and the II Canadian Corps commander, Lieutenant General Guy Simonds, which was captured by British media.[25]

The final revelation was slipped to the Germans on 31 May, when agent Brutus reported that Patton had taken over FUSAG. This was the first hard news German intelligence had of his role. The Germans were skeptical and had reason to be after the so-called Knutsford Incident at the end of April. On 25 April Patton had spoken to the opening of a welcome club for US servicemen. Although he worded his remarks carefully, the press reported Patton speculating on how Britain and the United States would rule the postwar world. This was seen as a calculated slight against Russia. American media, already sensitive to Patton after the slapping incident in Sicily, had a field day. "General Patton has progressed from simple assaults on individuals," an editorial in the *Washington Post* commented, "to collective assault on entire nationalities."[26] Patton was even denounced in Congress. General George Marshall, chief of the US General Staff, gave Eisenhower complete discretion over Patton's fate. Ike came within an ace of sacking him, and Bradley, too, wanted Patton sent home. But as Marshall reminded Eisenhower, Patton was the only combat-experienced army commander he had. Patton got a reprieve.

The Germans were able to track all this through the international media. It says a great deal about how the managers of Fortitude South played this that on 10 May Garbo, the dominant voice of the Fortitude deception scheme, confirmed to the Germans that Bradley was still in command of FUSAG. As May wore on, however, it was clear that it would be necessary to "move" Bradley away from FUSAG, since he would soon turn up in Normandy in command of US First Army. Patton was an excellent choice if, as it seems, the Germans "feared" him, so minor agent Brutus passed the information along to them on 31 May. Significantly, the German intelligence service, Abwer, refused to believe Brutus's claim. Only when Garbo confirmed Patton's "appointment" to command of FUSAG on 12 June did Abwer finally accept.[27] In the early phase of the Normandy campaign, therefore, when it was vital for Operation Fortitude to keep reinforcements away from Normandy, Patton's role was unclear at best. Rather, the crucial role at this stage of Fortitude South appears to have been played by First Canadian Army, which was concentrated opposite the Pas de Calais.

As II Canadian Corps wound through the back roads of southern England in late April to draw off the panzers in its own way, the prospects for Overlord were still good. But they were changing fast, and for the worse. Rommel's efforts to fortify the shoreline greatly augmented the combat power of the two coast defense divisions, 711th and 716th, between the Orne and the Cotentin Peninsula. These small, two-regiment divisions (13,000 all ranks) were virtually without motor transport, their firepower was largely fixed, and a large portion of their personnel were non-Germans, including some full battalions of Osttruppen (ex-Russian prisoners of war [POWs]). In April 1944 one small, fully operational first-rate infantry division (13,000 men), 352nd, was also known to be lodged around St. Lô, behind Omaha Beach.

Coastal forces and infantry divisions were not the primary concern: only panzer and panzer grenadier (PG) divisions possessed the speed and impact to threaten Overlord with catastrophic destruction. Although there were plenty of German infantry formations in France, few of them were considered "field divisions," and all of them (including the 352nd) were primarily horse-drawn. As a 21st Army Group intelligence memo explained in late February 1944, "From the point of view of counterattack the fundamental distinction between PG and inf divs lies in the latter's horse drawn artillery, and its ineptitude for assault."[28] Horse-drawn formations could cordon off the beaches and delay the Allied advance inland, but they could not counterattack effectively—as the fate of 352nd Division's attempt on 6 June against

50th British Division would reveal. Only panzer and PG divisions had the punch to attack and destroy the assault force.[29] Knowing where the armor was, therefore, became the key focus of intelligence activity in the weeks prior to 6 June 1944.

The task was not easy, and on the eve of D-Day, specifics remained elusive. The trend, however, was very clear by early May: the panzer threat to D-Day was growing by the day. In the early spring of 1944, Allied intelligence estimated that there were nine panzer divisions and one PG division in the west (France and Belgium). Four of these were considered up to strength and battle ready (rated "A" or "A-B" category); the rest either were rebuilding after service on the eastern front or were "upgraded reserve panzer divisions." This was probably a conservative estimate. The designated commander of Panzer Group West, General der Panzertruppen Leo Geyr von Schweppenburg, commented after the war, "The statement [by Hans Speidel, Rommel's chief of staff] that the six panzer divisions in A Grp B [Army Group B] area were 'unready' is erroneous." According to Schweppenburg, "All ten panzer divisions in the west on 6 Jun 44, except the Leibstandarte [1st SS Panzer Division], were long past the stage of reorganization or rehabilitation. In material they were almost entirely up to full strength; in the matter of training, ready to be committed."[30]

Until the end of April 1944, Allied intelligence considered that the greatest threat to Overlord came from the four panzer and one PG divisions in France known to be fully operational. The most immediate danger was 12th SS Panzer Division (Hitler Youth). Early that month it had replaced the 10th SS "Frundsberg" Panzer Division, which had been garrisoned around Lisieux fifty kilometers east of Caen. The 12th SS was positioned slightly farther east, in keeping with Schweppenburg's idea that the panzers should be withheld until the focus of the Allied effort (Normandy or the Pas de Calais) was clear. The bulk of 12th SS, its panzer regiment and one PG regiment, was therefore garrisoned on the south bank of the Seine between Elbeuf and Houdan (west of Paris), ready to go north or west. The division's other infantry regiment settled in farther west around Bernay-Orbec-Vimoutiers.[31] This regiment might start arriving near the beaches north of Caen by noon on D-Day. With a total strength of 23,000 personnel, 12th SS was also well equipped with transport and armored vehicles, with over-strength infantry companies, led by a battle-hardened cadre from 1st SS Panzer Division (Leibstandarte Adolph Hitler) and composed of youthful Nazi fanatics. It was, however, seriously deficient in noncommissioned officers and weak in junior officers. Allied intelligence rated 12th SS as "one of the best divisions in the west."

Among the other panzer divisions in France in April 1944, 116th Panzer Division (a recent amalgamation of 16th PG Division and 179th Reserve Panzer Division) was still under training at Mantes west of Paris. A few units within it were considered battle ready, and so the Joint Intelligence Committee (JIC) rated it a category "C" formation. British MI 14 nonetheless expected 116th Panzer to be fully operational by May.[32] Thus, at the end of April, one first-rate panzer division, 12th SS, posed a direct threat to the Overlord beaches in the British sector, with another, 116th Panzer, in the offing.

The main threat to the American sector at the end of April 1944 came from 21st Panzer, garrisoned at Rennes at the base of the Brittany peninsula. It arrived there in late March as part of what the British official history described as a "striking reinforcement of the coastal zone" in late winter. According to Allied intelligence, 21st Panzer was "well equipped and at full strength," composed of "cadres from experienced divisions and recruits from training units who should be thoroughly trained." Although its order of battle of 15,000 all ranks made 21st Panzer smaller than 12th SS, its two tank battalions were believed to be up to strength. As a result, 21st Panzer also earned an "A" rating. As late as 6 May, SHAEF expected 21st Panzer to move to La Hayes du Puits to seal off the Cotentin, contain the American landings, and help secure Cherbourg. In fact, the operational order for 3rd Canadian Division, issued on 12 May, still lists 21st Panzer at Rennes.

Of the other panzer divisions in France in mid-April, only 2nd Panzer, re-forming since early 1944 in northern France and Belgium, was rated as first quality ("A"), with a strength of 15,500 personnel. The rest were all either recently arrived "battered" eastern front units (1st SS, expected to arrive soon to rebuild), seriously understrength (2nd SS, at Bordeaux), or "reserve panzer divisions" such as 273rd at Bordeaux and 155th at Nimes. None were ready for battle.[33] The only PG division in western France, 17th SS south of Tours, was rated highly ("A-B"), but it lacked transport, was short of officers and noncommissioned officers, and was nearly 50 percent non-German. It, too, would take some time arriving.

It was expected that the armor close to the beaches, 21st Panzer in the American sector and 12th SS Panzer in the Anglo-Canadian zone, would assist infantry divisions in their areas to contain the landings. Limited counterattacks by up to four panzer divisions would commence by D+1, and by D+2 a further panzer division and one PG division would join in the attacks. It was anticipated that the Germans would try to regain or hold Carentan, Bayeux, and Caen, to split the Allied beaches, and to secure Cherbourg from capture. By D+6 enough German infantry divisions would have arrived to remove the panzer divisions from the containment role and allow them to concentrate for the "full blooded" counterattack. This estimate of German dispositions and likely responses was issued in early May, just as the final Overlord operational orders were being compiled.[34]

However, by the time Montgomery rose in St. Paul's School on 15 May to deliver his famous D-Day briefing, the situation in lower Normandy was undergoing changes that would profoundly affect his plans.

The Germans, too, faced enormous challenges as the long-anticipated assault on France approached. Hitler's directive of 3 November 1943 sought to buy time with space in the east while concentrating forces in the west to defeat the landings. Additional men were to be combed out of rear areas and from supply and administrative units to form new combat units, and by early 1944 orders were issued to harden troops in the west through ideological indoctrination in Nazism.[35] One manifestation of the latter process was the transfer of combat veterans from the eastern front to France and Belgium. In 1943, only roughly one-quarter of officers in France had fought on the eastern front; by early 1944, this figure rose to about 60 percent. The NCO cadre of the western army was also "easternized," and Nazi "commissars" were appointed to oversee the indoctrination. German soldiers were reminded of their obligation to National Socialism, and that the Western Allies were ruthless murderers. Not only were the British and Americans terror-bombing their families, apparently Western Allied armies generally refused to accept the surrender of German soldiers. Russell Hart contends that this program of nazification of the Wehrmacht in the west, coupled with intensified combat training, contributed notice-

Field Marshal Gerd von Rundstedt visits 12th SS Hitler Youth Division, Belgium, January 1944. Left to right: Rundstedt; Kurt Meyer, commander 25th Panzer Grenadier Regiment; Fritz Witt, commander 12th SS Division; and Sepp Dietrich, commander 1st SS Panzer Corps. (Bundesarchive Bild 101 I-297-1739-16A)

ably to the protracted and bloody nature of the fighting in Normandy that followed.[36] Certainly the Canadians who survived the campaign could affirm that Waffen SS troops heard and absorbed the message.

While perhaps all Germans could agree on the need to prepare the Wehrmacht for the coming invasion, there was no consensus on how to employ it. Senior German generals understood—as did Overlord planners—that the ultimate outcome of the struggle to defeat the landings depended on the employment of mobile reserves. Throughout 1943 and early 1944, the Germans wrested with two quite different theories about how this might be done: kill the assault quickly on the beaches, before the Allies could get established, or allow the Allies to penetrate deep inland and then destroy them in a mobile battle. They never did entirely resolve the issue.

Field Marshal Gerd von Rundstedt, commander in chief, west, and Schweppenburg, who was to command Panzer Group West (once the

General der Panzertruppen Leo Geyr von Schweppenburg, commander of Panzer Group West. (AHEC)

invasion started), believed that Germany's strength lay in fast-paced, fluid battles. This, after all, had been the basis of its success since 1939. Rundstedt and Schweppenburg preferred to draw the Allies deep into France, beyond range of their naval fire support, and then "blitz" them with a massive panzer counterblow. Rommel, commander of Army Group B stretching from the Netherlands to the Loire, wanted to kill the Allied landings on the beach.[37] His appointment in December 1943 to the task of defending the Atlantic Wall brought renewed energy and purpose to the tons of concrete, steel, wire, mines, and weapons laid along the coast. It also suited his conception of how the Allies must be beaten: as close to the beaches as possible. At best the Atlantic Wall was simply an elaborate trip wire. The Western Allies could pick their time and place, overwhelm fixed defenses, and get ashore. The key to destroying the invasion, according to Rommel, was to hit it hard just after it was weakened by the beach defenders and before it could fully consolidate ashore. That meant keeping reserve formations, especially panzers, close to the coast or within a few hours' travel. Rommel knew the Western Allies and cautioned his colleagues against letting them get ashore:

> Our friends from the east cannot imagine what they are facing here. It is not a matter of fanatical hordes to be driven forward in masses against our line. . . . Here we are facing an enemy who applies all his native intelligence to the use of his many technical resources. . . . It is obvious that if the enemy once gets his foot in, he'll put every anti-tank gun and tank he can into the bridge-head and let us beat our heads against it, as he did at Medenine. To break through such a front you have to attack slowly and methodically under cover of massed artillery, but we, of course, thanks to the Allied air forces, will have nothing there in time.[38]

As usual, Hitler hedged his bets and split his armored reserves. He allowed Rommel, as commander of Army Group B, to have three panzer divisions (21st, 2nd, and 116th) and gave three to Army Group G in the south of France as well. The cream of panzer formations in France was left in Panzer Group West under Schweppenburg.[39] These latter included 1st SS, 12th SS, 17th SS PG, and the newly arrived

Panzer Lehr (discussed later) grouped as 1st SS Panzer Corps. Hitler's solution therefore divided overall command of panzer forces in France into three, to everyone's dismay.

By the spring of 1944 both Rommel and Hitler were convinced that a landing in lower Normandy was imminent. It might not be the main landing, but it would be the first, and it would take place in the Baie de Seine. As a result, Rommel was given more latitude to move forces closer to the coast. By the time Montgomery gave his briefing at St. Paul's School on 15 May, Ultra had already revealed that two more panzer divisions had arrived in or near the landing zone. Panzer Lehr, a newly formed and well-equipped division of 23,000 men created from training units and larded with battle-experienced cadres, was rumored to be en route for France for some time. On 8 May, Ultra signals confirmed its arrival at Chartres, about 200 kilometers from the Normandy coast.[40] Although the division had not yet fought as a formation, Allied intelligence rated Panzer Lehr highly ("A-B").[41]

More alarming, perhaps, was the news on 14 May that 21st Panzer had moved from Rennes to somewhere around Caen.[42] Monty revealed this much in his briefing the next day, but that was just about all he knew. Indeed, virtually nothing was known of the precise location of 21st Panzer's units or even the nature of its equipment. The evacuation of all but a few civilians from the coastal area sharply reduced the local intelligence network. All the Allies knew was that 21st Panzer had moved in around Caen; they had some sense of its size and general equipment state by the number of railcars in reconnaissance photos and scars left on the open terrain west and north of Caen by tracked vehicles. The nature of 21st Panzer's equipment and strength was not fully discerned until 9 June from captured documents.

Things only got worse in the days that followed. In late May, Ultra revealed what the British history of intelligence described as "the completion of a considerable reinforcement of the Cotentin" Peninsula. This had begun in April with the allocation of the 6th Parachute Regiment to the Cherbourg area. Subsequently, the northern sector of the Cotentin was reinforced by 206th Panzer Battalion (composed of Russian, French, and German light tanks) and 17th Machine Gun Battalion. Farther south, at the base of the peninsula, Rommel deployed the Seventh Army Sturm Battalion at La Haye du Puis, the 101st Stellungswerfer Regiment was split between the east and west coasts, and 91st Infantry Division headed for Nantes was diverted to the Cotentin. These latter deployments were intended to defend against parachute landings. The 100th Panzer Replacement Battalion, some thirty French light tanks at Carentan, was also placed on alert "for action against airborne troops."[43] Perhaps even more alarming was the move of elements of 352nd Infantry from St. Lô to the coast north of Bayeux, which until then was thinly held by 716th Division. The impact of that move on the American landings on 6 June is one of the dominant themes of the D-Day story, but at the end of May it was the reinforcement of the Cotentin Peninsula that really worried Eisenhower.

By the end of May 1944, the situation in lower Normandy for the Allies had deteriorated sharply. The 21st Army Group weekly intelligence review for 28 May estimated that as early as D+1 perhaps four panzer divisions (12th SS, 21st Panzer, Panzer Lehr, and 116th Panzer) would be available for immediate counterattacks. By D+6, when it was estimated that the main panzer blow would fall, perhaps eight panzer and PG divisions would be available, supported by up to nine field grade infantry divisions.[44] It was a grim, worst-case assessment. COSSAC had set a figure of no more than twelve first-class divisions in France as the crucial limit for launching Overlord. Senior Allied commanders agreed in late winter of 1944 not to hold to that figure: it was just as well. On 20 May, British intelligence reported to Churchill that perhaps as many as sixteen first-class divisions awaited the Allies in France.[45]

It was not just that there were more German divisions in France than planners had hoped; it was where they were and what kind they were. All the COSSAC estimates, war games, and "German staff appreciations" of late 1943 put the panzer threat primarily on the open countryside west of Caen. The expansion of the assault from the Orne to the Vire Rivers confounded subsequent planning and estimates. But German redeployments in the final weeks before D-Day revealed that the original COSSAC estimates were correct: the Germans garrisoned the bocage with infantry and focused their panzer counterattack forces around Caen.

In those frantic final weeks of preparation, COSSAC's worst fears, and those of other Allied planners, therefore came to pass. Not only did the Germans reinforce lower Normandy, they deployed one first-class panzer division (21st Panzer) virtually on the coast at Caen, where it could be supported within hours by one of Nazi Germany's elite panzer divisions (12th SS) and, if all went well, within a day or so by a new elite panzer formation (Panzer Lehr) as well as the new 116th Panzer. The Allies knew, rightly enough, that both 12th SS and Panzer Lehr were enormously powerful, over-strength elite formations. But their intelligence also believed that 21st Panzer's organization and equipment were "exceptional."[46] The best guess at the end of May was that 21st Panzer consisted of 240 Panthers, Mk IVs, and Tigers, as well as forty assault guns.[47] This proved to be wildly wrong, but in May 1944 no one in Allied intelligence knew that. If Rommel had had his way in May 1944, all four of those panzer divisions would have been echeloned south and west of Caen for immediate action on either side of the Mue River.

Intelligence revelations and estimates of German tank strength in the Caen sector in the days just before the assault must have sent a chill down the spines of anyone in the know. How much of this news got down to the troops is unclear. The presence of some of 352nd Division on the bluff overlooking Omaha Beach certainly came as a surprise to many Americans, and it appears—since nothing could now be done in any event—that the assault formations landing at Omaha were simply not told. In the event, most of 352nd Division was not at Omaha, just one battalion of it, but the rest was ominously close. Perhaps more important, unknown to Allied intelligence, as Steve Zolaga has discovered most of 352nd Division's artillery was deployed behind Omaha Beach and had preregistered its targets along the shoreline.

Senior Anglo-Canadian officers were clearly aware of the challenge that now faced their troops. The official historian of British intelligence in the Second World War, Harry Hinsley, suggests that the intelligence on these German forward deployments just prior to D-Day was not "spelled out with sufficient emphasis when relayed to the Commands."[48] Perhaps. In late May, Second British Army estimated that of the roughly 900 German tanks in the area between the Loire and Seine Rivers, 550 of them were concentrated in the Caen-Bayeux area. Worse still for the men of I British Corps, most of these, some 540 (21st and 12th SS), were thought to be around Caen. According to intelligence estimates, these included a large number of both Panthers and the heavy Tiger tank with its lethal 88mm gun. First British Corps was warned of this intelligence estimate on 22 May.[49]

There is no indication from the surviving intelligence or planning documents that this revelation changed anything for the Allies. The open fields north and west of Caen had long been identified as the crucial ground for a major panzer counterattack by the Allies and the Germans alike. Rommel's redeployment of forces in the spring of 1944 confirms that, as would his reactions to the landings. By May the operational orders had been issued, and everything was moving at a frantic pace. The I Corps plan had already been adjusted to allow for the failure of 3rd British Division to capture Caen in a coup de main on D-Day: 51st Highland Division and 4th Armoured Brigade would finish the task as soon as they got ashore. The scale and complexity of Overlord precluded any last-minute adaptation of the plan as May wore on. All that remained to be confirmed in late May were the American airborne landings. The infusion of forces into the lower Cotentin Peninsula put them at serious risk, and the final decision lay with Eisenhower.

As for the rest, it was much too late to change. It had already taken four weeks of frantic effort to rewrite the plan to land at low tide. How long would it take to find the landing craft, equip and train new assault divisions, and alter the plan to allow for more panzers around Caen? Indeed, would the delay be worth it? There was a limit to how big the landings could be, how much they could carry, and delay allowed the Germans to reinforce lower Normandy even more. It may be that Hinsley was right, that the importance of the changed operational situation by late May was not conveyed effectively to lower commands. What could they do with the news anyway? By the end of May, there was nothing to be done except launch the assault and hope that it all worked out.

If the increase in armored formations in front of 1st British Corps bothered Eisenhower, he never mentioned it, then or subsequently. Perhaps the secrecy around Ultra played a role in this. But the requirement for holding Ultra close did not mask his anxiety in the final weeks before D-Day about the plan to drop two American divisions at the base of the Cotentin Peninsula. As late as 29 May, SHAEF's air commander,

Major General Rod Keller, general officer, commanding, 3rd Canadian Infantry Division, gets the point from his immediate superior, the commander of I British Corps, Lieutenant General Sir John Crocker. In the spring of 1944, Keller was considered (by some) to be a "soldier's general": tough and plainspoken. By the time this photo was taken in late June, Keller was "jumpy," and Crocker had lost faith in him. (LAC PA-129170)

Air Chief Marshal Sir Trafford Leigh-Mallory, urged that the drops be canceled. The Germans had heavily reinforced the area with infantry divisions and flak batteries. Sending the airborne troops into that area would, in Leigh-Mallory's words, be "futile slaughter," with casualties as high as 70 percent.

The decision to go ahead with the drop of 82nd and 101st Airborne Divisions was Eisenhower's, and his alone. His senior air commander had made a strong recommendation against it. Eisenhower then ruminated for a day before ordering the drops to proceed. On the eve of D-Day, his work as supreme commander done for the moment, Ike went to the airfield at Newbury to see the 101st board its C-47s. There was, Eric Larabee wrote, an uneasy awareness that some of these men were about to die—how many no one knew—and that Eisenhower was ultimately responsible for their fate (as indeed he was for every man in the assault). British reporter Goronwy Rees observed later that during Eisenhower's visit to the paratroops, it was unclear who was reinforcing whom. Ike shook hands with as many as he could, asked names, and inquired about hometowns and family. He stayed until the last C-47 lifted off and then turned, with tears in his eyes, and said quietly, "Well, it's on."[50]

Montgomery had already steeled his troops for frightful casualties, perhaps 75 percent, he had warned 3rd Canadian Division in February. But while Monty exuded confidence, as indeed he was obliged to do, Ike had to carry the burden if Overlord failed. Guarding against the worst, he drafted a letter taking full responsibility for the failure of the whole operation and tucked it in his pocket. "Our landings in the Cherbourg-Le Havre area have failed," the letter read. "If any blame or fault attaches to the attempt it is mine alone." Historians have attributed this anxiety to the perilous airdrops over the Cotentin, the dreadful weather in the Channel, and the myriad of things that might rob Allies of success. Curiously, no historian seems to have connected Eisenhower's fears on the eve of Overlord to the 540 panzers that intelligence concluded at the end of May were massing around Caen. Some of the assaulting formations had determined to take no notice of them either. Yet those panzers would have to be stopped if Overlord was to succeed.

3

The Assault, 6 June

That is no place for soldiers with weak hearts;
The minenwerfers have it to the inch.
Edmund Blunden, *The Zonnebeke Road*

IN THE EARLY MOMENTS of 6 June 1944, paratroopers and gliders began falling from the sky across lower Normandy. Bombardment of the
landing beaches followed at around 0530 hours, and then the first amphibious landings commenced, rolling like a wave along the shore from
the Vire River estuary in the west at 0630 and sweeping east along
eighty kilometers of coastline with the set of the tide. By 0830 hours,
along the stretch from Pont L'Abbe and the Merderet River at the base
of the Cotentin Peninsula to the bridges over the Dives south of Ca-
bourg in the east, thousands of men were locked in desperate struggle.
By the end of the day, Allied hopes, and not Eisenhower's secret fears,
were realized. The landings succeeded. In fact, they succeeded beyond
almost everyone's expectations, and with the sole exception of Omaha
Beach, Allied casualties were much lower than anticipated.

But not everything went according to plan, and it was fortunate that
the Germans, too, were forced to muddle through the confusion. Fears
of a catastrophe befalling the American airborne drops into the lower
Cotentin were nearly realized; the German response was hesitant and
uncertain, and defenses canalized attackers in unforeseen ways. Fears
that the storm surge in the Channel would affect the landings came
true, in ways not noticed by historians. All of these events affected
the fortunes of 3rd Canadian Division. In particular, counterattacks
diverted the axes of thrusts inland by 3rd British Division to the Canadians' east and 50th British Division to their west. As a result, when
the Canadians drove a deep salient into the German lines the next day,
their flanks were exposed and they were left to fight the bridgehead
battles that followed virtually on their own. This fact, perhaps more

than anything else, also isolated the story of 3rd Canadian Division from the larger Normandy narrative.

The Allied assault on France came as no surprise to anyone on either side of the Channel: indeed, the whole world knew it had to come in the spring of 1944. Hitler, Rommel, and Rundstedt—in fact, all of Germany—waited in anxious anticipation for the landings. Great faith was placed in Rommel's ability to achieve a stunning victory, and most senior leaders saw the invasion, in the words of the German official history, as "a unique opportunity to turn the tide of the war in Germany's favour."[1] As one historian of the German public mood explained, "A majority of Germans had daily expected and yearned for this operation for weeks and months."[2] The sooner, the better. Allied, Axis, and international press all speculated openly on where and when.

Because it was an open secret that France would be invaded in 1944, precisely where and precisely when were the only crucial questions. The Allies protected those secrets with what Churchill dubbed "a bodyguard of lies." Allied deception operations, code-named Operation Fortitude, played to German fear in hopes of holding forces in place elsewhere: in Norway, Holland, and especially the Pas de Calais. The deception scheme was superbly executed. Ralph Ingersoll, an American journalist turned soldier who was sharply critical of the British in many things, saw the operation from the inside as a representative of the US Army. He concluded that the deception operation was "brilliantly conceived by the British" and made the difference between success and catastrophe.[3] The primary focus was on the Pas de Calais, where nineteen divisions of the German Fifteenth Army lay within easy reach of lower Normandy. But other threats were nurtured. The Canadian official history notes that in the weeks and days prior to D-Day, II Canadian Corps was busy exercising amphibious assaults across the tidal estuary of the Medway River. These, Charles Stacey wrote, were training exercises for the eventual deployment of the Canadians on the left flank of the Allied armies, along the coast, and therefore preparation for crossing the Seine, the Somme, and the Scheldt estuaries.[4] But since the summer of 1943, First Canadian Army had been developing plans for a descent on Antwerp. By the late fall the cover plan for Operation Overlord, which became Operation Fortitude South in 1944, specified that the need was to keep the Germans fixed "in or EAST of the PAS DE

CALAIS area."[5] Even during the first days of the Normandy campaign, the exercises in the Medway, disguised on the radio to mimic units of 3rd Canadian Division, continued. The Germans remained anxious about the Belgian coast and, as we shall see, on 6 June fretted about a possible landing near Antwerp.[6]

The importance of the Canadians to Fortitude South and the notion of a descent upon Antwept are not far-fetched. The British had landed at Antwerp in September 1914, behind the German army as it swept through Belgium. Nor was a Canadian role in large-scale deception unique in May 1944. As Overlord prepared to launch, so too did a massive Allied holding action in Italy, designed to fix German divisions there and if possible syphon off some from France. In support of Operation Diadem, the breaching of the Cassino line south of Rome, I Canadian Corps was kept back from the initial assault in order to deceive the Germans into believing that it, "reinforced" by 36th US Division, was preparing to land at Civitavechia northwest of Rome. As with Operation Fortitude, the Canadians were only part of a much larger scheme that fixed German reserves farther north. However, "In the plot framed by General Alexander's playwrights," the Canadian official history of the Italian campaign concluded, "the leading role was given to the 1st Canadian Corps."[7] It seems that the Germans were anxious in the spring of 1944, just as they had been in 1917–1918, to know where the Canadians were.[8]

The ultimate purpose of Operation Fortitude was to allow an acceptable level of operational surprise, since there were really only two places where the Allies could land. These could be determined by simply scribing an arc of the ranges of Spitfires and P-47s from air bases in southern England. That left only the Pas de Calais or the Calvados region of lower Normandy. By the spring of 1944, both Hitler and Rommel agreed that the *first* Allied landing would take place in lower Normandy, along the Baie de la Seine. The question that remained unresolved was whether the first one would be the real assault or just a feint for the real landing in the Pas de Calais.

What complicated German reading of Allied intent was not just geography and fighter ranges. The "Transportation Plan" launched by Allied air forces to destroy rail and road communications in western France put as much effort into isolating the Pas de Calais as it did lower

Normandy. Further, a major objective of the deception plan was to convince the Germans that the Allies had more capability than they really possessed. By the end of May 1944, German intelligence—carefully nurtured by British deception—believed that there were seventy-nine combat-ready Allied divisions in Britain and assault craft available to lift fifteen at a time. Given this scale of capability, two major landings were entirely feasible. Of course, the German estimate was vastly inflated. In the spring of 1944, there were fifty-two divisions in the United Kingdom, most of them American and most not yet ready for battle, and amphibious lift for only six.[9] Operational surprise was therefore possible if the meaning of the initial landing's purpose in Calvados was unclear.

In the event, all the Allies could be reasonably sure of was tactical surprise. The weather delivered that. Overlord was initially scheduled for Monday, 5 June, and the weather during those first days of the month had been spectacular, clear, bright, and summery. As forces began to move on 3 June, the forecast called for high winds and heavy seas in the Channel on 5 June. At 0430 hours on the morning of 4 June, Eisenhower then ordered a twenty-four-hour delay, perhaps more if the weather did not abate. Anything beyond forty-eight hours put the whole operation in jeopardy. The great advantage that the Allies enjoyed over the Germans was that in the Northern Hemisphere weather generally moves from west to east, so the Allies had excellent forecasting information. At 2130 hours on 4 June, the SHAEF's brilliant weatherman, the dour and humorless Scot Group-Captain James M. Stagg, RAF (described by one British admiral as "six foot two of Stagg, and six foot one of gloom"),[10] advised Eisenhower that conditions would moderate slightly beginning Monday afternoon and into Tuesday, 6 June. Winds would ease to twenty-five to thirty knots westerly, and the cloud cover would lift from 500 feet to perhaps 3,000 feet and clear by about 50 percent. The air force did not like the forecast, but the navy and Montgomery were prepared to go. So was Eisenhower. "I'm quite positive we must give the order," he said quietly to his senior staff when conditions were reviewed at Southwick House outside Portsmouth on the evening of 4 June. "I don't like it, but there it is. . . . I don't see how we can possibly do anything else."[11] The order was issued at 2145 hours, and by midnight the whole vast armada was on the move—again.

It simply remained to confirm the forecast and the decision to go, which was done at 0430 hours on Monday, 5 June. As the staff assembled again, Eisenhower looked at the lanky RAF officer and said quietly, "Go ahead, Stagg." The weather, it seems, would moderate more than was previously thought on 6 June and then on 7 June deteriorate again, which might trap the assault on the shore without chance of reinforcement or withdrawal. Eisenhower pondered the risk, discussed it with his staff, and then said, "OK, let's go." Now there was no turning back.

Across the Channel the onset of dreadful weather lulled the Germans into a false sense of security, which was fortunate because German intelligence knew that the Allies were on their way. They had broken the coded messages sent via the BBC to the French resistance warning of the imminent invasion and had received the initial warning message on 1 June. Several intermediate alerts were issued over the next few days, and then the final alert at 2215 hours on 5 June, just as Eisenhower was seeing off the men of 101st Airborne. Rommel dismissed the warning of 1 June as a ruse, not least because he believed the Allies would land later in the month. By the time of the final alert he was hundreds of miles away, having set off on 4 June for Germany to visit Hitler, leaving a little early so as to drop in on his wife on her birthday, 6 June.

The weather on Monday, 5 June, seemed to confirm Rommel's view. After weeks of exceptional weather it was incomprehensible that the Allies would cross the Channel under conditions "that you would not even send a dog out in."[12] Naval and air reconnaissance were canceled for 6 June as a result. Rundstedt's intelligence officer was on leave, and the German naval commander in the west went on an inspection tour to Bordeaux. Even the senior officers of Seventh Army defending lower Normandy were ordered away. When the planned "training alert" scheduled for 5 June was canceled, they were all summoned to a war game in Rennes for the next day in which they were to defeat a combined airborne and seaborne assault. The war game was canceled by Seventh Army's chief of staff, Major General Max Pemsel, at the last minute, so only a few actually were on the road when events began to unfold. Despite the weather, Pemsel was convinced that the Allies were coming on 6 June, and because of his initiative, the German response was, as William F. Buckingham observed, "efficient work in the circumstances."[13]

The first Allied troops landed shortly after midnight, when three gliders of the British airborne's Deadstick Force crash-landed within yards of the bridge over the Caen canal at Benouville—famous thereafter as Pegasus Bridge. About the same time pathfinders from British 6th Airborne Division started dropping east of the Orne, marking landing zones for the 9th Airborne Brigade, which began to fall by 0050 hours. Poor weather, flak, and flooded terrain dispersed and disrupted the British airborne landing (which included the 1st Canadian Parachute Battalion). However, enemy troop concentrations east of the Orne were low, and the airborne landings were sufficiently concentrated that objectives were largely completed.

The same cannot be said for the American airborne assault on the base of the Cotentin Peninsula. The American 82nd and 101st Airborne Divisions had the toughest assignment of the airborne troops. Their landing areas lay amid landscape broken by bocage and flooded river valleys, in an area heavily garrisoned by troops trained to expect an airborne landing. The first wave, 6,900 troops of the 101st carried in 433 C-47s, was supposed to drop from 600 feet in dense formation in drop zones behind Utah Beach. In the event, cloud cover, heavy flak, and inexperienced C-47 pilots conspired to disperse the 101st all over the Cotentin Peninsula, from Cherbourg to St. Lô. Many heavily laden paratroopers plunged into the flooded areas and were drowned, while others leaped from C-47s flying too low for their chutes to open. The 82nd Airborne Division, coming in the second wave to secure crossings of the flooded Merderet River, suffered a similar fate. The dispersion of these airborne landings, coupled with the dropping of 200 dummy parachutists (supported by two RAF Special Air Service teams equipped with pyrotechnics and radios) west of St. Lô designed to simulate the landing of a whole division, totally confused the Germans about the purpose and focus of the attack.

By 0215 hours on the morning of 6 June, alerts had been issued across the invasion front. According to Buckingham, "The unintended dispersion and aggressive behaviour of airborne troops," coupled with the use of dummy parachutists (some south of Caen and across the Dives as well), "reinforced German confusion."[14] The first reaction of

84th Corps at 0211 hours was to order 709th Coast Division, 91st Luftwaffe Division, 243rd Infantry Division, 6th Parachute Regiment, and the 100th Ersatz Panzer Battalion (thirty Mk IIIs and French R35 tanks) to seal off and destroy the American airborne landings. At 0325 hours Task Group Meyer, 84th Corps' strategic reserve composed of the 915th Regiment (two battalions) of 352nd Division supported by the divisions' fusilier battalion, was alerted for a move south of Carentan to deal with American parachutists.[15]

By 0350 hours it was clear to the Germans from the scale of the Allied airdrops that they were not simply a diversion: a landing along the shoreline between the Orne and the Vire was imminent. While infantry forces moved to seal off the US air landings, 21st Panzer Division was released at 0430 hours to support 716th Infantry in dealing with the British airborne forces northeast of Caen. However, in the darkness of early morning it was unclear just what 21st Panzer should do. The bulk of its forces (about two-thirds of the division) laagered south of Caen. If they moved east of the city to attack the parachute and glider troops at the bridges across the Orne River and Caen canal, and on the high ground to the east, their tanks would be cut off from the beaches north of Caen—where the main landing would surely come. If they swung northwest of the city, to join the Kampfgruppe already deployed there, to attack the bridges from the west, then a simple demolition of those bridges would secure the airborne landings from counterattack. Moreover, attacking even airborne troops in close country at night with tanks was a perilous undertaking. As Buckingham concluded, deciding what to do with 21st Panzer was no easy matter, and the situation called for some caution—not the typical German response.[16]

Things became clearer just after 0500 hours. As daylight filtered through the clouds, German defenders gaped in awe at a sea literally covered with ships. Warning orders went out to the closest units of Panzer Group West, 12th SS and Panzer Lehr, in the minutes that followed. If there was any doubt about the Allies' intent, that was dispelled at 0530 hours when the naval bombardment began, "with what one eyewitness described as a single ripple of flashes running across the entire horizon."[17] The big ships—battleships and cruisers—engaged the major shore batteries, striving to make it as safe as possible for the little ships that would land the men. Waves of bombers then dropped their payloads along the assault beaches. As H hour closed in, destroyers and specialized landing craft equipped with rockets and, along the British and Canadian beaches, LCTs carrying the self-propelled artillery regiments of the assaulting divisions drenched the beach defenses with fire. As the infantry in landing craft approached, so too did other LCTs carrying amphibious tanks: they were supposed to swim ashore, then stop in the surf to fire on strongpoints just prior to the infantry assault. The tanks were to be joined by special gun-equipped landing craft, which were to run onto the beaches and pour even more direct fire into enemy pillboxes and gun positions.

Not all of it worked according to the carefully orchestrated plan, but all the assault divisions got ashore. The American experience was both the best and the worst. Fourth US Infantry Division landed on the west side of the Vire virtually unopposed, except for some machine gun positions in the line of dunes that formed the beach. It helped that it landed on the wrong beach, closer to the Vire, where the defenses were weaker. For 4th Division the major obstacles were a flooded coastal plain behind the line of dunes, crossed by several roads that now formed causeways, and the brooding high ground that lay behind it. Massive coastal batteries dominated Utah Beach from three sides: from the north around St. Vaast de Hogue, from the high ground behind the landing beach at Crisbeq and Azeville, and—it was thought—from the south at Pointe du Hoc. The dune along the beach was too thin to provide any depth to the local defenses, but there were significant German defenses at the beach exits of the causeways.

The infantry of 4th Division landed almost unopposed, and in the words of the American official history, they "had no immediate need" for the duplex drive (DD) tanks of 70th Battalion, which were deposited directly on the beach a few minutes later.[18] Unfortunately, American airborne forces were both too dispersed and too heavily attacked to secure the landward ends of the causeways. Forcing a way across the causeways and the flooded polder was an infantry task. It drew murderous fire, but 4th Division established small lodgments on the high ground and rested content there.

The situation on Omaha Beach is a familiar tale of tragedy and heroism. Not only was it a formidable obstacle itself, but three other factors combined to bring the landings of 1st and 29th US Divisions close to failure. The first was American army doctrine, organization, planning, and execution. The assault on Omaha was conceived primarily as an infantry task with—by Anglo-Canadian standards—modest armored and artillery support. Infantry assault companies were reorganized late in their training to provide them with more integral engineer support. The idea was sound, but the reorganization disrupted unit cohesion. The work of breaching beach obstacles was given to reinforced combat engineer companies operating on foot. The British offer of specialized engineer assault vehicles from 79th Division was reviewed by a board of senior engineer, ordnance, and artillery officers from First US Army. They recommended adoption of all of them, except the Flail tank (which beat the ground ahead of it with chains on a rotating drum). Bradley approved the recommendation and then nothing was done. The history of First US Army concluded that "American planners, in the end, turned against the 79th devices; except for the amphibious tank . . . the decision not to adopt most of the tanks offered by the British would be highly controversial."[19]

The focus on infantry, and perhaps a reluctance to rely on British technology, meant that the whole American assault on D-Day was "light" by Anglo-Canadian standards. This may well reflect the differences in anticipated German opposition as well as geography. The British expected to meet German armor on the plains around Caen, while the close country of the bocage from Bayeux west was better suited to infantry than massed armor. Whatever the reason, 1st and 29th US Divisions landing on Omaha were poorly supported by armor. Two tank battalions, 741st and 743rd, each composed of fifty-three Shermans and a squadron of M3 light tanks, were assigned to the initial assault. This was about two-thirds the size of the armor brigade (each of three regiments) landing with the Anglo-Canadian divisions. Furthermore, the four regiments of M7s that landed on Juno Beach brought with them the equivalent of an entire armored regiment of Sherman tanks (fifty) as observation posts armed with 75mm guns plus a few command vehicles (typically fitted with dummy guns to allow for more radios in the turret). And of course the combat engineers and special vehicles of 79th Division landing in the assault waves of Gold, Juno, and Sword were also armored: Flails, Dustbins, mine plows, fascine layers, flamethrowers, armored bulldozers, and so forth. Compared

Splendid shot of a "Dustbin," a spigot mortar-carrying "armored vehicle, Royal Engineers" Churchill tank. Such specialized armor was crucial to success on the Anglo-Canadian beaches on D-Day. In fact, the Churchill was the only Allied tank that could crush every German beach obstacle except the huge "Belgian Gates." The weapon on this variant fired a shaped charge (which had to be loaded externally) designed for bunker-busting. (AHEC)

with the American beaches, those of the Anglo-Canadians were awash in armored vehicles.

Moreover, most artillery assigned to Omaha Beach was towed.[20] Both the 16th Regimental Combat Team (RCT, a combined arms American equivalent of the more ad hoc German Kampfgruppe) landing on the left and the attached 116th RCT (from 29th Division) on the right were each supported by thirty guns: twelve from a towed field artillery battalion and eighteen M7s from a self-propelled battalion.[21] The towed guns were carried in amphibious trucks (DUKWs) to be craned out and deployed on the beach; the M7s landed from LCTs. The balance of the guns slated to land on Omaha on D-Day—five more battalions plus the cannon companies of the infantry regiments (six per regiment)—were all towed. In theory, well over a hundred 105mm guns were scheduled to be landed on Omaha on D-Day, but only thirty-six were self-propelled.

The second factor impacting the Omaha assault was that the sea swallowed much of what little armor there was—and its crucial firepower. The decision to launch the DD Shermans 6,000 yards offshore was occasioned by anxiety about getting too deep into the Baie du Grand Vay and catching cross fire from batteries on the Cherbourg peninsula. That and the heavy sea produced disastrous results for both armor and artillery. The 741st Tank Battalion, supporting 16th RCT on the left, launched its Shermans at 6,000 yards for their swim to the shore: all but two were swamped and sunk. The naval lieutenant in charge of launching the 743rd, landing in support of 29th Division's 116th RCT on the right, ignored his orders and landed his two companies of DD tanks on the beach.

American artillery fared worse. Most of the DUKWs carrying the artillery pieces were swamped. The 111th Field Artillery got one gun ashore, 7th Field Artillery six, and the cannon company of 116th RCT one. Most of those that did arrive were M7s: by 1900 hours, 116th RCT had only six guns firing in support.[22] The US 29th Division landed only twenty-nine guns from four different battalions on D-Day. Gordon Harrison in the US Army official history is blunt in his conclusion: "The artillery that was planned to support the infantry attack particularly in the advance inland did not reach the shore."[23] In the end, American infantrymen and combat engineers had to take Omaha Beach the hard way: with small arms, satchel charges, and whatever battalion heavy weapons they managed to muscle ashore. In the end, what saved the Omaha landings was direct naval fire support provided by the half dozen destroyers that pushed well inshore. As the US Navy official history concluded, "Their fire afforded the troops the only artillery support they had during most of D-day. They filled the breach created by terrific loss of tanks and of dukws [amphibious trucks] carrying Army guns."[24]

The American task on Omaha was made significantly harder by a third factor: the presence of elements of 352nd German Infantry Division. The idea that the Americans faced *all* of the 352nd on D-Day probably owes its origins to Eisenhower's initial report to General George Marshall in Washington on 8 June. Whether disingenuously or not, Eisenhower told Marshall that opposition on Omaha "was unexpectedly heavy due to the presence on the beaches *of a full Ger-*

man division which was on manoeuvers."[25] This was, in fact, a gross exaggeration.

The 352nd Division, a small, seven-battalion formation (three two-battalion regiments plus an independent "fusilier battalion"), was the only fully combat-capable German infantry division in lower Normandy. Three of its battalions were on the coast on 6 June, supported by the division's five artillery battalions (some sixty guns). It was the 2nd Battalion of 916th Grenadier Regiment (GR) that was on the bluffs overlooking Omaha on D-Day, alongside 726th GR of 716th Coast Division. Both battalions were supported by 1st Battalion (twelve guns) of Artillery Regiment 352 under Werner Pluskat—the character made famous in the Hollywood epic *The Longest Day*, reporting from the bunker at Longue-sur-mer. Pluskat's guns had pre-registered targets along Omaha Beach, and their presence was apparently unknown to Allied intelligence. Panzerjäger-Abteilung 352, with twenty-four assault guns, was ten kilometers south of Vierville. So, one battalion of 352nd Division, a third of its artillery, and its only armor were at Omaha (or close) when the assault came in. A second battalion of 352nd Division arrived late in the morning.

The rest of 352nd was spread between the Vire River and le Hamel, on Gold Beach. In fact, 1st Battalion of 916th GR was east of Bayeux, headquartered on the Sommervieu-Bazenville ridge at Ryes, due south of Arromanches. At least some portion of the battalion—perhaps all—was in the beach defenses at le Hamel alongside the 726th GR. The 3rd Battalion of Artillery Regiment 352 provided support. The 914th GR was deployed to the west, around Isigny. Its 1st Battalion was near the beach at Grandcamp—close enough to attack the Ranger landing at Pointe du Hoc—and the 2nd Battalion was on the banks of the Vire closer to Utah Beach than Omaha Beach. The division's third regiment, 915th GR, and its fusilier battalion were concentrated south of Bayeux in the early hours of 6 June. Dubbed "Kampfgruppe Meyer" after the 915th GR's commanding officer, this full regiment of first-quality German infantry formed the only strategic reserve for 84th Corps. Mounted on bicycles and requisitioned French civilian trucks, like the rest of 352nd Division, Kampfgruppe Meyer had limited mobility.

So, there never was a "full German Division on manoeuvers" at Omaha on D-Day, but there were certainly enough—when coupled with the other problems mentioned—to bring the landing close to failure. For our purposes here it is the movement of elements of 352nd Division not committed to Omaha Beach, specifically those fought by 50th British Division on D-Day, that had impact on the Canadian battle against the panzers in the early days of the Normandy campaign.

A gap of sixteen kilometers characterized by high vertical cliffs separated Omaha from the nearest British beach, Gold, northeast of Bayeux. Next to Utah, Gold was arguably the least defended, least urbanized, and most open of the D-Day beaches. It was, and remains, a long arc of sand between the coastal villages of La Riviere in the east and le Hamel in the west. This was the central beach of the 1943 COSSAC plan. It is backed by low ground that rises on the east and south into the Sommervieu-Bazenville ridge, and in the west into low ridges that overlook Arromanches, with an easy run to Bayeux in between. It is primarily open farmland.

British 50th Division's assault was powerful and well executed. The division was ostensibly a northern England formation, composed of battalions from Durham and Yorkshire. But it had recently traded one of its brigades for 231st "Malta" Brigade, battle-hardened professionals, veterans of three recent amphibious assaults in the Mediterranean. For the assault 50th Division had an additional infantry brigade attached, allowing for a two-brigade front with four battalions in the initial assault, and a powerful following reserve. In keeping with British Commonwealth doctrine, the assault was supported by the full weight of armor. This included flail, bridging, ramp-laying, and fascine-carrying tanks of 79th Armoured Division, armored vehicles, Royal Engineers (AVREs) including Churchill tanks with special bunker-busting spigot mortars in the turret to fire huge shaped charges that shattered concrete, armored bulldozers of the Royal Engineers, SPs from both the Royal Artillery and the Royal Marines, and, of course, two regiments of DD Sherman tanks. The latter were put ashore directly from their LCTs because it was unsafe to launch them at sea, and as a result they arrived late. By then the specialized armor was already at work clearing obstacles. German defenses took a heavy toll on these vehicles but were unable to stop them, which in turn allowed the infantry to get forward.

Landings began on Gold at 0725 hours, fifty minutes after Omaha, and by noon all the brigade groups were ashore. In the east, facing the Green Howards and East Yorkshire battalions of 69th Brigade on King Beach, were two companies of the 441st Ost Battalion—formerly Russian POWs—and one company from 736th GR of 716th Division. They were well dug in around La Riviere and gave a good account of themselves but were no match for British assault troops. Elements of 1st Battalion of 916th GR of 352nd Division and a battalion of 725th GR held the western sector of Gold, including the strongpoint at le Hamel: they fought well. Sixty-Ninth Brigade's task was to secure the battery positions at Mont Fleury and Ver-sur-mer on the eastern flank, push on to Creully, connect with the Canadians, and then sever the Caen-Bayeux highway at Ste.-Croix-Grand-Tonne. The highway to the west, between Ste.-Croix and Bayeux, was the objective of 151st Brigade, while the attached 56th Brigade captured Bayeux and pushed through to the Drome River to link up with 1st US Division. It fell to 231st Brigade to move west along the coast and attack Arromanches from the rear to secure the site for one of the artificial harbors. Meanwhile, 47th Royal Marine Commando was to pass through 231st Brigade to capture the small harbor of Port-en-Bessin. In theory, the thrust lines of 50th Division were both south and west.

The British on Gold fought exceptionally well, but they were also fortunate to have struck a seam between German formations. Gold was in the sector to be reinforced by 21st Panzer in the event of invasion, but by 0800 hours that division was already caught up in the battle for the Orne bridges. All that 21st Panzer could do was send some of its 200th Heavy Anti-Tank Battalion, 88mm guns on towed mountings, to the line of the Seulles River south of Courseulles and try to hold the British there. Because 50th Division had no intention of crossing the Seulles at that point, the only opposition these guns of 21st Panzer met was the Canadians.

The one force that might have threatened either Omaha or Gold early in the day was the 84th Corps reserve, the three battalions of Kampfgruppe Meyer from 352nd Division billeted south of Bayeux. Fortunately for both Allied beaches, by the time the amphibious assaults started, Kampfgruppe Meyer was miles away chasing "Gummipuppen"—rubber dummies simulating paratroops—south of Isigny. Meyer's force, borne on requisitioned French commercial transportation and bicycles, seems to have been joined by the 352nd's Panzerjäger-Abteilung of twenty-four Marders and Stug IIIs in their search for the elusive rubber men. This was probably the greatest success ever achieved by this rather eccentric deception: they kept a third of 352nd's combat power, including its only armor—and 84th Corps' only reserve—away from the beaches at a critical time.[26]

At 0819 hours one of Meyer's battalions was diverted to help at Omaha Beach. General Frederick Marcks, commander of 84th Corps, and other senior officers in the area probably thought that would be enough to finish off the Americans trapped in the dunes below the bluff. Fifteen minutes later Marcks ordered the rest of Kampfgruppe Meyer and Panzerjäger-Abteilung 352 to counterattack toward Asnelles, into the western flank of Gold Beach, where the situation was now "difficult." So Kampfgruppe Meyer and the armor of 352nd Division began an arduous fifty-kilometer daylight trek to an assembly area on the Sommervieu-Bazenville ridge: just where COSSAC planners had estimated a panzer attack from the Bayeux area would go. As the French civilian trucks broke down or were destroyed by air attacks, the Kampfgruppe became weaker and more men walked. Finally, by 1530 hours, Meyer reported contact with 1st Battalion of 916th GR, which was already fighting the British, and the Stugs of Panzerjäger-Abteilung 352. Assembly for the counterattack was nearly complete.

All we know with certainty is that Kampfgruppe Meyer's encounter battle with 69th British Brigade late on the afternoon of D-Day was a complete disaster. The last report from Meyer was logged at 1600 hours, saying that he was going to attack and that British tanks had broken through to the south around Creully. Ninety minutes later the Kampfgruppe reported failure "in the face of a superior enemy." The fusilier battalion had retreated, the Stugs, too; contact with Meyer's 1st Battalion near Bazenville had been lost, and Meyer was believed wounded and captured. In fact, he was dead, and so was his artillery commander. At 2255 hours Kampfgruppe Meyer reported that only forty men of the fusilier battalion and fifty from 1st Battalion 916th GR had returned from the attack; four Stugs had been lost.

The destruction of the 84th Corps reserve force is one of the great unheralded moments of D-Day. Kampfgruppe Meyer had attacked along the Sommervieu-Bazenville ridge, as COSSAC planners anticipated, although apparently only ten Stugs made it to the start line. But

British 69th Brigade did not know that. It had stopped just short of its D-Day objective at Ste.-Croix-Grand-Tonne (on the Caen-Bayeux highway) and reported encountering "forty SPs of the 1352nd Assault Gun Battalion [1st Battalion 352nd Artillery Regiment]."[27] Because all the guns of 1352nd Artillery were horse-drawn, it is likely that the "forty SPs" were the Stug IIIs of the Panzerjäger-Abteilung supporting Kampfgruppe Meyer and perhaps some Marders of the Panzerjäger battalion. By the time this was recorded in the 50th Division war diary, the attack was by "forty tanks." Regardless of what transpired and what the British believed they saw, the attack by Kampfgruppe Meyer was enough to stop 69th Brigade and focus its attention westward, away from the Canadians. This would have an impact on Canadian operations for the next few days.

Meanwhile, 231st Brigade captured Arromanches, 56th and 151st Brigades stopped on the outskirts of Bayeux, and 47th Royal Marines (RM) Commando was checked just short of Port-en-Bessin. Although few of 50th Division's D-Day objectives were secured, it had done exceptionally well: virtually all of its D-Day objectives fell with a quick push the next day. It was also fully in command of the crucial Sommervieu-Bazenville ridge, with the Seulles River as a moat to the south and the leading elements of British 7th Armoured Division coming ashore behind it.

By the end of the day, 50th British Division, the lead formation of XXX Corps, was in contact with the Canadians (and therefore I British Corps) to their east, at least as far inland as Creully. Farther south things were less tight. The Canadians, too, were delayed getting forward, and as a result contact between the leading elements of 50th Division and 3rd Canadian Division on D+1 was tenuous at best. This left the Canadians' western flank in the air.

Although Juno Beach, where 3rd Canadian Division landed, lay immediately east of Gold, this was the one place where the landing sequence did not follow the set of the tide. An extensive reef just offshore, Les Iles des Bernieres, required a little more water for the assault to clear. And so the next landings after Gold actually took place farther east, on Sword Beach, near the Orne estuary.

The assault on Sword went adrift more than that on any other beach except Omaha, and with equally good reason. Of all the landings on

D-Day, 3rd British Division had the most complex tasks, and it lacked the combat power to complete them. The critical timings associated with 3rd British Division's movement inland were undone by a narrow beach and the fact that Sword was the only assault zone where the Germans had fully developed a second defensive line. And if all this were not enough, 3rd British Division received the only serious panzer counterattack of the day. That counterattack was "seen off" superbly. But coming at the end of an arduous day and seemingly a portent of more to come, the attack forced 3rd British Division to consolidate on good ground for the night. It all conspired to push 3rd British Division east, tight to the Orne River and Caen canal—leaving Caen and the Canadians both well out of sight by the end of the day.

Landings at Sword were also affected by reefs close to shore. In this case, a gap in the reef that lay opposite a largely undeveloped stretch of beach provided an opening for landing craft. The narrowness of the gap in the reef and the beach opposition invited an assault by four brigades echeloned, one right after the other. The leading brigade landed on a two-battalion front, the smallest frontage on any D-Day assault beach. Then three more brigades (one of them Commandos) were to pass through in quick succession. In theory it was a good idea, but timing was crucial. The beach and its exits had to be cleared quickly, so too routes inland, and then movement had to be swift.

None of this happened. Sword was defended by 3rd Battalion of 736th GR, one company from 642th GR, a half dozen artillery batteries (including two from 21st Panzer), and some miscellaneous units—including the ubiquitous Ost Battalions. The beach itself was dominated by a series of strongpoints. To the west, strongpoint "Trout," WN-21, consisted of one 75mm and two 50mm guns in reinforced concrete, supported by the usual machine gun positions, wire, mines, and obstacles. In the center, between Queen Red and Queen White beaches, lay WN-20, code-named "Cod." Its 88mm and three 50mm guns were a formidable threat to the assault. A kilometer or so east of Cod was a small strongpoint, WN-18, containing two emplaced guns. The coastal town of Ouistreham at the mouth of the Orne River was a fortress. Its various strongpoints guarded not only the beach but also WN-12 ("Daimler"), with its four powerful 155mm guns, and just southwest of Daimler another WN with five or six 155mm guns. Farther inland, on the high ground three kilometers south of the assault beach near Colleville-sur-Orne, lay strongpoint "Morris," with four 100mm guns, and behind it strongpoint "Hillman," with two 105mm guns. Both Morris and Hillman were "second-line" defensive positions. Tucked in safely behind the flat crest of Periers ridge still farther south lay two batteries of artillery from 21st Panzer's 155th Battalion. Ken Ford described the British assault forced that landed on Sword as "one of the most powerful divisions that had ever left Britain."[28] Given the task it faced, it had to be.

The initial assault on Sword fell to 8th British Infantry Brigade on a two-battalion front, supported by DD tanks of 13th/18th Hussars and all the panoply of Royal Engineer and 79th Division specialized armor. Opening moves went largely according to plan. The prelanding bombardment was the best of the day, most of the DD tanks arrived well before the infantry, and the specialized assault and engineer armor did its job. Landings started at 0730 hours, and by 0830 hours all of 8th Brigade was ashore. It was quickly followed by more than a brigade of Commandos to clear the shoreline to the east to connect with the Canadians, and 1st Special Service Brigade, RM, to capture Ouistreham. Once that was done, the Commandos were to advance up the Caen canal and make contact with airborne forces holding the bridges at Benouville.

The next formation to land was 185th Brigade. It was to set out "with speed and boldness" to capture Caen. Second Battalion, King's Shropshire Light Infantry (KSLI) carried on the back of tanks of the Staffordshire Yeomanry, supported by M10 antitank guns, and flail tanks from the 22nd Dragoons formed the spearhead, while the other two battalions advanced on the flanks on foot. The reserve brigade, the 9th, landed last. It was to secure the division's right flank and make contact with 3rd Canadian Division. If 185th Brigade failed to take Caen, 9th Brigade was to attempt its capture from the *west*. Unfortunately, congestion and enemy fire on the beach delayed the concentration of 185th Brigade, and then Hillman and Morris had to be cleared. By noon, time was running down fast, and little progress toward Caen had been made.

Meanwhile, around 0745 hours, 3rd Canadian Division finally began landing on Juno: the last assault division to arrive. The full weight of the Canadian attack fell astride the Seulles River at Courseulles-sur-mer and around Bernieres farther east. Like 50th British Division on Gold, the Canadians attacked on a two-brigade front with two battalions per brigade in the leading wave, followed by a third battalion in reserve. One brigade was in reserve, to be landed after the beach had been won for the dash inland. Seventh Canadian Infantry Brigade, the "Western Brigade" composed of the Canadian Scottish from Vancouver Island, the Regina Rifles, and the Royal Winnipeg Rifles from the Prairies, attacked the strongpoint at Courseulles-sur-mer. Along with Port-en-Bessin and Ouistreham, Courseulles was one of three key small ports in the landing area, and therefore was a designated German "fortress." The result was generally considered to be the toughest waterline defenses assaulted on D-Day. Five massive concrete gun positions straddled the small entrance to the harbor at the high-water mark, ensuring overlapping fire across the nearby beaches. One of the nine guns in the assault area was an 88mm sited to sweep in front of Courseulles itself. None of these bunkers were vulnerable to naval gunfire: all presented a thick, steel-reinforced concrete side to the sea, and all were sited to fire along the beach and defeat a landing. All survived the initial bombardments, and all had to be taken by infantry attack. Survivors of the Canadian assault battalions later cursed the navy for failing to destroy the positions, but the navy never said it could. Targets at the waterline were laced by fire from supporting destroyers, but their shells were too small to penetrate the massive bunkers at Courseulles or anywhere else. All the navy ever promised was enough harassing fire on the emplacements to stun and concuss the defenders for twelve minutes. The infantry had to get there before the Germans regained their wits.[29]

Two full battalions manned the Courseulles defenses. The 441st Ost Battalion was deployed just southwest of Courseulles, and most of it seems to have fled. It is possible, however, that the battalion caught the full force of the Canadian artillery's drenching fire—which everywhere landed too far inland to affect the beach defenses. Second Battalion of 736th GR, manning the forward defenses of Courseulles, fought well. Nine field guns supported the Courseulles fortress. The coastal defense batteries at Ver-sur-mer and Mont Fleury, objectives of 50th Division on D-Day, overlooked the port. Some artillery from 21st Panzer Division was within range.

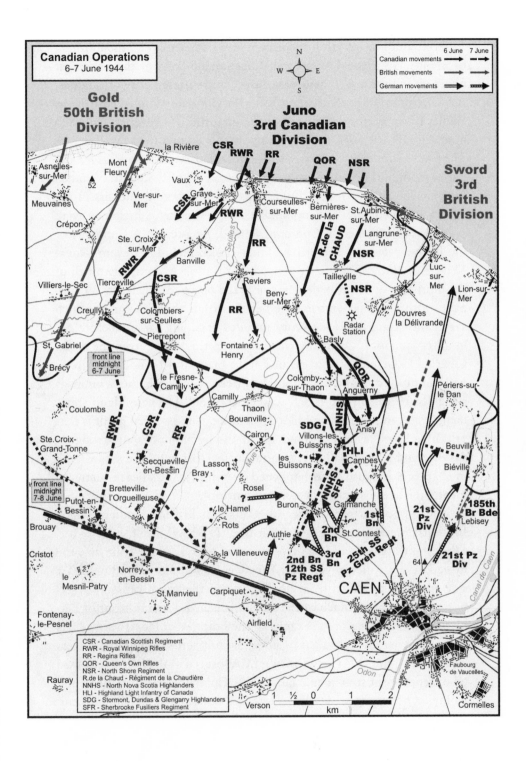

Canadian Operations
6–7 June 1944

	6 June	7 June
Canadian movements		
British movements		
German movements		

Gold
50th British
Division

Juno
3rd Canadian
Division

Sword
3rd
British
Division

N
W — E
S

Asnelles-sur-Mer

Mont Fleury

la Rivière

CSR
RWR
RR

QOR
NSR

Meuvaines

52

Vaux

Ver-sur-Mer

Graye-sur-Mer

CSR

RWR

Courseulles-sur-Mer

Bernières-sur-Mer

St. Aubin-sur-Mer

Langrune-sur-Mer

Luc-sur-Mer

Lion-sur-Mer

Crépon

Ste. Croix-sur-Mer

Banville

RR

R. de la CHAUD

NSR

Tailleville

Villiers-le-Sec

Tierceville

RWR

CSR

Colombiers-sur-Seulles

Reviers

Beny-sur-Mer

NSR

Radar Station

Douvres la Délivrande

Périers-sur-le Dan

St. Gabriel

Creully

Pierrepont

RR

Fontaine Henry

Basly

QOR

Anguerny

Brécy

front line midnight 6–7 June

le Fresne-Camilly

Camilly

Colomby-sur-Thaon

NNHS

Beuville

Coulombs

Thaon

Bouanville

Cairon

SDG

Villons-les-Buissons

Anisy

Ste. Croix-Grand-Tonne

RWR

CSR

RR

Secqueville-en-Bessin

Lasson

Bray

les Buissons

HLI

Cambes

Biéville

front line midnight 7–8 June

Bretteville-l'Orgueilleuse

Rosel

NNHS
SFR

Galmanche

21st Pz Div

185th Br Bde

Lebisey

Putot-en-Bessin

le Hamel

?

Buron

1st Bn

Brouay

Rots

2nd Bn

St. Contest

Cristot

Authie

3rd Bn

2nd Bn 12th SS Pz Regt

25th SS Pz Gren Regt

21st Pz Div

le Mesnil-Patry

Norrey-en-Bessin

la Villeneuve

64

Fontenay-le-Pesnel

St. Manvieu

Carpiquet

CAEN

Rauray

Airfield

Faubourg de Vaucelles

CSR - Canadian Scottish Regiment
RWR - Royal Winnipeg Rifles
RR - Regina Rifles
QOR - Queen's Own Rifles
NSR - North Shore Regiment
R. de la Chaud - Régiment de la Chaudière
NNHS - North Nova Scotia Highlanders
HLI - Highland Light Infantry of Canada
SDG - Stormont, Dundas & Glengarry Highlanders
SFR - Sherbrooke Fusiliers Regiment

Verson

1   ½   0   1   2
km

Odon

Cormelles

Two battalions of 7th Brigade captured Courseulles on the morning of 6 June. The Royal Winnipeg Rifles landed west of the harbor at about 0745 hours, well before the tanks, and suffered heavy casualties. A few minutes later the Regina Rifles' A Company landed east of the Seulles River, in front of the village. B Squadron, 1st Hussars, launched nineteen DD Sherman tanks to support this company of the Reginas. They were supposed to arrive before the infantry and suppress the defenses from hull-down positions in the sea. Five of B Squadron's tanks sank on the way in (one, "Bold," has been recovered and sits in the square at Courseulles as a monument), the rest either were late or were swept eastward where B Company landed. As a result, A Company of the Reginas stormed the beach alone. Tanks, including several Royal Marine Centaurs, eventually arrived, but it took A Company much of the morning to clear the defenses near the beach. To the east, B Company of the Reginas enjoyed the benefit of DD tanks, some of which sat in the rising tide for twenty minutes engaging targets before the infantry landed. B Company was soon into the village from the flank. Clearing Courseulles went according to plan, and by noon the Reginas had pushed inland and cleared Reviers, meanwhile the Winnipegs struggled to get off the beach west of the Seulles. These bland statements mask much hard and bloody fighting. The essential point is that 7th Brigade was ashore and moving inland by noon, despite strong resistance and a few small counterattacks. Its story is told in some detail in chapter 6 because what happened on 7th Brigade's beach mattered greatly to the subsequent beachhead battles.

The same was true of the 8th Canadian Brigade landing, which straddled the town of Bernieres-sur-mer. The town itself, heavily fortified along its seawall, was the objective of a Toronto regiment, the Queen's Own Rifles of Canada. They were supposed to land on either side and take the town from the flanks. But the storm caused navigation problems, and much of the assault touched down in front of Bernieres—and long before the tanks of the Fort Garry Horse arrived. As a result, Bernieres was taken by direct assault across about fifty meters of flat, wet sand. One Queen's Own LCA lost ten of the first eleven men who stepped out to machine gun fire; A Company left forty dead and wounded below the wrack line. Here, as elsewhere, skill, commitment, and daring saved the day, and Bernieres was taken.

Eighth Brigade's other assault battalion, the North Shore (New Brunswick) Regiment (NSR), landed west of Bernieres village on either side of Gap N7 in the little hamlet of La Rive Plage. Its objective was the strongpoint on Cap Romain at St. Aubin, which it was to take from the flank. The plan worked reasonably well. The assaulting infantry of A Company got through the defenses west of N7 like a hot knife through butter: its landing is immortalized in the only surviving Allied footage of the actual assault landing by infantry. But B Company landing on the left of N7 was trapped on the beach by murderous fire from the strongpoint on the headland. The beach was soon littered with dead and wounded—and with armored bulldozers, AVREs, Royal Marine Centaur SPs, and Shermans from the Fort Garry Horse all looking for an exit. Finally, the tank squadron commander simply drove through the minefield in Gap N7, followed by the rest of his tanks: three were knocked out, but a route was opened, and soon troops, tanks, SPs, and other vehicles poured into the flank and rear of St. Aubin. Unfortunately, just as this was being done, 48th Commando RM arrived in wooden assault boats and was badly mauled by machine gun fire from the headland.

The NSR and the Royal Marines (who fought through the eastern part of St. Aubin on their way to link up with 3rd British Division) found St. Aubin a rabbit warren of tunnels, trenches, and gun positions stoutly defended by both troops from 736th GR and Ostruppen (who in this case fought well). Centaurs from 2nd RM Assault Squadron fired supporting barrages from as little as 600 meters, while Fort Garry tanks fought through the village's narrow streets. The defenses of St. Aubin were so elaborate, so well defended, and so well connected by tunnels to points inland that the NSR had to leave a platoon in the village overnight to finish the job. What the Canadians discovered later, as the NSR fought through Tailleville to the south and attempted to capture the Douvres radar station, was that they had attacked the western edge of a fully developed coastal defense system. The radar station, Tailleville, St. Aubin, and Bernieres, as well as the Tailleville forest farther south, were all connected by tunnels. Tailleville, the forest, and the radar station contained elaborate underground steel-reinforced concrete complexes: barracks, command headquarters, kitchens, radio rooms, storage, and even a stable.

More specialized armor: a Centaur of 2nd Royal Marine Assault Squadron
supports the Regina Rifles in the streets of Courseulles-sur-mer, 6 June 1944.
(LCMSDS)

The NSR was supposed to take St. Aubin, Tailleville, the forest, and
the radar station in a series of company-level attacks. Nineteenth RCA,
less three M7s lost when an LCT took a direct hit, was soon ashore to
support the NSR and by noon was pounding Tailleville and the radar
station. But the NSR attack stalled at Tailleville, whose underground
complex had to be cleared six times because of repeated infiltration
from other sites. Only when a flamethrower was employed did things
go quiet in the underground complex. As for the radar station, a vast,
heavily defended site built around a five-story-deep, steel-reinforced
concrete bunker, it was left for the next day. The problems of clearing
the left flank of the Canadian landings on D-Day had a serious impact
on the events of D+1.

Eighth Brigade's reserve battalion, La Regiment de la Chaudiere,
began landing at 0830 hours at Bernieres. By then the rising sea cov-

ered many of the beach obstacles, and several of the Chauds' LCAs foundered. The men simply stripped off their equipment and swam ashore. As one of their officers commented, "They still had their knives and were quite willing to fight with this weapon."[30] The Chauds spent "some time" on the beach waiting for the Queen's Own to clear Bernieres, and then movement through the tight village streets was cautious and slow. It then took the Chaudieres an inordinate amount of time to consolidate and get moving—they were still in their assembly area just south of Bernieres at 1356 hours. As the next chapter explains, it seems that elements of 21st Panzer may have been responsible for the critical delay moving south from Bernieres.

The problem of advancing south of Bernieres lay partly in the nature of the ground: there was simply no cover. South of the village, then as now, lies a flat, open field from horizon to horizon, rising to a flat, clear crest line on the Tailleville-Beny road about two kilometers distant. The first three M7s of 14th RCA to deploy south of Bernieres were immediately destroyed by guns firing from west of Tailleville more than 2,000 meters away. With mines, mortar rounds, and small arms ammunition stacked four feet high over their engine compartments, the SPs disappeared in shattering explosions. The Fort Garry tanks declined to move into the open south of Berniers until the guns were silenced. Fourteenth RCA settled for a gun position near the beach.[31] The tardiness of 8th Brigade's move inland, and the storm surge, compounded 3rd Canadian Division's problems.

In this sector the chaos and confusion only got worse as the morning wore on. By 1000 hours Major General Rod Keller was weighing his options for landing his reserve brigade, the 9th, which he needed for the drive to the D-Day objective at Carpiquet. According to the plan, he had two choices: land it behind 8th Brigade at Bernieres and St. Aubin, or behind 7th Brigade at Courseulles. As will be seen in chapter 6, the situation at Courseulles was not good at 1000 hours, nor by that time had the NSR managed to clear Cap Romain, the strongpoint overlooking Gap N7 at St. Aubin. So Keller chose the "third" option: push the whole brigade through Bernieres.

The result was mayhem. There is only one road between the beach in front of Bernieres and the open country to the south. It winds and snakes its way through the village and, near the church at the southern

The M7 Priest "Evelyn," No. 4 gun of F Troop, 14th RCA, in its LCT at Portsmouth, 5 June 1944: loaded and ready to go. Note the ammunition for drenching fire stacked on the deck of the landing craft, and the Sherman tank also of 14th RCA in the LCT behind. (LAC PA-191019)

end, narrows to barely a dozen feet between stone walls. With most of 8th Brigade stalled in Bernieres because of the 88mm guns near Tailleville, 9th Brigade began to land there at around 1140 hours. By then the rising tide and the storm surge had narrowed the beach to a sliver. The normal spring tide on this stretch of the coast is twenty feet, leaving a narrow but usable strip of sand. The storm surge pushed the tide higher still, virtually eliminating the beach. Moreover, spring tides in the Baie de la Seine stand at high water for well over an hour, nearly two hours on a neap tide. So all along the coast, the storm surge and the long period of standing water at high tide affected the progress of the landings.[32]

The vanguard of 9th Brigade, the North Nova Scotia Highlanders (NNSH), began landing at Bernieres about an hour behind schedule. "The beach was crowded and confusion reigned," Will Bird wrote in

The Stormont, Dundas, and Glengarry Highlanders of 9th Canadian Infantry Brigade landing at Bernieres, late morning of 6 June 1944. Note the bicycles for the "dash" inland and how the narrowness of the beach at high tide restricts access to the bridge over the sea wall. (LAC PA-131506)

the Novas' history.[33] Beach masters and officers barked orders, but no one listened. Fortunately, the Germans did not shell the area. As the Novas moved into Bernieres, "every lane and road and street and garden was jammed with troops." Meanwhile, Keller appealed to the navy to tackle the antitank guns delaying the advance inland. It is not clear that he was successful in getting naval help, so the stalemate at Bernieres dragged on into the afternoon.

The guns covering the open ground south of Bernieres were probably 88s from 21st Panzer's Heavy Anti-Tank Battalion 200. The troops who captured them, A Company of the Chaudieres, thought they were.[34] The Chauds also captured the "Beny-sur-mer" battery of four 100mm Czech guns, and Stacey intimates that the two were confused. Some Queen's Own thought the guns near Tailleville were 75mm. Whatever they were, they were powerful enough to reach across two kilometers of farmland and kill tanks, and the 88s of 21st Panzer were the only mobile guns of that caliber along the whole stretch of the Normandy landings. On the morning of 6 June, Heavy Anti-Tank Battalion 200 guarded the good tank country along the Mue and Seulles Rivers. The Canadian official history shows the three companies of the battalion garrisoned at Putot, Ste.-Croix, and Camilly (in front of 7th Brigade) prior to D-Day. But these guns were pushed forward in late morning to try to stem the assault. Stacey's fold-out map of German defenses shows them again—without explanation—in their deployed positions on D-Day along the Seulles River, south of Beny and (perhaps) west of Tailleville.[35] The range at which the 14th RCA Priests were destroyed suggests that the guns near Tailleville were 88s.

These Pak 43/41s were powerful weapons. At nearly twenty-two feet long, the gun was the L/71 version being fitted to the King Tiger. The huge gun and the ersatz towed mounting weighed more than four metric tons, and the gun was so ungainly it was dubbed the "Barndoor" by German troops. But the Pak 43/4 was low, and the gun was lethal: easily capable of killing T-34s on the eastern front at 3,500 meters.[36] The Canadians would fight these guns throughout the initial beachhead battles, and on 6 June they may have been enough to keep 8th Canadian Infantry Brigade and its supporting tanks cowering in Bernieres for far too long—anyone who has seen the ground will understand the problem.[37]

While infantry and armor waited for someone to deal with the 88mm guns, sea conditions—powerful wave action at the height of the tide—prevented 3rd Canadian Division's antitank regiments from landing most of its guns. The forty-eight guns of 3rd Anti-Tank Regiment, RCA, half towed 6-pounders and half self-propelled M10 "tank destroyers" with a 3-inch gun, were integral to the Overlord plan. The M10s provided mobile firepower, and their 3-inch fifty-caliber American gun was lethal to most German tanks at 1,000 yards. All sixteen of the regiment's M10s had been combined for the assault in 105th Battery, to help secure the advance to Carpiquet. They were to be the first to land at Bernieres, but it seems that only one M10 landed there on D-Day. It made a perilous transfer to a Rhino ferry, a large, flat barge propelled by outboard motors, at noon and did not come ashore

Traffic jam in Bernieres-sur-mer, 6 June 1944. (LAC PA-133740)

until 1600 hours. The rest of the M10 battery did not land until the next morning.[38]

A similar fate befell 3rd RCA Anti-Tank's 6-pounders. As Stan Medland, commander of 52nd Battery from Weymouth, Nova Scotia, recalled, "The role of the 6-pounder was unique. To be effective, they needed to be moved up quickly into each new area taken by the infantry to prepare for a counter attack."[39] The key to the importance of the 6-pounder was its new "armor-piercing, discarding sabot" ammunition. Developed by the French at the start of the war and carried to England by escaping engineers, the round consisted of a small tungsten dart embedded in a full-bore "shoe" (hence the French word *sabot*), which fell away once the round left the barrel. That allowed the full charge to propel the dart at 4,050 feet per second and penetrate 143 millimeters of armor plate. The dart had just enough kinetic energy to penetrate a tank but usually not enough to escape out the other side. So once inside, it rattled around at frightening speed, with results that can only be imagined. Because the 6-pounder was low, small, and easily handled, it was deployed well forward and used to engage targets at 900 yards or less—in fact, seldom more than 500 yards. At that distance the tungsten dart reached its target in about an eighth of a second: no German armor could stop it.[40]

But getting towed antitank guns ashore on Juno Beach was nearly impossible: the sea was simply too rough. The first craft trying to land 6-pounders of 3rd Anti-Tank RCA foundered and sank. By late morning the surf was running so high that it was not possible to put a towed 6-pounder gun ashore from a large landing craft because the Bren carrier pulling it—despite raised sides to help keep out the surf—would run off the ramp and disappear in the sea. So it was decided to try transferring the guns from landing craft (LCTs) onto Rhino ferries at sea and transshipping them to the beach. This perilous undertaking was done only once, at Courseulles (described in chapter 6). The rest of 3rd RCA Anti-Tank had to wait until D+1.

The rock upon which the German panzer assault would ultimately break was 62nd Anti-Tank Regiment, RA, with its forty-eight 17-pounder guns. The 62nd RA was also organized into four batteries of twelve guns each: two towed (246th and 247th) and two of the M10 variants "Achilles" (245th and 248th). All four were slated to land on D-Day: two in a fluid reserve role under Brigadier Todd, the CRA, at Bernieres behind the 8th Brigade, and two (246th and 248th) with 7th Brigade. All arrived off Juno safely and on time: only eight guns got ashore on D-Day, all of them at Courseulles. None of 62nd Anti-Tank Regiment's guns landed in support of 8th and 9th Brigades on D-Day. In fact, the first to do so, the towed 17-pounders of 247th Battery, did not arrive until the afternoon of D+1. The M10 Achilles did not arrive in this sector until D+3. The tardy arrival of these guns, and those of 3rd RCA, was one of the unknown costs of landing in bad weather.

The congestion in Bernieres did not begin to ease until early afternoon. At 1440 hours the Chaudieres and Fort Garry tanks, supported by 14th RCA, moved on Beny, which they captured less than an hour later. This cleared the way for the vanguard of 9th Brigade, the NNSH, to move toward Beny at around 1700 hours, where they met tanks of the Sherbrooke Fusiliers. By 1820 hours, the advance to Carpiquet, the operation practiced two months earlier in Exercise Pedal II, finally began. However, this time the vanguard's FOOs came from 14th RCA, which moved up to the gun area at Beny to provide support. The rest of 9th Brigade moved in support as well.[41]

Terry Copp, who has studied the Canadian landings more thoroughly than anyone else, concluded that "there is little doubt that the 9th Brigade could reach Carpiquet" before dark (approximately 2230 hours) on D-Day.[42] By 2013 hours it had reached Villons-les-Buissons and run into some opposition, but the commander of Second British Army, General Sir Miles Dempsey, ordered everyone to stop about that time. Given that none of the antitank artillery assigned to the covering position at Carpiquet was yet ashore, the decision to stop was a good one. However, apart from exhausted men and delays on the beach, what Dempsey was really worried about was the attack on 3rd British Division by a large group of tanks.

Third British Division's struggle to get off the beach and capture Caen, and the German reaction to both it and the airborne landings east of the Orne River, shaped the course of the next three days on the I Corps front. As noted earlier, in the early morning 21st Panzer was ordered to attack the airborne bridgehead on the east side of the Orne. Most of the division, two-thirds of its combat power, was laagered south of Caen, so it approached 6th British Airborne from the south and east of the city. Only the Kampfgruppe commanded by Lieutenant Colonel Joseph Rauch, billeted northwest of Caen around Cussy, Buron, Cairon, and spots along the Caen-Bayeux highway, moved across the north side of Caen. Twenty-First Panzer's concentration against 6th Airborne was not yet complete when the priority changed. The news of Canadian movement off the beach coupled with that of 3rd British resulted in a cancellation of the attack on the airborne bridgehead and a shift to striking directly toward Sword Beach. Kampfgruppe Rauch was already largely in position north of the city. But there was no time to move the bulk of 21st Panzer's armor around Caen to the west, while the approach to Sword from the east was blocked by the British airborne's control of the bridges at Benouville. The only way to get the armor north of Caen was through its winding streets. It took five and a half hours to do so. It is interesting to speculate on what might have happened to 21st Panzer—and the subsequent beachhead battles—if Caen had fallen quickly on D-Day. Freddie Morgan wanted to drop an airborne division on it: he may have been right.

As the day dragged on, the British airborne drove off halfhearted attacks by elements of 21st Panzer, especially by the Kampfgruppe of Hans von Luck, which remained east of Caen to contain the paratroopers, while the division shifted its weight to the plains north of the city. Defenses along the beach sector, especially those in the second line, covered the delay in assembling the counterattack by fighting desperately. Eighth British Brigade did not close with the second line position Morris, and force its surrender, until 1300 hours, and Hillman held out until after 2000 hours. Sword was not declared "clear" until 1600 hours. By then the storm surge and the narrow beach had created yet another traffic jam, and the Staffordshires, who were supposed to be carrying the KSLI on the dash to Caen, were caught in the snarl. The 185th Brigade, setting off for Caen on foot and without its supporting tanks, was soon stymied by strongpoint "Rover," an infantry position on the crown of a small hill a mile south of Hillman. The brigade reached Beuville and Blieville before stopping to wait for the tanks. It's well it did.

Assembling in front of 185th Brigade, shielded from sight by Lebisey ridge, was the armored might of 21st Panzer organized into two Kampfgruppen. Kampfgruppe Oppeln was the mailed fist of the attack: two battalions of Mk IV tanks of 22nd Panzer Regiment (PR), supported by one battalion of 192nd Panzer Grenadier Regiment (PGR). The other, Kampfgruppe Rauch, consisted of the other two battalions of 192nd PGR, plus division engineers and self-propelled artillery. Both Kampfgruppen were liberally equipped with half-tracks, and some of the division's towed and self-propelled antitank artillery were echeloned in support. The attack was considered so important that 84th Corps' commander, General Marcks, was at Lebisey to see them off. Oppeln's tanks were to make for Periers ridge to control the high ground that dominated the beaches, while Rauch and his infantry made the dash to Lion-sur-mer. The objective was clear. "Oppeln," Marcks said quietly to his tank commander, "if you don't succeed in driving the English into the sea, we've lost the war."[43]

Marcks believed—and hoped—that elements of 192nd PGR were still in possession of Periers ridge: he was wrong. The ridge already was occupied by 2nd Battalion KSLI, the Staffordshire Shermans, and twenty antitank guns of 41st Anti-Tank Regiment, RA. Kampfgruppe Oppeln's attack lapped along the face of Periers ridge like a long ocean swell rolling down a beach, and like a wave it broke as it went. The 22nd PR's 2nd Battalion on the right was the first to feel the effects of fire from C Squadron of the Staffordshires and their supporting anti-tank guns. Hits in quick succession forced the attackers west, across the face of the Staffordshires' A Squadron, which took its own toll on 2nd Battalion. The 1st Battalion, 22nd PR, was in line to the west and approached the western spur of Periers ridge from the south. As they crested the ridge, Staffordshire tanks and antitank guns in defilade shot them to pieces. When 1st Battalion withdrew, shifted left, and then mounted the ridge from the west, it got the same treatment. By the time it was over, fourteen German tanks were destroyed and fifteen others damaged, with little loss to the British. The fist of 21st Panzer had not been broken, but it was badly bruised.

Meanwhile, Kampfgruppe Rauch, starting from St. Contest, reached the sea at Lion-sur-mer without serious incident. Its presence, just to the east of Douvres, was probably the reason the North Shore Regiment stopped at Tailleville for the night: to secure the Canadians' open flank. Marcks made plans to reinforce this success, but these were undone by airborne troops. At 2100 hours the first wave of a scheduled reinforcement of the airborne bridgehead darkened the sky north of Caen. The appearance of Allied aerial power clearly impressed senior German officers. When the second wave flew over at 2130 hours, they panicked and recalled both Kampfgruppen to their start lines north of Caen. This is probably the only instance in the war when an armored division retreated in the face of airborne troops. Oppeln brought his shattered force back, while Rauch dispatched at least one company of infantry into the radar station at Douvres during his retreat.

The massive radar station at Douvres, 7 June 1944. The village of Douvres-la-Deliverand is at the bottom left. The wooded area at the bottom right is the Tailleville forest, which harbored an extensive bunker complex, including underground stables, for German artillery operating on this stretch of the coast. The main part of the station in the center of the photo sits atop a five-story underground bunker. The station was finally taken on 17 June by 4th Special Service Brigade, Royal Marines. (LCMSDS)

Thus ended what Buckingham has rightly described as "the strongest and most dangerous threat to emerge anywhere along the Allied invasion front on 6 June."[44] Had 3rd British Division been able to dash into Caen, or had Morgan's plan for an airdrop on Caen not been abandoned, it would never have happened. Certainly COSSAC planners were well aware of the good tank country north of the city; the plain between the sea and the city at times looks like a prairie.

Fearing the worst, and with the armor of 21st Panzer loose on its western flank during the evening of 6 June, 3rd British Division also stopped for the night. It has since been chided by historians, mostly American and most recently the German official history,[45] for lack of aggression and for failing to push on to Caen. This is an idle criticism. Third Division had seen off the largest and potentially most deadly counterattack launched on the day, but 21st Panzer had not been destroyed. On the evening of D-Day it was still roaming freely across the wide plain between Caen and the sea, and between 3rd British Division and 3rd Canadian Division. Everything Allied intelligence knew about 21st Panzer at the time suggested it was a uniquely powerful formation, with Tiger tanks and probably a regiment of Panthers. On the evening of D-Day there was no way that Major General Tom Rennie or the I Corps commander, Lieutenant General John Crocker, or their staffs could know that the Mk IVs brushed away from the slopes of Periers ridge with such ease were the best that 21st Panzer possessed. Moreover, intelligence distributed on the eve of D-Day that I Corps faced possibly 540 German tanks in its zone of operations meant that the 50 seen from the Staffordshires' position were just the tip of the spear: more, and bigger and better, were surely en route. In these circumstances, consolidation on Periers ridge was prudent.

In the event, more panzers were en route. The two closest panzer divisions, 12th SS spread out from Houdan just west of Paris to Vimoutiers in lower Normandy and Panzer Lehr in garrison around Charters, belonged to the panzer reserve controlled by Oberkommando der Wehrmacht (OKW), the German army headquarters. Von Rundstedt, the commander in chief, west, had asked for release of these divisions to his control at 0445 hours and was denied. All OKW would allow was to put the panzer divisions on standby. For its part, 12th SS was not content to wait, and it sent its reconnaissance elements out; some went west into lower Normandy, others north of the Seine. By the time the division was ordered to "stand by," its reconnaissance units had reached Bayeux. Shortly thereafter, 12th SS was allocated to 84th Corps for operations and ordered to assemble at Lisieux. This order drew 25th SS PGR, garrisoned around Bernay-Obec-Vimoutiers and therefore only a few hours' drive from the coast at Caen, north and away from the landings. By 1000 hours units began to concentrate for the move. Then, for the next five hours, uncertainty reigned.

Indecision over when and how to release the panzer reserve stemmed largely from uncertainty over what the Allied landings in Calvados really meant. As noted, they were not a surprise. But through much of 6 June, senior German leadership, including Hitler and his staff, debated whether the landings in lower Normandy were just a feint. When Rommel returned to his headquarters at Roch Guyon west of Paris late on 6 June, after an arduous, high-speed car ride, he focused attention on defense of the Fifteenth Army sector in the Pas de Calais, where the real attack was expected. Moreover, it was anticipated that the assault in the Fifteenth Army sector would be supported, in the words of the German official history, by "an imminent attack on Antwerp."[46]

Eventually it was decided to release panzer divisions south of the Seine to deal with the landings that had already occurred. At 1400 hours on 6 June, 1st SS Panzer Corps was subordinated to Army Group B (Rommel) to control the panzers, and an hour later both 12th SS and Panzer Lehr were released to 1st SS Corps headquarters. The decision was confirmed within minutes by Rundstedt, who added 21st Panzer and 716th Divisions to 1st SS Corps as well.[47]

The man now charged with defeating the landings was Oberstgruppenführer (Colonel-General) Joseph "Sepp" Dietrich, an ardent Nazi. Milton Shulman, a Canadian intelligence officer who interviewed many senior German generals immediately after the war, described Dietrich as short and squat, and resembling "a battered bar-tender in appearance." A sergeant in the Great War and a member of Hitler's "bullying gangs" during the Nazi rise to power, Dietrich was a survivor by 1944. Shulman described him as "crude, conceited and garrulous." Nazi propaganda and his "hard and ruthless energy" had elevated Dietrich to legendary status that by 1944 rivaled Rommel's. Now, at the crisis of the war in the west, he was charged with orchestrating a panzer corps attack from his headquarters in Brussels 300 kilometers away from the battlefield. With a little luck and skill he might have done it. But Dietrich had none of the former in the early stages of the Normandy campaign and possessed little of the latter. Shulman, who was in a position to know, accepted von Rundstedt's assessment of Dietrich: "He is decent, but stupid."[48]

The task of Dietrich's 1st SS Panzer Corps was clear: the landings in Calvados were to be destroyed that day because, in the words of Rundstedt's chief of staff at 1655 hours, "there was the danger of strong airborne and sea landings" in the Pas de Calais.[49] By the time the decision was made to launch the panzer corps at the landings, however, it was already too late to achieve a decisive result on 6 June. Panzer Lehr was simply too far away, and by then the counterattack by 21st Panzer was already under way. Moreover, the decision at 1000 hours to concentrate 12th SS at Lisieux, ready to operate north or south of the Seine, had wasted precious time. In preparation for the attack on forces landing near Caen, 12th SS was now ordered to concentrate at Evrecy, southwest of the city. British historian Michael Reynolds estimated that had Evrecy been assigned as the concentration area from the outset, 12th SS could have had 25th PGR assembled there and ready to attack by 1500 hours on 6 June. In the event, 25th PGR spent hours moving north to Lisieux and then had to retrace its steps south to Evrecy. Its sister regiment, 26th PGR, now had a full 200 kilometers to travel and could not be ready until late on 7 June at the earliest. Twelfth SS finally began to move into the battle zone by 1740 hours.[50] Clearly, Allied deception operations had already bought crucial time for the assault troops to get ashore and consolidate. These delays proved critical in allowing 7th Canadian Infantry Brigade, in particular, to fully occupy its covering position around Putot-Bretteville-Norrey on 7 June in preparation for the panzer assault.

Twelfth SS established headquarters at Moutier-en-Cinglas in the Forest of Grimbosq north of Falaise by 1800 hours on D-Day, and its forces gathered to the north around Evrecy. The advanced headquarters of 1st SS Panzer Corps lay nearby, just outside Falaise, and 21st Panzer headquarters was to the east at St. Pierres-dur-Dives. Only Panzer Lehr was missing. Contact with it was established at 2400 hours, and its leading elements (reconnaissance troops) were expected to reach Thury-Harcourt by dawn. Panzer Lehr's movement to the front, not much longer in road miles than that of 12th SS, was difficult, and it took nearly two days to assemble it in front of the Canadians west of the Mue River.

Meanwhile, the leading elements of 25th PGR of the 12th SS began arriving around Evrecy by 2300 hours, and losses on the move—to all units of the division—were minimal. However, the SS had not budgeted its fuel effectively, and the Panther battalion of SS 12th PR ran out of gas east of the Orne. This was just the first example of sloppy staff work and command and control that characterized 12th SS Division's experience in the beachhead battles. Kurt Meyer, commander of 25th PGR and later the division commander, blamed Allied fighter-bombers for the fuel shortage. Perhaps. General Major Edgar Feuchtinger, commander of 21st Panzer, commented after the war that there was plenty of fuel available, but the SS were either too arrogant or too stupid to ask.[51] "I could have given him all he wanted if he had asked me for it," Feuchtinger commented. When asked about this after the war, Dietrich cut to the heart of the matter that dogged coordination of German reaction to the landings. "It is easy for Feuchtinger now to say that he would have given Meyer petrol on 7 June," Dietrich told Milt Shulman in September 1945, "but on the morning his answer to such a request would have been 'I haven't got any.'"[52] In fact, Dietrich's comment reflects the pervasive tension between the Wehrmacht and the SS that crippled so much of Germany's war effort.

The antipathy between Feuchtinger and the SS was therefore mutual and by no means unique. When Meyer arrived at the new 12th SS HQ in the Forest of Grimbosq, he was angered that Feuchtinger was forward with his own division and out of touch with his headquarters. Later, in his memoirs, Meyer castigated Feuchtinger for botching the battle on D-Day. Recrimination between losing generals is a common phenomenon, especially when those generals have been accustomed to setting the tempo of their battles. The one thing that the Anglo-Canadians had learned from two generations of fighting Germans was their reliance on speed and audacity to upset the enemy and turn the battle into one of movement. Indeed, the whole of German army organization, equipment, and doctrine was predicated on managed chaos. The Germans needed to get the battle to tumble into a rout, so they needed

General Major Edgar Feuchtinger, commanding officer of 21st Panzer Division. (AHEC)

to hit hard and hit fast. On 6 June 1944 they were unable to do that, and throughout the months that followed, they were never able to get the Allies to dance to their tune. And it was not all Hitler's fault.

The task for 1st SS Panzer Corps was to destroy the Allied landings as soon as possible. It was generally believed that the fate of Overlord would be decided on the plains north and west of Caen. Only there could a crushing blow be delivered, only there could the panzers cause the battle to tumble into chaos. With the Anglo-Canadian forces destroyed in an armored blitz, it would then be possible to cordon off the Americans and eliminate them, too. This wishful thinking seemed to take no account of Allied naval and air superiority, but the threat of the panzers was real. It was, in the end, Germany's only hope of defeating the landings. At midnight on 6 June, Dietrich ordered a three-division panzer counterattack in the 716th Division area: their objective was the sea.

No one really expected this could happen, except perhaps Kurt Meyer. Meyer finally caught up with Feuchtinger at the headquarters of 716th Division at midnight. The headquarters was located in a tunnel in a quarry north of Caen (now the museum and commemorative site "Le memorial," with the 716th headquarters tunnel part of the exhibit space), which was also being used as a field hospital: the dying and wounded clogged the passageways. The mood was somber. Major General Richter, 716th's commander, was there, as was a liaison group from Panzer Lehr—all the elements of 1st SS Panzer Corps. The news was not good. Units were holding out in the beach zone, especially the radar station at Douvres, but the Allies were ashore in strength. Feuchtinger in particular cautioned the group about the power of their enemy, which he had just witnessed at Periers ridge. Meyer was unimpressed. As Feuchtinger recalled in 1945, "Meyer studied the map, turned to me with a confident air and said, 'Little fish! We'll throw them back into the sea in the morning.'"[53]

4

9th Brigade Advances
The Morning of 7 June

We shoved on again and it was a breeze, nothing but
infantry until we were fired on by A/T guns to our right.
Sergeant T. C. Reid, C Squadron, Sherbrooke Fusiliers

NIGHTS ARE SHORT in the Norman summer. The lingering twilight
lasts until late in the evening, close to 11:00 on modern watches, and
by 5:00 the next morning sunlight is already filtering in across the eastern sky. But even these short hours of darkness gave little rest and re-
cuperation for the men on both sides in the Normandy beachhead. For
Allied assault troops, many of whom had been without proper sleep
now for forty-eight hours, 7 June offered the prospect of intense and
bloody fighting as they struggled to reach objectives that should have
fallen the day before.

As the Germans rushed reserves to the front to stabilize the hemor-
rhage and throw the Allies back into the sea, Montgomery urged haste
in securing the final D-Day objectives. The situation around Caen was
so confused on D+1 that he could do little more than admonish. Terry
Copp concluded that "higher command could play no role in the day's
events."[1] Men on the ground knew what they had to do, and many
were already on the move as dawn broke. As the Canadian official
history states—and the Overlord operational orders made clear—by
D+1 the Canadians were to be in their fortress positions astride the
Caen-Bayeux highway "to meet the anticipated counter attack."[2]

The two infantry divisions of I British Corps, 3rd British and 3rd
Canadian, were supposed to be shoulder to shoulder by the end of
D-Day. But as the sun rose on 7 June, the only units operating on
the Canadian left were elements of 21st Panzer, roaming the miles of
rolling, open countryside between Caen and the sea. The 3rd British

Division D-Day plan called for 185th Brigade to make the assault on Caen, with 9th British Brigade linking up with its Canadian counterparts to the west, and the whole broad front advancing south. Caen was an entirely British objective, and so was the string of villages to its northwest and west: Cambes, Galmanche, St. Contest, Bitot, Cussy, the Abbey d'Ardennes, and St. Germaine-la-Blanch-Herbe. In fact, the division boundary between 3rd Canadian and 3rd British ran barely a thousand meters east of the route that the vanguard of 9th Canadian Brigade was to follow on D+1. Had things gone better on D-Day, the British would be in contact and keeping pace with the vanguard of 9th Canadian Brigade. In fact, 3rd British Division was not even trying to close the gap. It was closed up to the Orne River in support of the airborne bridgehead, bracing for another panzer attack that Major General Rennie expected first thing in the morning. No advance on Caen or linking with the Canadians was going to happen until 21st Panzer showed its hand.

As a result, at daybreak on 7 June, 8th Canadian Brigade held a long and troubled left flank. One platoon of the North Shore Regiment was still sitting on the beach defenses in St. Aubin-sur-mer, where it was not clear if all the resistance had ended. The rest of the battalion was three kilometers inland at Tailleville, preparing to capture Tailleville wood and then tackle the Douvres radar station—which stuck like a thorn in the side of the Canadian position. The North Shores were the only Canadian assault battalion still fighting in the beach defenses on D+1. Farther south, the rest of 8th Brigade (the Queen's Own Rifles and the Chaudieres) held the high ground around Anguerny. If this was not enough to give the Canadian division commander Major General Rod Keller pause, many of the antitank units assigned to this flank of his division had not even landed by the morning of 7 June. In particular, none of the two towed batteries of 17-pounder guns from 62nd Anti-Tank, RA, began to land before the afternoon of D+1, and only a few of the towed 6-pounders from 3rd Anti-Tank, RCA were ashore. Fortunately, most of the M10s of the 105th (Composite) Battery of 3rd Anti-Tank, RCA were landed, and L Troop was ready to roll with the vanguard on the morning of D+1. Only the infantry battalions' 6-pounders, the remaining tanks of Fort Garry Horse, the unbloodied Sherbrooke Fusiliers who landed in the reserve wave, and the guns

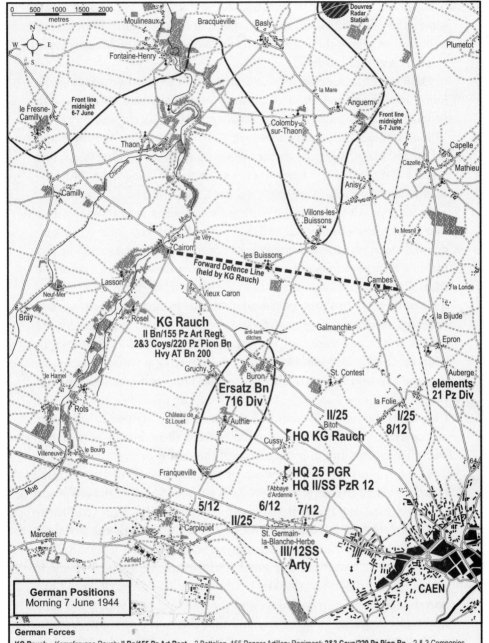

German Positions
Morning 7 June 1944

German Forces

KG Rauch – Kampfgruppe Rauch; **II Bn/155 Pz Art Regt** – 2 Battalion, 155 Panzer Artillery Regiment; **2&3 Coys/220 Pz Pion Bn** – 2 & 3 Companies, 220 Panzer Pioneer Battalion; **Hvy AT Bn 200** – 200 Heavy Anti-Tank Battalion; **25th PGR** – 25th Panzer Grenadier Regiment; **I/25, II/25, III/25** – 1st, 2nd & 3rd Battalions, 25th SS Panzer Grenadier Regiment; **II/SS PzR 12** – 2nd Battalion, 12th SS Panzer Regiment; **5/12, 6/12, 7/12, 8/12** – 5, 6, 7 & 8 Companies, 2nd Battalion, 12th SS Panzer Regiment, III/12SS Arty – 3rd Battalion, 12 SS Artillery Regiment of 14th and 19th RCA were available for the day's demanding tasks: secure the open left flank, march inland, and then establish the covering position where the plain east of the Mue met the highway west of Caen. It was a tall order.

Despite all this uncertainty, at sunrise the vanguard of 9th Brigade, built around one battalion of infantry and a regiment of tanks with supporting arms from various regiments, was poised just north of Villons-les-Buissons, ready to move south down what is now route D220 and seize its objective: the village and airfield at Carpiquet, just seven kilometers away. Resistance was expected to be light. No German panzer divisions were expected until the next day.

In view of what transpired during the day, it is important to stress that the D-Day operational order remained in effect until 3rd Canadian Division was consolidated on its covering position. On 7 June this meant a continuation of a two-brigade thrust down either side of the Mue River to positions astride the Caen-Bayeux highway from Carpiquet in the east to Putot in the west. It also meant that each brigade operated separately, and that their fire support was managed by the separate 12th and 14th Field Group, RCA, commanders operating in support of each brigade. Only when the covering position was secure was the division to be fought as a single unit, and only then would Brigadier Stanley Todd take control of all the division's guns. So the Canadians did not "push boldly" inland on D+1 "despite" the danger of powerful German forces moving toward them but in accordance with their orders and in *anticipation* of the enemy arriving.

The Germans were well aware of the importance of this terrain. Historians note that 21st Panzer was garrisoned south of the city prior to D-Day, and they focus on the division's counterattack on 3rd British and 6th Airborne Divisions. However, about a third of the division, especially its towed artillery and many of its SPs, its half-tracks, and its heavy antitank battalion, was north and west of the city on D-Day. It is suggestive of German thinking that 21st Panzer's Heavy Anti-Tank Battalion 200 was garrisoned west of the Mue, where a wide plain runs down to the sea at Courseulles, and that the heavy antitank platoon (1 Zug) of 8 Company of the 192nd PGR was astride the Mue near Cairon. About a third of 21st Panzer's artillery—all the towed companies of Panzer Artillery Regiment 155, twelve guns including eight ex-Russian 122mm—was also deployed north of Caen. They were supported by the 192nd PGR commanded by Lieutenant Colonel Joseph Rauch.[3] On D-Day the mounted elements of these units shifted east to attack 3rd British Division and then, as Kampfgruppe Rauch, attacked to the sea. As they did, more of the division shifted into the area around Buron-St. Contest, including some of its self-propelled antitank guns and artillery. This included what remained of Heavy Anti-Tank Battalion 200 with its massive 88mm guns, the half-tracks of 1st Battalion, 192nd PGR (one company of this regiment, it will be recalled, had gone into the radar station at Douvres to reinforce its garrison), an uncertain amount of Pioneer Battalion 220 equipped with half-tracks and 1.8mm "Granatenwerfer," and about a third of the division's self-propelled artillery.[4]

On 7 June a significant portion of 21st Panzer therefore remained west of Caen. It was well equipped and well trained, and it stood in the path of 9th Canadian Infantry Brigade east of the Mue. The Canadian official historian, Charles Stacey, was unaware of the presence of 21st Panzer forces in front of 3rd Canadian Division on 7 June.[5] As we will see, 21st Panzer had its own reasons to forget its involvement in this battle.

The advance of the vanguard of 9th Brigade was like stepping off into the dark. The 7th Canadian Infantry Brigade, advancing down the west side of the Mue River to its covering position, was out of touch and out of sight. The two Canadian brigades were divided by the wooded valley and therefore were not mutually supporting. As it turned out, 7th Brigade, too, then advanced in isolation. Contact with 50th Division to the west was firm as far south as Creully, but beyond that the pull of battle—especially the ill-fated counterattack late on D-Day by Kampfgruppe Meyer of 352nd Division—had drawn the British west and away from the Canadians. So on the morning of 7 June both Canadians flanks were "in the air." It was assumed, of course, that this problem would be resolved during the day and that the two Canadian brigades would themselves establish firm contact once the final D-Day objectives were secured. On the morning of 7 June this was about as much as Major General Rod Keller and his brigadiers knew.

The lack of British support—or even presence—on the Canadian flanks was not an excuse for inaction. Brigadier D. G. Cunningham's orders for his 9th Canadian Infantry Brigade were clear: get onto its D-Day objective.[6] These orders were passed on to the North Nova Scotia Highlanders at 0645 hours. There was, however, one note of caution. If heavy resistance was experienced at Carpiquet, a major German airfield ringed by 88mm guns, close defenses, wire, and massive bunkers, the vanguard was to take and hold its interim objective: the 80-meter contour—traced on the 1/25,000 maps—in the open field southeast of Buron.

It took nearly an hour to get the 9th Brigade vanguard into form after a nighttime excitement. There had been no rest. At about 0200 hours German infantry in half-tracks attacked both the Novas and the Chaudieres, killing, wounding, or capturing a whole platoon of the Chauds.[7] "Paratroopers," young soldiers in the full camouflage uniforms of the 12th SS were often reported as paratroopers at this stage, were reported infiltrating the Canadian positions during the night, and German vehicles seemed to stumble through the lines in all directions. Finally, at 0740 hours the Novas and the rest of the 9th Brigade vanguard set off down the D220 toward Carpiquet. This was a practiced move. The major elements of the advance had been training together for this moment since the previous fall, they had rehearsed it in April in Exercise Pedal II, and they had conducted the initial phase with success the day before.

The advance—and "defeat"—of the vanguard of 9th Brigade on 7 June became one of the iconic moments of the early stages of the Normandy campaign. Kurt Meyer, who fought against the vanguard, described in his 1956 memoir, *Grenadiere*, how he saw the Canadians passing through Buron and Authie like a road move, oblivious to the presence of his 25th PGR and its supporting tanks and artillery. Very cleverly, Meyer ambushed the Canadians and sent them reeling. The Canadian official history, published four years later, did nothing to refute the view that the novice Canadians were suddenly struck and beaten. Charles Stacey devoted seven pages to the battle: four and a half setting it up, and most of two analyzing why the brigade "had been caught off balance and defeated in detail."[8] In Stacey's view, the Canadians fought with "courage and spirit, but somewhat clumsily" against "an unusually efficient German force of about its own strength, it had come off second best." The result was a "severe local reverse" that—in words that damned the whole of 3rd Division's efforts for seventy years—"helped to ensure that Caen remained in German hands." In fact, Stacey never did a thorough workup on the battle, probably because the critical failure of Canadian artillery support for the vanguard of 9th Brigade on 7 June made it impossible for him to do so.

The vanguard force consisted of the North Nova Scotia Highlanders (a battalion) with companies at assault strength of about 119 men,[9] supported by fifty Sherman tanks of the Sherbrooke Fusiliers, four Vickers machine guns of No. 11 Platoon of the Cameron Highlanders of Ottawa,[10] and a troop of M10 tank destroyers of the 3rd Anti-Tank Regiment, RCA. The vanguard deployed in a wide arrow formation with the D220 forming the shaft. The Sherbrookes' reconnaissance troop of Stuart light tanks formed the tip of the arrow. Behind them on the D220 came C Company of the Novas borne by the battalion's Bren gun carrier platoon, supported by the Camerons. Major Don Learment, a twenty-five-year-old native of Truro, Nova Scotia, commanded the whole leading party, passing control of his C Company to Captain F. C. Fraser. The Novas' B Company moved across the open ground to the left of the road carried on the tanks of the Sherbrookes' B Squadron, while A Company did the same with A Squadron on the right. D Company (drawn largely from the Prince Edward Island Highlanders) and C Squadron of the tanks, as well as the Novas' support company, its four 6-pounder guns, and battalion headquarters under Lieutenant Colonel Charles Petch brought up the rear. Petch, wearing his Murray of Atholl tartan kilt into battle, was in overall command of the vanguard.

Artillery support for the vanguard was provided by 14th Field Regiment, RCA. These gunners had trained for this operation since the fall of 1943 alongside the Novas and the Sherbrookes, and the units knew each other well. Major Learment later recalled that 14th RCA was "practically one of us" and that Jake Beer, one of the forward observation officers who joined them that morning, was a fellow Maritimer from Charlottetown.[11] That said, 14th RCA had missed the final training exercise for the advance, Pedal II, in April: whether that had any impact on what unfolded during the day remains unknown. The regiment's twenty-one remaining 105mm SPs were near Beny-sur-mer (roughly where the Canadian cemetery now stands) at 0745 hours and were to move forward to a new gun position at La Mare, just north-

Lieutenant Colonel Charles Petch (right), commanding officer of the North Nova Scotia Highlanders and of the vanguard of 9th Canadian Infantry Brigade on 7 June 1944. To his right is Major C. F. Kennedy, commander of the Novas' D Company. (LAC PA-133733)

west of Anguerney, by noon. The regiment was to leapfrog forward by batteries, and at no point was the vanguard to be without immediate fire support.

According to the D-Day operational order, the Novas ought to have picked up four FOOs, one for each company,[12] from both regiments of 14th Field Group, RCA. In the event, they went forward on 7 June with only two. Why remains a mystery, but clearly casualties and over-commitments played a role. At this stage 14th Field Group, RCA, was still composed of only the two assault regiments, 14th and 19th RCA:

Command post for D Troop, 14th RCA, early in the campaign: still under canvas alongside the CP Sherman. Lieutenant Garth Webb, the troop commander, is standing to the right of the plot, which is being worked by Corporal Doug Allen, while Gunner Cowie monitors the radio. Gunners soon learned to dig their CPs into the ground. (Author's collection)

79th Medium Regiment, RA, was not slated to land until D+2, and the final regiment of the group, 191st Field Regiment, RA, not until D+3. Both 19th RCA and its FOOs ought to have been available on 7 June to support the vanguard, but they were not. That regiment was tasked on 7 June to support the North Shore Regiment's attempt to capture the radar complex at Douvres. Instead of having a FOO with every infantry company, the vanguard had only two in total. They attached themselves to the battalion headquarters, in accordance with normal British Commonwealth practice. Petch also had a forward officer, bombardment (FOB) from the Royal Navy, who could call down fire from two cruisers assigned to the Canadian beaches: the nine 6-inch guns of HMS *Belfast* and eight 5.25-inch guns of HMS *Diadem,* which were the equivalent of two medium regiments of artillery. So the 9th Brigade vanguard was well provided with on-call artillery support, especially for an advance against light opposition.

In the event, opposition proved anything but light. Obersharführer Bernhard Meitzel, the ordnance officer of 12th SS, testified at Kurt Meyer's war crimes trial in 1945 that remnants of the 736th Grenadier Regiment of 716th Division were reorganized into a battalion that fought in the Canadian sector on 7 June.[13] It held Buron, Authie, and Franqueville as part of a reinforced Kampfgruppe Rauch, which was ordered to a defensive line between Cairon and Cambes on 7 June.[14] Apart from the one company of infantry sent into the radar station at Douvres after its retreat from the sea on the evening of D-Day, Rauch retained most of his infantry, all his armored vehicles, and the 3rd Battery (four 10cm Czech guns on SPs) of Artillery Regiment 1716 (which had formed gun position "Waldersee"). It would seem, based on anecdotal evidence, that the bulk of Rauch's own 192 GR garrisoned Galmanche, Cambes, and possibly St. Contest. Meitzel testified that the 88mm Pak 43/41 guns of 21st Panzer remained in the area as well (eventually under command of 12th SS) "throughout the first days of the invasion."[15] Other detachments from 21st Panzer were also there. These included eighteen SPs of the 2nd Battalion of Panzer Artillery Regiment 155 (on converted French tank chassis, "Schutzwagen Lorraine-Schleppers") and the self-propelled artillery of 21st Panzer's "Sturmgeschutz-Abteilung 200." The latter was garrisoned southeast of Caen, at Cagny, prior to D-Day and was composed of seventeen Pak 40 7.5cm self-propelled antitank guns and twenty-four 105mm self-propelled howitzers. Both the self-propelled antitank guns, the Fahrgestell-Panzerkampwagen 38H9(f) with their long barrels protruding from a boxy armored superstructure and the Geschutzwagen 38H(f) howitzer with its stubby 105mm in a similar mounting, were built on French tank chassis. To tired men in their first battle, both looked a whole lot like tanks. The 2nd (half-track mounted) Company

Soldiers of 21st Panzer Division, summer 1944, wearing their shelter halves as camouflage smocks. (Bundesarchive Bild 101 I-722-0405-05)

of Panzer Pioneer Battalion 220 was also in front of 9th Brigade's van-guard, and Meitzel claimed in 1945 that Luftwaffe troops continued to man their antiaircraft positions near Franqueville.[16]

These German units did not constitute a well-organized and coor-dinated force, but they were well equipped and well trained, and the vanguard had to fight them nonetheless. The guns of the heavy anti-tank battalion in particular proved exceptionally deadly, while artil-lery from 21st Panzer and 716th Division played an important role throughout the battle. Moreover, although historians have been rather dismissive of 21st Panzer Division's efforts to throw back the landings and of its ersatz self-propelled gun, its equipment was good and the di-vision was very well trained. Certainly, Lieutenant Colonel Rauch was an experienced combat veteran from the eastern front and is known to have trained his regiment, the 192nd, to a high level. This included intense exercises on the ground over which they now fought.[17]

The secondary road that Kampfgruppe Rauch guarded and that was followed by 9th Brigade on 7 June ran south across a wide, rolling plain, dotted with agricultural villages composed of stone houses and barns, surrounded by high stone walls and orchards. The ground south of Villons-les-Buissons is basically flat, rising gently to a kidney-shaped flat ridge that runs east-west north of Buron and St. Contest. The ground is open to the east toward Cambes and Galmanche, and to the west slopes down toward the Mue River. About a kilometer south of Villons-les-Buissons, the village of les Buissons lies a few hundred me-ters to the right (west) of the main road. The junction of the lane to the hamlet and the road south to Buron was later dubbed "Hell's Corner." South of les Buissons the ground rises gently for about a kilometer to-ward a broad, flat crest, before dipping down into Buron. Just south of the crest the Germans had dug an antitank ditch for a hundred yards on either side of the road. The rooftops of modern homes now crowd the skyline south of les Buissons, but in 1944 both St. Contest and Buron lay out of sight—except for the church steeples—from Hell's Corner. To the west, in front of the hamlet of les Buissons itself, the crest flattens and dips away into low ground around Vieux Cairon and the Mue River.

In 1944 there was little in Buron north of the intersection with the major east-west road through the village (now the D22) except a long stone wall across the back of the houses that line that main road. Then, as now, the D22 was a significant road connecting to Caen through St. Contest, Buron, and Vieux Cairon to Creully in the west. Buron had largely developed along its axis. South of its main intersection with the D22, the D220 passes through the Buron village square and takes two tight ninety-degree turns between buildings and chateau walls, before it emerges once again heading south across flat open fields.

South of Buron the road runs straight, across a plain (with a barely perceptible rise about halfway) for a kilometer to Authie. This whole area is overlooked from St. Contest, and even more so from the towers of the Abbey d'Ardennes a kilometer and a half to the east, but it is completely out of sight from les Buissons. About halfway between Buron and Authie another road from Caen (now route D126) intersects the D220, passing west to Gruchy and the Mue River valley. Gruchy lies about a kilometer west of this intersection, which meant that it was just a little too far away for the vanguard to dominate it. In 1944 Authie straggled along either side of route D220 for about 500 meters in the middle of an essentially flat plain. West of Authie lies four or five square kilometers of open farmland that slopes gently down to the Mue River. This was designated gun area "Dorothy," where 14th Field Artillery Group would deploy once Carpiquet was secured.

South of Authie the fields and the road dip a little, with Franqueville on a slight rise to the right, before reaching the lip of the plain just above the Caen-Bayeux highway and rail line. From that point Carpiquet and its airport are overlooked. The edge of the plain is not reflected well on the Ordnance Survey maps in use in 1944 and is seldom mentioned by historians. But it is clearly visible on the ground, and it runs right around behind the Abbey d'Ardennes and across the northern perimeter of Caen. In sum, the vanguard of 9th Brigade advanced down a gently rolling but open plain that dipped down at Buron into dead ground over which the Germans had excellent observation and fields of fire. Moreover, the plain around Buron, Authie, St. Contest, and Gruchy where the battle was primarily fought dropped abruptly farther south into superb dead ground, where the Germans could deploy their artillery and hide their counterattack force.[18]

The first intimation that elements of 21st Panzer lay along the road to Carpiquet was the explosion of a Sherbrooke reconnaissance tank

The northern end of Authie just before the war. The road in the foreground runs to Cussy and the abbey, and that to the right to Buron. The square of the village is near the intersection. Gun area "Dorothy" designated for 14th Field Group, RCA, lies between the village and the wooded Mue River on the horizon. (Courtesy M. Villalba, Authie)

north of les Buissons. When that happened, the leading elements of the vanguard responded with trained professionalism. While the infantry of the Novas' C Company dismounted and continued on foot, the mortar platoon dropped twelve 3-inch bombs on the gun position, and the carrier platoon did a flanking move. Captain Errol Stewart Gray, commanding the carriers, led the attack, which took the 88mm gun in a shower of grenades. While that was going on, another 88mm gun hit Sergeant Allsop's Stuart tank. The second gun was taken out by 37mm and machine gun fire from the Recce Troop, which killed the crew.[19] The advance into les Buissons then continued, where three half-tracks—one equipped with a rocket projector, which indicates the presence of 3rd Company, Panzer Pioneer Battalion 220—were destroyed in the village.[20] Meanwhile, in the fields nearby, B Squadron accounted for another rocket-equipped half-track, a motorcycle and sidecar, and a truck filled with 155mm artillery ammunition.[21] With orders to "leave

The Authie-Buron battlefield, photographed a month later, just prior to its recapture. Buron is at the top, Authie is at bottom center, Gruchy is in the upper left corner, and Cussy and the Abbey d'Ardennes are just out of the frame at the bottom right. The rectangular hedged area between Authie and Buron where Major Rhodenizer's two platoons of A Company held out is clearly visible, as is the small wooded area at the southern end of Authie where Captain Fraser and two platoons of C Company, plus supporting arms, fought. The heavily bombed square area in the bottom right is an antiaircraft position associated with Carpiquet airfield. (LCMSDS)

the heavy mopping up to others,"[22] the hamlet of les Buissons was reported secure by 0900 hours. However, when the Stormont, Dundas, and Glengarry Highlanders entered les Buissons at about 1000 hours, they had to clear it again.[23]

To the west of les Buissons, toward the Mue River valley, A Company of the Novas under Major L. M. Rhodenizer ran into more grenadiers from 21st Panzer holding a small wood with machine guns and a self-propelled gun. They were quickly overcome. As Rhodenizer walked through the newly prepared position, a German emerged from the thicket to surrender and guided him to several wounded. As they were taken charge of, several more enemy infantry were rooted out or surrendered. It was at this point that Rhodenizer realized that clearing a position of Germans was tougher than he expected: he was not the only Canadian to learn that lesson on 7 June. By the time A Company was clear of the small copse and back in the open, the leading elements of the vanguard were already well ahead of them.[24]

After clearing les Buissons—or so they thought—Major Learment and C Company remounted their carriers and, led by Shermans of No. 2 Troop, C Squadron, set off for Buron. The reconnaissance troop's Stuart tanks entered Buron at about 1000 hours and then sent word for the vanguard to come forward. The Sherbrookes' tanks moved first. According to Sergeant T. C. Reid, a troop sergeant in C Squadron, his tanks destroyed another 88mm gun and two "hornets"—a euphemism for other tanks, but probably SPs of Sturmgeschutz Abteilung 200—as they entered the village. With the armored and heavy guns cleared, the tanks then waited for the infantry to follow.[25]

The Novas arrived to find Buron "alive with snipers and machine guns and it took some time to get a foothold in the place."[26] Don Learment later recalled that the enemy, at this stage both 716th and 21st Panzer Division troops, "were showing a growing tendency to fight to the last man rather than choosing to either surrender or run."[27] Nonetheless, many prisoners were taken, a second self-propelled gun was destroyed in the village, and another 88mm gun was taken out. The latter was claimed by the carrier platoon led by Captain Gray, his second 88 of the morning. For his "great personal courage on a number of occasions by going forward on foot under fire in order to maintain progress," and for leading the charge to take out two 88mm guns,

The Sherman-killer on the Authie-Buron battlefield: a Pak 43/41 88mm, France, winter 1944. (Bundesarchive Bild 101 I-297-1722-34)

Virtually no photos exist of the advance of the vanguard of 9th Canadian Brigade on 7 June, but a glimpse of what it looked like can be gleaned from photos of Exercise Pedal II—the final rehearsal for that advance—in April 1944. Bren carriers of the NNSH on the move during Exercise Pedal II. (LAC e011108373)

Gray was awarded the Military Cross. The self-propelled gun was probably accounted for by Lieutenant J. H. Langley and his platoon, who were sent to sweep the eastern end of Buron. They surprised the German crew and knocked out the gun with a shower of grenades and small arms fire. It all went so well, Will Bird wrote, that it encouraged Langely and his men to be more aggressive, "killing or capturing every German they could find." In the midst of it all, an air battle developed over Buron, when a dozen Luftwaffe fighters were intercepted by Spit-fires. One British fighter crash-landed close enough for Lieutenant Jack Veness to rescue the pilot from the battlefield.[28]

Buron was declared "secure"—the first time—at 1200 hours, just as the Novas' commanding officer, Lieutenant Colonel Charles Petch, arrived with the headquarters company. They had been delayed by the need to fight through les Buissons again. This included a very personal skirmish between Petch and his intelligence officer, Lieutenant Cunningham, and a group of the enemy—four of whom were killed by Cunningham using a Bren gun snatched from Petch's driver.[29]

While the spearpoint cleared Buron, things were not going so well for B Company and the Sherbrookes' B Squadron on the left. They advanced across a wide-open plain between route D220 and the road through Cambes, Galmanche, and St. Contest which lay in the 3rd British Division's zone. As they moved east of les Buissons, this wing of the Canadian advance drew heavy fire from Galmanche and St. Contest. This was a portent. Both villages were heavily garrisoned by men of the 21st Panzer, and they knew their business. The Novas' B Company infantry were quickly driven off the Sherbrookes' tanks by shell, mortar, and machine gun fire, which stopped shortly after the Novas dismounted. Following a pause, and some speculative fire directed at the Germans, the Novas remounted the tanks, and they all began moving again. That drew another hail of fire, driving the infantry to ground again, inflicting casualties, and scattering one of the platoons. B Company then made its way into the east end of Buron on foot.

Goaded by the fire from Galmanche, Major G. S. Mahon, commander of the Sherbrookes' B Squadron, decided to push the Germans off. One of his troop leaders, Lieutenant L. N. Davies, commented in his after-action report that they "opened fire on various enemy targets, these were tanks, half-tracks, 88s, men, cycles and plenty of movement." C Squadron, moving along the D220, tried to organize a "squadron shoot" in support, lining up its tanks and firing like artillery as B Squadron moved to engage targets with direct fire. But accurate German shell fire broke up C Squadron and forced it to move, leaving Mahon and his tanks to advance on their own. Within minutes, three Shermans of B Squadron, including Mahon's, were knocked out. At least one of these hits was believed to come from an 88mm antitank gun. It is possible they all did, although 21st Panzer also possessed lethal 7.5cm Pak 40 guns on its Geschutzenwagens. By the time B Squadron disengaged, it had lost two more tanks, and command of the remaining ten passed to Captain Merritt Bateman.[30] The presence of such German forces to the east appears to have done little to unsettle the vanguard, but they meant that Brigadier Cunningham had to take

Infantry of the North Nova Scotia Highlanders clamber onto a Canadian
Ram Mk II of the Sherbrooke Fusiliers during Exercise Pedal II. (LAC
e011084139)

care to secure his left flank as he moved: the British were nowhere to
be seen.

It seems that the only German whom the Sherbrookes drove off the
battlefield with certainty around noon on 7 June was the commanding
officer of 25th PGR of 12th SS Hitler Youth Panzer Division, Standartenführer Kurt Meyer. Twelfth SS was freed to move from its lodgments east of Caen by 0500 hours on the morning of 6 June, but its
initial orders to concentrate at Lisieux and then Evrecy delayed its arrival west of Caen. The first units of the vaunted Hitler Youth division
did not arrive around the Abbey d'Ardennes until the early hours of 7
June. The first to do so were the three over-strength battalions of 25th
PGR and their supporting artillery. By 0900 hours German time (0800
British) on 7 June, half of the infantry of 12th SS and a third of its
artillery were therefore in place on the left flank of 9th Brigade's vanguard. Meyer made his headquarters in the Abbey d'Ardennes, a huge

walled compound, where the view from towers of the abbey church commanded the whole battlefield. Meyer's Kampfgruppe was completed around 1000 hours, when fifty Mk IV tanks of 2nd Battalion, 12th SS PR, rolled in.

Meyer's artillery support was 3rd Battalion of SS Artillery Regiment 12, the heavy battalion of his division's artillery. In fact, 12th SS Panzer had more and larger field artillery guns than would normally support a British Commonwealth division, and in keeping with German practice each of the division's rifle battalions had an integral four-gun 75mm artillery battery. The 3rd Battalion, SS Artillery Regiment 12, was equipped with sixteen towed guns in all, twelve of them 150mm (medium artillery by Allied standards) and the other four 100mm. The two heavy companies of 150mm guns deployed in the dead ground south of the abbey around the village of St. Germain-la-Blanche-Herbe, and the four 100mm guns settled in near Venoix south of the Odon River.[31] The twelve 75mm guns of 25th PGR worked closely with their units.

The presence of these elements of 12th SS added enormous power to what was already a strong German force in front of the vanguard of 9th Brigade. Kampfgruppe Rauch was supported by twenty-four 105mm self-propelled artillery pieces of the 2nd Battalion, Panzer Artillery Regiment 155, and four 100mm guns of Artillery Regiment 1716. Where the guns of 21st and 716th Divisions were deployed is uncertain, although anecdotal evidence from Canadians suggests that some were in the Mue River valley.

What is clear is that by late morning on 7 June, the 12th SS Artilleriekommandeur (Arko) in the tower of the Abbey d'Ardennes controlled more than fifty field artillery pieces within range of the Canadian vanguard. His location was superb. From the abbey tower it was (and still is) possible to see from the high ground south of Caen right around to Juno Beach and the sea. German oversight of the battlefield was also greatly enhanced by observers in the radar station at Douvres, who remained in contact with Caen through buried telephone cable. Continued possession of the radar station allowed the Germans to see the whole rear of the Canadian positions east of the Mue.

Meyer arrived to find the front held by Kampfgruppe Rauch, with its headquarters in the hamlet of Cussy, just north of the abbey. When the officers of 21st Panzer could not provide him with a clear picture

The commanding view from the top of the church of the Abbey d'Ardennes: forward observation officers of 12th SS artillery in the south tower on 7 June. This view looks southward toward Carpiquet airfield, which is just beyond the tree line. (LCMSDS)

of what lay to his front, Meyer did his own reconnaissance toward Buron. As he approached, he was fired on by tanks of the Sherbrookes. These were likely Stuart tanks of the reconnaissance squadron, which reported an action with enemy vehicles south of St. Contest around noon.[32] Meyer beat a hasty retreat to the abbey and climbed one of the towers to get a better view of things. He arrived just in time to see the Canadian vanguard move on Authie.[33]

About the time Meyer was being driven off the battlefield, Lieutenant Colonel Petch was being petitioned by B Company officers on his left flank to put down artillery fire on St. Contest, and by A Company on his right to hit Gruchy.[34] The Canadian official history says nothing about this initial request by the vanguard for supporting fire, although it does observe that 14th RCA had begun to move forward from its positions at Beny "at noon," and later, when the battle shifted to Authie, Stacey wrote that the guns were "out of range from their old position."[35] Moreover, according to Stacey, the new position assigned to 14th RCA at La Mare, just north of Anguerney, was under mortar, machine gun, and antitank gunfire from the radar station at Douvres.[36] Copp asserts, based on the 14th RCA's war diary, that this harassing fire from Douvres meant that "for two crucial hours they were unable to meet requests for fire support."[37]

But St. Contest was not out of range of 105mm guns from positions at Beny, and the lapse in fire support lasted until the evening. The maximum range of the 105mm as fitted to the M7 (which slightly reduced the gun's ability to elevate) was 11,400 yards. The distance from the gun position at Beny, essentially where the Canadian war cemetery now stands, to St. Contest is 11,000 yards and to Gruchy 10,000 yards. These are not optimum ranges for field artillery: trajectories will be flat, and the impact area will be more of an ellipse than a tight circle. But the original gun position at Beny—for both 14th and 19th Field Regiments—was not out of range when Petch first called for fire support. Nor, contrary to what the Canadian official history asserts, was the harassing fire from the Douvres radar station a serious impediment to the operation of the battery deployed at La Mare by noon. David Struther, the gun position officer of C Troop at La Mare on that day, recalled that fire from the Douvres radar station "didn't bother us." Wes Alkenbrack, the commander of gun D4 (fourth gun of D Troop), later confirmed this, saying they were "not endangered on the 7th. . . . Some mortar fire. . . . Sporadic."[38] In any event, the guns were supposed to move forward in bounds with at least one battery on call for immediate fire. As it turned out, the vanguard was not without fire support for two hours: the failure lasted all day.

At noon in the smoldering village of Buron, Petch's FOO informed him that the guns were "unavailable"—whatever that meant. Things might well have gone better had both regiments of 14th Field Group, RCA, been available to support the vanguard, as the operational order specified. But 19th RCA's FOOs remained committed to supporting the North Shore Regiment's futile attempts to capture the radar station. That massive ten-acre site was composed of thirty steel-reinforced concrete positions, some as big as anything along the Atlantic wall, while the main bunker complex extended five stories deep into the ground. The station was ringed by wire, trenches, an antitank ditch, minefields, machine positions, antitank guns, and a flak battery. Padre Miles Hickey, of the NSR, remembered that firing 105mm shells at the Douvres defenses was "like blowing soap bubbles against Gibraltar."[39] The North Shore never even tried to take the radar station on 7 June. In fact, no one did.[40]

With his supporting artillery "unavailable," Petch turned to his naval FOB, to put naval fire support down on St. Contest and Gruchy. In theory the FOB was in contact with HMS *Belfast* and HMS *Diadem*, whose guns firing at a high rate would have shattered German positions on the vanguard's flanks. Unfortunately, radio contact with the cruisers also failed and was never established that day. It was said that the FOB was reduced to tears of frustration over the failure of his radio link. So, even Petch's fallback fire support failed him. All that he could arrange at noon to suppress enemy fire from St. Contest were the puny 37mm guns of the Sherbrookes' three remaining Stuart reconnaissance tanks and the 3-inch gun of one M10 tank destroyer: it's not clear the Germans noticed.[41]

Otherwise, things were going reasonably well for the vanguard. By midday three of the Novas four infantry companies were concentrated in and around Buron, well supported by the Sherbrookes' tanks: C held the center and east of the village overlooking St. Contest, A was deployed on the western outskirts overlooking Gruchy, and B was in the center of Buron preparing to move south. Despite this strong presence in the village, Petch now ordered D Company in to Buron to clear it again—a job that produced more prisoners but still failed to get all the Germans.[42] From this point on, Buron, squeezed between the Germans in St. Contest and Gruchy, was a bottleneck for further advance and under constant shell and mortar fire.[43] Sergeant T. C. Reid of the Sherbrookes described it as "the heaviest mortar fire I could ever have imagined."[44]

In retrospect the vanguard ought to have stopped at this point to secure its flanks before moving on. St. Contest was a particular thorn in 9th Brigade's side and would remain so for the rest of the day. Had things gone according to plan, it should have been captured by 2nd Battalion of the King's Own Scottish Borders by noon. But at that point of the day they were fighting their way southward, toward the little hamlet of le Bois du Mesnil, four kilometers to the north. Petch had no way of knowing when the British would capture St. Contest, that his artillery support would remain off-line for the next seven hours, or that half of 12th SS Panzer Division was already deployed in front of his force. We have no record of the vanguard's casualties up to this point, but they appear to have been very light.

Moreover, although it had taken more than four hours to move from Villons-les-Buissons to Buron—a drive that today takes a matter of minutes—the vanguard had fought well. Drills for flanking movements on enemy positions, for infantry coordination with the tanks, and for house clearing all worked superbly. Indeed, the whole day indicates that the men of the vanguard were exceptionally well trained, very professional, and very motivated troops. With the Glens now tucked in behind them at les Buissons, there was no good reason to stop the Novas at Buron. Besides, the vanguard's alternative objective—the eighty-meter contour south of Buron—was just ahead.

The push toward Authie began with a probe by three Bren carriers, which returned after taking small arms and machine gun fire from the orchard north of the village. Once it was clear that Authie was defended, Petch ordered B Company, supported by tanks from the Sherbrookes' B Squadron, to make the first move. B Company began by deploying in the large orchard on the southwest corner of Buron to provide fire support, while the tanks advanced to the crossroads with the D126 halfway to Authie. From there the tanks destroyed the machine gun positions on the northern outskirts of the village.[45] Then, supported by fire from B Company and the tanks at the crossroads, two carrier-mounted platoons of the Novas' C Company rolled toward Authie and dismounted on the outskirts. Captain Gray, once again out in front with the carriers, called out to the platoon commander, "Start clearing up. I'll call up some tanks and support you on the left flank." Gray ordered one section of carriers to flank Authie to the left and meet the infantry as they emerged at the south end. He sent the other carrier section by the same route to probe as far as Franqueville. When the third carrier section with the rest of C Company arrived (it had missed the movement order in Buron), the infantry dismounted and deployed on the road north of Authie, and their carriers too were sent south toward Franqueville. All the carriers were quickly driven back by mortar fire and soon reassembled north of Authie.[46]

Meanwhile, two platoons of the Novas' C Company worked their way through Authie: Lieutenant Herb Langley's on the west side of the road and Lieutenant Jack Veness's on the east. The enemy, apparently from 716th Division, elected flight rather than fight, but that did not save all of them. Captain Gray's call for help from the Sherbrookes brought B Squadron out of its positions at the crossroads between Buron and Authie, and into position on the east side of the village. There, in Will Bird's words, they shot down "groups of the enemy in all directions."[47] Lieutenant Davies of B Squadron confirmed Bird's estimation, noting in his after-action summary that they had "lots of fun as we kept going."[48] C Squadron, too, supported the attack on Authie. As Sergeant Reid described it in his after-action report, they just "kept knocking off fleeing infantry who kept popping up in front and instead of surrendering, just either shot it out or ran." When Reid's fire drove the enemy from the first house in Authie, they "got smacked down" by the tanks nearby. "We shoved on again," Reid wrote, "and it was a breeze, nothing but infantry until we were fired on by A/T guns to our right."[49]

As Authie was cleared by the infantry, the Sherbrookes' A Squadron commanded by Major E. W. L. Arnold was sent freewheeling to the west, between Authie and the valley of the Mue. The squadron looped one troop through Gruchy, which drew fire, and then pushed past Authie, through the little Hameau de St. Louet, and to the west side of Franqueville. According to the Sherbrookes' regimental history, the tanks of A Squadron reached a point overlooking the hangers at Carpiquet airfield, from which they could "bring fire to bear on them."[50]

Meanwhile, at roughly 1330 hours, Langley's and Vaness's platoons reached the southern end of Authie and stopped for lunch.[51] Shortly afterward, as the Sherbrookes' Shermans probed toward Franqueville, enemy tanks were seen 800 yards east of Authie by B Squadron and south of Authie by A Squadron, followed a few minutes later by tanks to the west of Franqueville, which engaged Major Arnold.[52] It was about this time that the whole area around Authie erupted under intense enemy artillery fire. The easy part of the day was now over for the vanguard of 9th Brigade.

5

Death in the Afternoon

The 12th SS Attacks, 7 June

Then the haze lifted. Bombing on the right
Down the old sap: machine guns on the left;
And stumbling figures looming out in front.
"O Christ, they're coming at us!" Bullets spat,
And he remembered his rifle . . . rapid fire . . .
And started blazing wildly . . .
        Siegfried Sassoon, *Counter-attack*

WHEN THE VANGUARD of 9th Canadian Infantry Brigade reached Authie, they expected to see some evidence of the British on their left or
7th Canadian Brigade on their right.[1] Neither was in sight. Instead
of being elbow to elbow with the Canadians, 9th British Brigade was
split between supporting the advance along the Orne and guarding the
western flank of Sword Beach. In fact all of 3rd British Division were
bracing for the next wave of panzers. As Ken Ford observed, the attack
by 21st Panzer late in the afternoon of D-Day caused "some lack of
nerve in the British camp," and "the rapid advance on Caen had been
abandoned for one of consolidation." That became 9th British Brigade's task for the next twenty-four hours. When the British advance
on Caen resumed at 0845 hours on 7 June, it consisted of a single battalion: all that Major General Rennie would risk. That battalion soon
became entangled with 21st Panzer in a prolonged and ultimately futile
battle in Lebisey wood. Only as the situation stabilized on D+1 did 9th
British Brigade begin probing its way west, toward the Canadians. By
noon they were still miles away.

Meanwhile (as discussed in detail in chapter 6), 7th Canadian Brigade moved onto its final D-Day objectives along the Caen-Bayeux
highway west of the Mue River at Putot and Bretteville around noon

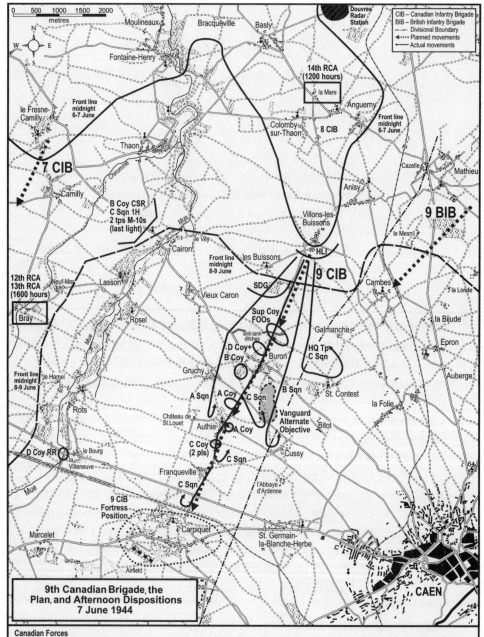

9th Canadian Brigade, the Plan, and Afternoon Dispositions 7 June 1944

0 500 1000 1500 2000
metres

CIB – Canadian Infantry Brigade
BIB – British Infantry Brigade
- - - - Divisional Boundary
▸▸▸▸ Planned movements
——— Actual movements

Douvres Radar Station

Moulineaux
Bracqueville
Basly

14th RCA (1200 hours)
la Mare

Fontaine-Henry

8 CIB

le Fresne-Camilly

Front line midnight 6-7 June

Colomby-sur-Thaon

Anguerny

Front line midnight 6-7 June

Thaon

Cazelle

Mathieu

7 CIB

Camilly

Chromme

Mue

B Coy CSR
C Sqn 1H
2 tps M-10s
(last light)

le Vey

Cairon

Front line midnight 8-9 June

les Buissons

Villons-les-Buissons

HLI

le Mesnil

9 BIB

12th RCA
13th RCA
(1600 hours)

Neuf-Mer

Lasson

Vieux Caron

SDG

9 CIB

Cambes

la Londe

Bray

Mue

Rosel

Sup Coy
FOOs

la Bijude

Galmanche

Epron

anti-tank ditches

D Coy+
B Coy

Buron

HQ Tp
C Sqn

Auberge.

Front line midnight 8-9 June

le Hamel

Gruchy

B Sqn

St. Contest

la Folie

Rots

A Sqn

A Coy

C Sqn

Vanguard Alternate Objective

Bitot

Mue

D Coy RR

le Bourg

la
Villeneuve

Authie

A Coy

C Coy
(2 pls)

C Sqn

Cussy

Franqueville

C Sqn

l'Abbaye d'Ardenne

64

Château de St.Louet

Marcelet

9 CIB
Fortress
Position

Carpiquet

St. Germain-la-Blanche-Herbe

CAEN

Airfield

Canadian Forces

A, B, C & D Coy – Companies of the North Nova Scotia Highlanders; **A, B & C Sqn** – Squadrons of the Sherbrooke Fusiliers Regiment; **1H** – First Hussars; **12th, 13th & 14th RCA** – Field Regiments, Royal Canadian Artillery; **CSR** – Canadian Scottish Regiment; **HLI** – Highland Light Infantry of Canada; **RR** – Regina Rifle Regiment; **SDG** – Stormont, Dundas and Glengarry Highlanders; **FOO** – Forward Observation Officer on D+1 without interference from the enemy. It also was out of sight and out of immediate contact with the vanguard of 9th Canadian Brigade on the other side of the wooded river valley. This was not what Allied planners had intended for D+1, but until 3rd Canadian Division reached its final D-Day objectives, the operational order for 6 June held firm. It was now up to 9th Brigade to reach its objective and establish a fortress position at Carpiquet. It might have done so had it not advanced into a hornet's nest of enemies.

As the leading elements of the Novas and Sherbrookes stopped for lunch in Authie around 1330 hours, everything was "going well." Significant, although unrecorded, casualties had been inflicted on the enemy, and a number of 88mm guns, half-tracks, and SPs were captured or destroyed. No one in 9th Brigade, certainly not Petch, knew that Authie and Buron were nearly surrounded by a much larger force of German infantry, guns, half-tracks, and tanks from both from 21st Panzer and 12th SS Panzer Division. While it certainly was Kampfgruppe Rauch's task to stop the Canadians, the 12th SS Division was there to attack. As COSSAC planners had foreseen in September 1943, both panzer divisions had been ordered to drive the "Little Fish into the sea" on D+1. What transpired in the afternoon of 7 June was an encounter battle between the advancing Canadians and the Germans they were supposed to stop. Kurt Meyer would soon discover that those Little Fish were more than his soldiers could handle.

It was clear that COSSAC planners had read their maps—and their enemy—well. Late on the afternoon of D-Day, 1st SS Panzer Corps ordered a major attack by three panzer divisions north and west of Caen to destroy the Anglo-Canadian beachhead. The 21st Panzer Division, already heavily engaged with 3rd British Division north of Caen and with 6th British Airborne Division east of the Orne River, and with the Canadians west of Caen, was to consolidate north of Caen and attack toward the sea down the east side of the Caen-Luc-sur-mer railway—across ground already littered with the wrecks of Mk IVs and half-tracks from its previous day's ill-fated attack. On their left, 12th SS Panzer Division (Hitler Youth), coming into line west of Caen, was to attack toward the sea down either side of the Mue River. Panzer Lehr, hustling west from its laagers around Chartres, was to join in to the west of the Mue as it arrived. The attack was scheduled for 1600 hours on 7 June, with instructions to "drive the enemy . . . into the sea and destroy him."[2]

The two panzer divisions slated to attack astride the Mue River were the most powerful German divisions in the west. Twelfth SS was composed of youthful fanatics of the Hitler Youth, seventeen to nineteen years old, led by veterans from 1st SS Panzer Division, Leibstandarte Adolf Hitler. Its actual strength on 6 June was probably only 17,000 all ranks, much less than its authorized 22,000, but 12th SS was exceptionally well equipped. British historian Max Hastings has called it "the most formidable of all German units now on their way to Normandy"[3]—all true, except that it was already there. Its tank regiment (12th SS Panzer) contained ninety-eight Mk IVs and sixty-six of the new Mark V "Panthers," considered by many the best tank of the war. All told, the division employed some 500 tanks and armored fighting vehicles.[4] The infantry units of 12th SS were over strength. Instead of the normal rifle company establishment of roughly 140 all ranks, the regular companies of the 25th and 26th PGRs numbered 190 officers and men, while the motorized company of the PGR boasted 225 all ranks. On 7 June each of those companies was further reinforced by platoons from the regimental Pioneer Companies, bringing the average infantry company strength to more than 210, and 250 for the motorized company.[5]

The exceptional size of the 12th SS infantry companies has gone completely unnoticed by historians. In fact, the Canadian official history states emphatically that the vanguard of 9th Brigade was stopped by a force roughly its own size. This is simply not true, even if only the confrontation between the vanguard and 12th SS is measured. Only in the number of tanks deployed on 7 June were the two forces equal. In every other aspect the Germans enjoyed an overwhelming advantage, and the reinforced infantry companies of 12th SS were an important feature of the early beachhead battles fought by the Canadians. Fortunately for the Novas, who did not have to fight their way across the beach, they were largely up to strength on 7 June, with 119 all ranks per company. As will be discussed in the next chapter, the battalions of 7th Canadian Infantry Brigade, which fought ashore and then fought the 26th PGR for three days, were not so fortunate. So the Canadian claims of "swarms" of Hitler Youth attacking, rather derided by historians as hyperbole from inexperienced troops, were not wrong: the Hitler Youth did come forward in inexplicable numbers.

The 12th SS's other units, including engineer and reconnaissance battalions, were also larger and more powerfully equipped than normal SS or Wehrmacht units. Its field artillery included sixty guns, exceptional by German standards. On 6 June only the division's jagdpanzer battalion was not fully equipped, and its battery of six 280mm *nebelwerfers* (11-inch rockets with a 180-pound warhead) had not yet appeared. In all other respects, 12th SS was an elite division even among elites, right down to its new camouflage-pattern uniforms.[6]

Panzer Lehr was equally formidable and was considered among the best in the German army. As its name indicates, it was formed from training units. Panzer Regiment 103 contained some 237 tanks, including eighty-nine Panthers, ninety-nine Mk IVs, and thirty-one Jagdpanzer IVs (the regiment's eight Tigers did not get to Normandy). All of Panzer Lehr's infantry battalions were equipped with half-tracks, 658 of which were operational on D-Day. Only its artillery, powerful enough, could be rated as ordinary. On 6 June Panzer Lehr was in the midst of a move to the eastern front, with its Panther battalion already on trains heading east. The rest of the division was available for operations in Normandy and by 7 June was on the move to the Canadian front.

The third panzer division committed to the 1st Panzer Corps attack on 7 June was, of course, 21st Panzer. Until 9 June its composition and equipment remained enigmatic to the Allies. Intelligence summaries from late May suggested that it was "specially" equipped, that it too probably operated Panthers and almost certainly Tigers. As we now know, it was equipped with about 100 Mk IVs, but its "special" equipment was a clever blend of German, Czech, and Russian guns mounted on former French tank chassis. Nonetheless, the division packed an enormous punch. Apart from the self-propelled artillery, the most lethal combination of captured equipment was the long-barreled 75mm Pak 40 mounted on a Hotchkiss chassis, the Lorraine Schlepper. Its 6.8kg shell traveled at 792 meters per second, and no Sherman armor could stop it at even two kilometers.[7] Covered in camouflage, the Lorraine Schlepper looked a lot like a tank—maybe even a Tiger, which the Canadians reported and which historians again dismiss as the "Tiger phobia" of experienced troops.[8] It seems that the Canadians were briefed to expect Tigers, and the first Panthers they saw were often misidentified as Tigers. But if the Tiger was not present around Authie and Buron on D+1, its gun was: the Pak 43/41 88mm of 21st Panzer's Heavy Anti-Tank 220. Given the prelanding intelligence estimates, the number of long-barreled "tanks" roaming the battlefield, and the destruction of Shermans at exceptional ranges, it was reasonable for Anglo-Canadian troops to believe on 7 June that they were fighting Tigers.

First Panzer Corps ordered its great attack toward the sea on 7 June to commence at 1600 hours (German time). It was the first of three major attempts to launch a decisive counterattack against the Allies down either side of the Mue River over the next three days. And like subsequent attempts it was doomed from the start. Twenty-First Panzer was too deeply committed to stopping the British to extract itself, and 12th SS was too slow to arrive. Meyer later claimed this was because of Allied air attacks and lack of fuel. The first is almost certainly correct, although 12th SS's losses on the approach march were minimal. Among the most important vehicles destroyed were fuel trucks. But 21st Panzer had plenty of fuel available, and all 12th SS had to do was ask for some: it did not. As a result, 26th PGR and the division's Panther battalion were delayed and did not enter the battle until 8 June. Meyer would later claim that this lack of fuel was the ultimate reason his troops failed to reach the sea on 7 June, a claim Major General Feuchtinger of 21st Panzer dismissed as a cover for the fact that Meyer's Kampfgruppe was shot to pieces by the Canadians.[9] The most important reason for the delay in assembling 12th SS west of Caen was the initial decision taken to concentrate it at Lisieux, for possible deployment north—to the Pas de Calais or the Scheldt—rather than Evrecy south of Caen. Operation Fortitude can take the credit for that.

For its part, Panzer Lehr struggled with delays imposed by air strikes and distance, too. As we will see in chapter 8, it was not fully assembled west of the Mue until 8 June. So by the time Kurt Meyer climbed the north tower of the church in the Abbey d'Ardennes around noon on 7 June, the corps-level panzer assault was already just a dream. The diary of Seventh German Army and Gordon Harrison was right: there was no corps-level German counterattack on 7 June; it would have to wait for another day.[10] But there was much hard fighting.

Meyer claimed that what he saw from the tower of the abbey church—the Canadian vanguard stretched out nose to tail on the road between Buron and Authie—was simply too good to pass up. So he preempted his orders for the corps attack and decided instead to launch an immediate attack on the Canadians. This view of events is entirely a postwar creation. What Meyer may have witnessed was a tactical pause, as the vanguard prepared for the final dash to Carpiquet. The vanguard was not strung out on the highway, motoring along like some movement exercise; it was fighting its way through Kampfgruppe Rauch.

It was probably at this point that the sixteen guns of the 2nd Battalion, SS Artillery Regiment 12, deployed behind the abbey around the village of St. Germain-la-Blanche-Herbe and near Venoix, joined the barrage falling on the 9th Brigade vanguard. While the Canadians were being softened up, Meyer climbed down from the abbey tower and made the rounds of his battalions, passing new orders. First Battalion, 25th PGR, with only five tanks but reinforced by 16th Pioneer Company, was waiting to the east of the abbey. It was pointed at Le Cambes, where the leading elements of 9th British Brigade were pressing south. Meyer's 2nd Battalion was just north of the abbey in the hamlet of Bitot with about twenty Mk IV tanks. His 3rd Battalion, with about twenty tanks, was echeloned to the left rear as a flank guard. It was deployed in the dead ground south of Franqueville.[11]

Third Battalion, 25th PGR, was commanded by a particularly murderous and incompetent Nazi, Lieutenant Colonel Karl-Heinz Milius. The diminutive Milius (at five feet seven inches, a full inch too short to join the Hitler Youth as a recruit) had joined the Nazi Party before 1933 and for two years commanded a platoon of guards at Dachau concentration camp. His most recent combat experience was in France in 1940, where he won distinction for bravery. He spent the next three years training recruits until joining 12th SS in October 1943. Aloof, overconfident, and obstinate, Milius was considered by his peers to be an ineffective commanding officer, unable to bond with or control his boy-soldiers. "These flaws," Howard Margolian writes, "coupled with the inevitable brutalizing effects of the two years he had served as the commander of concentration camp guards, did not bode well for Milius's ability to control either his junior officers or his teenaged troops once they had experienced the first shock of combat."[12] The good news for the soldiers of 3rd Canadian Division in all this was that Milius's incompetence as a battlefield commander was not unique in 12th SS. The bad news was that his murderous tendencies, and those of his troops in 3rd Battalion, were not either.

The attack on the Canadian vanguard is usually portrayed as Meyer being opportunistic, taking advantage of Canadian carelessness to strike an enemy strung out along the road. Russell Hart calls it an ambush, in which the Canadians were quickly overrun. Hart can be excused his view because Charles Stacey, the Canadian official historian, implies as much, giving this phase of the vanguard battle about six lines. But Meyer's hand was forced. His counterattack toward the sea was not slated to move for several hours yet, and now Milius's battalion—assigned to screen the left flank—and its supporting armor were about to be revealed by the vanguard's advance. What followed was anything but an ambush. It was the commencement of six hours of intense and often brutal fighting.

By early afternoon the Sherbrooke Fusiliers had begun a pincer operation toward Franqueville, with B Squadron moving east of Authie and A Squadron to the west. It was about to close when, according to Captain Errol Gray of the Novas' carrier platoon, "intense shelling and mortaring began to break loose on AUTHIE." Lieutenant Colonel Petch recalled in 1945, during Kurt Meyer's trial for war crimes, that the artillery fire came in from *both* flanks and the front, which means that it came from more than the batteries of 12th SS at St. Germain-la-Blanch-Herbe and Venoix.[13] Whether all guns available to the Germans were firing at this stage we will never know, but more than fifty artillery pieces (roughly equivalent to the normal artillery of a British Commonwealth division) were both within range and under command of "Arko" of 12th SS in the tower of the abbey church. The twelve 75mm infantry guns of the 25th PGR and any number of mortars and rockets (from 21st Panzer) added to the din.

It was clear to everyone in the Canadian vanguard that the dramatic increase in the volume of fire signaled a counterattack. This did not occasion panic but rather careful preparation as Petch moved to consolidate in Buron and especially Authie. In the event, the full-scale German counterattack was preceded by a tank-on-tank battle that lasted for

As close as any Canadian cameraman got to the action on 7 June 1944: tanks of the Sherbrooke Fusiliers in action near Gruchy. (LAC PA-137444)

about two hours.[14] The Sherbrookes' A Squadron dueled with tanks west of Authie, destroying three Mk IVs in the first exchange of fire before the Germans began to hit, too. Meanwhile, B Squadron fought on deadly ground east of Authie. Lieutenant L. N. Davies, with what was left of B Squadron, moved up with six Shermans at about 1400 hours and soon saw seven or eight enemy tanks to his left. He immediately killed three with his 17-pounder, and then "all hell broke loose." With "trace and 75mm gun flashes all over the place," the remainder of B Squadron moved to Davies's left to cover his two troops. They were all

Newsreel cameramen followed 12th SS into battle on 7 June, and stills from their footage provide some of the best photographic coverage of the action. This is Captain Merrit "Bomber" Bateman's tank of B Squadron, Sherbrookes, burning and abandoned, 7 June 1944. (British Pathé)

soon under heavy and accurate fire. "Tanks were hit and burning all around us by then," Davies wrote in his after-action report a few days later. It was "impossible to keep track of who was who, one was hit directly in front of me, one right of me," and 88mm fire "was cutting down trees all over the place." Davies withdrew, driving through a group of enemy soldiers running from Authie in the process. When B Squadron rallied later at les Buissons, it had five tanks left.[15]

C Squadron of the Sherbrookes fared little better. It pushed forward in support of B Squadron and got caught in the same "tank trap" east of Authie: a pair of guns, almost certainly the 88mm deployed near Cussy, which could not be seen.[16] Sydney Radley-Walters, a troop commander in C Squadron, recalled, "Everyone was calling for artillery to help them get out of this mess but did not get any supporting fire from the guns." By the time C Squadron returned to les Buissons, the war diary records that it was down to six tanks: Radley-Walters recalls three.[17]

The infantry of 9th Brigade watched this developing tank-on-tank battle with interest but without undue alarm. David Dickson, a Nova officer seconded to the 9th Brigade staff, recalled many years later that the tanks initially fought at some distance from the infantry positions. And, while that was clearly of interest, at least Dickson and the men around him were rather distracted by a stallion in a nearby field that mounted a series of mares during the tank battle. If anyone was ambushed on 7 June 1944, it was clearly not the Novas' battle group.

What Lieutenant Colonel Petch thought about the stallion's antics we will never know, but we do know he had time during the tank battle to prepare for what was to follow. He ordered C Company of the Novas to dig in at the southern end of Authie, and he consolidated B Company, the carrier platoon, and Lieutenant Graves's platoon of C Company in Buron. Major Learment came back from Authie with the carriers to consult with Petch and then found himself stranded with Graves's platoon in Buron by the heavy shelling. But the intensification of the shelling and the sudden appearance of German tanks did nothing to unsettle the vanguard. In fact, "the picture had its bright side," Captain Errol Gray explained to an army historian in late June.[18] The Sherbrookes were engaged with enemy tanks, as the doctrine prescribed. Meanwhile, a section of Vickers machine guns from the Camerons under Lieutenant Couper went forward into Authie, and flail tanks and pioneers from supporting engineer units—delayed by a traffic jam in Buron—were also on their way.

So, too, was A Company of the Novas. By early afternoon it had swept through Buron, clearing it yet again, and was moving to a position west of the village when the intense bombardment of Authie commenced. Major L. M. Rhodenizer held two of his platoons east of Buron and sent Lieutenant Sutherland's platoon on the backs of a troop of Shermans from C Squadron toward Authie to help. Sutherland's men took up positions east of Authie on the road to Cussy. Shortly afterward, according to Captain Gray, "the entire troop of Shermans which brought them there was knocked out." This is not strictly true. Lieutenant M. J. Fitzpatrick later reported that two of his three tanks were destroyed in sixty seconds by an 88mm gun firing from St. Contest. Now on his own, Fitzpatrick moved his Sherman Firefly—with its powerful 17-pounder gun—to the southern end of Authie and joined C Company. Meanwhile, Major Rhodenizer followed with the rest of A Company on foot to a large, rectangular hedged area halfway between Buron and Authie and dug in.

Petch had to decide whether to reinforce Authie and try to hold it, or to extract C Company. The brigade plan called for the vanguard to press on to Carpiquet only if there was "no serious opposition." Those same orders also specified that "if there was heavy opposition the North Novas were to consolidate on high ground between Buron and Authie as a base for further attacks on the objective."[19] The problem, perhaps now realized by Petch but certainly never noticed by historians, is that there is no high ground between Buron and Authie. The 1944 1/25,000 Ordnance Survey map of the area shows a little kidney-shaped bump inside an 80-meter contour about a grid square to the east of the Buron-Authie road. It does not appear on the 1/50,000 maps, and if it ever existed, it is not discernible today. The ground east of the Buron-Authie road is as flat as a billiard table and dominated completely by the slight rise of St. Contest. So there was no alternate position to hold south of Buron, and the Germans held the high ground to the east.[20]

By early afternoon of 7 June, the open, flat fields between Buron and Authie were being plowed by a steady stream of bullets, shells, and shrapnel. Petch's own alternate position, at the crossroads north of Authie, was a death trap. B Company learned this to its peril when it tried to take up position on the east side of the road across from the hedged area held by A Company. They, and a mortar section under Sergeant Cossons, were driven back by intense and accurate mortar fire. When Petch ordered B Company to try again, Major J. W. Douglas went forward to speak to Major Rhodenizer, who "was digging in and content to remain." Douglas, who had lived something of a charmed life under fire up to that point, was wounded on the return trip, and command of the company passed to Captain A. J. Wilson. Petch ordered Wilson to try again, so he—like Douglas before him—scampered out to check with Rhodenizer to see just where his company might dig in. Wilson could find no good spot on the east side of the road. In the meantime,

Petch decided to send B Company straight into Authie in the battalion's Bren carriers. Through the radio in Lieutenant Fitzpatrick's tank, Petch told Captain F. C. Fraser, and his platoons of C Company dug in at the southern end of the village, to hold on—reinforcements were on their way.[21]

Now more than ever, Petch really needed help from the guns. Naval fire support, which would have served well in a counterbattery role, was still off-line. It was later discovered that interference from a myriad of other radio transmissions, and not German jamming, was primarily responsible for the failure to contact supporting cruisers on 7 June, and that the radio sets carried by FOBs needed relay stations to ensure that their signals reached the ships.[22]

Nor could Petch get help from 14th Field Regiment, RCA. By early afternoon it was clear that the artillery plan for the vanguard's advance had simply fallen apart. Although half of the planned firepower, 19th RCA, was distracted on 7 June to deal with the radar station at Douvres, the support of 14th RCA should have been enough. Moreover, in a real crisis FOOs from 14th RCA could have asked for support from both regiments, and indeed all artillery regiments within range: as the artillery is fond is saying, it is not the gun that is the weapon, it's the shell. The gunners of 3rd Canadian Division had been working with their infantry counterparts for nearly a year on the Overlord project. It all ought to have worked despite the fact that 14th RCA missed the final exercise for the advance of the vanguard in April. What Petch desperately needed by early afternoon were FOOs with good radio links to their guns and to the artillery radio net. According to the Overlord plan, each of the Novas companies should have had a FOO: none did.

What we know with certainty is that by 1400 hours the two FOOs of 14th RCA attached to the vanguard gave up trying to get forward. They were traveling with Petch and the battalion headquarters, according to normal Anglo-Canadian practice. Caught in the traffic muddle of Buron's narrow streets, under a shower of mortar and artillery fire, and unable to contact their guns, the 14th RCA's FOOs "withdrew to get observation to the A/Tk ditch" north of Buron.[23] This effectively removed them from the battle for the next four hours or more, and even from contact with the Novas' headquarters.

The essential problem is that 14th RCA's gunners, who resolutely stuck to their embattled forward position at La Mare, received no orders to fire in support of the vanguard during the crucial afternoon battle with 12th SS. Malcolm Langille, the Novas' intelligence sergeant at the time, recalled in 2003 that he tried repeatedly during the day to raise 14th RCA through various radio networks and failed.[24] He was not alone. The Stormont, Dundas, and Glengarry Highlanders (the Glens), who back-stopped the Novas at les Buissons on 7 June, eventually relied on the brigade radio net to get supporting artillery.[25]

It was widely suspected that superb German radio counterintelligence was to blame. A complete copy of the Canadian operational order had fallen into German hands on D-Day when a Sherbrooke officer was captured.[26] It contained all the radio frequencies allocated to units for the initial phase, including those of the artillery, as well as call signs. German divisions, including 12th SS, had dedicated radio intelligence and jamming units in their order of battle, so the general failure of artillery communications on the 9th Brigade front for much of 7 June may have been the result. Certainly the Sherbrookes were unable to get through on the armored brigade net. Malcolm Langille believed that this is what happened. If he was right, then having a FOO with each company would not have achieved much in any event.

There is a final twist to the artillery failure on the 9th Brigade front on 7 June. By 1600 hours both 12th and 13th RCA were in position on the west side of the Mue River valley at Bray, a mere 5,000 to 6,000 meters from Buron and Authie. One might have expected the CRA, Brigadier Stanley Todd, to grip the 9th Brigade battle and arrange fire from other artillery regiments. His headquarters was ashore by the evening of D-Day. However, he did not. In all likelihood this was because the operational orders were clear that control of artillery in the advance to the final D-Day objectives was in the hands of the artillery group commanders. Only when the brigade fortresses were established on the Caen-Bayeux highway would Todd take control of his guns: on 7 June Todd was still watching from the sidelines.

We will never know what Todd and his headquarters thought of all this. The war diary for Todd's headquarters was discovered in 1945 to be "a complete blank between 6 Jun to 18 Jun."[27] What exists in the files today is nonsense written in July 1945 on the orders of the army historical section to fulfill the requirement for completion of the document. In later years Todd never alluded to any problems with fire support on 7 June. When asked directly by Jean Portugal, during her extensive interviews published in *We Were There*, if there was a "breakdown in communications following the landings," Todd flatly denied it. "I doubt it," he replied. "Confusion is more likely . . . what is known as 'The Fog of War.' . . . Communications are inclined to get mixed up and guys are so busy defending themselves that they don't think of sending back reports, when if they did, they'd get the artillery support they required."[28] Todd was, by all accounts, a superb gunner, one of the best. But his statement to Portugal is simply obfuscation. The fundamental doctrine of the army he served was built around indirect fire support, and never more so than in the beachhead battles after D-Day. On 7 June that system failed completely for at least seven crucial hours on the 9th Brigade front. It was not supposed to be that way.

During the war crimes trial in 1945, Petch explained that he had no worries about the troops forward in Authie in the early afternoon because they "had not been committed."[29] "No one was worrying too much," the Novas' regimental history recorded, at least "none of those dug in at Authie." By the time German shells "began to scream overhead in salvoes," a sign that the infantry attack was imminent, two platoons of C Company under Captain Fraser were secure in an orchard on the southern edge of the village. The two-gun Vickers section of the Cameron Highlanders of Ottawa and the platoon headquarters group under Lieutenant Couper had failed to reach them: Couper and his men were all wounded or killed by shellfire while trying to get forward. Lieutenant Jack Veness recovered one Vickers machine gun and its Bren carrier from a shell hole in Authie and drove it into the orchard.[30] Some machine guns were removed from disabled tanks and added to the infantry positions. Lieutenant Fitzpatrick's Sherman Firefly with its disabled 17-pounder was also there. It was later determined that the gun's failure to fire was caused by too much oil shorting the electrical firing mechanism: one of the perils of going into battle with an unfamiliar weapon.[31] Whether Fitzpatrick got his 17-pounder going again is unclear, but his machine guns added to the firepower of Captain Fraser's desperate little band of men, as did "several" other tanks. Meanwhile, just to Fraser's north, on the road east out of Authie, one

"Chase," a Firefly of C Squadron, Sherbrooke Fusiliers, lies derelict on the battlefield, with another Sherman in the background, 7 June 1944. An earlier clip of Chase from the newsreel footage shows the Gerry cans tied to the glacis of the tank. In the interim someone has made use of the gasoline. (British Pathé)

platoon of A Company was dug in, and two more under Major Rhodenizer held the rectangular hedge north of the village. Historians have long known that they fought without artillery support. But they should have had antitank guns, too; that was also the plan.

The absence of antitank guns with the forward elements of the vanguard had a lot to do with weather. Historians are quick to excuse German failings because of difficulties getting to the battlefield; they might extend the same courtesy to the Allies. Virtually all the heavy antitank guns assigned to the 9th Brigade sector were either still afloat or just crossing the beach on the afternoon of 7 June: the perils of landing in the midst of a gale. What these guns might have accomplished on the Buron-Authie plain on 7 June is unclear, but what they did on the

Vickers heavy machine gun of the Cameron Highlanders of Ottawa, on exercise in England, April 1944. Heavy and bulky, the water-cooled Vickers could fire all day, and it was critical to Anglo-Canadian defensive doctrine. (LAC e006581362)

same ground a month later is suggestive. When 3rd Canadian Division finally captured Buron, Authie, and the abbey from the 12th SS for good on 8 July, eight Achilles 17-pounder SPs of 245th Battery, 62nd Anti-Tank Regiment, RA, were hustled into position along the southern edge of Buron to meet the counterattack. "In the brief engagement that followed," Terry Copp has written, "thirteen German tanks were destroyed in one of the most successful Allied anti-tank engagements of the Normandy campaign."[32] Had they been there on 7 June (more precisely, had their towed counterparts assigned to 9th Brigade been there), more Panzer Mk IVs of 12th SS would have been destroyed, and more tanks of the Sherbrookes would have survived to parry the German infantry assault. In the absence of supporting Canadian artillery fire, however, it is unlikely that the presence of antitank batteries could have preserved the Canadian positions forward of les Buissons, but it would have been a very different battle.

When increased German artillery fire signaled the imminent attack, B Company made one final valiant effort to get forward from Buron. Supported by four tanks, two of the company's platoons, plus some of Lieutenant Graves's men of the missing platoon of C Company and a mortar section reached the hedge at the northern end of Authie. One tank was destroyed by 88mm fire from St. Contest in the process, and the whole group was mortared intensely. Unable to find shelter or a defensible position, the company once again retreated, this time to the comparative safety of the large orchard at the southwestern end of Buron.

By midafternoon Petch finally had reason to be anxious. His battalion was stretched out and pounded by a circle of German mortars and medium and heavy artillery, and was sniped at by tanks and 88mm guns. Most of A and C Companies were in and around Authie; B Company, for the moment, was in the orchard southwest of Buron; Major Learment's small group (largely Lieutenant Graves's platoon of C Company) was dug in just north of Buron to the east of the road; and D Company was dug in north of Buron, halfway back to the antitank ditch. The Novas' support company, the battalion 6-pounder antitank guns, and a section of the Camerons' Vickers guns held the antitank trench itself. By 1400 hours the Glens had cleared les Buissons—again—while the Highland Light Infantry, the brigade's third battalion, held the refused left flank just south of Villons-les-Buissons. Stacey's criticism that the vanguard and the brigade were strung out like a string of pearls is right, although it is not clear what Brigadier Cunningham could have done about it.

Canadian accounts generally agree that the tank duel between the Sherbrookes and the Mk IVs of 12th SS preceded the main counterattack with infantry by as much as two hours. It seems to have been pretty much a draw, at least in tank-on-tank duels, but the 88mm guns of 21st Panzer firing from "offstage" destroyed many Canadian tanks. It is likely that SPs from Kampfgruppe Rauch also participated in the action, especially the long-barreled 75mm Pak 40s. How many of these were destroyed by Canadian Shermans will never be known, since the only German accounting for vehicles lost in the battle comes from 12th SS. Assertions by historians that the Sherbrookes' claims for kills were exaggerated fail to account for the presence of armor from 21st Panzer.

And because the Germans were left in possession of the battlefield, their losses do not include tanks recovered, while recoverable Canadian Shermans fell into enemy hands.

Accounts of the German assault on the vanguard's forward positions invariably claim it commenced with an attack on Captain Fraser's two platoons of C Company and their supporters south of Authie. Maps of the battle typically show the Germans coming into Authie from the southeast. However, in 1945 Petch was clear that the main tank battle was *west* of Authie, between Buron and Gruchy, and that this was where the infantry assault on the vanguard began. The attack, launched by an unknown force that included tanks and infantry mounted in half-tracks, fell on A Company in the field north of Authie and B Company in the orchard at the western end of Buron.[33] This claim is echoed in the Novas' regimental history, and the attack stopped the final attempt by Petch to push B Company into Authie.[34] This was followed by news that C Company and Lieutenant Sutherland's platoon of A Company on the road east of Authie were under attack by tanks and a battalion of infantry from the southeast.

And so at roughly 1530 hours the vanguard was simultaneously attacked from two flanks. According to Petch's testimony at Kurt Meyer's trial, "At this time the remainder of the battalion was attacked from the direction of Gruchy by armour and infantry who dismounted from half tracks."[35] Who this was remains a mystery, but because none of the battalions of 25th PGR were equipped with half-tracks (only 3rd Battalion of 26th PGR was), it was likely elements of 21st Panzer's Pioneer Battalion 220. Their half-tracks had already been encountered at les Buissons, and Meyer later commented on seeing at least one (knocked out) in Rots, in the Mue River valley, two days later.

The attack on Authie was made by Milius's 3rd Battalion, 25th PGR, and some twenty tanks, and seems to have enveloped the village: this is the only attack historians note. It should never have succeeded. The Germans had to cross about 1,200 meters of open ground to reach Authie, and with 14th RCA online they would never had done it. But Captain Fraser and his men had to weather the storm on their own, tucked into a small orchard and surrounded by a hedge at the southeast corner of Authie. Lieutenant Fitzpatrick watched them come from

Off to war, "Frisch und Frolic": Hitler Youth in their distinctive camouflage uniform advance through a grain field, 7 June 1944. (British Pathé)

the turret of his Sherman: "two waves of infantry and then the tanks moving forward slowly and with determination."[36]

The Hitler Youth were met by withering fire from everything the Canadians at the south end of Authie could muster. "First groups of the enemy simply melted away before the murderous hail," the Novas' regimental historian wrote. "Time and again the enemy seemed but yards from the hedge and then they were blown down or hurled back. It seemed incredible that so small a force could keep back such weight and strength, but it was being done."[37] Lieutenant Sutherland's platoon—scarcely thirty men—of A Company on the Authie-Cussy road to the north was "forced back by a tidal wave of the enemy too numerous to halt." It is customary for regimental histories to deal in hyperbole, but in this case descriptions of "a tidal wave of the enemy" and the weight of the German attack are appropriate. Between them Fraser and Sutherland had about a company of infantry (perhaps 120 men), plus a few supporting arms and tanks. The four companies of Milius's battalion numbered 210 men each, totaling 840: the Canadians in Authie were outnumbered about six to one.

Eventually C Company's position withered, and the men were ordered to slip away in small groups to make their escape. Captain F. C. Fraser and Lieutenant Langley's platoon fought to the bitter end as a rear guard, "taking a dreadful toll on the fanatical S.S. troops." Fraser and Langley were both killed.[38] As the rear guard was overwhelmed, the survivors of C Company fled through the village. Some resisted, trying to make a stand in Authie. Others tried to surrender in what quickly became an orgy of unrestrained violence. "Already trigger happy," Howard Margolian wrote, "Milius's men went on a rampage, killing randomly, savagely, manically." Wounded Canadians were bayoneted to death, executed, or—in one case—bludgeoned to death where they lay, while those trying to surrender were shot down. It was all witnessed by other Canadians and by the people of the village.[39]

Once the fighting subsided in Authie, the survivors of Fraser's company were marched northward into the village, where one group of eight POWs sitting under guard near the main square was simply shot. Not satisfied with that, the murderers then dragged two of the bodies onto the main road in hopes that they would be run over. Civilians who tried to remove the corpses were stopped, while the Hitler Youth arranged for an Mk IV tank to run back and forth over them. Other Canadian POWs watched the unfolding scene in horror. Constance Raymond Guilbert, an Authie civilian who witnessed all this, later got permission to remove the bodies from the street: he needed a shovel. As Margolian concluded, the scene in Authie was "apocalyptic," with mutilated Canadian bodies in the street, buildings on fire, and the SS troops "whooping it up like drunken pirates." A white flare rose up over Authie at 1730 hours, which Major Learment in Buron interpreted as a signal that the village was now in German hands.[40]

While the battle for Authie raged, Petch had to deal with the attack on Buron, and the danger that he was being outflanked from the west. B Company was therefore sent back north of Buron. One platoon took up positions behind the village in a series of abandoned German trenches. These had been sited to defend Buron from the north, and they had very poor fields of fire toward the south because of their proximity to the stone walls and buildings of the village. Nonetheless, it was felt that this position prevented the village from being outflanked from the west. Two other platoons of B Company under the acting company commander, Captain A. J. Wilson, withdrew to the antitank ditch where, along with the others there, they "made ready to fight to the finish."[41]

With Authie now in enemy hands and most of B and D Companies north of Buron, the remnant of A Company in the hedged area north of Authie was completely cut off: isolated in the middle of an open, fire-swept field, under full observation by the enemy. Major Rhodenizer had no order to retire. And after his position was sprayed by gun and machine gun fire from six tanks on their way from Gruchy to Buron, his radio could no longer receive.[42] His company eventually ran out of men, ammunition, and will. It took a cordon of tanks and infantry from Milius's 11th Company some time to wear them down. As the wounded accumulated inside Rhodenizer's perimeter and the remaining stocks of ammunition dwindled, SS soldiers infiltrated closer through the grain. When the barrage on the position suddenly ceased, Major Rhodenizer stood up to see what was happening. He was greeted by two Germans who simply said, "Come." Another German shouted "Surrender!" just as a group of SS with machine guns rose from a ditch thirty yards away. Rhodenizer's weary men complied. Just when this happened remains unclear. The Novas' history says it was "near sundown,"[43] but this seems unlikely. Based on testimony at Kurt Meyer's trial in 1945, it probably occurred sometime around 1700 hours, about the time Major Learment recorded the white flare over Authie.

If Rhodenizer thought that surrender meant the end of the killing, he was soon disabused of his genteel notions. As his men were searched, a sudden burst of machine gun fire from the SS murdered two Canadian POWs. This was just the beginning. During the march into Authie, three more Novas were shot at short range by their guards. Once in the village the carnage of the struggle was evident, and if the Novas' postwar testimony is right, the bulk of the dead wore German uniforms. "The dust and smoke had settled," Will Bird wrote of Authie as Rhodenizer's men marched in, "and German bodies were lying in alleys and in the street and in the fields, everywhere, especially by the entrance to the orchard." Bird claimed that the lifting of the smoke of battle had "showed the casualties inflicted by C Company, and this so enraged the Germans that they crowded around and shot several prisoners in cold blood." They also shot French civilians who attempted to tend the wounded. Fortunately, Major Rhodenizer spoke fluent German and calmed the situation—for the moment, at least in Authie.[44]

Once Authie and the A Company position had fallen, elements of the 3rd Battalion of 25th PGR and more Mk IV tanks joined the surge around the western edge of Buron. They drew lethal fire from the remnants of B Company holding the trenches on the western fringes of the village, and finally from Canadian antitank guns firing across the flat plain (in this sector) from positions outside les Buissons. "Four Panzer IVs of my platoon were immediately on fire," Sturmmann Hans Fenn later recalled. As he watched them burn, a round slammed into his tank from a Canadian gun 1,500 to 2,000 meters away, probably from a 17-pounder of the Sherbrooke Fusiliers. The shell ripped off his commander's leg and set the tank on fire. Scorched and burned, Fenn scrambled out the loader's hatch. The whole 1st Platoon of the 6th Company of 12th SS Panzer Regiment had been quickly destroyed.[45]

What tipped the balance in the battle for Buron was the commitment of the 2nd Battalion of 25th PGR—another thousand infantry—and more tanks, SPs, and half-tracks, from Bitot to the east. It was about this time that Canadian POWs in Authie reported seeing "a fresh German battalion marching towards Buron in close formation."[46] Radley-Walters, ordered by the Sherbrookes' commanding officer, Lieutenant Colonel Mel Gordon, to take C Squadron out toward St. Contest to hold the vanguard's flank, had a front-row seat for this phase of the attack. "I had no squadron," he said decades later, "only three of us," but he went anyway and took position on some high ground overlooking St. Contest and the eastern approaches to Buron. "We saw the German infantry advancing on Buron and we fired at them with our machine guns."[47] Then, as the German tanks got closer, Radley-Walters and his two companions fired at them as well. "With the 75mm it was pointless to fire until they were 600 or 700 yards from you," he later recalled. "But the German tanks kept moving and never stopped until we knocked them out." His first action "was straight from the book. The order was, '75! Traverse Right! Steady. . . . ON! 600. Tank! Fire!'" How many they accounted for will

A tank burns in the open ground between Buron (left) and St. Contest (right) around 2000 hours, 7 June 1944. The field around it is filled with tracks and swirls from maneuvering armored vehicles. (LCMSDS 303-4353)

never be known. But it is likely that Radley-Walters's three tank kills were what briefly stopped this advance and in the process decapitated the commander of 2nd Battalion, 25th PGR, Sturmbannführer Hans Scappini.[48]

By this stage the main part of Buron had been abandoned by the Canadians, so the first to feel the weight of the assault by 25th PGR's 2nd Battalion was Major Learment's small group dug in east of route D220 north of the village. These positions also had poor fields of fire, and Learment's men were practically out of ammunition. They were easily overcome. The collapse of Learment's position opened the back door to the rump of B Company on the west side of the road. Lieutenant S. F. Campbell and his men, supported by fire from les Buissons, had checked every German attempt to get around behind Buron from the west. Now they too were forced to surrender, although in the subsequent confusion many escaped.[49] The Novas were now down to D

Company and two platoons of B, dug in at the antitank ditch with the support company and a few others.

Learment and eighteen or twenty of his men were marched into Buron and lined up in the village square, where the Hitler Youth searched them. Most were looking for personal loot. The young fanatics were, in Learment's words, "wildly excited and erratic and nobody seemed to be actually in charge. . . . They were continually yelling and screeching to one another. . . . I actually thought they must have been taking drugs."[50] Personal papers, pay books, and field dressings were simply thrown on the ground. Sulfa drugs and morphine syrettes, along with watches, rings, and other personal items of value were confiscated. So, too, was the Novas' emergency chocolate ration, which was consumed on the spot. All this went on while the village was being shelled. When Private J. Metcalfe, who was standing next to Learment, was found to have something in his pocket—perhaps a grenade, but Canadian eyewitnesses say it was his tin of chocolate—the youth searching him let out "one of those screeches they are noted for" and then shot Metcalfe with his submachine gun. When that burst failed to kill the Canadian, a second burst to his head finished the job.

What followed over the next hours was a murderous rampage that eclipsed what had happened earlier in Authie. There is no point in repeating the details: Howard Margolian lays it all out painstakingly in his book on the 12th SS war crimes. But it is important to emphasize both the "tone" of this battle—which set the standard for future encounters between the Canadians and 12th SS, and may explain why the 21st Panzer Division historians say so little about their role in it—and to explain why the Canadian death toll was so high. In addition to the individuals shot in cold blood, including a medic from the Sherbrookes and the wounded man he was tending, at least three further groups of Canadian POWs (beyond the eight POWs killed initially in Authie) were murdered after Buron fell. When Canadian shelling of the area intensified, six men marching south from Buron in the evening were hustled into a kitchen in Authie, lined up against the wall, and shot in the head. Nine more men died when their column, marching along the road from Authie to Cussy, encountered an SS unit moving up. The officer in charge of the unit angrily berated the Canadians and then began to shoot them with his pistol, at which point his men joined

Canadian POWs march past the newsreel cameraman to an uncertain fate, 7 June 1944. The footage was taken near the Abbey d'Ardennes, whose walls are just visible on the right. (British Pathé)

in the firing. Finally, most of the Canadians who were escorted into Meyer's headquarters at the Abbey d'Ardennes for interrogation on 7 June and the next day, eighteen in all, were summarily executed with a single pistol shot to the head (two more suffered a similar fate several days later).

Perhaps the most reprehensible incident occurred when a Red Cross truck from 12th SS swerved across a wide road and deliberately ran into a group of Canadian POWs: two Novas died. Even the Germans were so appalled by the incident that they publicly announced that Privates R. MacRae and D. Tobin died of wounds, and buried them with full military honors at Bretteville-sur-Odon—in front of German newsreel cameramen.[51]

As the position in Buron crumbled under the weight of two over-strength battalions of Hitler Youth, dozens of 12th SS tanks, and elements of 21st Panzer, the surviving members of the 9th Brigade vanguard retreated. "We watched as one tank would move back," Radley-Walters recalled, "then another two and some infantry." When his squadron commander, Major Walsh, ordered Radley-Walters to retreat as well, he had to pick up Walsh and his crew en route after the major's tank broke down. As Radley-Walters rolled back, he passed a slit trench with a dead German soldier lying on the lip with a commando knife in his back. "In the trench beside him was a sergeant from the North Novas," Radley-Walters recalled, "and as I went by him he smiled and gave me the victory sign."[52]

As the tanks pulled back, support from 14th Field Regiment, RCA, finally arrived in the form of a FOO party led by Major A. W. Duguid, commander of 34th Battery. Doug Hope, an ardent amateur historian who has pursued the story of 14th RCA on 7 June for a decade and a half, interviewed many veterans. Two of these, Glen Clemet and Don Jamieson, were with Major Duguid on 7 June and were sent forward late in the afternoon to support the vanguard. As Hope writes, "They were just coming up and getting ready to begin observation at the anti-tank ditch north of Buron, when the Sherbrookes' tanks were pulling back from Buron to les Buissons. They were sure that this was at the same time as the tanks' withdrawal, because one of them came tearing through a hedge and almost ran over Glen Clemet."[53]

In the event, Major Duguid withdrew his FOO party to les Buissons and began to call down fire. The 14th RCA war diary reports its first targets of the day—"Mike" targets, the whole regiment firing—at 1800 hours. David Struther, the gun position officer for C Troop of 14th RCA on 7 June, told Doug Hope that these were "scale 50": fifty rounds per gun, which put more than a thousand 105mm shells on a single target.[54] Where they fell we may never know, but there is a fair chance that they landed on Germans. Certainly, Canadian POWs trapped in Buron and Authie reported intense artillery fire on the villages by early evening.

By about 1900 hours on 7 June 1944, what remained of the 9th Brigade vanguard stood to around the antitank ditch halfway between Buron and les Buissons ready to meet the enemy. The Prince Edward Islanders who made up most of D Company and stragglers from the other companies held trenches out in front of the ditch, supported by

The timely arrival of Major A. W. Duguid, commander of 34th Battery, 14th RCA (seen here sitting for the cameraman during Exercise Manners II, 20 April 1944), in the late afternoon of 7 June saved the North Nova Scotia Highlanders from virtual annihilation. (DHH)

two mortars and two Vickers machine guns of the Camerons and the antitank platoon of the Novas with two 6-pounder guns.[55] About a dozen surviving Shermans of the Sherbrookes backed them up. Behind them, in and around the hamlet of les Buissons, the Stormont, Dundas, and Glenngarry Highlanders were ready to support the last desperate stand of the vanguard. And Major Duguid and his FOO party were in firm contact with 14th RCA. How much of 3rd Anti-Tank was forward with the Glens is unclear, although the entire regiment (minus the guns lost at sea on D-Day) was now ashore. The twelve towed 17-pounder guns of 247th Battery, 62nd Anti-Tank Regiment, RA, were hustling forward to Villons-les-Buissons as the battle died down. So not all the elements of a proper brigade fortress were in place at les Buissons in the early evening of 7 June, but there were enough.

As the Hitler Youth surged up the gentle slope from Buron, mortar and machine gun fire laced their ranks, while tanks and antitank guns, some from les Buissons, struck at German tanks moving around the western flank. When the Camerons' machine guns ran out of ammunition, they withdrew, and so did a number of Novas. But D Company held on, and finally—after a long day's wait—the first rounds of Canadian artillery landed in front of the vanguard's position at the antitank ditch.[56]

The remnants of the 9th Brigade vanguard wanted to "stand and cheer!" as Canadian artillery "routed the Germans." According to the Novas' history, the tanks of the 12th SS "vanished at first sound of artillery on the scene and the enemy were hounded all the way back to Authie, dying in groups all over the field."[57] With the Hitler Youth clearly in retreat, what remained of the vanguard counterattacked. The twelve remaining tanks of the Sherbrookes joined in and found the Hitler Youth fleeing in wild confusion, "in some instances the enemy being so numerous they were run over by them."[58] Radley-Walters's Sherman joined the attack with Major Walsh, his squadron commander, as his gunner: "We shot up Buron with everything we had." The survivors of the vanguard recaptured Buron and drove the remnants of 12th SS back to Authie, St. Contest, and Bitot.

The recapture of Buron was a signal victory for Petch's exhausted men, but it could not be held. The British 9th Brigade did not start its move in support of its Canadian opposite number until 1400 hours. It got as far as Cambes, from which it was driven by 12th SS's 1st Battalion. The British contented themselves with crushing the SS using artillery and naval gunfire,[59] leaving Cambes, Galmanche, and St. Contest in German hands. That meant that Buron, on a forward slope overlooked by the enemy, was untenable. Contact with 7th Canadian Brigade, across the wooded Mue valley, remained tenuous at best. So what was left of the Novas withdrew from Buron and settled in around "Hell's Corner" at les Buissons for the night, with the Glens to their right in the village and the Highland Light Infantry behind them. Meanwhile, the Hitler Youth, who took some time to discover that Buron had been abandoned, distracted themselves with their petulant shooting spree of Canadian wounded and POWs. Later that evening the whole area of Buron, Authie, the abbey, and St. Contest was smothered by naval gunfire, leaving a lasting impression on the Hitler Youth.

It is clear that the 9th Brigade vanguard was up against forces it could not hope to match on 7 June. Although a proper accounting of the role of 21st Panzer and 716th Divisions in the battle has never been done, their presence was highly significant. The Sherbrookes' claim that all their tank losses (twenty-two unrecovered, six damaged) fell to 88mm guns was not "Tiger phobia."[60] The long-range killing power of the 88mm Pak 43/41 was a factor on the battlefield. So, too, was the artillery power of 21st Panzer, while its troops and armored vehicles, and the remnants of 716th Division helped shape the battle long before 12th SS attacked. In the end, 302 Canadians were killed, wounded, or missing following the battle, roughly the equivalent of the losses inflicted on the 12th SS alone, which are recorded as 300.[61] Of the 110 Canadian dead on the day, 37 were murdered POWs (the 18 Canadian POWs shot at the headquarters of 25th PGR on 7–8 June would be among the missing in the figures for D+1). The people of Authie knew what had happened. After the war they renamed their main street the "Rue des 37 Canadians."

Because no casualty returns have ever been published for 21st Panzer and 716th Divisions for this battle, it seems likely that the final figure of German killed, wounded, and missing is significantly higher than 300. There was good reason for 21st Panzer to distance itself from events on the Canadian front on 7 June. At the war crimes trial of Kurt Meyer convened in December 1945, military lawyers attempted to distinguish between the murderers and the innocent by the uniforms they wore. Canadian survivors were frequently asked by the defense for Meyer if the Germans who shot their comrades wore camouflage smocks (21st Panzer) or camouflage uniforms (12th SS). Many witnesses were not really sure. The only certainty—and therefore the only successful prosecution—was that murders had occurred at Meyer's headquarters at the abbey while he was present.

As a result, most historians, the Canadian official history included, are only dimly aware of the presence of Kampfgruppe Rauch in the battle against the 9th Brigade vanguard, and therefore they accept casualty figures from 12th SS as the measure of the German loss. Nothing the vanguard accomplished prior to 1330 hours is accounted for in the reckoning. B and C Squadrons of the Sherbrookes alone in their after-action reports claim to have killed or wounded more than 100 of the enemy with machine gun fire: casualties inflicted by the other two squadrons were probably comparable.[62] We have no idea what casualties the Novas inflicted on the ersatz battalion of 716th Division or 21st Panzer Kampfgruppe. As for the vehicles destroyed, historians dismiss the Sherbrookes' claims as wildly exaggerated. In the end, 12th SS admitted to losing nine MK IV tanks, leaving the Canadians' claim of "thirty-one Panzers including eleven Tigers," in Buckingham's words, as "another early example of Allied Tigerphobia."[63] But the Canadians never claimed that all thirty-one "Panzers" were from 12th SS, and there clearly was confusion (natural on the day) between SPs and tanks, especially the long-barreled self-propelled 75mm variety. "Hornets" were Hornets. Finally, because the Germans were left in command of the battlefield, the tanks that they recovered do not enter into their accounting.

And while historians have lauded the 12th SS for its "spectacular combat debut,"[64] it was anything but. As the Novas' history observed decades ago about the defeat of A Company, it took the Germans "a large part of an afternoon to overrun a position held by a fifth of their number."[65] Clearly, the vanguard was not "thrown back in confusion," as some historians claim. The situation remained tense and controlled until the vanguard was swarmed by two over-strength battalions of 12th SS and their supporting artillery fire. Once Canadian supporting artillery fire arrived, the remnants of the vanguard drove the Germans off most of the battlefield. In fact, Feuchtinger concluded dismissively that Meyer "had made a short spurt with some fifty tanks, but was driven back" by antitank fire.[66] He was not impressed by the SS. Neither was British historian Michael Reynolds. German command and control of the battle was poor. "It would seem," Reynolds wrote, "that just as there was a failure to coordinate on the Canadian side, Meyer, Witt and Feuchtinger failed to get their act together at this important time."[67] In the end, 12th SS never got close to the sea: indeed, it never got much beyond its initial gains in the first hour or so.

That the 9th Brigade vanguard was driven back on 7 June by a force more than three times its size supported by superior firepower fighting on ground the enemy knew well should not surprise us. The result was not a reflection of incompetence of Allied leadership or tactical ineptness among the troops, an interpretation favored by historians and analysts since 1945. Rather, the Nova battle group fought well on 7 June 1944: the petulant fury of 12th SS in the immediate aftermath of the battle is evidence of that.[68] Maybe, in the end, there was something in Max Hastings's stereotyping of Canadian soldiers. They were tough and they were brawlers—in the words of Dick Raymond, the American serving in the Camerons of Ottawa, they went at it "like hockey players." As Hastings wrote, Raymond had professed himself "scornful of their indiscipline and doubtful of their quality" until he saw the Canadians fight on 7 June. "The strength of that Canadian army," Raymond concluded, "was as close-in fighters."[69] More evidence of that would emerge over the next few days.

Just as important, at the end of 7 June, 9th Canadian Infantry Brigade was secure on the only piece of ground that made sense. Unless and until the British seized St. Contest and, more important, Caen, Carpiquet was untenable, and there was no suitable ground to hold between it and les Buissons. The so-called alternate position for Petch's battle group, the "high ground" between Buron and Authie, was a mapmaker's fiction: it did not exist. More important, the initial panzer assault on the crucial ground west of Caen had been forestalled, and the preemptive German assault on the Canadian advance had been beaten. Meyer and his regiment had gone as far as they could go. Indeed, had the storm in the channel not delayed the completion of the vanguard's antitank artillery, and had Canadian field artillery or the naval fire support been online, Meyer's battle group would have been shattered.

Early the next morning the commander of Second British Army, General Sir Miles Dempsey, came ashore to steady his troops. His first stop was General Crocker's I British Corps headquarters in Courseulles, where Dempsey admonished Crocker to get the artillery and armor of both 3rd British and 3rd Canadian Divisions "organized and under control." He then went on to see Major General Rod Keller at Beny-sur-mer at 0930 hours to make the point even firmer to the Canadians.[70] It is likely that neither Keller nor his CRA, Brigadier Todd, needed reminding. The guns had failed on D+1, a combination of many factors, not least being a rigid adherence to the Overlord operational order (as Dempsey must have known). The Canadians would not make that mistake again.

Having failed to drive the "Little Fish" into the sea, the Germans now faced the task of getting 7th Canadian Brigade to abandon its positions astride the Caen-Bayeux highway on the west side of the Mue River as part of the larger panzer corps plan. They would find that, too, an insurmountable task.

6

According to Plan

The Advance of 7th Brigade, 7 June

Gloucester, 'tis true that we are in great danger;
The greater therefore should our courage be.
William Shakespeare, *Henry V* i.1

WHILE THE VANGUARD of 9th Brigade drew the full fury of the German assault on the beachhead on 7 June, the Canadian advance on the west side of the wooded Mue River valley went off virtually without opposition and pretty much according to plan. Although it was a busy and often fretful day for the men of the "Western Brigade" and their supporting arms, by noon they were on the division covering position astride the Caen-Bayeux highway. In fact, things went so well that in the early afternoon warning orders were given to bounce the crossings over the Odon River and turn 2nd Canadian Armoured Brigade loose on the heights of Point 112 overlooking Caen from the south.

That optimism quickly changed as the day wore on. As the smoke of battle darkened the sky to the east, details of 9th Brigade's bloody encounter with 21st Panzer and 12th SS echoed through division radio nets. Tank crews of the 1st Hussars and Fort Garry Horse of 2nd Canadian Armored Brigade could follow the fortunes of the Sherbrooke Fusiliers on their headsets. By evening, 7th Brigade was under no illusions about what lay ahead. There would be no dash to the Orne and the heights beyond. Instead, Canadians west of the Mue prepared to do what their operational orders required: defend the beachhead against a panzer assault. Fire plans were worked out, signal wire laid, antitank guns positioned, and barbed wire and mines hustled forward as infantry companies dug deep into the soil around the villages of Putot, Bretteville, and Norrey. Over the next three days the Western

Brigade and its supporting arms broke the back of the panzer threat to the D-Day landings.

It was fortunate that 7th Brigade had a full day to prepare for the onslaught. D-Day at Courseulles-sur-mer was bloody, and it did not go as well as historians have assumed. And here, too, the fortunes of battle drew the adjoining British formation, in this case 50th Division, away from the Canadian flank. Moreover, 7th Brigade had to do it all: make the initial assault, fight its way inland, consolidate on the covering position, and then defeat the panzers. No reserve brigade landed behind them to add weight to their advance. According to the plan, the Western Brigade should have completed the first three of these tasks by the end of D-Day. But on the beaches astride the Seulles estuary, as elsewhere along Normandy's Calvados coast on D-Day, the intricate timing of things was thrown off by both the enemy and the sea. By the time 7th Brigade settled down on its D-Day objective late on 7 June, it was a tired and much weakened force. Fortunately, the delay in the arrival of two panzer divisions in precisely the same area allowed 7th Brigade to consolidate its fortress position just in time.

The story of the landings at Courseulles-sur-mer has been told well many times, but some important points bear repeating here because of the influence they had on later events. The 7th Canadian Infantry Brigade landed on a two-battalion front on either side of the Seulles River estuary, supported by DD tanks of 1st Hussars from London, Ontario. The strongpoint here was the heaviest waterline position assaulted by the Allies on D-Day, with a series of massive concrete emplacements on the beach. Both of 7th Brigade's leading battalions, the Royal Winnipeg Rifles from Manitoba attacking the west side of the Seulles River (Mike Red and Mike Green Beaches, technically at Gray-sur-mer) and the Regina Rifles from Saskatchewan landing in front of Courseulles-sur-mer to the east (Nan Green Beach), suffered heavy casualties during the assault.

The Reginas' A Company landed right in front of the Courseulles strongpoint. B Squadron of 1st Hussars ought to have been there first, but the fourteen tanks that made it to the beach drifted farther east. So A Company, with an assault strength of just 119 all ranks, tackled the beach defenses alone, until a few Royal Marine centaurs arrived. It then took them all morning to clear the lower end of Courseulles.

By noon, eighty men of the company lay dead or wounded, and there was still much to be done. The remnants of A Company, reinforced by elements of the Reginas' support company, continued to fight in Courseulles throughout the early afternoon.[1]

Fortunately the Reginas' B and C Companies had an easier landing just east of Courseulles. B Company made the initial assault and arrived to find the tanks of 1st Hussars' B Squadron in the surf, firing away at targets—just as the tactical plan envisaged. One Hussar Sherman fired twenty-five 75mm rounds into a nearby pillbox before it was swamped by the sea. B Company, too, had its section of Courseulles to clear, but its casualties that morning were mercifully light. C Company came in behind B and was soon also in Courseulles fighting from house to house.

The final Regina company to land was D. Its task was to bypass Courseulles completely to the east and take the bridges over the Seulles River three kilometers south near Reviers. By the time D Company's five LCAs approached the beach, the storm surge had covered many of the obstacles, and the company suffered heavy casualties even before getting ashore. One LCA grounded in ten feet of water, and another was impaled on an obstacle. Many of the men who tried to get ashore from these stricken landing craft drowned: few got ashore with more than their battle dress and boots. Meanwhile, Major J. V. Love's LCA suffered the fate feared by all: it struck a mine and blew up, killing most of the thirty-six men in it. Only two men from Love's LCA made it to the beach safely. Major Love was not one of them. The other two LCAs carrying what was left of D Company made it to the beach. All that Lieutenant Hector L. Jones, the senior surviving subaltern, could muster for D Company's task at Reviers was forty-nine men, but they secured the bridges over the Seulles by 1100 hours.[2]

The tank squadron landing in front of Courseulles fared poorly, too: only ten Shermans of B Squadron, 1st Hussars, cleared the beach at Nan Green. They, and a few Centaurs from 2nd RMAS, were soon helping the Reginas clear Courseulles. The village was a poor place for tanks, and the 1st Hussars lost several tank commanders to snipers. When Sergeant Leo Gariepy caught a glimpse of a muzzle flash from a second-story window he grabbed a Sten gun, jumped from his tank, and raced up to the room. Kicking the door open, he found a girl with a rifle in her hands and immediately cut her down with a burst of fire. According to the story, her German boyfriend had been killed that morning by Canadians.[3] Once Courseulles was cleared, the Hussar tanks moved south to their rally point with the Reginas at Reviers. There, after consulting with Major Stew Tubb of the Reginas' C Company, the ten Shermans of B Squadron under Captain John Smuck pushed alone up the open ground toward Camilly-Pierrepont-Fontaine-Henry. They should have waited. A lone 88mm gun, probably from 21st Panzer's heavy antitank battalion (which deployed guns in the area by noon), destroyed six Shermans in quick succession. The 88 was finally destroyed by Sergeant Gariepy, who fired two quick rounds from his 75mm and then charged the gun.[4] Four Shermans, all that remained of B Squadron, returned to Reviers in the late afternoon.[5]

The bulk of 7th Brigade landed on the west bank of the Seulles, on Mike Red and Mike Green Beaches. Here, too, massive concrete positions lay among the dunes just above the wrack line, and here too delays and casualties disrupted landings and the movement inland. B Company of the Royal Winnipeg Rifle (RWR) assaulted the heavily fortified dunes just west of the estuary: three large bunkers, at least twelve machine gun positions, and a network of trenches and wire. The tanks were late, and so the infantry went in cold. Murderous fire hit the LCAs while they were still 200 yards from the beach, and it tore through their ranks as the men sprinted for enemy emplacements. Even with the storm surge shortening the distance between the low-tide mark and the line of dunes, it would have taken the heavily laden Winnipegs several minutes—an eternity under fire—to wade from their LCAs, cross the open sand, and reach the dunes. By the time they did this and cleared the bunkers and machine positions, B Company, with an assault strength of 119 all ranks, was down to Captain P. E. Gower and twenty-six men.[6]

Major L. Fulton's D Company of the Winnipegs was more fortunate. It landed west of B Company, just outside the main belt of the strongpoint at Courseulles and along a stretch of open beach. Fulton's men virtually sprinted through the defenses on Mike Green and by 0900 hours were clear of them, over the flat interval behind the beach and up on the rising ground approaching Banville. Farther west still, C Company of the Canadian Scottish Regiment (CSR), a Victoria, British

Columbia, regiment known to the Canadian army as the "Can Scots," under Major D. G. Crofton, landed with the very specific task of eliminating a single massive bunker right on the waterline (it is now almost in the sea) at Vaux. It commanded much of Mike Beach with a 75mm gun and needed to be captured quickly. The Can Scots' company did that, and then, like D Company of the Winnipegs to its left, it pushed quickly inland to take the hamlet of Ste.-Croix and its château. That is where its real troubles began.

The high ground behind Mike Green was home to 2nd Battalion, 726th PGR, the 441st Ost Battalion, and eighteen field guns—twelve of them in concrete positions around Ver-sur-Mer (a 50th British Division objective). As they moved inland, Major Fulton's and Major Crofton's companies met heavy machine gun fire and were stopped cold by a force of infantry many times their own strength. They needed help to get forward.

That took time to arrive because the tanks could not get off the beach. The 1st Hussars' A Squadron landed on Mike Red and Mike Green, slightly behind the infantry. A couple of tanks foundered during the run-in or were swamped when they dropped their flotation screens: several made it only because the driver locked the throttle and then climbed out of the tank to join the rest of the crew holding the flotation screen in place. One LCT took a direct hit from a mortar round and sank, leaving two DD tanks floating inside the vessel. Nine of the squadron's sixteen tanks survived the assault, only to find themselves trapped on the beach. On Mike Red and Mike Green an arm of the Seulles River meanders behind the line of dunes for nearly a full grid square (1,000 meters). There were no crossing points suitable for tanks, so once A Squadron reached the beach, there was nowhere to go. When C Squadron, composed of all the regiment's Firefly tanks, began landing on Mike Beach at 0820 hours, it too was trapped. The need to cross this water obstacle had been anticipated, so a scissors bridge was loaded into the LCT carrying the regimental headquarters. By 0820 hours that LCT was stranded on a sandbar in deep water well off Mike Red.

The young naval lieutenant in charge of the LCT carrying the Hussars' regimental headquarters and its bridge had made a hash of the landing. He lowered the vessel's ramp too early, overran it, and got it stuck on a sandbar, which nearly swamped the LCT. The young man compounded his error by then declaring that the moment his LCT floated free it would go straight back to England. The Hussars on board had other ideas. They put the naval lieutenant under guard and passed command to his New Zealand sublieutenant, who got the LCT clear and landed both the bridge and the regimental HQ. Soon Hussar tanks were pouring inland to support the infantry stalled in front of Banville.[7]

While the Hussars struggled to get off the beach west of the Seulles, the brigade's reserve infantry battalion landed on Mike Red. The CSR was the spearhead of 7th Brigade's advance to the D-Day objective, and the three companies landing at 0830 hours swarmed ashore carrying bicycles for the dash inland. In short order two companies, A and D, and the battalion headquarters consolidated at La Valette in preparation for the move. The leading elements, two platoons of D Company, duly set off on their bicycles to secure the bridge over the Seulles southwest of Reviers, over which B Company was due to pass. Other platoons set off on bicycles to secure the bridge at Columbiers-sur-Seulles.

The CSR's race to the final objective on the Caen-Bayeux highway was undone by the inability of the Winnipegs and their own C Company to take Ste.-Croix and Banville promptly. The villages lay across open, gently rising fields at the seaward end of the Sommervieu-Bazenville ridge, where it ran down toward Courseulles-sur-mer. The ground in front of the two villages was swept by intense mortar and small arms fire and supported by dug-in heavy guns. By the time the rest of the CSR landed at 0830 hours, C Company had cleared the Château Vaux after a nasty fight and was engaged with the HQ element and three platoons of 2nd Battalion, 726th PGR, near Ste.-Croix. To their east the Winnipegs were stalled in front of Banville, and large numbers of Germans (about two battalions by Major Crofton's estimate) could be seen moving around in and between the villages. Crofton, commander of the CSR's C Company, later remarked, "I realized that this area of the beachhead was in danger of being overrun by the enemy."[8] The Can Scots sent A Company to support Crofton's dwindling force, while he asked his forward observation officer to provide whatever fire support he could. Fortunately, the guns were online and ready to fire.

Getting the guns ashore was crucial to securing the landings, and there could be no advance inland without them. Every company that assaulted the beach on D-Day had its own FOO consisting of a "walk-ing party" of a captain, his "able"—a FOO's assistant—and a signaler carrying an Mk 18 radio set. As a rule, FOOs from 12th RCA ac-companied the Winnipegs, as did 12th RCA's headquarters, while 13th RCA supported the Reginas. The CSR, as the reserve battalion, had FOOs from both regiments. Unit reconnaissance parties of both regi-ments landed with the reserve companies of the Reginas and the Win-nipegs to guide the guns to their designated positions around Banville.

So there were FOOs ashore from the outset, but they were not much use without guns to draw fire from—and not much use if they became casualties. The first guns ashore were the Centaurs of the 2nd Royal Marine Assault Squadron, and the FOOs of both Canadian artillery regiments called on their 95mm guns to help infantry fight through the defenses. The first 105mm M7 SPs of the Canadian field artillery to land were the four guns of B Troop, 12th RCA, on Mike Green west of the Seulles River at 0845 hours; the rest of the regiment followed over the next fifteen minutes. At this time the beach exits were still blocked, and the dunes were clogged with tanks and armored engineer vehicles waiting to move forward across the one bridge available. And so, 12th RCA deployed its twenty-four M7s on the beach, between the high-water mark and the dunes. Their first target was just 1,400 yards away. By the time Major Crofton called for support in front of Ste.-Croix around 1000 hours, 12th RCA had already been firing for an hour.

The decision to deploy 12th RCA along the beach at Mike Green was crucial in unhinging the powerful German positions around Ste.-Croix and Banville, but that deployment compounded delays already experienced in getting other elements ashore and moving inland.[9] The incoming tide and storm surge quickly covered obstacles that engineers were supposed to clear. This made the approach to the beach perilous and contributed to the wrecked landing craft jamming it. The surge also narrowed the beach itself, leaving a thin strand between the surf, which rose as the tide did, and the line of dunes—a line that on Mike Green was filled by twenty-four SPs firing constantly. As a result, the other artillery regiment supporting 7th Brigade, 13th RCA, was unable to land on time. One battery, the 44th, was finally put ashore east of Courseulles at noon to help the Reginas get forward, while the rest of 13th RCA circled offshore in their LCTs. The remaining two batteries of 13th RCA had to wait for 12th Field to clear Mike Beach, and so did not begin to land until 1500 hours. The whole of 13th RCA was not consolidated in gun area "Mary" north of Banville until about 1800 hours.[10] By then all the guns from both regiments were there: none were lost on D-Day. But they were late.

The most serious losses to 12th and 13th RCA on D-Day were in personnel. Lieutenant Colonel R. H. Webb of 12th RCA later recalled that his second in command, Major E. Pickering, as well as a battery commander and two FOOs were wounded.[11] Casualties in 13th RCA were much worse. Five officers landed at Courseulles-sur-mer with the Reginas in the assault wave, but only one remained with the battalion by the end of the day. The 13th RCA's second in command, Major G. F. Rainie, a corporal, and two gunners of the advanced headquarters party landed alongside the Reginas' headquarters: all were killed when they either detonated a mine or were struck by a shell. Major J. D. Young, commanding officer of 22nd Battery (and the unit deployment officer responsible for getting the regiment into action) and his signaler never reached the beach: they were killed when a shell struck their landing craft. Of the four FOOs with the Reginas, three were killed or wounded by sunset. Captain W. M. Dirks drowned when his assault craft struck a mine and sank. His signaler swam ashore, and his able (or assistant) was picked up by the navy and taken back to England. Captain J. Else was wounded crossing the beach, and his able, Gunner J. F. Robinson, was killed. Else carried on, supporting the Reginas' battle through Courseulles before being struck again and evacuated. That left Else's signaler, Gunner J. Holtzman, to carry on, which he did, calling down fire from two Centaurs of "S" troop, 2nd RMAS, on a beachfront blockhouse that was delaying the Reginas. Holtzman earned the Military Medal for his efforts. Later that evening Captain A. F. Wrenshall was wounded and evacuated. The only FOO with the Reginas to make it through D-Day was Captain W. J. G. Steele.

The final officer casualty from 13th RCA on D-Day was Lieutenant J. M. Doohan, the command post and reconnaissance officer for 22nd Battery. Doohan's command post tent was pitched at the bottom of a thirty-foot-deep hole created by a 16-inch shell from the monitor HMS *Roberts*. The position was guarded by sentries, and William McCrie, the battery signaler, recalled being startled just before midnight by a burst from the sentry's Bren gun. This was immediately followed by Lieutenant Jimmy Doohan collapsing through the tent flap, seriously wounded. Apparently Doohan had been tardy with the response to the password for the day, and Gunner Kubay fired a burst at him. Doohan was struck six times, four bullets in the leg, one in the chest—which fortuitously struck his cigarette case—and one that severed a finger on his right hand. He may well have been clutching his helmet at the time, since it was reported to have several holes in it. Doohan's war was over, and he was evacuated. He was much better at remembering his lines later as the iconic engineer "Scotty" in the 1960s TV series *Star Trek*.

In all, seven officers of 13th RCA were killed or wounded on D-Day, and it might well have been worse. Fortunately, Lieutenant Colonel Frederick P. T. Clifford and the regimental headquarters, two other FOO parties, and Major R. K. Mackenzie (78th Battery commander) landed unscathed alongside the CSR on Mike Green at 0830 hours.[12] Gunner Bill Milner of the 13th RCA headquarters defense section was the first off the landing craft. Taller than most, he was given the end of a rope and ordered by a sergeant to take it ashore and tie it off on a beach obstacle so the rest could come ashore safely—especially Clifford, who was scarcely more the five feet tall. Milner plunged off the LCT ramp into water neck deep and did as ordered. When he paused in a safe spot amid the dunes to fieldstrip his wet weapon, a Thompson submachine gun from one of the M7s, he was kicked by the same sergeant and told, "Get to hell off the beach: There's a war on!"

Although 13th RCA's personnel casualties on D-Day were small compared with those of the infantry, Major Mackenzie recalled that they caused significant disruption to the regiment for days.[13] Major Young, for example, had the unique task of bringing the batteries and troops together as a unit amid the chaos. With Young dead, Major J. D. Baird, commander of 44th Battery, assumed that job and the task of second in command.[14] It says a great deal about the nature of the early beachhead battles that 49 of the 167 casualties suffered by 13th RCA during the entire northwest Europe campaign occurred between 6 and 12 June—including all the officer fatalities. With officers dispersed across the front in liaison and FOO roles, it took some time to identify and fill the gaps in command and control of 13th RCA.

Lieutenant J. M. Doohan, command post and reconnaissance officer of 22nd Battery, 13th RCA, one of the many officer casualties suffered by the regiment on D-Day. Doohan was shot by his own sentry after being a little slow with the password, but survived and later had a successful acting career. (LCMSAS)

These losses, and the delay in landing 13th RCA itself, may account in part for why the Reginas did not begin their advance inland until 1700 hours. They were to lead the eastern flank of 7th Brigade's advance to the D-Day objective. The delay is traditionally blamed on the tardy arrival of the shattered A Company, while Lieutenant Colonel Foster Matheson, the Reginas' commanding officer, later commented that he was simply waiting for orders from brigade to move. But the Reginas also needed guns and FOOs to secure their advance. Thirteenth RCA's commanding officer, Lieutenant Colonel Freddie Clifford, and his headquarters party attached themselves to the Reginas' headquarters shortly after landing in the morning and remained there for the forthcoming battles. But until late afternoon Clifford had only one battery, the 44th, ashore, and several of the Reginas' companies were without FOOs. By the afternoon Captain Steele with C Company and Captain Wrenshall with A Company were the only FOOs left, and the rest of 13th RCA was just beginning to land. Lieutenant T. J. O'Brennan was hustled forward to join the Reginas' B Company, and Lieutenant R. J. Macdonald joined what was left of D. So the delay to the advance inland may well have been caused by the tardy arrival of supporting artillery regiments and the need to sort out FOOs.

Congestion and delays on the beach also delayed the arrival of the final, crucial element of the plan to stop the panzers: the antitank regiments. In addition to the 6-pounders of the infantry battalions (six per battalion), the ninety-six guns of the two attached antitank regiments were the real tank killers. Third Anti-Tank Regiment, RCA, was integral to the division. It was equipped with a mix of towed 6-pounder guns and self-propelled M10 "tank destroyers" with a 3-inch gun. The M10s provided mobile firepower, and their 3-inch 50-caliber American gun was lethal to most German tanks at 1,000 yards. Two of 3rd Anti-Tank RCA's 6-pounder batteries were to land with the assault brigades: 52nd Battery with the 8th Brigade and 94th Battery with the 7th Brigade (with 4th Battery in reserve and, it will be recalled, the M10s of 105th Battery assigned to 9th Brigade). These little guns were the real frontline panzer killers. As Stan Medland, commander of 52nd Battery from Weymouth, Nova Scotia, recalled, "The role of the 6-pounder was unique. To be effective, they needed to be moved up quickly into each new area taken by the infantry to prepare for a counter attack."[15]

While the 6-pounder with the new ammunition was lethal at short range, the ultimate panzer killing power of the Anglo-Canadians in Normandy lay in their lethal 17-pounders. Twenty-four of these guns were scattered throughout 2nd Canadian Armoured Brigade in Sherman Mk Vc Firefly tanks, one for each troop. However, the rock upon which any German panzer assault would ultimately break was 62nd Anti-Tank Regiment, RA, with its forty-eight 17-pounder guns. Like 3rd Anti-Tank, RCA, 62nd was organized into four batteries of twelve guns each: two of these (246th and 247th) were towed, while the other two (245th and 248th) were equipped with Achilles, the 17-pounder on an M10 chassis. Two of these batteries, the 246th and 248th, were slated to land with 7th Brigade. All ninety-six of the Canadians' supporting antitank guns arrived off Juno safely and on time, but only a handful landed on D-Day.

The storm surge, breaking seas, and narrow beaches made getting towed antitank guns ashore on D-Day problematic. When the first landing craft trying to put 6-pounders of 3rd Anti-Tank RCA ashore foundered and sank, and it was clear that the surf was running too high to permit any Bren carrier to pull a towed 6-pounder gun from a large landing craft, desperate measures were resorted to. It was decided to try transferring the 6-pounder guns from their LCTs onto Rhino ferries at sea and transship them to the beach that way. This perilous undertaking was done only once, at Courseulles, trying to get 94th Battery ashore.

Rhinos were massive flat steel barges powered by two Johnson outboard engines and, as W. T. Jones later recalled, "crewed by two RN or REs who looked about 40 years old!"[16] The Rhino assigned to bring Jones's H Troop of 6-pounders ashore met them beyond the line of breaking surf, where the ramp of the LCT was lowered onto the ferry's deck. In the heaving sea, four guns towed by steel-tracked Bren carriers skittered onto the sea-drenched deck of the ferry, followed by their crews in steel-shod boots. En route to the beach, one of the Rhino's outboards (built in Canada, Jones noted, with a touch of irony) quit, leaving the ferry slowly turning in circles. A combination of cursing by the gunners "and the REs calling for the wrath of God brought it back to life." The guns drove off as soon as the ferry touched the beach, leaving their crews scrambling after them through the dunes. No one was willing to try this again. As a result, the four guns of H Troop appear to be the only towed equipment of 3rd Anti-Tank RCA to land on D-Day. Apart from the three troops of M10s that got ashore with 9th Brigade in the afternoon, the rest of the regiment—some twenty guns—had to wait for 7 June and calmer seas.

The 62nd Anti-Tank RA fared little better. None of Brigadier Todd's antitank reserve slated to land at Bernieres arrived at all on D-Day. The first to do so, the towed guns of 247th Battery, did not land until the afternoon of 7 June. They reached Villons-les-Buissons just as the initial battle between the vanguard of 9th Brigade and 12th SS was dying down. The 17-pounder M10s of 245th Battery assigned to the eastern side of the Mue River did not get ashore until 9 June. The only guns from 62nd Anti-Tank to land on D-Day came ashore at Courseulles in support of 7th Brigade: two troops of M10s (eight guns in all) from 248th Battery in midafternoon. One troop went forward to support the Reginas, the other to the Winnipegs. Fortunately, the third troop of 248th Battery and all of 246th Battery (towed) were able to land on 7 June: they were then hustled forward to help secure the covering position. As a result, all twenty-four guns of 62nd Anti-Tank assigned to support 7th Brigade on the west side of the Mue were in place only by late in the day on 7 June. It was fortunate, indeed, that the Germans had their own troubles getting into action.

So the march of 7th Brigade inland from Courseulles on D-Day was delayed by the enemy and the sea. The Reginas finally began to move at 1700 hours. The Canadian thrust inland on this front was puny: basically the equivalent of two reinforced companies, four M10s from 62nd RA, the four surviving Shermans of the 1st Hussars B Squadron, and a troop from C Squadron sent to help. Only their artillery, the full regiment of 13th RCA now in position and ready to fire, was as it should be.

Seventh Brigade's strength lay on its right flank, where the Winnipegs and the Can Scots, the equivalent of seven companies, struck south across the northern tip of the Sommervieu-Bazenville ridge. They were supported by the rest of the 1st Hussars, a troop of M10s from 62nd RA, and the guns of 12th RCA (as well as 13th RCA) in gun area "Mary" around Banville. On the right the Winnipegs crossed the high, open plain toward the picturesque medieval château and village of Creully (soon to become 21st Army Group headquarters) on the Seulles River. To their west elements of 50th British Division were advancing through Crepon toward the Caen-Bayeux highway around St.-Leger/Ste.-Croix-Grand-Tonne. When the RWR reached Creully, it stopped and dug in.

Contact between the Winnipegs and the British was made at Creully at 1800 hours, but the two forces were drifting apart. Fiftieth Division had its eyes on Bayeux, while its left wing, 69th Brigade, had shifted its axis from south to southwest along the Sommervieu-Bazenville ridge. The shift in British focus was at least partly in response to the counterattack by Kampfgruppe Meyer of 352nd Division. By British reckoning they had been attacked by some fifty tanks or Stugs. This was a wild overestimation, but well in keeping with the COSSAC and SHAEF appreciations of likely German actions, which had long identified the ridge as a high threat area for panzer counterattacks. Meanwhile, the Winnipegs and the rest of 7th Brigade remained oriented south, toward their covering position around Putot. So as with the Canadian eastern flank, where 3rd British Division was forced away by circumstance and counterattack, the British formation to the Canadians' west was drawn away from them by the need to capture a key city and also by German counterattacks on D-Day. And as was the case with the fate of 9th Canadian Brigade, what happened over the next two days to 7th Brigade was shaped by its tenuous contact with adjacent forces.

In the center of the 7th Brigade front, the CSR pushed across the Seulles on bridges west of Reviers and at Columbiers-sur-seulles (captured by their cycle-borne companies) in the afternoon of D-Day, and onto the high ground around Le Fresne-Camilly. There they bumped into the leading elements of the Reginas. The Reginas had moved forward with two companies up and the remnants of D in reserve, leaving the battered A Company—now down to forty men—and six Centaurs of the Royal Marines to guard the bridges at Reviers. The leading companies ran into resistance near Le Fresne-Camilly, where the 88mm gun had destroyed much of what was left of B Squadron of 1st Hussars earlier in the day. Battalion mortars and fire from the Centaurs pounded the German position, while D Company flanked it to the east. During the action the commander, second in command, and several men of B Company were killed.[17]

By the evening both the CSR and the Reginas were preparing to make the dash to the final objective, "Oak," on the Caen-Bayeux highway, when General Sir Miles Dempsey ordered all his troops of Second British Army to stop for the night.

Brigadier Harry Foster, commander of 7th Brigade, agreed with Dempsey's decision. "The men were bushed. Some hadn't slept in three days," he recalled. "They were stuffed with wake-up pills and just about dead on their feet." He was also warned about the movement of 12th SS into his area and told by division headquarters to expect counterattacks in the morning. "All in all I thought it had been a pretty good day," Foster said after the war. "The outstanding features of the day were, first, the admirable spirit of the men and second, the excellent fire support of the artillery. No request for support went unanswered and many infantry professed to understand for the first time that the gunner's role was something more than to block traffic."[18]

It was also necessary to reconstitute shattered units. All the assaulting battalions had reserves in the D-Day pipeline, already kitted out in the regimental livery. But not all of them got to their units, and not all got ashore. The first group of four officers and sixty-nine men allocated to the North Shore Regiment of 8th Brigade arrived off Courseulles at midnight, a long way from their parent unit at the other end of Juno Beach. When the LCT grounded hard in six feet of water, none of the men were prepared to wait for the tide or the sea to solve their problem, and they were not going back to England. Heavily laden with weapons and equipment, no one expected to swim to shore. But as men from a rural coastal community, they knew a lot about beaches and sandbars, so they walked to the beach. The taller men bobbed off the bottom, gasping for air when they surfaced, until they could stand fully. The shorter men removed the bolts from their Lee Enfields and walked underwater using the inverted rifle as a snorkel. Only three men drowned. It was two days, and brief stints in other units, before they reached the NSR. That same evening five officers and seventy-eight other ranks found their way to the Winnipegs at Creully. All eighty-three went into what was left of B Company. Meanwhile, survivors from the sunken landing craft of the Reginas' D Company drifted into the battalion. They arrived without weapons or equipment, and so were outfitted with captured German weapons. And A Company of the Reginas, which like all assault companies had begun with a strength of 119 all ranks, received about 100 replacements. By morning the Reginas were largely reconstituted.[19]

As night settled in and tired men in countless slit trenches fought off sleep, a few Germans, and mosquitoes, 7th Brigade's senior officers were called to an "Orders Group" at Foster's headquarters in Columbiers-sur-Seulles at 0130 hours on 7 June. The advance, he told his senior officers, would continue at 0600 hours. The Winnipegs on the right would move first, followed an hour later by the Reginas; both would be supported by the 1st Hussars. The CSR would remain dug in on the high ground south of Pierrepont to form a solid base in the event of a counterattack.[20] The guns of 12th and 13th RCA would move forward in stages to cover the advance, making sure they always had batteries ready to fire.

The 7th Brigade advance on 7 June started a little late, the Winnipegs leaving their positions around Creully at 0615 and the Reginas following an hour later. Neither had tank support. The battle log of the brigade noted at 0735 that the 1st Hussars, in nighttime harbor at Pierrepont, were delayed because of lack of fuel.[21] The Canadian official history simply states that the Hussars were not ready to move, and that since the advance encountered no resistance, it did not matter anyway. Perhaps. But 2nd Canadian Armoured Brigade fancied itself an arm of exploitation, destined for a grand sweep onto the slopes of Point 112 south of Caen. Close support of the infantry was a job for the antitank regiments. Fortunately, the two troops of 17-pounder M10s from 248th Battery, 62nd Anti-Tank Regiment, were ready to go. They moved with the infantry battalions and provided mobile antitank support.

When the Hussars finally did get rolling, it appears they had not learned the lesson from B Squadron's ill-fated dash inland the previous afternoon, when a single 88mm gun had destroyed six tanks in short order. On D+1 they advanced in cavalry style again without the infantry and did a sweep south. This time they were lucky. Having reorganized following the losses on D-Day into two squadrons, A and a composite

A fine public relations shot of two Canadian Scottish Regiment captains, Johnson and Gordon, on exercise in England, 28 April 1944, and all geared up for the landings: new helmets, high-top combat boots (which eliminated the need for gaiters), and the invasion vest, which replaced webbing for the assault. (LAC PA e32542)

of B and C, the Hussar tanks drove through Bretteville-l'Orgueilleuse and Norrey-en-Bessin in the late morning and reported no troops—Canadian or German.[22]

The infantry was not far behind, and they were moving quickly. By 0850 hours it was clear that nothing of substance stood in front of the Western Brigade. The CSR were ordered to move, and all battalions were told to "go flat out for their objectives."[23] By 1030 hours the leading elements of the Reginas reported themselves on the northern edge of Bretteville (Oak Alpha), and the Winnipegs did the same for Putot twenty minutes later. Both battalions signaled "Oak Charlie," the forward edge of the brigade-covering position, shortly after 1200 hours. The CSR and the 1st Hussars were in the brigade reserve position at Secqueville-en-Bessin by 1230 hours. With no Germans to their front, the carrier platoon of the CSR was warned at 1310 hours to prepare to bounce the Odon River.

The only serious fighting during the advance of the brigade took place on the east flank, along the valley of the Mue River, where elements of 21st Panzer were already in place. Details of the action remain unclear, but both B and D Companies of the Reginas reported fairly heavy fighting and that they needed fire support from both battalion mortars and Centaurs during the day. Most of the Reginas' casualties on 7 June—one dead and eleven wounded—probably occurred on this part of the front.[24]

The gunners of 12th and 13th RCA covered the advance in a series of bounds, making sure that at least one battery from each was in position to fire at all times while the rest moved forward. Royal Marine Centaurs did the same. Survey parties from both regiments roamed ahead, laying out alternate gun positions. Thirteenth RCA (about which we know more because its records are the most complete for this period) moved forward from Banville to a position halfway between Pierrepont and Fontaine-Henry, to cover the brigade's final advance on its objective. Because there appears to have been no call for fire support, we can only assume that the communications problems that plagued 9th Brigade on this day were not a problem for the forces west of the Mue. The final advance of 13th RCA to gun area "Nora," three grid squares around the hamlet of Bray, began at 1600 hours. Anecdotal evidence suggests that 12th RCA arrived in Nora shortly afterward.

Gun position Nora was a good one: open, close to the front, and secure from direct enemy observation. Barely a mile north of Bretteville-l'Orgueilleuse, Bray is nestled into a little flat reentrant west of the Mue River shaped by one of its tributaries, a small stream called Chiromme brook (scarcely a ditch by North American standards). Bray sits just below the fifty-meter contour line on its east and west sides. To the west is the broad, flat plain that runs north from Bretteville to the sea: the focus of both COSSAC and German planning for counterattacks. Gun area Nora was open to Bretteville across flat fields to the south but sheltered from the Mue River 1,000 meters east by a broad, flat crest of open farmland. The 13th was assigned the grid square around Bray itself and deployed 22nd Battery to the south and 78th Battery to the east, both commanding open ground, and tucked 44th Battery behind

Photos of Canadian—or any Allied—artillery in the Normandy campaign are rare because cameramen were expressly forbidden to photograph guns tactically deployed. This one, from 28 June 1944, shows an M7 Priest (No. 4 gun, E Troop) of 13th RCA, firing into Carpiquet from a gun position near Lasson. (LAC PA-114577).

the village with the regimental headquarters in the middle. The 13th RCA's war diary observed that "the gun posn at BRAY was most satisfactory and defensively ideal with good tk killing ground forward," at least until 12th RCA deployed in the open ground directly in front of 22nd and 78th Batteries. The fortress plan assigned the grid square just north of the village of le Hamel on the edge of the Mue River valley to 12th RCA, but it appears that the regiment preferred to stay close to

Bray. The result, according to 13th RCA, was "a dangerously cramped Gp posn without any advantage of perimeter fire!"[25] In the event, 12th RCA provided that perimeter fire to the south, where German tanks would soon appear.

Had things gone differently on the 9th Brigade front on 7 June, the wooded Mue River valley and the open ground to its east would have been under Canadian control by the time 12th Field Group, RCA, settled in around Bray. More specifically, 14th and 19th RCA would have been nestled into gun area "Dorothy" just two grid squares away behind Authie. But on the afternoon of D+1, only Nora was occupied by Canadian guns, and the position was far from secure. The Mue River, with a good secondary road threading through its wooded valley from Rots to Cairon, was no-man's-land. On the afternoon of D+1 no one in 7th Brigade—least of all the gunners—knew who controlled the Mue River valley.

A mounted patrol from both 12th and 13th RCA set off late in the afternoon to find out. It probed as far as Rots, finding the château occupied by the enemy and recording the positions of a number of 88mm flak batteries just a few kilometers from the gun positions at Bray. The artillery regiments then mounted their own local defense and local observation posts on the crest east of Bray to deal with infiltrations. As it turned out, the gun positions were under constant fire from the time they deployed. Mortars, machine gun fire, snipers, and 88mm air burst were constant dangers—and soon tanks, too. The Centaurs of 2nd Royal Marine Assault Squadron were supposed to be forward of Nora, providing countermortar and counterbattery fire. The war diary of 2nd RMAS records that some Centaurs were deployed on 7 June with the field artillery groups, but most were still fighting in the beach defenses between St. Aubin and Lion-sur-mer. There is no record of their activity along the Canadian front line before 9 June.

The two gun positions, Nora and Dorothy, had been chosen with care. Both lay in the heart of the whole British Second Army sector. From there 105mm and 25-pounder field guns of the Canadian and British regiments attached to 3rd Canadian Division could engage targets as far south as Esquay across the Odon River southwest of Caen, east nearly to the Orne River crossings at Benouville (Pegasus Bridge), and west to within a few kilometers of Bayeux. The 79th Medium Regiment, RA, with its sixteen 4.5-inch guns assigned to Dorothy in the operational order, could range nearly twice as far. During the course of the next few days, the guns positioned at Bray did fire continuously in all directions, on at least one occasion on an arc of 245 degrees.

However, the primary task of 12th Field Group was to help defend the 7th Brigade covering position. The plan for defense of the brigade fortress called for 13th RCA to work closely with the Regina Rifles in Bretteville, while 12th RCA worked with the Royal Winnipeg Rifles holding Putot. The CSR apparently had only one FOO during most of 7 June and asked for more: perhaps their FOOs were supposed to come from 6th RA, which, as will be noted, was late arriving.

Artillery was a key component of the whole plan to defend the covering position. This is well illustrated by the example of 13th RCA. Lieutenant Colonel Clifford, the diminutive, wiry, and tough professional gunner who commanded 13th RCA, and a small group of headquarters personnel settled in with Lieutenant Colonel F. M. Matheson at the Reginas' headquarters, a small château beside the church of St. Germain in the eastern end of Bretteville. FOOs from 13th RCA were deployed with each of Matheson's companies, in accordance with the operational order. The hastily rebuilt A Company in the heart of the village had Captain Wrenshall, the sole 13th RCA FOO to survive D-Day, with them. FOO parties, no longer walking but now armored and mobile in their own Sherman tank, were assigned to companies in forward positions: Captain W. J. G. Steele with C Company in Norrey, Lieutenant T. J. O'Brennan with B Company in the open ground east of Bretteville and Norrey, and Lieutenant R. J. Macdonald with what remained of D Company near la Villeneuve. In these static roles, the Sherman observation post tank was usually established in an overwatch position, while the FOO, his able, and a signaler went forward to a good vantage point with a telephone line, leaving the other signaler in the tank to act as the radio link.

Although the guns, FOOs, and headquarters party were all in basically static positions, their dispersal and the general work of the artillery required many men of the artillery regiments to be in constant motion. Ammunition needed to be brought forward from the beach, which became possible once the B echelon vehicles landed on 7 June. Alternate gun positions had to be surveyed in case they were forced to move (about thirty were surveyed during the first week ashore for 13th RCA alone), land lines to FOOs and various headquarters laid and maintained, reliefs and meals provided for those serving forward, liaison maintained with neighboring formations, and dispatches and personnel moved between headquarters at all levels.

The situation was made even worse for the regiments at Bray because 7th Brigade occupied a narrow and deep salient, with enemy forces on both flanks. As the 13th RCA regimental history observed, "A few wrong turns, while travelling to the forward positions, would quickly take the unfortunate map reader into enemy territory."[26] Harold Merrick, a gunner with 22nd Battery, recalled being frightened of losing his way when detailed to drive two battery officers from Bray forward to the Reginas' headquarters in Bretteville early one morning. He had to navigate the short distance in the dark with one of the officers reading a map with a penlight. They took one wrong turn but got there eventually. The return trip in the dawn light was perhaps even more harrowing, since the scenes of battle littered the road.[27] On at least one occasion, signalmen from 13th RCA were nearly in Carpiquet before being called back. Others were not so fortunate. Late on 7 June, Bombardier C. A. McDonald, signal NCO of Fox Troop, was killed by enemy infantry while returning from the observation post in Putot.

While 9th Brigade fought a fierce battle just a few kilometers away, 7 June was a day of battle preparation for 7th Brigade, and it used it well. For the artillery this meant organizing fire plans in cooperation with the forward battalions and Foster's brigade headquarters (established at Le Haut de Bretteville, just behind the forward lines). The intelligence log of 13th RCA, the only one that seems to survive for this period, records thirty-three defensive fire (DF), emergency close support (SOS), and Mike (regimental) targets prepared on 7 June: we can presume that 12th RCA did the same. Defensive fire tasks, which included enemy forming-up areas, lines of communications, and likely approach routes, were selected by battalion and brigade staffs in consultation with the gunners. Most of these in the 7th Brigade plan fell into two general categories: the western approaches to the brigade fortress in the open ground west and southwest of Putot, and targets south of Norrey, including the most likely enemy concentration and

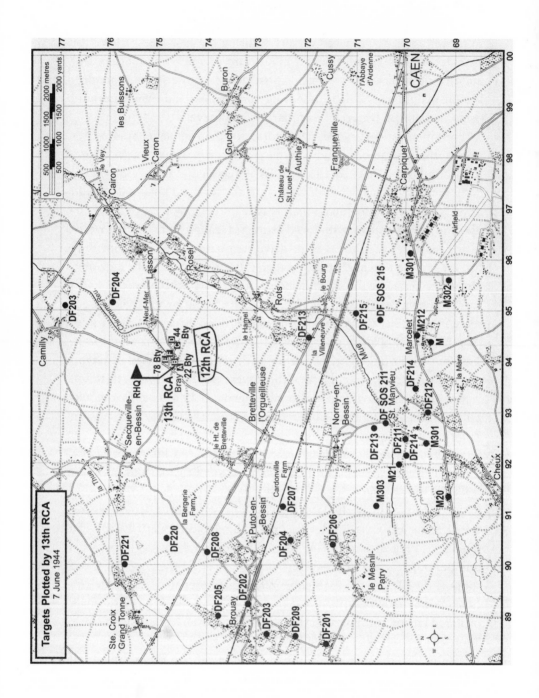

Targets Plotted by 13th RCA
7 June 1944

approach routes around Cheux, St. Manvieu, and Marcelet. SOS fire tasks, to be brought down when the defending infantry were closely engaged, were arranged with the rifle companies to cover forward defense lines and areas immediately to the front that could not be swept by infantry weapons.[28] The great advantage of prepared and numbered DF and SOS tasks was that they could be called in by FOOs quickly and, if necessary, preregistered by the gunners, so fire would be fast and accurate. When the enemy arrived on 7th Brigade's front, the gunners were ready.

So, too, were the antitank regiments. While the brigade moved to its covering position on 7 June, its supporting antitank units landed and hustled forward to join them. The job of laying out the division's antitank gun plan fell to Lieutenant Colonel J. Phin, commanding officer of 3rd Anti-Tank Regiment, RCA. By the afternoon all of the 6-pounders from Phin's 94th Battery, as well as the 17-pounders of 62nd Anti-Tank, RA assigned to the 7th Brigade front, had arrived. Phin deployed G and L Troops, eight guns in all, overlooking the eastern approaches to Bretteville, sent H Troop to Putot to help the Winnipegs, and ordered D Troop of 62nd RA to deploy its four towed 17-pounders in Bretteville. The six-pounders of the infantry battalions covered other approaches within their sectors, especially south of Norrey, between Norrey and Bretteville, and the so-called Brouay railway crossing west of Putot. Phin used the remainder of his 17-pounders, 246th (towed) and 248th (M10) batteries, to cover wider arcs of fire on the open west flank, especially in the plain between Putot and Secqueville.[29] Some of these powerful long-range tank killers deployed with the CSR near Secqueville, and some settled into a copse of trees in the middle of the plain near La Bergerie farm, from where the 17-pounders could dominate the whole area. A number of 6-pounders from 3rd Anti-Tank Regiment, RCA, were deployed in the copse as well. This, as it turned out, was an adaption of the operational order occasioned by the fact that by the end of D+1 no British forces were in sight on the brigade's west flank.

With the artillery and antitank guns in place, the Shermans of 2nd Canadian Armoured Brigade were supposed to settle into their reserve and counterattack assembly area on the high ground north of Bray, in an area designated as "Jill." However, the brigade had suffered heavily

Panzer-killer: 17-pounder of 62nd Anti-Tank Regiment, RA, deploying in
Normandy, early June 1944. (LAC PA-128793)

on D-Day, losing about half its strength, and for the moment no replacement tanks were getting ashore—another consequence of the bad
weather. So the mailed fist that 3rd Canadian Division was supposed
to possess for the beachhead battles no longer existed. Moreover, the
shallowness of the Canadian position east of the Mue and the threat
there from 12th SS on 7 June forced Major General Keller to concentrate what was left of 1st Hussars, Fort Garry Horse, and—after 7
June—the Sherbrooke Fusiliers and the M10s of 3rd Anti-Tank Regiment on the high ground near Anguerney. That meant that 4th British
Armoured Brigade, in the process of landing on 7 June and dedicated
for the renewed assault on Caen, was concentrated behind 7th Canadian Brigade instead.

Preparations went on throughout the day in the 7th Brigade fortress,
as guns and ammunition came forward, and perimeter defenses were
prepared. Contact with the beach was established by the supply ech-

elon of the artillery regiments, and the hard work of delivering shells to the gun positions began. In Bretteville, the gunners attached to the Reginas' headquarters in the château behind Bretteville's church made themselves useful. Gunner Bill Milner, a qualified machine gunner toting a Thompson submachine gun, spent at least some time on 7 June attaching signal wire to antitank mines and laying these out so they could be drawn across the road. Observation posts were established in support of the forward companies, signal wire laid, and communications checked.

Meanwhile, the infantry companies of the brigade dug in. The operational order called for the brigade to defend Bretteville and Putot along the rail line, using it as a barrier: either a raised embankment over which the Germans would have to come, or as a ditch where the line ran through a cutting in the soft Norman soil south of Putot. But the lay of the land necessitated some adjustments. The most important of these was the decision by Major Tubb of C Company of the Reginas to occupy Norrey-en-Bessin, about one kilometer south of Bretteville. It took Tubb only a few minutes to realize that Norrey, ten meters higher than Bretteville and surrounded by open fields, stood like a bastion. To its east and south the approaches to Norrey sloped away gently across open fields like the glacis of a fort, and to the west the ground was open and flat. The northern approaches to Norrey from Bretteville were largely covered from enemy view. From the top stories of Norrey's larger houses, the Reginas could see the Carpiquet airfield and the open ground around Buron-Authie-St. Contest to the east, and around St. Manvieu and Cheux to the south, and west to le Mesnil-Patry. Norrey became the forward keep of the Reginas' main position in Bretteville, with gun area Nora only four grid squares away.

Lieutenant Colonel Foster Matheson, the Reginas' CO, immediately supported Tubb's decision to hold Norrey. It helped that of all the Reginas' companies, C was at full strength: still about 119 men. In consultation with Phin, Matheson pushed two of the battalion's six 6-pounder antitank guns forward in support of Tubb. The detachment for each gun was fifteen men, including a Bren gun section to protect it, so the two guns effectively added a fourth platoon to Tubb's force in Norrey. He placed the guns on the southeastern edge of the village, overlooking the road to St. Mauvieu and the Mue River valley.

In the open ground to the northeast of Norrey, toward the road and rail crossings over the Mue at la Villeneuve and arcing back to Bretteville, Matheson deployed what was left of his B Company. They were down to about seventy all ranks and by 7 June were commanded by one of the company's captains, John C. Treleaven. He took over after the company commander and second in command were both killed, and the senior subaltern and the company sergeant major were wounded. Treleaven's tough initiation into war as a company commander was mirrored a half kilometer farther east, at la Villeneuve, where the Reginas' ill-fated D Company dug in. During the day, D Company received about fifty reinforcements, some of them more stragglers from the destroyed landing craft. Its position at la Villeneuve was precarious, well removed from the main weight of the battalion, and well beyond support from the other companies. It was, at best, a trip wire. But D Company was backed by some of the battalion mortars in a small copse of trees to the rear of B Company northeast of Norrey. A Company, along with battalion headquarters and the commanding officer of 13th RCA, secured Bretteville itself.[30] Apart from a shift of D Company (discussed later), these were the positions from which the Reginas fought the initial beachhead battles.

The Winnipegs were much less fortunate in the ground they had to defend and the circumstances of their open flank. The sixty-meter contour that wrapped around Norrey and allowed it to dominate the fields nearby runs west to le Mesnil-Patry and then north as a spur to Putot. North of Putot the ground gently slopes away into the wide and open fields west of Bretteville along the Caen-Bayeux highway. The village itself is a loose assembly of farm buildings: even today it has a barely discernible center. Farmhouses and their compounds are generally surrounded by high stone walls, into which barns and storage sheds are built. Shade trees and small orchards surround these farmsteads.

On a map, Putot looks like a good, defensible spot: on 7 June 1944 it was not. Just south of Putot the sixty-meter contour is cut through by the Caen-Bayeux railway. On the face of it, the rail cutting (perhaps fifteen or twenty feet at its greatest depth) was an advantage. Certainly, it was an impassable tank obstacle. And as long as Canadian antitank guns in the heart of the brigade fortress covered the rail line east of Putot, where it ran between Bretteville and Norrey on a raised bed,

no tanks could come that way either. But there were no good fields
of fire between the farm compounds of the village and the rail line to
the south. Unless the lip of the rail cutting was held in force, it was no
obstacle at all to infantry. More important still, west of Putot, toward
the village of Brouay, the rail line ran across slightly rolling and lightly
wooded countryside, with no easy observation, no clear fields of fire,
and no real obstacles to vehicle movement. And finally, in the open
fields to the west there was still no sign of the British 50th Division.

The expectation that the British would close up on the Winnipegs'
western flank helps explain Lieutenant Colonel J. M. Meldram's dispositions on 7 June. He deployed three companies along the rail line
and held one in reserve. To the west, where the road from Secqueville-en-Bessin crossed the railway cutting over a small bridge (known
as the Brouay crossing), he placed A Company. Along the rail cutting
immediately south of Putot, C Company was deployed, while D held
the eastern end of the rail line where the cutting ended. B Company,
with nearly 100 reinforcements to absorb, was in reserve in the village
near the battalion headquarters. The Winnipegs' carrier platoon was
pushed forward to the southeast to occupy Cardonville farm as an out-
post in the gap between Putot and Norrey. A troop of M10s probably
from 62nd Anti-Tank, RA, a platoon of Vickers machine guns and
4.2-inch mortars from the Cameron Highlanders, and two FOOs and
a battery commander from 12th RCA also provided support.[31]

Meldram has been criticized for his deployment at Putot: too
stretched and too far forward. "The Winnipegs found themselves in a
classic dilemma," Terry Copp wrote about Meldram's problem. Quite
apart from the problems of the ground, "They were to fight on both
a division and a corps boundary."[32] There was every reason to expect
that the British 69th Brigade either would be in Brouay or would close
up during the day. In fact, at 1316 hours on 7 June, Meldram was ordered by Brigadier Foster to send out a patrol to Brouay in expectation
of contacting 5th Battalion, East Yorkshire Regiment.[33] Major Fred
Hodge, the strapping six-foot-three commander of A Company, sent
Lieutenant Frank Battershill's platoon on the mission. It found nothing and withdrew to the north side of the rail line at Brouay to await
events. Nearly a kilometer to the east, Hodge's other two platoons
guarded the northern, wooded side of the Brouay crossing. Because

An M10 Achilles of 245th Battery, 62nd Anti-Tank Regiment, RA, being inspected by men of the 21st Panzer Division near Caen in late June 1944. The 17-pounder gun of the Achilles was lethal, but its armor—and even its gun mantle, which has also been struck here—was not proof against 88mm rounds. (Bundesarchive 101 I-299-1818-05)

nearly everyone in A Company was killed—in one fashion or another, as we will see—over the next twenty-four hours, details of its deployments and action are scarce.[34]

Holding fast to the Brouay crossing made sense at the time. But A Company's fields of fire were severely restricted, and behind them the open plain running back toward Secqueville (where the Canadian Scottish were held in reserve) and the beach were held only by antitank guns and whatever fire FOOs could bring to bear. The RWR was the extreme right unit of not just 3rd Canadian Division but the entire I British Corps. They were where they were supposed to be on D+1. It was now 50th British Division's job to reach its objectives and close the gap.

Historians generally observe that British 50th Division "made contact" with the Canadians on 7 June and leave it at that. While this was true at Creully, nine kilometers south at Putot the forward areas between the Canadians and 50th Division remained a no-man's-land occupied fleetingly by reconnaissance regiments of both sides. The 7th Brigade war diary records that at 0705 hours, 69th British Brigade reported that it had reached its objective at St. Leger, six kilometers northwest of Putot on the highway to Bayeux, so it was not unreasonable for Brigadier Foster and Lieutenant Colonel Meldram to expect it in Brouay by early afternoon. But British infantry seem not to have gone farther east during the day. The reconnaissance regiment of 12th SS operated between St. Leger and Putot on 7 June. It had taken up a position at the Château d'Audrieux, a grand eighteenth-century palatial home about six kilometers south of St. Leger, with a commanding view to the north. The reconnaissance unit of I British Corps (the Inns of Court Regiment), a reconnaissance troop of the 24th Lancers of the 8th British Armoured Brigade (50th Division), and the reconnaissance regiment of Panzer Lehr also roved through the area on 7 June. The thrust of 50th British Division's effort on 7 June was south, toward Villers-Bocage. The only infantry in the gap between 3rd Canadian and 50th British divisions on this day belonged to Panzer Lehr. Its 1st Battalion, 902nd Panzer Grenadier Lehr Regiment (PGLR), arrived in the small wooded area south of Brouay that evening.

For Brigadier Foster the immediate threat on 7 June lay to the east, where the battle between 9th Brigade and 12th SS raged. By the evening it was clear that 9th Brigade's vanguard had been driven back to les Buissons, and that 7th Brigade's left flank along the Mue River north to Cairon was now in the air, too. By late afternoon the Reginas' new positions were being probed by reconnaissance elements from 12th SS. Around 1800 hours two SS patrols approached D Company's position at la Villeneuve, one down the road from Caen and the other along the country lane from the south (St. Manvieu). The group on the main road was allowed into the village and then, according to 16 Platoon commander Lieutenant Dick Roberts, they were all killed in a hail of small arms fire. Anecdotal evidence suggests that the other group fared little better. At 1900 hours Foster took action to secure his flank and protect his supporting artillery. He ordered two squadrons of 1st Hussars and B Company of the Can Scots to positions along the Mue River north of gun area Nora, on the high ground northwest of Cairon.

Few photos convey the broad horizons of the plains on either side of the Mue River better than this one of the Regiment de la Chaudiere dug in north of Cairon on 8–9 June 1944. (LAC e011084138)

By sunset on 7 June 1944, 7th Brigade was ready for battle. Unlike the misfortune that struck 9th Brigade that day, the Westerners had had time and opportunity to establish their fortress, solidify its direct and indirect fire support, and—with the bulk of its heavy antitank guns to the west and tanks, infantry, and two regiments of M7s along the Mue River valley—secure (to some extent) its exposed flanks. The infantry battalions, weakened by loss and days of intense exertion, were well dug in: some reinforcements had arrived, and companies shattered the day before had been hastily reconstituted. Given the circumstances, it is not clear what more could be done. In the event, it proved to be enough.

The first attack on the 7th Brigade fortress came late in the day, if the RWR regimental history is to be believed, when one tank and a group of Germans appeared south of the Brouay crossing around 2100 hours (still daylight). The RWR claims the Germans were "the vanguard of Kurt Meyer's Hitler Youth Division," but the attack is unrecorded in the 12th SS history. It would not be the last time that mystery forces attacked the Canadians: these may well have been from the Panzer Lehr battalion, which arrived south of Brouay about that time. We will never know: most of the Panzer Lehr battalion died the next day, too. According to the regimental history, the Winnipegs saw them off with light casualties.[35]

As darkness descended on 7 June, few of the men in the 7th Brigade fortress could have harbored any doubts about what lay ahead. While all around them the sights and sounds of battle raged, they had gotten a free pass: a whole day to prepare for the storm to come. As night fell, the forward companies pushed out patrols, probing the enemy to discern what lay in store. At 0140 hours on 8 June, the brigade war diary noted, "Extremely quiet now. . . ." It would not stay that way for very much longer.

7

Putot, 8 June

It was still possible in the morning of 8 June to deal the British a severe blow in the vicinity of Courseulles-sur-mer.

General der Panzertruppen Leo Geyr von Schweppenburg, commander, Panzergruppe West

BY THE EARLY HOURS of Thursday, 8 June, the "schwerpunkt" of the Normandy campaign lay west of Caen. This had been foreseen by COSSAC planners ten months before. Indeed, the earliest staff appreciations by COSSAC of likely German responses to a landing in lower Normandy, completed in the late summer and fall of 1943, identified the plains on either side of the Mue as the likely location for a Panzer counterattack. Even after Montgomery expanded the assault in early 1944, COSSAC planners remained convinced that the Panzers would mass astride the Mue and strike north to the sea. Given a little more time, they conceded at the end of January, the Germans might prefer to secure the Bayeux pivot "by sheer weight" and then attack along the Sommervieu-Bazenville ridge.[1] But Rommel was in command of the forces trying to push the Allies back into the sea, and experience told him there was no time to waste. An immediate counterattack was the plan. This was just what 3rd Canadian Division came powerfully equipped to stop.

It was well it did, for if Field Marshall Erwin Rommel had had his way in May 1944, three panzer divisions would have been astride the Mue River by 6 June. His wishes were thwarted by the confused and conflicting views of Hitler and his senior generals. All he managed to accomplish was the shift of 21st Panzer from Rennes to Caen a few weeks before the invasion. But the ground west of Caen drew armor like bees to honey, and the German command system—conflicting, muddled, indecisive, and confused—managed to concentrate two panzer divisions there by 8 June. Two more were en route to that area by noon that day. Anglo-American historians, busy with explaining the operations of their own countrymen and focused on narrative story-telling, have failed to notice. Therefore, 8 June was the day of decision for both the Germans and the Allies.

Nothing that happened during the course of 7 June altered the German intent to launch a panzer corps counterattack over the ground west of Caen held by 3rd Canadian Division. Intense fighting on both the east and west flanks of the Allied beachhead on that day was focused on securing—or denying—local D-Day objectives. To the east, attempts by 3rd British Division to force its way into Caen across the dreadful glacis in front of Lebisey Wood faltered, as did attempts by 21st Panzer to crush the airborne bridgehead east of the Orne. Paratrooper and glider forces, ill-equipped and outnumbered, but reinforced late on D-Day by the glider-borne 6th Airlanding Brigade and supported by increasingly strong artillery, fought the Germans to a standstill. The only major setback east of the Orne was the loss of Escoville by the Oxfordshire and Buckinghamshire Regiment after intense fighting. To help them, 51st Highland Division, previously tasked with taking Caen from the west along with 4th Armoured Brigade, was sent east to help secure the airborne bridgehead.

To the far west, at the base of the Cotentin Peninsula, 7 June was a day of confused fighting in the broken country of the bocage and the flooded Vire and Merderet River valleys. In behind Utah Beach, infantry from 709th Coast and 91st Luftwaffe Divisions, supported by a company of assault guns from the 7th Armee Sturm Abteilung and about thirty antiquated French light tanks from the Panzer Ersatz Battalion 100 (a training unit), struggled to retake Ste.-Mere-Eglise from American paratroopers. Meanwhile, 4th US Infantry Division moved cautiously inland, securing the massive batteries at Crisbecq and Azeville, as tank units found their way forward to help both line and airborne infantry. The singular American success of the day was the expansion of the Omaha beachhead. This was greatly facilitated by the rapid movement of the British on their left and the capture of Bayeux, and because 84th Corps had no major reinforcements to offer the embattled 352nd Division. All that the 352nd received for help on 7 June was a bicycle-mounted battalion of "Schnell Brigade 30" late in the day. It was used to try to stem the breakout of 1st US Division between the Aure and the Drome Rivers. The toughest fight of the day in the Omaha beachhead was the unsuccessful struggle to relieve the Rangers trapped and under heavy attack on the promontory of Pointe du Hoc.

In the center of the Allied assault, 7 June went superbly for XXX British Corps. Bayeux was captured by 50th Division in a virtual coup de main, which helped unhinge the defenses in front of Omaha.[2] The capture of Bayeux was a major accomplishment and an underestimated triumph. Without Bayeux the Germans could not use the Sommervieu-Bazenville ridge for a major panzer counterattack. That left the corridor astride the Mue as the only viable option for a decisive attack on the landings. By 8 June 50th Division was shifting forces south and east, down the axis of the Caen-Bayeux highway in a tentative attempt to link up with the Canadians somewhere near Brouay, and due south to get forces through Tilley-sur-seulles and astride the Caen-Vire highway at Villers-Bocage.

While the Germans struggled to contain, and if possible destroy, the Allied assault in lower Normandy on 7 June, they remained uncertain about whether the landings were the real thing or just a diversion. The only certainty for the moment was that the Anglo-Canadian landings around Caen posed a serious threat to Paris if they ever broke out. As the Allied Inter-Service Information Series Report on France study on Normandy reported in May 1943, the "Campagne" area around Caen "affords an approach from the west towards the Seine valley and from the Seine estuary south-east towards Paris." Only the heavily wooded chalk plateau between the Dives and the Risle Rivers, an area hard to secure against infiltration, stood between the Caen and the Paris basin.[3] So the orders for 1st SS Panzer Corps for 8 June were roughly similar to those issued twenty-four hours earlier: crush the Anglo-Canadian landings with a panzer thrust to the sea.

Perhaps the only important change in German intent on 8 June was that the general objective had shifted west. The plan for Sepp Dietrich's three panzer divisions of 1st SS Panzer Corps on 7 June had been to concentrate east of the Mue and target the sea at Lyon-sur-mer. On 8 June the weight of the attack shifted west, to either side of the Mue, and the target became the coast between St. Aubin and Courseulles, and to secure the line of the Seulles River inland to Creully. This would, of course, require the complete destruction of 3rd Canadian Division and 2nd Canadian Armoured Brigade, and the I British Corps reserve assembling behind them around Amblie. Although Dietrich may not have known this, it would also force all the headquarters of Allied higher formations in the eastern sector of the assault to decamp. By then I British Corps had its headquarters in Courseulles, Second British was just across the Seulles River at Banville, and Monty's advanced headquarters for 21st Army Group was at Creully.[4]

The plan on 8 June reduced 21st Panzer's attack north of Caen to a supporting role, while two panzer divisions astride the Mue River struck the heavy blows. Twelfth SS would lead on the east side of the river, with Panzer Lehr echeloned behind 12th SS's left on the west bank of the Mue, to exploit the Canadian's open flank and secure Courseulles. Armored reconnaissance units would secure 1st SS Panzer Corps' left flank from intervention by XXX British Corps.[5]

It is clear that the Germans believed that recapturing the shoreline between Courseulles and St. Aubin was critical to throwing the Allies back into the sea. The pre-Overlord debate among senior German commanders had focused on two scenarios for defeating the landings: stop them on the beaches or in the coastal battle zone very quickly, or draw the Allies inland and inflict a blitzkrieg-style defeat that would then produce another Dunkerque. Rommel understood that the window for achieving the first scenario was very tight, and even Allied planners worked on a quick attack scenario within three to five days of the landings. Schweppenburg agreed that the only real chance to throw the Allies back into the sea was probably on or before 8 June. Indeed, he commented after the war, "It was still possible in the morning of 8 June to deal the British a severe blow in the vicinity of Courseulles-sur-mer."[6] Moreover, it had to be done with crushing strength, which is why Rommel wanted four panzer divisions massed south of Caen in May. As dramatic and intense as the fighting between the Canadians and the 12th SS was between 7 and 10 June, that panzer division was stopped by forward elements of the Canadian division supported by intense artillery and naval gunfire. In short, one panzer division scarcely dented the crust of the Allied defenses. Had the forward Canadian units been overrun by the Hitler Youth, there were still significant Anglo-Canadian reserves ashore behind them by 8 June, including about one and a half armored brigades, several brigades of infantry, virtually all of 62nd Anti-Tank with forty-eight 17-pounders, and most of 7th Armoured Division concentrating behind the Sommervieu-Bazenville ridge.

Perhaps more significant, any armored assault approaching the beach would have been met by massive naval fire support, as one battalion of Panzer Lehr discovered to its great misfortune west of Putot. Here, the lessons of Gela and Salerno suggest the vulnerability of panzer forces to concentrated naval gunfire. The greatest danger to the Allies may have been the potential for command and control disruption, since all the higher-formation headquarters of Second British Army were echeloned behind the Canadians. Assuming that the panzers reached the coast in strength, they would then have to divide and attack east and west to roll up the Anglo-Canadian landings. The Seulles River presents a significant tank obstacle to movement west from the Canadian rear (which was why COSSAC choose the area of Gold beach initially as the main landing site), just as the Orne River and Caen canal secured its eastern flank from panzer assault. The problems the British later encountered in moving armor quickly across the Orne bridges in Operation Goodwood in July are suggestive here. In any event, recapturing the coast between Courseulles and St. Aubin could only be phase one.

It seems, in the end, that the key to a successful panzer assault on the Normandy landings was ultimately control of the air. So long as the Allies held it, the navy could stay in tight to the coast and provide an umbrella of fire that prevented German mobile forces from operating with impunity within range of their guns. Some German officers, like Rommel, understood this only too well. Others came to realize it as the Normandy campaign unfolded, and as they did so, appeals were made to Hitler—all in vain—to withdraw inland beyond the range of naval gunfire. It is conceivable that the destruction of the Anglo-Canadian beachheads, and the freedom it would have given the Germans to concentrate everything on the Americans, might have led to a total defeat of Operation Overlord. It would not have been an easy task. But that is clearly what the Germans believed was possible, and the way to make it happen lay on the plains astride the Mue River.

The plan for 1st SS Panzer Corps on 8 June was almost precisely the scenario envisaged in COSSAC's 4 September 1943 "Memorandum on Possible Course of Action Open to German Reserves on D-Day or D Plus 1" Option C.[7] It will be recalled that this variation anticipated a slight pause in the German response to the landings, to D+2 or D+3, in order to assemble two panzer, one mechanized, and one infantry division along the Caen-Bayeux highway on either side of the Mue River, with the armor weighted on the east side. By this stage of the COSSAC assault plan, the British "dash to Caen" would be complete, so the panzer attack in Option C did not immediately put the Germans into the main COSSAC landing zones west of the Seulles River. Morgan's planners therefore conceived of this German counterattack in two phases: secure ground up to the coast and the Seulles River in phase one, and then an assault across the Seulles onto Sommervieu-Bazenville ridge and into the side of the assault beaches in phase two. Sepp Dietrich's plan for 1st SS Panzer Corps on 8 June was virtually identical: phase one was targeted at the sea at Courseulles and the line of Seulles as far south as Creully, and then attacks radiating from there in subsequent phases. The only difference between COSSAC's Option C of September 1943 and the plan of 1st SS Panzer Corps on D+2 was that the weight of the panzer assault was astride the Mue River.

Like all the other plans made by the Germans in the early days of the Normandy campaign, the 1st SS Panzer Corps plan for 8 June was based on poor intelligence and a lot of wishful thinking, and it reflected a completely muddled command and control structure. Allied control of the air, radio jamming, and targeted attacks at German transmitters (and often the headquarters associated with them) effectively blinded German intelligence and crippled their command and control at crucial moments. This much was an Allied triumph. But the larger issue of the byzantine German command structure and the paralyzing effects of fear, nepotism, Nazism, and an army verging on defeat were entirely self-inflicted. The commander of Panzer Group West, Schweppenburg, later opined that it required six levels of command—from the panzer corps headquarters, through Panzer Group West, to Seventh Army and up the chain to Army Group B, then to commander in chief, west, Gerd von Rundstedt, and finally to OKW—just to move the three armored divisions.[8] As it turned out, 84th Corps ordered the initial panzer attack by 21st Panzer on D-Day, 1st SS Panzer Corps ordered the second and third attacks for D+1 and D+2, and Panzer Group West ordered the fourth for 10 June, which Rommel—the commander of Seventh Army—had already disrupted by moving Panzer Lehr west before Schweppenburg could assert his authority.

It is clear that by 1944 Schweppenburg had grown weary of the internal politics of army senior commands and of the interference of Nazi generals, including the upstart wunderkind of the Third Reich, Field Marshall Erwin Rommel. Schweppenburg had been among the clique of senior officers arguing for the concentration of panzer forces away from the beach in order to attack the Allies once they were well inshore, and thereby defeat them in a mobile battle. His stellar career as commander of armored forces in Poland, France, and the Soviet Union and his impeccable pedigree as a Westphalian nobleman made him an ideal candidate for commander of Panzer Group West in early 1944. But it is also clear from the tone of his postwar testimony that Schweppenburg was difficult, arrogant, and opinionated. He had little good to say of his Wehrmacht colleagues, and one can only imagine how this elegant, accomplished, and egotistical aristocratic officer felt about working alongside the SS.

Regardless, as a professional soldier Schweppenburg had a job to do. Although notionally in command of panzer forces in Normandy on 8 June, he was still in the process of moving Panzer Group West's headquarters from Paris to La Caine (north of Thury-Harcourt, about twenty-five kilometers south of Caen) and had not yet taken control of panzer forces in Normandy. In the interim, no one gripped the battle. "The first action of the staff of 1st SS Panzer Corps," Schweppenburg complained after the war, "should have been to ignore the confusion of contradictory orders, especially since no one in higher headquarters had the slightest conception of tank tactics, except perhaps Rommel and his staff." But for Schweppenburg, who had quarreled with Rommel over how to use tanks to meet the invasion, the Desert Fox was out of his depth. "Normandy was not Africa," he commented,[9] and Rommel was too fearful of airpower. For Schweppenburg, the landscape and weather of northern France still permitted careful movement.

The movement of Panzer Lehr to the front would seem to make—or refute—Schweppenburg's point, depending on how it is viewed. Panzer

Panzer Lehr on the march, ca. 7–8 June, led by a Mk IV tank with the "Wespe" 105mm self-propelled gun covered in brush following the motorcycle. (British Pathé)

Lehr was garrisoned around le Mans-Chartres, some 270 kilometers by road southeast of Caen. The division arrived from Hungary at the end of April in anticipation of the invasion. Indeed, that had been the rationale for its creation from the demonstration units of various schools. As the inspector general of panzer forces had told the division's commanding officer, Generalleutnant Fritz Bayerlein, "Your objective is not the coast! It is the sea!" To help make that happen, Panzer Lehr was fully armored and mechanized, the only German division to be 100 percent so. Its four infantry battalions (organized into two regiments) were all carried in and supported by half-tracks, and one of the two tank battalions of 130th Panzer Lehr Regiment was equipped with Panthers.[10] Despite this, and much to the dismay of von Rundstedt and others in the west, Hitler had recently ordered Panzer Lehr to the eastern front. On 6 June the Panther battalion was sitting on railcars in southern Germany headed to the Russian front: the rest of the division would have followed had the Allies not landed.

Panzer Lehr's commanding officer, Fritz Bayerlein, was also fearful of Allied airpower. He had been Rommel's chief of staff in North Africa and like his mentor had a healthy respect for Allied fighter-bombers. If Panzer Lehr was to deploy its combat power effectively, any move to the coast needed to be conducted with care and preferably at night. On 6 June Bayerlein was ordered by Generaloberst F. Dollman, commander of Seventh Army, to start his move toward Caen at 1700 hours. Bayerlein protested that moving his division in daylight would be, as the Panzer Lehr history says, "a death sentence," but he was told to get on with it. As Dollman reiterated, "Caen is of the greatest importance to us."[11]

Despite Bayerlein's best efforts at caution, speed, and routing, nothing could mask the huge columns of dust thrown up by the vehicles of Panzer Lehr as they snaked west along five designated routes. In all some 229 tanks and assault guns, 658 half-tracks, and more than 1,000 wheeled vehicles set off for Normandy. Strict radio silence did nothing to hide the division from prowling fighter-bombers, which swarmed the routes. "Soon, the bombers were loitering over the roads, destroying crossings, villages, and cities that were along the advance route and diving on snaking vehicles columns," Bayerlein recalled after the war. "At 2300 hrs we passed through the village of Sees. It was lit up like a 'Christmas tree' and heavy bombs were already burst in the small town. Get through!" By the time he reached Argentan, "it was as light as day from the fires and explosions."[12]

The Mk IV tanks of Helmut Ritgen's II Battalion of 130th Panzer Lehr Regiment were found by a couple of fighter-bombers in Alençon while refueling just after dawn. The strafing and bombing killed a few men and set tanks and fuel trucks on fire: the pall of smoke simply attracted more attacks. But Ritgen was ultimately dismissive of the impact of the air assault on Panzer Lehr's strength. The "first loss reports" from the march of Panzer Lehr, he observed, were inflated under the principle "Always double them!" Postwar historians inflated the losses again. The best estimate in the literature (Buckingham) is that the move cost Panzer Lehr five tanks, eighty-four half-tracks, and ninety wheeled vehicles. However, the figure of half-tracks lost in the march to Normandy—

Generalleutenant Fritz Bayerlein, commanding officer of Panzer Lehr
Division. (AHEC)

eighty-four—is actually the total lost from the whole month of June.[13] Panzer Lehr's history, which described the Chaumont-Villers-Bocage road as "a scene from hell," declined to give firm numbers.[14] Anthony Beevor is a little more emphatic: figures given for Panzer Lehr's losses on 7–8 June are "almost certainly a gross exaggeration."[15]

The greatest blow inflicted on Panzer Lehr by the forced march may be the confusion resulting from the radio silence, the dispersion and delay caused by the routes taken and the air attacks, and the loss of perhaps fifty armored fuel tankers. Certainly Bayerlein struggled to locate Dietrich's 1st SS Corps advanced headquarters near Thury-Harcourt and only managed to do so late in the afternoon of 7 June. There he was told to mass two battle groups, one built around 901st PGLR with tanks at Norrey and another with 902nd PGLR and tanks at Brouay, and be ready to attack the next morning (8 June), alongside 12th SS and 21st Panzer. On his return from this meeting Bayerlein's vehicle was attacked by aircraft and destroyed and his driver killed: Panzer Lehr's commander barely escaped with his life.[16]

Dietrich's orders for Panzer Lehr to assemble in front of 7th Canadian Brigade led to disastrous confusion that sapped the power of the panzer assault on 8 June. The original order for an attack by 1st SS Panzer Corps, issued by 84th Corps in the evening of 6 June, assigned the ground west of the Mue River to 26th PGR of 12th SS. That order was apparently never rescinded. As a result, 26th PGR and the leading elements of Panzer Lehr arrived opposite 7th Canadian Brigade about the same time late on 7 June and in the early hours the following day. Meanwhile, armored reconnaissance elements of both divisions operated, apparently without cooperation, west of Putot, in the gap between the Canadians and 50th British Division. When the heart of Panzer Lehr's eastern battle group, 1st Battalion of 901st PGLR, arrived north of Cheux, it encountered the 1st Battalion of 26th PGR preparing for an attack on Norrey: the Panzer Lehr infantry sought cover and awaited events.[17] To the west, the 2nd Battalion of 902nd PGLR, reinforced by tanks of the 2nd Battalion PLR, pushed to Brouay, where they got entangled in a nasty fight—presumably with a platoon of the Winnipegs. With the rest of Panzer Lehr Division deployed to the rear, along the Caen-Villers-Bocage road, forward divisional headquarters was established at either le Mesnil-Patry—within rifle shot of the

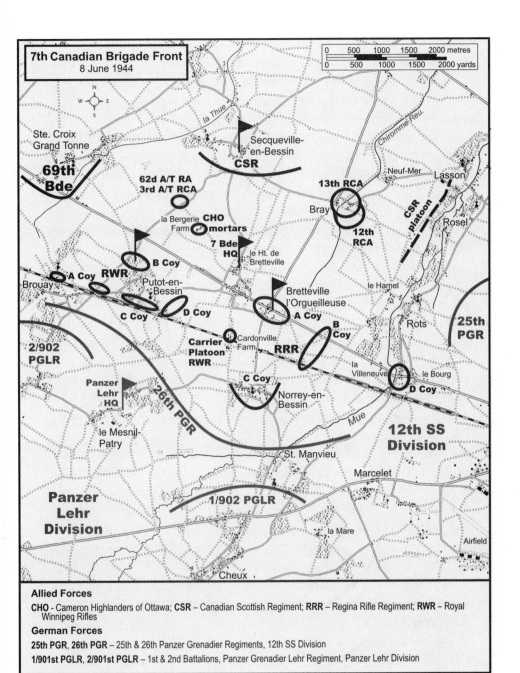

7th Canadian Brigade Front
8 June 1944

| 0 | 500 | 1000 | 1500 | 2000 metres |
| 0 | 500 | 1000 | 1500 | 2000 yards |

la Thue

Ste. Croix
Grand Tonne

Secqueville-
en-Bessin

CSR

Chiromme-Reu.

Neuf-Mer

Lasson

**69th
Bde**

62d A/T RA
3rd A/T RCA

13th RCA

Bray

Rosel

la Bergerie
Farm

**CHO
mortars**

7 Bde
HQ

le Ht. de
Bretteville

12th
RCA

**CSR
platoon**

B Coy

le Hamel

A Coy **RWR**

Brouay

Putot-en-
Bessin

Bretteville
l'Orgueilleuse

C Coy

D Coy

A Coy

B
Coy

Rots

**25th
PGR**

**2/902
PGLR**

**Carrier
Platoon
RWR**

Cardonville
Farm

RRR

la
Villeneuve

le Bourg

D Coy

**Panzer
Lehr
HQ**

26th PGR

C Coy

Norrey-en-
Bessin

**12th SS
Division**

le Mesnil-
Patry

St. Manvieu

Mue

Marcelet

**Panzer
Lehr
Division**

1/902 PGLR

la Mare

Airfield

Cheux

Allied Forces

CHO - Cameron Highlanders of Ottawa; **CSR** – Canadian Scottish Regiment; **RRR** – Regina Rifle Regiment; **RWR** – Royal
Winnipeg Rifles

German Forces

25th PGR, **26th PGR** – 25th & 26th Panzer Grenadier Regiments, 12th SS Division
1/901st PGLR, **2/901st PGLR** – 1st & 2nd Battalions, Panzer Grenadier Lehr Regiment, Panzer Lehr Division

Winnipegs' forward positions at Putot—or, according to some, slightly farther back at Cheux opposite the Reginas.[18]

The net result of this confusion in command and control was, nonetheless, to accomplish just what COSSAC planners feared in September 1943 that the Germans might do: assemble two panzer divisions astride the Mue River within days of the landings. Fortunately for the Allies, and especially for the Canadians, the result was not a massive armored thrust to the sea but the reduction of most of Panzer Lehr to idleness on 8 June. As Helmut Ritgen observed in his memoirs, Panzer Lehr "was unable to strike or to shift its sector" on that crucial day.[19] The Allies could take no credit for this muddle. Schweppenburg lamented after the war that the chaos of 8 June was a self-inflicted wound.

The tide that rose against 7th Brigade on 8 June 1944 was therefore smaller than it might have been, but it was bad enough. It came over the next forty-eight hours in a series of waves, all badly coordinated and all ultimately failures. The fighting was intense and brutal, all the same, and witnessed the first mass use of Panthers in the Normandy campaign. When it was finished, the Canadians retained control of the corridors to the sea astride the Mue, and the immediate panzer threat to the Normandy beachhead was thwarted. The plan had worked.

The attack on 7th Canadian Brigade's fortress position on 8 June was primarily the work of 26th PGR of the 12th SS. Like its counterpart the 25th PGR east of the Mue, this regiment was much more powerful than a normal Anglo-Canadian infantry brigade. Twenty-Sixth PGR also had reinforced companies: 190 men, plus their supporting arms in 1st and 2nd Battalions, and 220 men in the motorized companies of 3rd Battalion. And although they had made a difficult and prolonged march to the front, none of these battalions had yet been in combat, and their losses were negligible. Compared with the Canadians they faced, the Hitler Youth were fresh and at full strength. Supporting artillery (some self-propelled) was in place: only the Panther tanks of 1st Battalion, 12th SS Panzer Regiment, arrived too late on 8 June to help in the initial attacks.

In a formation notorious for its ardent Nazis and battlefield brutality, 26th PGR was commanded by a particularly violent sociopath, Lieutenant Colonel Wilhelm Mohnke. His incompetence and murderous behavior undermined the success of the attack on the Canadians for the

Brouay (bottom) and Putot (top center), with the "Brouay" rail crossing in the center. The railway cutting south of Putot shows clearly in this photo. (LCMSDS)

next thirty-six hours. An early convert to Nazism and a longtime member of the SS, Mohnke had fought with distinction in France in 1940 and had lost a foot in action in the Balkans in 1941. "Acknowledged as a skillful and courageous soldier," Howard Margolian wrote in his book on SS atrocities in Normandy, "Mohnke nonetheless was a man about whom even his fellow officers had nothing good to say." He was, Margolian asserts, "prey to ungovernable rages." In France in 1940 this had manifested itself in the deliberate machine-gunning of more than 100 British POWs. By 1944 Mohnke's volatile rages were fueled by a morphine addiction resulting from his amputation. The irrational behavior of this "madman" would not only affect the battle itself. He and the equally murderous Major Gerhard Bremer, in command of the 12th SS Reconnaissance Battalion, shaped the fate of more than sixty Canadian POWs.[20]

Attacks on the 7th Brigade fortress started in earnest in the early hours of 8 June, when three companies of the 1st Battalion of Mohnke's 26th PGR moved north from St. Mauvieu (rendered "St. Manvieu" on wartime maps) to push the Reginas out of Norrey and Bretteville. This initial attack was an attempt to clear the Canadians off the planned start line (the Caen-Bayeux highway) for the major panzer thrust to the sea, and an attempt by Mohnke to bring his regiment into line with Meyer's 25th PGR, which held positions around Buron farther north. While 1st Battalion cleared Norrey, Mohnke's 2nd Battalion was to brush the Winnipegs out of Putot. The motorized 3rd Battalion was to secure the western flank of the attack. According to the 1st Panzer Corps order for 8 June, only after 26th PGR had cleared Putot-Bretteville-Norrey was Panzer Lehr to follow through as the exploiting force toward Courseulles.[21]

The attack of the 1st Battalion of 26th PGR on the morning of 8 June was a complete failure. Major Stu Tubb, the lanky, bookish commander of the Reginas' C Company, had thought that the village was a little big for one company to hold, but it commanded superb fields of fire, and he refused to abandon it. Events soon proved him right. While his three rifle platoons defended the perimeter of the village—east, south, and west—Tubb kept his headquarters around the church as a reserve, and with two 6-pounders on the southeast corner of the village he had some antitank support and the equivalent of another platoon of men. He also had Captain W. P. G. Steele, the FOO from 13th RCA, in the church. Steele and Tubb had worked together to lay on DF and SOS fire tasks around the village and the approaches to it.[22] In addition, B Company, which is often erroneously placed in the Mue River at this stage, held the open ground to the northeast between Norrey and Bretteville, while the remnant of D Company guarded the bridges over the Mue at la Villeneuve.

The third company of Mohnke's 1st Battalion moved straight on Norrey at about 0300 hours on 8 June, driving in Tubb's outposts

Lieutenant Colonel Foster Matheson, commanding officer of the Regina Rifle Regiment, poses while on exercise in April 1944. The simple French gray patch of 3rd Canadian Infantry Division shows clearly on his right shoulder. (LAC PA-171257)

before the attack was halted by withering small arms and artillery fire. The Hitler Youth had, of course, walked into the prearranged DF tasks of 13th RCA. Checked in their direct advance on Norrey, the battalion's first company tried to slip around the village to the east. There they ran into the antitank guns positioned at the southeast corner of Norrey, and eventually into B Company. The fighting here was close and intense. One of the 6-pounders was overrun and nearly captured, while the Hitler Youth got close enough to exchange hand grenades and rifle butts with B Company. Mortars tucked in behind B Company fired through the night and much of the next day. Sergeant A. H. J. James's citation for a Mention in Despatches, written at the time he was killed during the crossing of the Leopold Canal in October, observed that his section "fired 500 bombs per mortar" that day "at a range of 300 yards." Given that the mortars were located 200 yards behind B Company's trenches, most of the bombs landed therefore directly in front of the company. James controlled much of this fire from inside the German positions. When his observation post was overrun and used as a German command post, James climbed a tree and brought fire down on it, "causing considerable damage to personnel there as borne out by their screams."[23]

On the B Company front, then, the assault of 8 June by the first company of the 1st Battalion, 26th PGR, was turned back by close fighting with small arms. At least some of the Germans succeeded in infiltrating the village, but they seem to have distracted themselves by murdering civilians.[24] This company of 12th SS eventually occupied the Mue River valley as far as Rots, clashing with D Company at la Ville-neuve as it did so. This put an enemy combat unit directly opposite the gun positions at Bray for the first time.

If this was not bad enough, tanks from 12th SS Panzer Regiment also probed the eastern flank of the 7th Brigade fortress on 8 June. In the afternoon, 2nd Canadian Armoured Brigade reported that "a strong force of German tanks worked around the LEFT flank of 7 Cdn Inf Bde" and approached the bridge over the Mue at Cairon.[25] This critical hinge between the two forward brigades of 3rd Canadian Division was screened by a small force of infantry from the Canadian Scottish Regiment, two troops of M10s (likely Achilles 17-pounders from 62nd Anti-Tank, RA), and what was left of the 1st Hussars's C Squadron. The defense of Cairon was little more than a screen. Second Canadian Armoured Brigade later reported that "the enemy appeared to be in considerable strength and the situation looked serious." "If he continued his adv [advance]," the brigade's report at the end of June observed, "there was nothing to stop him between there and the beaches." Entirely fortuitously, what was left of the Sherbrooke Fu-siliers happened to be passing Cairon on their way to Camilly, and shortly afterward fifteen replacement tanks headed for the 1st Hussars arrived on the scene. The sudden, and very visible, reinforcement of the Canadian position at Cairon caused the Germans to withdraw. The probe had failed, but only by a narrow margin.[26]

Meanwhile, with the third company of 26th PGR stalled in front of Norrey and the first probing the eastern flank of the Reginas' position along the Mue, the second company of the 1st Battalion attacked west of Norrey but stopped south of the rail line just short of Cardonville farm—held by the carrier platoon of the Winnipegs—when the other attacks faltered.

The Reginas' war diary records this first attack by 26th PGR on the morning of 8 June as minor, presumably because very little of it got beyond C Company's positions in Norrey. "The enemy carried out a counterattack during the night on the positions of B-, C-, and D-Company," the war diary recorded laconically. "It was repulsed by our troops."[27] Even the 12th SS historian, Hubert Meyer, at the time the division's chief of staff, commented that the Canadians scarcely noticed the attack. Stu Tubb's postwar testimony makes no mention of it, nor does it feature in any of the regimental accounts. Apparently Captain Jack Treleaven, the new acting commander of B Company, neglected to report what his troops endured, for anecdotal evidence indicates that the fighting there was close and intense. Moreover, it was not a minor attack, and it lasted for some six to eight hours. It simply was checked by effective small arms and artillery fire. As the history of the 12th SS records, "The positions of the whole [1st] Battalion were covered with brisk artillery and mortar fire throughout the day. It slowed any kind of movement."[28]

Artillery support was crucial. The intelligence log of 13th RCA records that the regiment fired 976 rounds between 1800 hours on 7 June and 0600 hours on 8 June. The regimental history claimed that a "curtain of fire" secured the Reginas' C Company's position at Norrey that day.[29] When asked about this many years later, the commanding officer of 13th RCA at the time, Colonel Freddie Clifford, described the idea of a curtain as "bullshit!"[30] The perimeter was maintained by a series of DF and Mike (regimental) shoots. One concentration on the road leading southeast from Norrey at 0500 hours on 8 June was fired at "scale 5" from both regiments at Bray—240 shells, almost four tons of steel and high explosive, on a single grid reference in a few short minutes. Two other Mike targets were fired in that area over the next few hours. Whatever their commitment to the führer, the callow youth of the 12th SS preferred their slit trenches to Canadian artillery fire: the 1st Battalion of 26th PGR remained still for much of the day. By one Canadian estimate, German casualties in front of C Company positions that day were eighty-six, seventeen of them dead. It is not clear if these figures include losses in the attack on B and D Companies.[31]

Unfortunately for the Canadians, things did not go so well to the west, at Putot. In summary, it began with a modest Canadian success, followed by the virtual destruction of the Royal Winnipeg Rifles, and ended with the Canadians in complete possession of the battlefield. In short, the brigade fortress fulfilled its function: 12th SS failed to clear the start line, Panzer Lehr never moved during the day, and so there was no panzer drive to Courseulles on 8 June.

But no one could know that as dawn broke over the dripping Normandy countryside. The Winnipegs were in a tough spot from the outset. By the morning of 8 June the British had still not closed up from the west. At dawn elements of 69th Brigade and their supporting armor remained only several kilometers west, at Ste.-Croix-Grand-Tonne. Seventh Brigade headquarters was so poorly informed of what the British were doing that, once the German assault on Putot began, British movements—especially those of tanks—were taken to be those of the enemy.[32] The brigade and the Winnipegs had every reason to be anxious. Not only was the right flank of the Canadian division still wide-open, but the Winnipegs' rifle companies were still weak from the casualties of D-Day, and the men were exhausted. Everyone had been on the go since 4 June: even a steady diet of Benzedrine (a stimulant) was not enough to keep some men awake.

Lieutenant Colonel John Meldram, in command of the Winnipegs, had put his best troops under the bright young Major Fred Hodge in the most exposed position: covering the railway bridge at Brouay. Hodge had a tough assignment, and he stretched his A Company thin. It will be recalled that his main position was astride the road just north of the rail bridge, with the bulk of his company on the east side and one platoon across the road. He also pushed one platoon a kilometer west along the railway to a position just north of the village of Brouay, where he hoped to meet the British. A Company was supported by a platoon of Vickers machine guns from the Camerons and two of the battalion's 6-pounder antitank guns, but Hodge and his men were out on a limb. The bulk of the Winnipegs remained grouped around Putot: C Company along the railway cutting in a string of platoons, D Company southeast of the village where the rail line came out of the cutting, and the newly rebuilt B Company and the battalion headquarters in an orchard north of village. Two FOOs and a battery commander from

Lieutenant Colonel Meldram, commanding officer, the Royal Winnipeg Rifles, seen here at le Mesnil-Patry on 12 June 1944. (LAC e011108441)

12th RCA were at Meldram's headquarters on 8 June, as was a troop of M10s.

Brigadier Harry Foster was well aware of the exposed western flank of his brigade and so added depth to the Winnipegs' position and covered the open plain to the west of Putot. In a small wooded area northwest of La Bergerie farm (one kilometer north of Putot on the road between Secqueville and the railway crossing at Brouay), he deployed a powerful force of antitank guns capable of sweeping the surrounding fields with effective fire. It consisted of four 17-pounders of E Troop, 62nd Anti-Tank RA, a platoon of machine guns and one of 4.2-inch mortars of the Camerons, eight 6-pounders of 94th Battery, 3rd Anti-Tank, RCA, and a platoon from the Can Scotts. The rest of Can Scots (less the company guarding the road on the brigade's eastern flank near Cairon) were in reserve at Secqueville. On the whole the Canadians had covered the ground and the options quite well.

The open ground west of the Winnipegs offered the Germans their best hope for success on 8 June. On the Winnipegs' front alone they deployed nearly half a panzer division. The reinforced 1st and 3rd Battalions—the latter fully armored, with its men and supporting weapons, including light guns, carried on half-tracks—of 26th PGR were enough to overwhelm the Canadian position. The 2nd Battalion of 902nd PGLR, waiting at Brouay, was also fully armored. They enjoyed the support of the armored reconnaissance battalions of both 12th SS and Panzer Lehr, and some of both divisions' artillery was in place. Meanwhile, the leading elements of Panzer Lehr's Mk IV tank battalion and the 130th Armoured Engineer Battalion were just an hour's drive away at the Château Monts-in-Bessin just north of the Caen-Villers-Bocage road. These tanks and armored engineers were resupplied upon arrival in the early morning of 8 June and waited all day for orders to move: none came.[33] Small wonder that Schweppenburg was apoplectic with anger over the handling of German forces in the opening stages of the Normandy campaign. Had the Allies muddled such a crucial operation in so decisive a campaign, historians would have been savage in their criticism.

The assault on Putot began with another German tactical defeat at the Brouay railway bridge. At approximately 0530 hours an advanced party, probably from Mohnke's 2nd Battalion but possibly troops from Panzer Lehr, supported by half-tracks and an Mk III tank approached the bridge. It was met by intense fire from Major Hodge's 8 Platoon, machine gun fire from the Camerons, artillery, and antitank fire, which knocked out the tank and an armored car. It was over within an hour, as the Germans retreated. So far, so good.

But the Germans now knew that the crossing was held in force. With that Mohnke's 2nd Battalion commander, SS Major Bernard Seibken, ordered a full-scale assault, with two companies up, supported by the battalion's heavy weapons company. At least one platoon of Panzer Lehr joined in this attack on the western flank, and so did an artillery battery commander from 12th SS, who supported the attack with indirect fire. The assault was conceived in two phases: securing the rail line, then the Caen-Bayeux highway roughly one kilometer farther north. The attack spread along the whole Winnipeg line, from A Company's position at the Brouay crossing to D Company at the east end of the village.

Mike Bechthold, the most recent historian to work through the details of the attack on Putot, argues that it began at 1000 hours and "was supported by a heavy artillery barrage and armour." The Winnipegs' history claims that twenty to thirty panzers, including Tiger tanks, engaged in the attack, but this is hyperbole.[34] Nonetheless, there was constant fear of panzers, and it is clear that armor was present. Just what German armor participated in the attack around Putot on 8 June remains unclear, but there was plenty around.

We do know with certainty—once again—that there were plenty of German infantry in the assault. As at Authie and Buron the day before, the SS youth came in waves, and the Canadians in Putot served them with everything available, including the battalion's 3-inch mortars, the Cameron's Vickers machine guns, and artillery fire directed by 12th RCA's Captain Ben Nixon, the FOO. The Winnipegs' regimental history compared it to a Great War assault, in which the attacking "Germans were cut down in swaths."[35] But again, as at Authie, all the fire that the Canadians could muster was not enough to stop the Hitler Youth. "Like their counterparts at Authie," Margolian writes, "Mohnke's troops were openly disdainful of the heavy Canadian fire and just kept coming, moving forward recklessly, arrogantly, inexorably."[36] And as at Authie and Buron, they were helped by artillery and mortar fire, which swept the Canadian positions, and by armor—tanks or assault guns, perhaps both, and certainly half-tracks.

At the east end of Putot, where the Germans had to cross the raised rail bed, Major Laughlin Fulton's D Company stopped them. Fulton's company had good fields of fire and help from its support arms. Nonetheless, D Company's successful defense of the east end of Putot cost it "4 killed and 20 wounded, nearly 25 percent casualties."[37] Westward, along the rail line, the other forward Winnipeg companies were not so fortunate. Major Hodge, at the other end of the cutting with his A Company, was attacked by both infantry and twelve to twenty armored vehicles, likely all half-tracks and some with heavy weapons

Major Laughlin "Lockie" Fulton, commander of D Company, Royal Winnipeg Rifles. (RWR Museum)

mounted.[38] The open flank of A Company's position also allowed infiltration into the rear of Hodge's platoons. The two forward 6-pounder guns of H Troop, 3rd Anti-Tank, RCA, so laboriously transferred to Rhino ferries at sea two days before in order to get ashore, were overrun. Sergeant Jack Rudd, commanding another gun from H Troop farther back, heard about the fate of the forward guns when Norman Johnstone and Bill Clarke ran into his position and announced, "They are all gone! They are all dead!" Rudd was just able to bury his gun's striker case (disabling the gun) before he, too, and twenty-three others were captured.[39]

Meanwhile, the nature of the rail cutting directly south of Putot, where C Company was dug in, made it all but impossible to stop the

Germans from reaching the southern lip, getting into the dead ground in front of the Winnipegs' trenches and up into the company positions. As young Nazis surged into the village from the west and south, effective German machine gun and artillery fire gradually isolated the forward Winnipeg companies. This took several hours to accomplish, and as the battle raged around Putot, 3rd Division's commander, Major General Rod Keller, began preparations to renew the Canadian attack in the Buron-Authie area by 9th Brigade. He was no doubt reassured by Meldram's steady reports that he and his Winnipeg Rifles were still in control of Putot. "As late as 1400 hrs," Bechthold writes, "well after the forward companies had been surrounded, Battalion Headquarters reported to Brigade that 'it expected to handle the situation.'"[40]

In fact, Meldram had lost control hours before. By noon the battle for Putot had become one with no clear front, as more and more Hitler Youth penetrated the village, turning it into an impassable barrier for the Winnipegs still holding out to the south who sought to retreat. What remained of A and C Companies clung to the rail line. Some men escaped to the rear, but most seem to have slipped west along the rail line, looking for a way out. Major Hodge and the remnants of A Company, surrounded and short of ammunition, were eventually forced to surrender to 3rd Battalion, 26th PGR shortly after noon. At some point Meldram committed B Company, his final reserve, to the fight for the village. It, too, was swallowed in the maelstrom, and much of it disappeared on the battlefield, men scattering or dying as fate determined. Captain Gower, B Company's acting commanding officer, surrendered when he and a half dozen others were surrounded. "It was," Rifleman Edward Johnson recalled many years later, "the act of a very courageous officer to save the lives of his men."[41] Only Major Fulton's D Company, which was never fully enveloped, was able to extricate itself and move back to support the battalion headquarters.

By early afternoon the rump of the Winnipegs—D Company, support company, stragglers, and the headquarters staff—held out around battalion headquarters at the northern edge of the village. Canadian artillery fired incessantly. Many Mike and Uncle (division-scale) targets were fired over an arc of 340 degrees on 8 June from the gun positions around Bray. The 13th RCA was nearly firing in a circle, requiring the use of two plotting boards. By early afternoon it was also dropping white phosphorus smoke rounds into Putot to help the stragglers from the Winnipegs escape. Contrary to what Jack English claims, there was no "flight": even at the worst of it, the Royal Winnipeg Rifles remained on the battlefield, fighting.[42]

The attack on Putot was supported by armor, but who and what they were has never been clarified: certainly no German tank unit claims a role. But the memories of the Winnipegs' survivors remained vivid years after the war. "SS tank crews took sadistic pleasure," the RWR history records, "in romping through trench positions of riflemen: they created slaughter by simply locking a tread over a slit trench and gyrating the heavy tank in a circle until all the slit trench was crushed."[43] When B Company was overrun, Sergeant Major Charles Belton was ordered to brave the gauntlet of fire and seek help, which led to a very close encounter with German armor that could easily be mistaken for tanks. As Belton raced down the highway toward Caen in a Bren carrier, he slipped between two German SPs sitting on either side of the road. Belton was moving so fast they could not get a clean shot at him, although some landed very close. "I remember this dirt flying all around and getting into the carrier," Belton said, "but I got away." He reported to brigade headquarters: "That was the first time Brigade had heard of what was going on."[44]

Others recalled the armor as well, especially Tony Foulds, a British subaltern of 62nd Anti-Tank RA. Foulds was part of E Troop, 246th Battery, commanded by Lieutenant Gerry Blanchard, whose four towed 17-pounders helped garrison the small wood northwest of La Bergerie farm. According to Foulds, at about 0945 hours "an enemy force of nine tanks and a supporting infantry appeared" to their front. Sergeant Major Belton, who witnessed the attack, described them as Mk IV tanks, while Captain Harold Gonder, who commanded the Camerons machine guns in the wood, believed them to be Panthers.[45] In all likelihood they were heavily camouflaged assault guns and SPs, perhaps from 2nd Battalion, 902nd PGLR, known to be at Brouay. Given the descriptions, they may even have been SPs from 21st Panzer. The German armor stopped about 1,200 yards away and, as Foulds recalled, "commenced plastering the wood with machine gun and mortar fire." This had the desired effect of goading two 17-pounders and two 6-pounders into opening fire. Four German tanks were soon hit, as were the two 17-pounders. Lieutenant Blanchard and Lieutenant Ray, from 3rd Anti-Tank, RCA, directed the manhandling of replacement guns from the rear of the position, "under intense fire," and got them into action. Then Blanchard helped resite the defenses of the wood to ensure better fields of fire. In the meantime, a troop of M10 17-pounders arrived, as did two platoons of Can Scots to reinforce the position. German movement stalled following the initial clash, and the rest of the day was spent trading fire.[46] For their efforts both Gonder and Blanchard won a Military Cross.

What ultimately stopped the assault at Putot was not simply stubborn Canadian resistance, including intense artillery fire, but German indecision and the arrival of the British on the battlefield. It seems that by noon the Germans felt the same about the progress of the battle as Lieutenant Colonel Meldram did: the Canadians were doing OK. It was time for a further push, and that might have come from Panzer Lehr. By 1200 reports reached Bayerlein at le Mesnil-Patry, virtually within the battle zone, that "all of the combat elements [of his division] had reached their designated staging areas." Bayerlein and his staff also learned that the attacks by 12th SS had not gone well. Apparently Bretteville "had been taken" but abandoned "due to heavy enemy pressure." As the Panzer Lehr history concludes, "The Corps staff wanted to await the arrival of the commanding general, General von Geyr [Schweppenburg], before making decisions. He was expected at any moment."[47]

All that had been accomplished by early afternoon was the partial destruction of a single Canadian battalion and the occupation of a village overlooked by the enemy. There was also a growing British menace from the west in the late afternoon, in particular from British tanks. They had been summoned following a chance encounter north of Brouay between Major Jimmy Jones, the Winnipegs' C Company commander who had escaped from Putot, and a reconnaissance tank of the 24th Lancers. Jones and the Lancers concocted a plan to unite the British tanks with the remnants of C Company and attack Putot from the west. Meldram knew that Jones was planning the attack, but he never learned of the outcome. The attack failed, but the sudden appearance of eighteen tanks on their western flank probably accounts for German caution in attempts to exploit their capture of Putot. The Lancers and their supporting Canadian infantry subsequently withdrew, taking between forty and seventy POWs with them.[48]

By then it seems that the fate of 2nd Battalion, 902nd PGLR, at Brouay, the only unit close enough to intervene quickly, and that of the German panzer attack in the seam between the Canadians and 50th British Division, had been sealed. The Panzer Lehr battalion's presence was revealed both by a reconnaissance troop from the British Inns of Court Regiment and by the leading elements of the 24th Lancers. The former captured several Panzer Lehr artillery officers and in one of the most notorious incidents of the Normandy campaign tied one of them to a scout car as a human shield. The car was later knocked out, and the officer, a Great War veteran with one arm, subsequently died in a German hospital. This incident, often attributed to Canadians in the German and American literature, was used as justification for the murder of several Canadian POWs at the headquarters of 2nd Battalion, 26th PGR, that followed.[49] At some point during the day the vehicle park of 2nd Battalion, 902nd PGLR, at Brouay came under fire from British tanks, and the battalion (whose presence was evidently unknown to the 12th SS) was attacked from behind by Monhke's 3rd Battalion, 26th PGR, and subjected to fire from the 12th SS artillery.

The final indignity for the Panzer Lehr battalion at Brouay was the arrival of a British artillery spotter plane—an Angel of Death if ever there was one—over its position in the early afternoon. It brought down fire from Canadian and British divisional artillery and, more devastating still, naval gunfire from a cruiser. The results were catastrophic. When men of Mohnke's regiment returned through the position later that day, they "were offered a glimpse of the most horrific face of war." "The enemy had systemically hacked an element of the Panzer-Lehr Division to pieces with heavy artillery," Oberscharführer Hans-Georg Kesslar recalled. "Beside the obliterated vehicles and weapons lay pieces of our Comrades. Others hung from the trees. It commanded a dreadful silence."[50] Reconnaissance units from both German armored divisions were also targeted. The destruction of 2nd Battalion of 902nd PGLR by Allied artillery on 8 June provides a glimpse into what might have befallen the massed companies of 25th PGR around Buron and Authie on 7 June had the artillery system functioned properly—and what might have befallen a concentrated force of panzers approaching the beaches.

By early evening it was clear, to both sides, that the attack on Putot was going nowhere. By 1800 hours elements of 50th British Division were on the move west of Audrieux and threatening to envelop the left flank of 12th SS. The 12th SS Reconnaissance Battalion, under SS Captain Gerhard Bremer, had patrolled this flank all day, pushing back probes by the British. Prisoners captured by 3rd Battalion of 26th PGR were also passed to Bremer's unit shortly after noon, presumably for interrogation. Among the POWs were Major Hodge, the other survivors of A Company (including most of 9 Platoon), and two British soldiers: twenty-six in all. They were taken to Bremer's headquarters at the Château d'Audrieux.

Bremer, who spoke fluent English, interrogated Hodge and two non-commissioned officers around 1400 hours and, having learned nothing, ordered them to be shot. The executioners, under SS Sergeant Stunn, carried out the order by shooting the men in the back. But Stunn's men were unsettled when two of Hodge's group turned defiantly toward the firing squad at the last moment. And so the next three POWs to be murdered, all Winnipegs, were ordered to lie on the ground and were shot in the back of the head at point-blank range. Stunn and his men then stopped for lunch, presumably while Bremer worked his way through the rest of the POWs. This was interrupted by an attack from the leading elements of British 50th Division, which the SS defeated. However, by late afternoon the 12th SS Reconnaissance Battalion's position around the Château d'Audrieux was precarious, and Bremer had no time to interrogate POWs. So the remaining twenty were simply herded into two groups—thirteen survivors of the Winnipegs' 9 Platoon in one and seven in another—and machine-gunned. The incidents were witnessed by locals, and the evidence was still on the ground when the British occupied the area several days later.[51]

What finally drove Bremer's unit from the village and the Château d'Audrieux was fire from three British field regiments and two battleships that started about 1900 hours. According to Hubert Meyer, "Within one hour, the village was destroyed." The fire shifted to the château grounds, "where the staff and the staff company" of the reconnaissance unit were located: "They were shot to pieces."[52] Mean-

Major Fred Hodge, commander of A Company, Royal Winnipeg Rifles, until his untimely death on 8 June at the hands of the SS. (RWR Museum)

while, Lieutenant Colonel F. N. Cabeldu of the Can Scots was alerted at Secqueville at 1830 hours to prepare his battalion for a counterattack: 7th Brigade was going to recapture Putot.

As the crushing effect of Anglo-Canadian artillery and naval fire support smashed into the leading German units around Putot and Audrieux—and weakened their resolve—Field Marshall Rommel turned up at Bayerlein's advanced headquarters. Franz Kurowski, the historian of Panzer Lehr, describes the "division command post" as being at le Mesnil-Patry, which is just two kilometers south of Putot. Others place the Panzer Lehr headquarters at Cheux, five kilometers south of Bretteville. Either way, it says a great deal about how the Germans viewed the initial beachhead battles that Rommel's first trip to the front was to the Canadian sector: to the ground that COSSAC had identified nearly a year earlier as the key.

It had taken Rommel most of three days to get to the front. Since German generals were forbidden to fly because of Allied air superiority, Rommel had raced back from Germany by car to his headquarters at Roch Guyon on D-Day. He then spent 7 June trying to muster forces to defeat the invasion and secure the Pas de Calais. Finally, on 8 June, the Desert Fox went forward to do what he did best: get a sense of the battle at the cutting edge. During the day Rommel worked his way down the line of panzer headquarters, starting at Panzer Group West at the Château La Caine, stopping at Sepp Dietrich's 1st SS Panzer Corps headquarters now at Amaye-sur-Orne fifteen kilometers south of Cheux, before reaching Bayerlein south of the Canadians around 1800 hours (1900 German time).

With Canadian 7th Brigade a few thousand yards away, and amid the sound of crashing artillery and the rattle of musketry, Rommel and his old Afrika Corps chief of staff discussed options. "Bayerlein, all of our positions have been turned aside," Rommel said, apparently slipping excitedly into his Swabian accent. "The British 50th Division, our familiar friends from Africa, has taken Bayeux." Bayerlein was ordered to regroup his division, move it west, and retake Bayeux.[53] He must have been relieved at the orders. The operations of 12th SS were little short of chaotic, and few in the Wehrmacht—Bayerlein among them—could have cherished the thought of working closely with such an incompetent gang of murderous Nazis.

The order to change the focus of Panzer Lehr's operations toward Bayeux was the genesis of the dreadful battles of Tilley-sur-Seulles that followed: one of the bloodiest episodes of the Normandy campaign. But it was not the end of serious attempts to launch a major panzer thrust against the Allied landings while they were still fragile. Shortly after Rommel left Bayerlein's headquarters on the evening of 8 June, what was left of the OKW Panzer reserve was released to Rundstedt's command.[54] Of these, 1st SS Panzer Division, Leibstandart Adolph Hitler (the parent formation of 12th SS), and Panzer Regiment Grossdeutchesland of 116th Panzer were assigned to 1st SS Panzer Corps. They were immediately ordered to concentrate west of Caen. Schweppenburg was unimpressed. The chance for decisive action had been missed on 8 June, when two panzer divisions were already lined up in front of the Canadians, and nothing decisive was attempted. After the war he blamed "the divergent influence of the high staffs" for the failure of 8 June, probably a euphemism for Rommel. But he was clear about the lost opportunity. "If one has to pass final judgement on the conduct of this Corps, it should be stated that it missed the psychological moment—and the bus."[55]

The final act at Putot on 8 June was played out in the soft evening light. The Canadian Scottish Regiment was tasked to retake the village supported by the fire of five field regiments—proof that Brigadier Stanley Todd, the CRA, had gripped the battle.[56] Artillery, and fire from the Cameron's 4.2-inch mortars, was to keep German infantry in the village down, isolate the battlefield with a smoke barrage, and "walk" the Can Scots in with a creeping barrage. Once the village was retaken, Canadian artillery was to maintain defensive fire to the south and west until the position was consolidated. Tanks from the 1st Hussars and M10 Achilles of the 62nd Anti-Tank RA would provide direct fire support to the attacking companies. Lieutenant Colonel Cabeldu's plan was to move his battalion on a two-company front on either side of the Secqueville-Brouay road: D on the left, A on the right. C Company would follow D, while the Can Scots' other company, B, hustled from its positions five kilometers away on the Cairon-Buron road to support. The start line lay just behind the small wood northwest of La Bergerie farm, which had been stoutly defended earlier in the day; the objective was the rail line. Cabeldu told his company commanders that Putot had to be retaken and that "there was no other infantry battalion between Putot and the beaches." This was not strictly true, but they were inspiring words to men who already knew that the fate of the landings depended on the defense of the beachhead.

Despite the tremendous supporting fire and the presence of friendly tanks, the advance of the Can Scots was a bitterly contested and bloody affair. The attack moved off smartly at 2030 hours, just two hours after the orders had been given. It took fifteen minutes for the Germans to notice through the dust and bursting shells that the Can Scots were attacking. They advanced across a flat wheat field, devoid of cover, against an enemy concealed in orchards and the village. German gunners and mortar men dropped their shells a few hundred yards behind the Canadian supporting barrage, so the Can Scots attacked in a shower of explosions. Their war diary records that "the men advanced without falter into a veritable wall of fire, their courage was magnificent . . . casualties were naturally heavy."[57] By the time D Company reached the rail line at Brouay, it was down to twenty-six men and had lost its commanding officer, second in command, and sergeant major. Major Plows and A Company arrived and took charge, organizing the two companies for defense. "For a time," Mike Bechthold writes, "the situation was so desperate and ammunition running so low, that the men were forced to use captured German machine guns and their ample stocks of ammunition to bolster the defence."[58] This, the Can Scots' history observed, "added sweetness to 'clobbering the enemy.'" Within an hour it was largely all over, and the Can Scots reported to brigade that they were mopping up final stragglers in Putot.

Putot was not lost again, although attempts were made to recapture it, and it remained under pressure for the next few days. In contrast to Meldram's deployment of the Winnipegs, Cabeldu concentrated his defenses in and around the village itself and used the fields between it and the rail line and the Sequeville-Brouay road as a killing ground. Patrols and concentrations of supporting artillery fire made the railway cutting untenable for the enemy. By 2230 hours Cabeldu reported that things were getting quiet. It was welcome news to Brigadier Foster. By then the Reginas were under attack again, this time by the Panther battalion of 12th SS and elements of Kurt Meyer's 25th PGR. If Mohnke's 26th PGR regiment now joined in the attack, things would get very dicey indeed for the men of 7th Brigade.

8

Bretteville and Cardonville, 8 June

For God's sake stay awake. We're being attacked by
tanks.

Captain Gordon Brown to his FOO,
Cardonville farm, 9 June 1944

ROMMEL'S DECISION late on 8 June to shift Panzer Lehr west, to recapture Bayeux, and the Canadian recapture of Putot only slightly
changed the larger strategic context of battle for access to the Mue
River plains. For the moment no corps-level panzer counterattack
was possible. But the German intent remained, and the means were
on their way. Late that day the remaining panzer reserve in the west
was released for service on the coast. Among these were 1st SS Panzer
Division, garrisoned near Brugge in Belgium; Panzer Regiment Gross-
deutschland of 116th Panzer, laagered at Mantes west of Paris; and
a number of infantry and other units for Army Group B, Rommel's
command. The panzer formations began to move on 9 June.[1] As the
history of 12th SS observes, on the evening of 8 June, "The terrain on
both sides of the Mue creek and the lower Seulles to its mouth at Courseulles-sur-mer was favorable for such an attack."[2] The task of 12th SS
was now to shorten its front and once again try to clear the start line
for the panzer corps attack.

The immediate concern for the Hitler Youth was to bring its two
infantry regiments, 25th PGR east of the Mue and 26th PGR west
of the river, into line together. Between them a gap snaked along the
Mue River valley held by a screen of reconnaissance, pioneer, and flak
troops. "If the right flank of Regiment 25 could be successfully moved
to the north of Rots," the 12th SS history observed, "the front would
have been shorted by 3.5 kilometers."[3] The capture of the villages of
Rots and la Villeneuve in the Mue valley, and Bretteville and Norrey to
the west would then allow German armor to get safely onto the open

ground beyond. So, clearing the Canadian bastion at Norrey and its supporting position at Bretteville became the task of 12th SS for the night of 8–9 June. It was now time to commit the Panther regiment.

The capture of Bretteville and Norrey called for coordinated action by the two infantry regiments of 12th SS, the division's artillery, and, for the first time, the Panther tanks of the 1st Battalion of 12th SS Panzer Regiment. Roundly considered the best tank of the war on either side, the Panther was making its Normandy debut, and 12th SS hoped to deploy forty or more for the attack. They had arrived in the Franqueville area during 8 June and immediately drew fire from Canadian guns. Canadian division and brigade staffs were well aware that they had not yet seen all that 12th SS had to offer.

As the Panthers prowled the open ground west of Authie and Buron on 8 June, the Mk IV tanks of 12th SS Panzer Regiment's 2nd Battalion and infantry of 25th PGR continued to probe the positions of 9th Brigade around les Buissons. The whole Canadian front east of the Mue was alive with milling panzers, while the forward elements of 9th Brigade were under constant artillery and mortar fire during the day, and Hitler Youth infantry pressed forward through the standing grain to test the Canadians' resolve.[4] The Canadian solution to the latter was to bring in Flail tanks to beat down the grain and deal with the snipers, including those still operating within and behind Canadian positions.[5] What was left of the Fort Garry Horse and the Sherbrooke Fusiliers, most of the M10s of 105th Battery, 3rd Anti-Tank Regiment, RCA, and 17-pounder batteries from 62nd Anti-Tank RA were already grouped around Hill 70 (Anguerney), and there they stayed until 10 June. "Sitting on the relatively exposed position of 'Hill 70' for over two and a half days was quite an exhausting ordeal," Captain W. E. McAleese wrote in the Garry's C Squadron diary a few days later, "for counter attacks supported by armour were expected hourly in this sector, and this commanding ground had to be held at all costs." McAleese believed that the visibility of tanks and guns around Anguerney was intended to discourage a German attack.[6]

Perhaps, but on 8 June it seemed to senior Allied commanders that the Germans were more interested in mobility across the front. After several days of uncertainty, the intelligence branch of 21st Army Group (still in the United Kingdom) had finally located 12th SS in the Carpi-

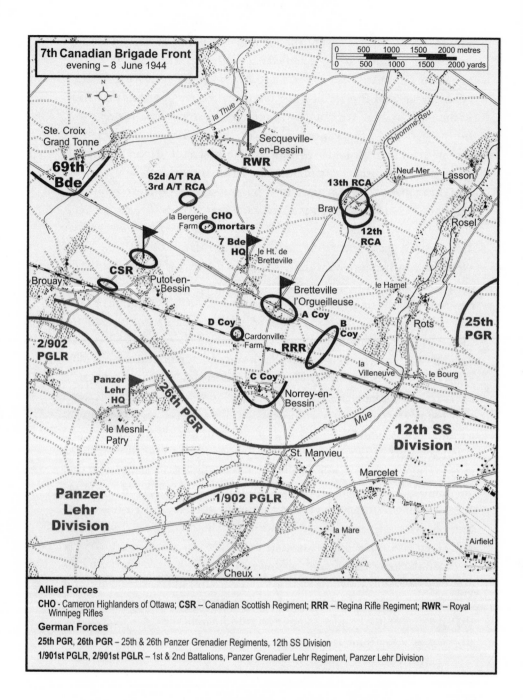

7th Canadian Brigade Front
evening – 8 June 1944

| 0 | 500 | 1000 | 1500 | 2000 metres |
| 0 | 500 | 1000 | 1500 | 2000 yards |

N
W E
S

Ste. Croix
Grand Tonne

la Thue

Secqueville-
en-Bessin

RWR

**69th
Bde**

Neuf-Mer

Lasson

**62d A/T RA
3rd A/T RCA**

13th RCA

Bray

Rosel

la Bergerie
Farm

**CHO
mortars**

**12th
RCA**

**7 Bde
HQ**

Je Ht. de
Bretteville

CSR

Brouay

Putot-en-
Bessin

le Hamel

Bretteville
l'Orgueilleuse

D Coy

A Coy

Cardonville
Farm

RRR

**B
Coy**

Rots

**25th
PGR**

**2/902
PGLR**

la
Villeneuve

le Bourg

26th PGR

C Coy

**Panzer
Lehr
HQ**

Norrey-en-
Bessin

Mue

**12th SS
Division**

le Mesnil-
Patry

St. Manvieu

Marcelet

**Panzer
Lehr
Division**

1/902 PGLR

la Mare

Airfield

Cheux

Allied Forces

CHO - Cameron Highlanders of Ottawa; **CSR** – Canadian Scottish Regiment; **RRR** – Regina Rifle Regiment; **RWR** – Royal
Winnipeg Rifles

German Forces

25th PGR, 26th PGR – 25th & 26th Panzer Grenadier Regiments, 12th SS Division

1/901st PGLR, 2/901st PGLR – 1st & 2nd Battalions, Panzer Grenadier Lehr Regiment, Panzer Lehr Division

quet area, and with 21st Panzer already operating north and east of Caen, it concluded: "The main weight of armour is being directed, although by no means fully committed yet, to the retention of Caen and the recapture of the Caen-Bayeux lateral."[7] The latter, of course, was not strictly true: the Germans had much grander ambitions for the attacks west of Caen than simply clearing the road. Canadian intelligence also believed that the Germans had not yet shown their full hand: the Hitler Youth still had Tigers to commit to the attack.[8]

The events of 8 June forced 7th Brigade to consolidate its infantry positions to make the fortress more secure, although this exposed its supporting artillery. The Can Scots company and the squadron from the 1st Hussars guarding the brigade's northeastern flank along the Mue River at Cairon, and the Can Scots' carrier platoon screening the artillery at Bray, had all been withdrawn for the counterattack on Putot late in the day. D Company of the Reginas also abandoned its position in the Mue valley near la Villeneuve, shifting to the farm at Cardonville between Putot and Norrey in relief of the Winnipegs' carrier platoon. This resulted in the virtual abandonment of Canadian presence in and along the western edge of the Mue River valley.

Cardonville farm secured the southwestern entrance into Bretteville, guarded the back of Norrey, and blocked the route north for the second company of 1st Battalion, 26th PGR, which was dug in just south of the railway tracks around its own—somewhat smaller—farm compound. The task of defending Cardonville was about as much as D Company could handle. Half of its strength had been lost just getting ashore two days earlier, and reinforcements brought it only up to around eighty all ranks. Even its commander, Captain Gordon Brown, was new to the job. Brown, previously the battalion transport officer, assumed command as D Company marched from la Villeneuve to Cardonville. "Having suddenly been thrust into the role of company commander," Brown recalled, "I was uncertain and very apprehensive."[9]

D Company's new position was a large enclosure roughly the size of a football field, surrounded by stone walls that were ten feet high and two feet thick. The Caen-Bayeux rail line lay just a few yards from the farm's southern wall, and a local road linking Le Haut de Bretteville to the north with both Norrey and le Mesnil-Patry to the south ran along its eastern face, over a level rail crossing. The main road connecting Bretteville and Norrey was about 500 meters east of the farm. Apart from the slightly raised rail bed and a gentle rise to the south, the fields around the farm were open and flat. The eastern part of the Cardonville compound centered on a two-story farmhouse, with barns, storage sheds, and an equipment yard clustered around it, and the main gate opening to the road. The western section of the compound—about two-thirds of the enclosed space—was a vegetable garden. About 100 meters north of the farm, on the road to Le Haut de Bretteville, was a rectangular orchard of about half an acre.

The house formed the central keep of Captain Brown's little fortress. From its upper story D Company's Bren gunners could cover most of the walls and the railway line east to west, but the view to the south was limited because of the roof. Brown put two of his platoons, perhaps sixty men, along the southern section of the wall facing the rail line and set them to cutting loopholes. Headquarters and supporting weapons occupied the farmhouse and covered the eastern wall along the road. Two Vickers machine guns from the Cameron Highlanders were also in the farmhouse or along the east wall.

The western wall at the far end of the garden and the northern wall facing Bretteville were left ungarrisoned. The wall was too high to scale easily, and there was no cover on the inside: the garden would be a trap for anyone foolish enough to drop down inside the wall. Two of the Reginas' 6-pounder antitank guns were positioned in the orchard covering the open ground around the farm, and the company carriers were also there under the trees. Lieutenant R. J. Macdonald, the FOO from 13th RCA, parked his Bren carrier in the orchard, just by the road. Presumably Macdonald ran a telephone wire to the second story of the farmhouse, where the observation was better, but it is clear that he stayed with the carrier. The guns, carriers, and FOO were supported by Brown's No. 17 Platoon, composed entirely of recent reinforcements of unknown number, which dug in around the orchard.[10]

The only other change in the Reginas' deployment was a shifting of Captain Jack Treleaven's B Company a little north, so that it now straddled the road east of Bretteville. A Company and the battalion headquarters remained in the center of the village, while Major Tubb's C Company held on in Norrey. The company positions were not as closely linked as Matheson would have liked: 800 meters separated

Cardonville farm from the center of Norrey, and Norrey was a full grid square plus—more than a thousand meters—south of A Company in Bretteville. Only the right flank of B Company and the left flank of C Company seem to have been close enough for mutual support. But the ground in between all of them was well covered by fire. Scattered among the companies was the remainder of the battalion's antitank guns, as were 6-pounders from 3rd Anti-Tank, RCA and Vickers machine guns of the Camerons. Two batteries of 17-pounders from 62nd Anti-Tank RA were deployed in depth behind Bretteville along the eastern flank of the brigade, and it seems—based on anecdotal evidence—that at least two towed 17-pounders were deployed to sweep the ground between Bretteville and Norrey. The forty-eight 105mm guns of 12th and 13th RCA were barely two kilometers north of Bretteville.

The abandonment of positions along the Mue River valley left the two Canadian field artillery regiments deployed around Bray fully exposed. For the moment they were left to defend themselves, but help was on the way. On 8 June Brigadier Todd recalled all the Centaur SPs of 2nd Royal Marine Assault Squadron to Canadian command for deployment around the gun area at Bray. Only about ten Centaurs, the survivors from five 2nd RMAS batteries, had stayed with 3rd Canadian Division after D-Day to fulfill their countermortar role around the Canadian gun concentrations. Three other batteries, X, Y, and Z, had been sent off to support the Royal Marines fighting in the coastal strip between Juno and Sword Beaches. These missing Centaur batteries were still at full strength, and their twelve 95mm guns were sorely needed. It helped, given the fluid nature of the flank along the Mue, that the Centaurs had fully enclosed tank turrets, making them less vulnerable to the mortars, airburst 88mm shells, and prowling infantry that increasingly characterized the eastern perimeter of gun area "Nora."[11]

Canadian firepower was further enhanced on 8 June by the arrival of 79th Medium Regiment, RA, with its sixteen 4.5-inch guns. Its landing, too, was delayed by bad weather, and the first medium guns did not start coming ashore until C Troop landed at Courseulles at 0800 hours on 8 June. The guns of C troop immediately went into action at Banville. The rest of the regiment landed in midafternoon. The 79th Medium could not assume its designated position as part of 14th Field

Group, RCA in gun area "Dorothy," west of Authie, because that was
now held by 12th SS. With the rest of 14th Field Group, RCA, in a
tight—and vulnerable—gun position near Basly, the British 4.5-inch
regiment finally settled in the middle of the Canadian front around
Thaon. By 1750 hours on 8 June the whole medium regiment was firing, and the effects were soon being felt—especially by the forward
companies of 26th PGR around Norrey.[12]

With the arrival of the antitank regiments, the landing of 79th Regiment, and the recall of the Centaurs by 8 June, 3rd Canadian Division
was close to assembling all the firepower assigned to it by Overlord
planners. Unfortunately, weather in the Channel continued to delay
the arrival of the final components of the division's artillery. In the end,
both 6th and 191st RA were so badly delayed that they missed all these
initial battles. These 25-pounder towed regiments completed landing
only on 10 June and did not fire their first targets until the next day.[13]
Third Canadian Division therefore fought the panzers from 7 to 10
June with only two-thirds of its assigned field artillery. The Germans,
however, certainly thought they had enough.

The concentration of tanks to the east of the Mue was watched with
interest on 8 June by Lieutenant Colonel Matheson and his men, and
B Company's FOO, Lieutenant O'Brennan, called down fire on them
during the day. So what was coming was hardly a surprise.

The 12th SS plan for the attack on Bretteville late on 8 June combined haste and arrogance in equal measure. An armored thrust would
attack just at dusk from the 25th PGR's positions in the Mue River
valley, westward along the Caen-Bayeux highway directly into Bretteville. This part was built around 1st and 4th Companies of the 12th SS
Panzer Regiment's 1st Panzer Battalion: Panther tanks. Historians cannot agree on just how many Panthers were committed to the assault.
The 12th SS history claims that only two companies were involved:
their full operational strength was twenty tanks each, so perhaps forty
in all. Because the division had not yet received its full complement of
Panthers, it is possible that the companies were not up to full strength.
However, the figure of about forty Panthers is confirmed by Canadian
evidence. Lieutenant Colonel Matheson counted twenty-two around
his battalion headquarters that night, while Captain Gordon Brown at
Cardonville farm counted twenty passing his position. There was prob-

Meyer, Witt, and Max Wunsche, commander 12th SS Panzer Regiment, Abbey d'Ardennes, probably 8 June 1944 (before Wunsche was wounded in the head). (Bundesarchive Bild 147-I-989-099-06)

ably some overlap in the Canadian counting. But either way there were a lot of Panthers committed to an attack on one Canadian battalion.

The Panthers were not alone. Their attack was coordinated and led by Kurt Meyer, commander of 25th PGR, and it would have infantry and artillery support. Meyer secured a battery of self-propelled 105mm "Wespe" guns but was unable to draw infantry from his own regiment. The battalion commanders of 25th PGR were all in a grim mood by 8 June and, according to Howard Margolian, "were not sanguine about the attack's prospects."[14] It was all they could do to hold the front; pulling troops away to support an attack to the west was unthinkable. Meyer was forced to assign a company of motorcycle infantry from the division reconnaissance regiment to work directly with the Panthers. In fact, the Kampfgruppe would be led personally by Standartenführer Meyer on a motorcycle. If all went well, the Grenadiers of Mohnke's 1st Battalion, 26th PGR, deployed in a circle around the perimeter of Norrey, would support the attack by rising from their trenches and sweeping into the Canadian-held villages. As it turned out, support from 26th PGR was more of an expectation than an order. Meyer was going to bounce the Canadians out of Bretteville and Norrey with shock, and he expected Mohnke's regiment to join in.

In his postwar memoir, *Grenadiers,* Kurt Meyer described the attack of his Kampfgruppe as something from Wagner's "Ride of the Valkyries." As it assembled west of Franqueville, Meyer went from tank to tank, "calling out to the boys" as they clambered aboard the Panthers. A year earlier, during training in Belgium, he had promised these reconnaissance troops (now commanded by his former adjutant, Captain von Buttner) that he would lead them into their first battle. Meyer now came clean on his promise, riding in a motorcycle sidecar driven by his old and trusted driver, Helmut Belke. One of the Panther companies was led by Hans Pfieffer, Hitler's former adjutant, while the whole Panther force was commanded by Max Wunsche, the handsome commander of 12th SS Panzer Regiment and something of a poster child for the Waffen SS. The mood was one of anxious excitement.

Around 2200 hours Meyer's Kampfgruppe crossed the bridge over the Mue at la Villeneuve, which the Reginas had not destroyed, and then shook out into a rough wedge shape. The spearhead was formed by 4th Company of 12th SS PR, with two Panthers on the road (one of them Pfeiffer's) and platoons on either side. Panthers of 1st Company deployed south of the road, into the space between Bretteville and Norrey. Immediately behind the tanks came Meyer on his motorcycle along with his FOO, supported by a small group of motorcycle-mounted infantry. The rest of 15th Company of the reconnaissance battalion followed 100 meters back on their motorcycles. Meyer thought of the attack as Wagnerian, but a modern audience would see it as more of a scene from a *Mad Max* movie, a wild charge of men and machines designed primarily to shock and overrun. "This is the way we fought in the East," Meyer wrote in his memoirs, "but will these surprise tactics achieve the same for us here?"[15]

The short answer was no.

The approach to Bretteville from the east along the Caen-Bayeux highway (now the D83c) is screened from the village by a small rise of open field about 300 meters away. Meyer's Kampfgruppe was largely secure from direct fire until it crested that hill, and then it was into

Bretteville and Norrey, July 1944. The high ground east of Bretteville, which the panzer attack of 8 June crested before encountering intense Canadian fire, shows clearly in the curve of the fields. A close look at the ground immediately south of the rail line about halfway between the station at the right edge of the photo reveals the results of Lieutenant Henry's work the next day: dead Panthers. (LCMSDS)

open ground totally devoid of cover: an ideal killing ground for Canadian fire. The Canadians spotted Meyer's Kampfgruppe on the move shortly before 2200 hours and deployed a section of Bren carriers on the south side of the road and two machine guns from the Camerons on the north side—on the high ground—in an attempt to disrupt the attack.[16] These units were overrun before they had time to dig in. But once the attack started down the open slope into Bretteville, it came under "murderous fire" from Canadian antitank guns and small arms.

One of the first Panthers hit and to explode in flames was Pfeiffer's. "We were surprised by the violent anti-tank fire," Lieutenant Fuss, an infantry platoon commander with the SS reconnaissance unit, observed shortly afterward. "A great number of anti-tank guns seemed to be in positions along the edge of town. Canadian infantry . . . peppered the mounted Grenadiers with wild rifle fire."[17] The antitank fire came from the 6-pounders of 94th Battery, 3rd Anti-Tank, RCA. G and K Troops (a total of eight guns) of the regiment were guarding the eastern flank of Bretteville in support of B Company.[18] K Troop was almost immediately overrun, losing most of its personnel, but G Troop fired effectively. Sergeant Herman Dumas manhandled his 6-pounder along a hedgerow, striking at least four Panthers at short range with the new discarding sabot round. The effort earned him a Military Medal. Meanwhile, Bombardier Cyril Askin stuck to his disabled gun when the crew abandoned it to fight as infantry. Askin got it working again and hit three more Panthers. He too was nominated for a Military Medal but was killed in action before it could be awarded. In the end, 3rd Anti-Tank, RCA claimed at least seven Panthers on the eastern edge of Bretteville. The claim was inflated, but it did kill several.[19] Sergeant T. V. Wood of the Reginas' 11 Platoon saw three Panthers hit and their crews bail out.[20]

As for the "wild rifle fire," it came largely from B Company, which was struck all along its front by the wave of tanks and motorcycles. The comment reflected the fact that Canadian infantry used their weapons, and very effectively. Contrary to the widely held belief fostered by S. L. A. Marshall's flawed research on the US Army, that Allied infantry seldom fired directly at the enemy, Canadian infantry were noted for heavy, aimed rifle fire.[21] It helped that the Lee Enfield Mk IV rifle was about as "semiautomatic" as a bolt-action could be. If the soldier's

A rare shot of a 6-pounder of 3rd Anti-Tank Regiment, RCA, deployed for action. The low profile of the gun shows clearly in this shot.
(LAC 340831 IB)

hand was big enough, it need never leave the stock: the bolt could be flicked up with the index finger and then slid home with the thumb. The Reginas also had excellent support from Vickers machine guns of the Camerons and widespread use of captured German automatic weapons.

It speaks well of the training and professionalism of these Canadian infantry that they stood to and did their job. Later that night, when things were close to unraveling, Brigadier Foster admonished his infantry battalions to "deal with the thin skins and let the hard shells go through to where we can deal with them."[22] He need not have bothered. As the initial wave of Kampfgruppe Meyer's attack hit them, the men of Captain Treleaven's B Company coolly allowed the tanks to roll past and then shot down the Grenadiers. Panthers rolled right over the top of Lieutenant J. McNinch's platoon, including one over his own slit trench, then his men rose and continued firing. "Nearly everyone had a German automatic weapon," he recalled.[23] Small arms fire, bursting mortar rounds, and artillery fire soon stripped the infantry from the back of Meyer's tanks and off their motorcycles, and drove the survivors to ground. Prearranged SOS barrages were soon falling all around the Reginas' companies.[24]

According to Meyer's memoir, he managed to get the attack moving again after it faltered, but at great cost: "Tears are running down my face, the old comrades become fewer and fewer." While Pfeiffer escaped his burning Panther, Meyer found von Buttner mortally wounded in the ditch, and moments later his driver Belke was killed beside him. It took about an hour to overwhelm B Company and the eastern defenses of Bretteville. Meanwhile, Meyer's supporting battery of 105mm Wespe SPs established themselves on the eastern outskirts of Bretteville, north of the Caen-Bayeux highway. Rallying his troops from his motorcycle, Meyer ordered tanks and infantry into the village. There, Meyer claims, they also overran the Reginas' headquarters. The Reginas' war diary simply records that by 2315 hours "3 Tigers" were prowling around it, and by 0030 hours it was "under attack." "The surprise attack is successful," Meyer trumpeted in his memoirs, but he was wrong. In fact, by this stage he was out of the battle. The gas tank on his motorcycle was shot through, spraying him with fuel, which then ignited—"burning like a torch." Only quick action by several Grenadiers pulled him clear and doused the flames.

Meanwhile, checked by the intensity and accuracy of the antitank fire, Wunsche ordered the Panthers of his 1st Company to swing south of Bretteville and attack the village from the area of Cardonville farm. Some of his tanks pushed down the rail line between Norrey and Bretteville, but it seems that most took the long route to Cardonville around the southern tip of Norrey. Three Panthers moving between the two villages were struck almost immediately by antitank fire. One burst into flame, illuminating the battlefield. Another took a round straight through the turret, badly wounding the loader and damaging the turret's electrical system. The third Panther was hit but also

Three-inch mortar of the Regina Rifles, still smoking from its latest round, Bretteville, 9 June 1944. Left to right (foreground): Ben Wilson, Sergeant Tom Holt, and George Cooper; left to right (background): Win Powell, "Swede" Renwick, and Dan Corturient. (LAC PA-128794)

remained operational: the two surviving Panthers withdrew to make repairs. Other Panthers slipping between Bretteville and Norrey were struck, but not destroyed.[25]

The Reginas' war diary claims that two further Panthers were destroyed or disabled by projectile, infantry antitank (PIAT) bombs fired by Company Sergeant Major Basil Currie near the regimental aid post and mortar positions southwest of Bretteville during the night. Irwin

Wood, who shared Currie's slit trench, later confirmed that the company sergeant major fired at the two nearest Panthers (about fifty yards away) with their PIAT. "Basil opened fire, firing as fast as I could slap the bombs on," Wood recalled. "He bounced bombs off both these tanks and with our last bomb he crippled the nearest tank." Armed only with pistols and hand grenades, Currie and Wood then watched in frustration as another Panther came up, and the crews dismounted to attach cables to the disabled tank and towed it away. Currie was later seriously wounded while bringing more PIAT bombs and a Bren gun back to their trench. He was awarded the Military Medal for his efforts. Wood stayed on and early the next morning watched a nearby 3rd Anti-Tank Regiment 6-pounder destroy a Panther near the road to Norrey.[26]

The Panthers that took the long route west, around Norrey, fared better, but only just. John Swityk counted six tanks roll past his anti-tank guns at the southeast corner of Norrey, one of which drove over his slit trench. With the 6-pounders pointed south, and the tanks virtually within the gun position, none of the Panthers were engaged before they disappeared into the night.[27] This group, which Gordon Brown counted off as about twenty, eventually crossed the rail line over the level crossing at Cardonville farm.

The notion that Meyer's surprise attack "was successful" would have come as news to the Reginas. Only a handful of German infantry made it into Bretteville, and the Canadians hunted them. The first Panther audacious enough to enter the village around midnight was destroyed by infantry. The story is by now a familiar one (to Canadians at least). It was hit by a PIAT bomb fired by Rifleman Joe LaPointe, a sentry at the gates to the château that housed Matheson's battalion headquarters. The PIAT was a heavy, ungainly weapon that used a spring and a 12-gauge shotgun shell to fire a 2.5-pound shaped charge about 100 meters. LaPointe fired from very close range, but his first PIAT bomb detonated without effect. The Panther then rolled a few more yards until it hit a string of grenades pulled across the road that broke the right track. At that moment LaPointe fired his second PIAT round and missed. LaPointe calmly reloaded again and hit the Panther with a killing shot. The final indignity for the Panther came when the tank behind it fired and hit it in the turret, starting a huge fire. LaPointe's

One of the iconic photos of the Normandy campaign: the Panther of 1st Company, 12th SS Panzer Regiment, destroyed by Rifleman LaPointe in front of the Regina Rifles headquarters, Bretteville, on the night of 8–9 June 1944. (LAC PA-130149)

Panther, the first destroyed by infantry in Normandy, is immortalized in one of the iconic photos of the whole campaign—although usually without context. It seems that one of Meyer's supporting SPs, an antiaircraft gun built on the chassis of a Czech T-38 tank, also entered the village, since the Reginas recorded the destruction of one "Czech" tank, and subsequent photos confirm it.

There is a final act to the story of LaPointe's Panther. Captain Tom Greenlees, the 13th RCA's survey officer, was crouching behind the stone wall at the entrance to the Reginas' headquarters when the Panther arrived and watched action unfold. "The crew bailed out," Greenlees recalls, "and I somewhat ineffectively engaged the fleeing figures with a Sten gun borrowed from my survey crew beforehand."[28] The Reginas' fire on the escaping Panther crewmen was more deadly. The tank's ammunition exploded and burned all night. Greenlees was therefore stunned the next morning when one fire-blackened crewman stuck his head out of the tank, "more dead than alive," and was promptly shot by a rifleman. For Greenlees it was a stark introduction to the tragedy of war.

The chaos, the fires, the parachute flares, the crash of explosions, and the rattle of small arms fire were vividly remembered by friend and foe alike. The Germans were particularly impressed with the Canadians' magnesium parachute flares that lit up the battlefield, made their tanks easy targets, and blinded tank crews.[29] Many of these were sent up by Rifleman Frank Wolfe, who stuck to his 2-inch mortar despite heavy fire. The crew of the nearby 6-pounder credited Wolfe's flares with allowing them to fire effectively.[30] The men of D Company, for the moment snug in their fortresslike compound at Cardonville, watched the pyrotechnics of the battle with interest. But those inside Bretteville had little time to take in the light show. Gunner Bill Milner, part of the security section of 13th RCA deployed with Lieutenant Colonel Clifford at the Reginas' headquarters, remembered a night punctuated by the ripping sound of armor-piercing rounds from Panthers firing petulantly over the stone wall against which he was sheltering. At one point Milner, still toting his Thompson submachine gun, had a chance to shoot some of the SS infantry to penetrate the village. Standing in an alleyway with his back pressed hard against a building and the Thompson clutched to his chest, Milner watched as an MG 42 section raced past him in the darkness and clambered over the stone wall at the end of the lane. Just as the last boot disappeared, Lieutenant Colonel Clifford swept around the corner and fired a few harmless shots from his revolver. Catching a glimpse of Gunner Milner and his Thompson, Clifford fired him a cold stare and a sharp "See me in the morning!" then disappeared into the night to find more Germans. A mild rebuke about duty and there "being a war on" followed in the early hours of 9 June for Milner.[31]

Matheson later recalled that the fighting in Bretteville was chaotic. Contact with all his companies was lost, "and several times the enemy seemed to believe that the resistance had faltered." Indeed, Meyer thought so, and he was clearly not alone. The SS eventually brought troops into the village in trucks, one of which was hit by a PIAT bomb in the street near Matheson's headquarters. At least one section of German infantry entered the church, overlooking the Reginas' headquarters, and occupied the bell tower: they were still there the next day and eventually escaped. Matheson himself shot a German off his motorcycle on the street. The most bizarre incident was probably the fate of the German staff officer who drove into Bretteville in his Kubelwagon, stopped in front of the Reginas' headquarters, and dismounted to have a look around. Rifleman LaPointe hit him square in the chest with a PIAT bomb. According to an unpublished postwar history of the Reginas, the officer "disappeared."[32]

"Panzer" Meyer's attack late on 8 June spilled over to the gun area around Bray. All night 12th and 13th RCA "stood to" and threw out a defensive perimeter equipped with small arms, Brens, and PIATs. "Tank Alert" was signaled at 0545 hours, and the No. 1 gun of Able Troop, 22nd Battery, 13th RCA, engaged a tank over open sights, with no apparent effect.[33] The intelligence log of 13th RCA records that 78th Battery fired forty-four rounds of M67 antitank ammunition that night. Given that the troop of Wespe 105mm SPs supporting Meyer's attack deployed north of the Caen-Bayeux highway barely a kilometer from the two Canadian self-propelled regiments at Bray, it is possible that the Canadian M7s fired on their German counterparts—if so, it was a unique situation indeed. "Each time we switched back to the tanks in front of us," the history of 12th RCA recounts, "the range would be shorter and the appeals of the FOOs more desperate. When we finally stopped them the range was just over 1,600 yards—much too close, especially when we were firing 8,000 yards in the opposite direction!"[34]

Meanwhile, 12th RCA, deployed in the open in front of 13th RCA, received a number of Reginas in their position, gave them ammunition, and watched them march back into the battle. The same regiment recounts firing an "Uncle" (division) target "directly in front of us"—which would have included the 13th, 14th, and 19th RCA. Uncle and Victor (all field guns in I British Corps, roughly 216) targets were engaged throughout 9 June on an arc of 180 degrees, from the front of 3rd British Infantry Division north of Caen to that of 50th Division to the west. James Moffat, a sergeant with 22nd Battery of 13th RCA, recalled many years later that that night they got an order to "keep firing until all your ammunition is gone!" "We could really fire," Moffat remembered, eight to ten rounds a minute, "and I have no eyelashes even today to prove it." A few weeks later, when the Reginas marched past the 13th RCA, a sergeant stepped over and kissed the barrel of Moffat's 105mm gun.[35]

Requests for fire support from FOOs with the Regina companies were constantly interrupted when the telephone lines forward were cut by tanks and shell fire. Lieutenant R. J. Macdonald, the FOO at Cardonville farm, lost his line at 2000 hours on 8 June, even before the attack started, and a line crew was immediately sent out to reconnect him.[36] As subsequent events reveal, they never did.

Macdonald and the men of Gordon Brown's D Company at Cardonville farm would soon need artillery support. The tanks that took the long route in their approach to Bretteville by passing south of Norrey rolled by the gate of Cardonville farm in the early hours of 9 June. Brown and his men watched silently (and almost certainly felt) as the Panthers passed, their long barrels clear against the fires and flares of the battle to the east. Once north of Cardonville, the Panthers fired into Bretteville as they waited for infantry from the second company of 1st Battalion, 26th PGR, to join them in the final assault on the Canadian position. So, too, did Meyer, who opined in his memoirs, "But where is 26th Regiment's infantry?"[37]

This question has never been answered, but two things are clear. The first is that the positions of 26th PGR were fired on through the night by Anglo-Canadian artillery, including the 79th Medium Regiment, RA. More important, it seems that the orders (or requests) never got through, probably because the 26th Regiment's commanding officer, Wilhelm Mohnke, was busy with other business on the night of 8 June. That evening Mohnke's primary focus was securing the western flank of his regiment in the aftermath of the British and Canadian attacks around Putot and Brouay. In the process he became totally distracted by efforts to ensure that his regiment took no prisoners.

It appears that Mohnke was diverted from his command role by an uncontrolled urge to murder prisoners on the night of 8–9 June. After learning that Siebken, commander of his 2nd Battalion, had dispatched a column of forty Canadians to the rear, Mohnke telephoned the battalion HQ and ordered Siebken to take no more prisoners. While Siebken phoned division HQ to see if this was a specific order, Mohnke set off to find the column of POWs. Around 2100 hours, about the time Mohnke ought to have been coordinating with Meyer for the attack on Bretteville and Norrey, Mohnke intercepted the prisoners. Springing from his staff car, he engaged the SS sergeant in charge of the escort in an agitated conversation. Witnesses later claimed that the conversation degenerated into a tirade by Mohnke, and that he threatened to shoot the sergeant. As Margolian wrote, the confrontation ended in angry gestures and "a torrent of orders to the hapless NCO."[38]

The column of Canadian POWs, mostly Winnipegs, was marched a little farther south, to a road junction a kilometer northeast of Fontenay-le-Pesnel. There they were led into a field and ordered to sit in three tightly bunched rows. It was clear what was about to happen, and several German speakers among the Canadians overheard the orders. When a half-track from a nearby armored column arrived, machine pistols and magazines were distributed to the escort, and the group approached the huddled prisoners. They stopped about thirty yards away but made no attempt to surround the Canadians. One of their executioners then said coldly, in good English, "Now you die!" and the SS opened fire. Only those in the rear had any chance: they broke and ran. Five men escaped, and although all five were recaptured soon afterward, they lived to tell the tale. According to Margolian, Mohnke was busy the rest of the night with ensuring that no more prisoners were taken, and that those who had been were shot. He was particularly incensed when he learned that evening of the incident in which the Panzer Lehr officer was used as a human shield by the Inns of Court Regiment earlier in the day. When he visited Siebken's headquarters during the night, Mohnke discovered that three Canadians were being held there. He insisted that they be shot: they were the next day.[39]

Mohnke's irrational and murderous behavior probably accounts for the failure of 1st Battalion, 26th PGR, to support Meyer's attack into Bretteville on the night of 8–9 June. It seems, however, that Siebken's battalion was ready to do its part, threatening the Can Scots at Putot in the early hours of 9 June. SOS fire was brought down on the "massing" troops, and nothing more was heard from that flank during the night.

Meanwhile, both Major Tubbs in Norrey and Captain Brown at Cardonville expected the infantry forces in front of them to move during the hours of darkness. After the Panthers rolled by Cardonville farm, then stopped and fired petulantly into Bretteville, Brown was uncertain of what to do. His first instinct was to bring fire down on the tanks, so he crawled out through the hole in the compound's north wall to find his FOO. He found Lieutenant Macdonald in the orchard, sitting upright in his Bren carrier, sound asleep. In what must be one of the most remarkable statements recorded in the midst of battle, Brown admonished Macdonald: "For God's sake stay awake. We're being attacked by tanks." "Sorry Sir," Macdonald replied, "I'm just so bloody tired." MacDonald got on the radio and tried to connect with 13th RCA. Brown moved on to find the sergeant in charge of the antitank gun section in the orchard and ordered him to redeploy the guns and engage the Panthers.[40]

Having done what he could to put effective fire onto the Panthers, Brown crawled back inside the compound, contacted Major Stu Tubb in Norrey by radio, and asked for advice. "Well, there's not much we CAN do," Tubb replied calmly. "We're just sitting here waiting for the infantry to attack us and that may be at any time, I suspect."[41] Tubb's platoon on the eastern edge of Norrey had been overrun by Panthers as they passed around the village, without serious losses, but his position had not yet come under attack. Tubb told Brown to sit still and wait for events to unfold. Brown thought it odd that the Germans would attack at night with tanks alone, without infantry support. He was not alone.

D Company watched the fireworks over and around Bretteville in nervous anticipation. Its situation grew more perilous around 0200 hours when six Panthers, returning from shelling Bretteville, took shelter in the orchard north of the farm where 17 Platoon and Brown's 6-pounders were dug in. Brown only became aware of this when he crawled out again into the orchard to check on the platoon and to find out why his antitank guns had not fired. Moving slowly on his hands and knees into almost total blackness, he eventually found the sergeant in charge of the antitank guns sheltering in the middle of the orchard. "When I demanded to know what had happened, and what he proposed to do about the attacking tanks, he said: 'What, Sir, are we going to do about the six tanks that now surround this orchard?'" Brown, sputtering, asked, "What tanks?" and the sergeant explained that there was now a Panther at each corner of the orchard and two along the sides. As Brown peered through the darkness, he soon made

Cardonville farm, photographed a month after the battle. Bretteville lies in the top left of the photo, Norrey on the right: Putot is just out of the frame at the bottom left. The farm compound lies just to the left of the rail line, with the orchard a hundred yards farther north. The German farm on the south side of the rail line shows clearly. (LCMSDS)

out the shapes; later he recalled, "In the silence I could hear the quiet idle of their motors."[42]

Brown and the sergeant now concocted a scheme to have two or three soldiers attack each tank, using "sticky grenades" on the turrets. "O.K. Sir, I'll do my best," the sergeant replied, and Brown made his way back to the farm. "Just as I reached the door, I heard the unmistakable chatter of a Sten gun," Brown remembered. "Someone had fired at the tanks in the orchard."

It seems that one or more of the tank commanders dismounted, prompting someone in 17 Platoon to shoot. At that point all hell broke loose in the orchard. "The tanks were firing wildly," Brown recalled, "and tracer bullets darted everywhere." In the midst of this the barn holding D Company's ammunition supply caught fire. Most of it was saved, but not the men or equipment in the orchard. As Brown observed, there was nothing they could do. "The tanks set all the vehicles on fire and were busy mopping up the slit trenches, running over weapons and crushing everyone and everything in their path." The last recorded messages from Lieutenant Macdonald were logged by 13th RCA at 0445 hours and 0450 hours, passed via 78th Battery, announcing that he was surrounded by tanks and needed "armour immediately." The Reginas echoed that appeal fifteen minutes later. "Div advised that enemy tks are cruising freely through our fwd positions," the radio log recorded laconically, "& and we expect a rather sticky time."[43]

Once the Panthers were finished in the orchard, they turned on the Cardonville farm compound. D Company stood its ground. When one Panther smashed the main gate and poked its nose in, the Reginas pelted it with small arms fire and stood ready with antitank grenades and mines. The Panther withdrew. For the next hour or so the angry cats prowled the perimeter of the compound, lashing out with the occasional blast of gunfire and stitching the inside, the walls, and the farmhouse with machine gun fire. Brown and his men just hoped the tanks would go away. "We adopted an almost passive strategy," he recalled, trying to ignore the tanks "mostly because we couldn't do anything about them anyway."[44] It seems that D Company had lost its PIAT guns coming ashore, too. But Brown could not prevent casualties from mounting. By the time the tanks rolled away at about first light, over the rail line and into the German positions, D Company and its supporting Camerons were down to under fifty men. Out of contact, unaware if their battalion still existed, Brown concentrated his remaining men in the farmhouse and the small stone paddock between it and the south wall. They had lots of ammunition and a stockpile of captured enemy weapons. But there seemed no way out. "Everyone realized . . . we were probably facing a fight to the finish."[45]

As dawn broke, the Panthers abandoned the battlefield and made their way back across the Mue River. Then the Germans compounded their folly by finally launching the infantry of Mohnke's 1st Battalion. The weight of this assault fell on what remained of Gordon Brown's D Company at Cardonville farm. Given the size of 12th SS's reinforced infantry companies, the remnants of D Company were now outnumbered about four to one. It seems that the Germans believed the Panthers had destroyed the garrison at Cardonville, since the initial attack across the rail line came in good order at a casual pace as if on exercise.[46] "It made no sense," Brown observed after the war. "If the infantry had not supported their tanks under the cover of darkness, who would launch an attack in broad daylight . . . without artillery or tank support?" The Reginas turned every automatic weapon they had on the Hitler Youth as they scrambled over the rail line, cutting them down in swaths. Sickened by the sight, Brown went into the farmhouse to consult with his second in command, Dick Roberts, and to see if his signaler had any luck connecting with Matheson at battalion HQ. "We're in serious trouble," Roberts told Brown. The SS were infiltrating around the compound, and they would soon be surrounded. "Hope we get through to the artillery soon," Roberts commented.

D Company's desperate defense of the Cardonville farm has all the hallmarks of a Hollywood drama, and had it happened to an American unit, Steven Spielberg would have made a movie about it. No matter how many of the SS the Reginas shot, more appeared to take their place. Germans could be seen "in hundreds," which was about right given the strength of companies in 12th SS. Around D Company's small perimeter, men seized every opportunity—and weapon—to maximize their firepower. One machine gunner from the Camerons, whose friend had been killed, simply picked up his Vickers tripod and all, moved it outside onto the road, and hosed Germans out of a nearby tree. When the gun jammed, he calmly picked it up and brought it back into the farm. Men nearby were struck down, but the Cameron escaped unscathed.

Just when it looked like things could not get much worse, German artillery or mortar fire began to land in the compound and on the roof of the farmhouse. When a shell blasted open the roof, Brown and Roberts were finally able to see clearly the source of their trouble: a smaller farm compound just south of the rail line, which was the German strongpoint. What was really needed now was an artillery barrage on the farm and the rail line.

Brown had just figured all this out when the next assault came in. "They're closing in on us now!" Company Sergeant Major Jacobs shouted. "We're in real trouble. They'll soon be throwing grenades over the wall." With many of the Reginas out of their slit trenches firing through loopholes in the wall, a shower of grenades inside the perimeter posed a real danger. Just then the call went out, "Hand grenades coming over the wall. Get into your trenches!" Jacobs quickly devised a warning system to tell the men when to take shelter and when to stand and fire: it worked, and the grenades soon stopped.

Hitler Youth in their mottled camouflage uniforms lay dead and dying all around the compound, and in rows along the railway and the south wall, but still the teenage soldiers of 12th SS came. Brown was soon down to "45 men and two officers," but they all had machine guns "of one sort or another (several German)."[47] When things looked darkest and while Brown surveyed the growing assembly of dead and dying in the farmhouse, his signaler suddenly shouted, "Good God, sir, it's Battalion headquarters!" Brown grabbed the headset and microphone and demanded to speak to "Big Sunray." "Sir, we can't hold out much longer," he told Lieutenant Colonel Matheson. "We need artillery and tank support." Matheson called Clifford, commander of 13th RCA, to the radio. "Where's your FOO?" Clifford barked. "I'm afraid he's been killed, we haven't been able to get into the orchard," Brown replied. "But I think everyone there is dead." Clifford asked how long D Company could last. Brown asked Dick Roberts and then reported, "About 20 minutes." When Brown passed the grid references for the artillery fire he wanted to Clifford, the gunner balked. "Brown, that's too close to your position. You sure you want it that way? Some rounds

The Canadian army did not send a photographer forward to Cardonville farm until the day after its heroic defense by the Reginas' D Company. Here Rifleman Daniel E. Corturient, formerly of the Regina Rifles' support company, stands in his slit trench behind the wall at Cardonville farm, 10 June 1944. (LAC PA-131423)

might hit your forward position." "We'll have to take that chance, sir," was Brown's cool response. Clifford warned Brown he only had about two minutes to take shelter before the first rounds fell. Roberts and Jacobs made a hasty trip around the tiny perimeter passing the warning. Within two minutes, the first rounds thundered in.

"God Almighty it was marvellous," Brown recalled. The first round landed squarely in the farm on the south side of the rail line, and then hundreds of shells exploded between the southern wall of Cardonville and the enemy positions. "I was never so pleased with anything," Brown said. "It was a work of art." Walter Keith, who joined 16 Platoon of D Company in October 1944, remembers that the Reginas were still talking about how that barrage creased the top of the farm compound wall on its way to the enemy.[48] The cheering of the men could be heard—barely—above the din: the sound was thunderous. The effect was devastating. The grain field back as far as the German-held farm smoldered, bodies lay strewn about, and the area looked like it had been plowed. Brown concluded, "The Germans had been thoroughly shaken by the artillery fire and now knew we had a lot of support." That said, he was not certain they had given up and asked for reinforcements and a few tanks: both were soon on the move. D Company, now down to thirty-seven all ranks, began to move its wounded back down the line.

The Germans did not come back that morning, although sniping and mortar fire remained a nuisance. The only event that marked the morning was almost inexplicable: a platoon of Germans came marching along the rail line from Putot, as if on parade. They were dispersed—and some killed and wounded—by a quick stonk of mortar rounds. No one could ever imagine how or why a platoon in marching order got onto the battlefield so casually.

Meanwhile, neither Brown nor Roberts wanted to inspect the orchard, where it appeared everyone from 17 Platoon and the antitank detachment lay dead. No one had ventured out there since the battle with the Panthers ended around 0430 hours. In the end, two men were found alive, and they confirmed that most of the rest had died in their trenches, which the tanks systematically raked with machine gun fire. Enough information was gleaned from the action to make five recommendations for awards. Among those killed were the FOO from 13th RCA, Lieutenant Macdonald, and his able, Gunner J. K. Jeffrey, both found in their bullet-riddled Bren carrier. Brown asked the battalion to collect his dead. But clearing the German dead fell to his own men. Days later D Company buried fifty-nine of the enemy in a common grave across the road from the farm gate. Brown recorded their names and units; most were Hitler Youth, and a few were from Panzer Lehr.[49]

For 12th SS it had been a frustrating, indeed futile, night. At least six Panthers were totally destroyed and an unknown number damaged. At one point, some twenty had surrounded the Reginas' HQ, but the Canadians had not panicked. Instead, they relied on their training, their doctrine, and their weapons. It all worked well. "Our

Riflemen Roy Pretty and Bert Caldwell watch Captain Gordon Brown
survey the scene beyond the Cardonville compound, 10 June 1944.
(LAC PA-129042)

confidence in ourselves and our weapons increased," the Reginas' war
diary recorded sometime after the event. "The dreaded Panther tank
was not invincible and could be knocked out by infantry who knew
how to use their weapons."[50] The same could be said of the 6-pounder
with its discarding sabot ammunition: it sliced through the Panther's
armor. Moreover, the Panthers had quit long before they reached the
17-pounders of 62nd Anti-Tank RA or the Fireflys of 2nd Canadian
Armoured Brigade. Only the outer edge of the Canadian defenses had
been tested.

It helped the Canadians enormously that the Panthers advanced
without effective infantry support. Tanks could take ground, but they

could not hold it, nor could they ferret out the Canadians who stalked them with PIAT guns. What Wunsche's Panthers needed was infantry support. One company on foot and motorcycles was not enough, and too few of them survived the Canadians' withering fire. The subsequent infantry assault on Cardonville by 26th PGR without tank support simply compounded the error. As the Canadian official history observed, "The German operations at this stage leave the impression of rather hasty and ineffective improvisation. The attacks were pressed with courage and determination but with no particular tactical skill. . . . The operations seem to have been locally conceived and control even on the divisional level was ineffective."[51] Meyer's Kampfgruppe and 26th PGR in front of Norrey lost 152 men on the night of 8–9 June.[52] The only noteworthy German accomplishment during the night was the occupation of Rots in the Mue valley by 1st Company of 1st Battalion, 26th PGR. This effectively linked 25th and 26th PGRs and put a major German combat unit within a kilometer of the guns deployed around Bray.

Meyer later claimed that as he drove through la Villeneuve and Rots on his way back to Authie, he was shown the site of an apparent murder of Germans by Canadian soldiers. Near a couple of destroyed vehicles lay ten bodies. These were probably the remains of the ill-fated SS patrol ambushed by D Company at la Villeneuve the day before. "They were all shot through the chest or head," Meyer claimed in 1945. Dick Roberts, who commanded the Reginas' 16 Platoon in that action, flatly denied allegations of murder. In the event, Meyer's story, told one way at his trial in 1945 and another in his memoir, is scarcely believable. The same is true of his apparent reaction to the murder of Canadian POWs when he returned to the Abbey d'Ardennes on 9 June. There he was confronted by two doctors from 25th PGR. They had found a group of some twenty Canadians lying in the garden of the abbey, all shot through the head at close range. Meyer testified at his trial that he was "incensed" and demanded to know how it could have happened.[53] Indeed. Had Meyer lingered on the battlefield east of Bretteville on the morning of 9 June, he would have found thirteen more murdered Canadian POWs, most from B Company of the Reginas. All were found lying disarmed, killed by bursts of submachine gun fire to the head and chest at short range (brass casings littered the chests of some of the men). By noon on 9 June, the tally of Canadian POWs murdered by the 12th SS had reached 130.

Canadians lay the blame for what became a "take no prisoners" attitude between themselves and the 12th SS squarely on the Hitler Youth, whose behavior on 7 June at Buron and Authie set the tone. Genuine hatred, and especially mistrust, of the Western Allies had, after all, been a key component of the "easternization" of German formations in the west over the previous six months. It was German soldiers who had been indoctrinated in the belief that the Western Allies took no prisoners. From the Canadian perspective, the murderous behavior of the Hitler Youth on 7 June was entirely unprovoked, and there was nothing in the subsequent behavior of 12th SS to suggest that the atrocities around Authie and Buron were exceptional. Indeed, quite the contrary. And so hatred and mistrust of the Hitler Youth characterized Canadian attitudes toward 12th SS for the balance of the campaign. As Gunner Milner recalled, when dealing with the Hitler Youth, "We had a saying in Normandy, 'Take these guys to the beach and be back in ten minutes!'" How much of that was youthful bravado and how much reality, we will never know.

Even the SS had to concede that the Reginas and their supporting arms had fought superbly on the night of 8–9 June. "The tactic of surprise, using mobile, fast infantry and Panzers even in small, numerically inferior Kampfgruppen, had often been practiced and proven in Russia," Hubert Meyer, the operations officer of 12th SS and the division's historian wrote in his 1994 book. "This tactic, however, had not resulted in the expected success here against a courageous and determined enemy, who was ready for defense and well equipped."[54] When asked about this in 2002, Colonel Clifford commented that the army's training and doctrine worked superbly. The artillery stripped away the enemy infantry or prevented them from moving, leaving their tanks vulnerable. His final conclusion on the night of 8–9 June was less circumspect than that of Hubert Meyer. "The Germans thought we were fucking Russians!" Clifford commented. "They did stupid things and we killed those bastards in large numbers."

9

Norrey, 9–10 June

The enemy seemed to have expected this . . .
Helmut Schuck, 12th SS Pioneer Battalion

ABOUT THE TIME Kurt Meyer led his ill-fated "Ride of the Valkyries" into Bretteville on the evening of 8 June, General Leo Geyr von Schweppenburg finally arrived at Château La Caine, five kilometers north of Thury-Harcourt, to activate Panzer Group West as an operational command. General Frederick Dollman, commander of Seventh Army, now passed total control of the panzer assault on the Allies to Schweppenburg. The commander, Panzer Group West, knew the ground well. Schweppenburg had been stationed in the area in September 1940 preparing for the invasion of England. The plan he now hatched would not have surprised Freddie Morgan and his COSSAC staff: they had envisioned it ten months earlier.

On 9 June 1944 Schweppenburg wanted a two-division panzer thrust down either side of the Mue River valley to the sea: this much had been tried twice already. He understood, however, that this could not be launched immediately, and so he hoped to take 9 June to complete two important preliminary tasks: regroup the divisions and try a third time to clear the start line. Schweppenburg now wanted 12th SS Panzer Division to concentrate east of the Mue, between the river and Caen. This would oblige Mohnke's 26th PGR and its supporting artillery to shift to the 9th Canadian Brigade's front. And he wanted Panzer Lehr to concentrate, as 84th Corps had ordered on 6 June and as had been accomplished on 8 June, on the west bank of the Mue in front of Putot-Norrey-Bretteville and 7th Canadian Brigade. As the historian of 12th SS Division, Craig Luther, concluded, "Such a deployment, Geyr reasoned, would enable the left wing of his Panzer Group to lay its assault across good tank country astride the Mue and the lower reaches of the Seulles, to its mouth at Courseulles." The task of 1st SS Panzer

Corps remained, as indeed it had been since D-Day, to "execute the decisive counterstroke against the Allied beachhead."[1]

Schweppenburg's plan to destroy the Allied landings with a corps-level attack, ordered for sunset on 10 June, was confirmed when he climbed the tower of the Abbey d'Ardennes with Kurt Meyer on the morning of 9 June. The ground dictated what needed to be done. As they surveyed the rolling plains west of Caen, Meyer opined that the next few days would be decisive. Schweppenburg cut him short. "My dear Meyer," the general said coldly, "the war can only now be won through political means."[2] Schweppenburg may well have known that his plans for a major counterattack under the cover of darkness by two powerful panzer divisions were already undone. Rommel had ordered Panzer Lehr to move west and attack toward Bayeux just the evening before, and Bayerlein was moving quickly.

By the time Schweppenburg and Meyer climbed the abbey tower, the last of the 12th SS Division's Panthers had arrived. From their vantage point the two men could see the 3rd Company, 12th SS PR, on the move toward the Mue River, in what Meyer told Schweppenburg was a local counterattack. As they watched the Panthers roll across the open ground west of Authie, Allied fighter-bombers and artillery struck them, confirming Schweppenburg's belief that only nighttime attacks could be successful. No one had told him that the SS were launching another, poorly coordinated assault on a major Canadian position. But because clearing the start line was one of the prerequisites for the corps attack on 10 June, Schweppenburg made no move to stop it.

Farther west, another attempt by 26th PGR to clear the Canadian Scottish Regiment out of Putot had already begun. Around 0900 hours, swarms of SS Panzer Grenadiers—supported by artillery and by tanks firing from hull down positions—struck the Can Scots from the south at the Brouay railway crossing. Major Arthur Plows, commanding the remnants of A and D Companies at the railway bridge, was told by Lieutenant Colonel Cabeldu that there would be no retreat. The bulk of the Can Scots was held farther back, around the village, and Cabeldu had placed his supporting arms—antitank guns, mortars, and heavy machine guns from the Camerons—in position to help the forward companies. It was the beginning of another daylong battle. Fortunately, the German tanks, from an unknown unit but possibly SPs, were reluctant to cross the rail line, and Canadian artillery pounded away at the enemy infantry. Mark Zuehlke, who has written the best account of this action, concluded that "artillery fire laid on by the FOO proved decisive."[3] And once again, effective infantry fire kept the enemy from closing the Canadian position. This action, which died down in the afternoon of 9 June, and the counterattack to re-take Putot the previous evening cost the Can Scots forty-five dead and eighty wounded. Since landing three days before they had lost a third of the battalion.[4]

The real problem for the Germans was not Putot but Norrey. Capturing it was an essential preliminary to securing the whole of the start line for the panzer corps attack. As Captain Stu Tubb had surmised two days earlier when he saw the ground for the first time, Norrey was like an outer bastion along a fortress wall. It dominated the ground around it, including Bretteville. No one knows who actually made the plan to assault it on 9 June and who gave the orders. Craig Luther claims that the scheme had Kurt Meyer's imprint all over it: hasty, impetuous, and poorly coordinated. However, Max Wunsche's testimony at the war crimes trials in 1945 suggests that he, as commander of the Panther battalion, was the author.[5] Certainly no one was willing to take responsibility in the immediate aftermath, and with good reason. The plan to attack Norrey at midday on 9 June was identical to the one that failed the night before on Bretteville. Panthers of 3rd Company, 12th SS Regiment, attacking Norrey from the east would carry a few soldiers of 25th PGR, while the bulk of the infantry (this time the division's engineer battalion) attacked from the south. Whether the subsequent attack on Cardonville was part of Wunsche's plan, or just developed locally, remains unclear.[6]

Once again the arrival of more Panthers on the battlefield west of Authie was noted by the Canadians, and, as Kurt Meyer and Schweppenburg watched from the tower of the abbey church, heavy fire was brought down on them. The Germans claim it was naval gunfire, but it might well have been the 4.5-inch guns of 79th Medium RA. It was a rude welcome to Normandy for 3rd Company of Wunsche's regiment, but miraculously the Panthers and their crews suffered no casualties. The Mk IV's of the division's 2nd Battalion who replaced them in the forward positions west of Authie were not so fortunate. Alois

Morawetz, in command of one of the Panthers, recalled looking back at the tanks of 2nd Battalion as they drove away. They were under intense artillery fire, and "the first Panzer IV began to burn."[7] The rest of Morawetz's day proved to be equally charmed.

The Canadians also called in tanks. According to Anglo-Canadian doctrine, as it was then practiced, tanks were primarily a mobile strike force. Their purpose was to attack, as they had alongside the 9th Brigade vanguard on 7 June or with the Can Scots at Putot late on 8 June, or to counterattack an armored thrust if it broke through the forward defenses. Antitank defense on the forward edge of the battle area was the job of antitank gunners. The operational order therefore called for the three regiments of 2nd Canadian Armoured Brigade to concentrate on the high ground west of Cairon, in an area designated "Jill."[8] There they were to form a kind of cavalry reserve, a mailed fist ready to strike any force that broke through the forward lines.

This never happened. Losses on D-Day, the failure to link up with British formations on either flank, and the battles of 7–8 June meant that what remained of 2nd Armoured Brigade's tanks was primarily concentrated on the high ground around Anguerney east of the Mue, with only what remained of the 1st Hussars laagered behind 7th Brigade. It also appears that the Sherbrooke Fusiliers were drawn into the battles around Putot and Bretteville on 8 June. By 9 June, 2nd Canadian Armoured Brigade did not exist as a massed counterattack force. Not only was it somewhat dispersed, but its tank losses had not yet been fully replaced. According to a brigade report of late June, it received thirty-one replacement tanks on the morning of 8 June and distributed these to the 1st Hussars and the Sherbrookes. That still left 2nd Canadian Armoured Brigade about a third short of its proper strength. As the history of the Royal Canadian Armoured Corps concluded, "At the end of the third day of fighting all three regiments of 2 Armoured Brigade had lost more than half their tanks and were rapidly approaching a state of ineffectiveness."[9]

Fortunately, the remnants of 2nd Canadian Armoured Brigade were not alone in their vigil around Anguerney. The massing of enemy tanks in the plain around the Abbey d'Ardennes and Authie was noted by Allied intelligence. This placed enemy armor opposite the narrowest portion of Second British Army's beachhead. The Canadians had already deployed the M10s of 3rd Anti-Tank Regiment, RCA, alongside the armored brigade to help concentrate its mobile reserves. And so General Sir Myles Dempsey shifted 4th British Armoured Brigade a little east, from its initial concentration near Amblie, to Colomby-sur-Thaon.[10] This placed them just four kilometers north of the 9th Canadian Brigade's positions around les Buissons and adjacent to the survivors of 2nd Canadian Armoured Brigade at Anguerney. There they stayed, ready to parry any panzer thrust to the sea, for a week or more.[11]

And so despite the Canadians' weakness in tanks when Lieutenant Colonel Matheson in Bretteville called for tank support on the morning of 9 June, the Canadian armored brigade responded positively. Six Shermans under Lieutenant Gordon Henry of C Squadron of 1st Hussars along with two troops (six tanks; troops were still composed of three each) of the Fort Garry Horse led by Captain C. D. A. Tweedale set off for Bretteville. Their timely arrival would help determine the outcome of the day.

In the meantime, with a company of 26th PGR now in Rots, 7th Brigade's eastern flank along the Mue—utterly unguarded by infantry—became a battlefield and put the brigade's supporting artillery regiments in serious jeopardy. Twelfth RCA had turned back PGs and some tanks or SPs with their 105mm guns at point-blank range over open sights the night before. By the morning of 9 June, gun position "Nora" at Bray was under attack. While 12th RCA dueled with German mortars sited in the valley of the Mue, shells from 88mm flak batteries of Carpiquet airfield defenses and 12th SS Division's own antiaircraft units deployed west of Authie fired airburst over the gun positions. The situation was eased somewhat by the final arrival of sixteen Centaurs of S, T, X, and Z Troops of 2nd RMAS, which were far better suited to dueling with the enemy at close range.[12]

However, despite support from the Centaurs, fire from 88s and mortars intensified during the day, with 12th RCA fighting a battle against a group of mortars just 1,700 yards away.[13] German fire eventually became too intense for the batteries of 13th RCA, packed tightly around the village. They moved across the road west of Bray (the regimental headquarters did not move) in the afternoon, into the grid square reserved for 6th RA (which was still at sea). By then the Queen's Own

Rifles of 8th Canadian Brigade was en route to secure this open flank, and planning began to clear the Hitler Youth out of the Mue River valley.[14] For the moment, 12th RCA hung on to its embattled positions south of Bray.

The attack on the Reginas' position at Norrey began at 1300 hours on 9 June. Panthers of the 3rd Company of 12th SS Panzer Regiment, supported by a few men from 25th PGR, slipped south under the rail bridge at la Villeneuve and shook out into attack formation in the dead ground east of Norrey. In their haste, the Panthers left some of their own infantry behind: the rest were stripped away by Canadian artillery fire. Meyer's history of the 12th SS recorded that "the whole sector was under concentrated enemy fire, some of it from ships' guns."[15] At least some of the fire was called in by Gunner E. Barton, 13th RCA. Barton was with 14 Platoon on the eastern edge of Norrey and moved forward to a vantage point in the field east of the village, carrying a field telephone and dragging a wire behind him through mortar and machine gun fire, as the attack commenced. When the wire to his carrier was cut, Gunner B. J. Bohn, the signaler, "ran the gauntlet" back to the radio with requests for fire.[16]

After a pause to organize, and amid a shower of bursting 105mm shells and dust, twelve Panthers of 3rd Company began their ascent of the kilometer of open, slightly rising farmland to Norrey. About halfway to the village they turned slightly south to present their thick frontal armor to the antitank guns supporting the Reginas' C Company. As they advanced, the Panthers rode over the right-hand elements of B Company, which had two of the Reginas' 6-pounders. One of these guns was already out of action. The sergeant in command of the disabled gun, Elof Granberg, noticed that the other gun was unmanned, so he crawled over to it and fired three rounds at close range at the attacking tanks. Every shot missed, passing just inches in front of them. No one had told Granberg—or apparently anyone in the battalion antitank platoon—that the new discarding sabot ammunition traveled so fast there was no need to lead the target. "We had never trained on the new ammunition," Granberg mused, "so that's why I missed." Granberg took cover as the tank rolled over his slit trench and through that section of B Company. Then suddenly the Panthers began to explode and burn.[17]

It was just at this moment when Lieutenant Gordon Henry and his mixed unit of 1st Hussar and Fort Garry tanks arrived in position south of Bretteville. The Hitler Youth riding to glory in Panthers in their first battle were less than 1,000 meters in front of Henry's tanks. What unfolded next was a nightmare for the Germans.

It says a great deal about the "ordinariness" of the Canadians' experience with all German tanks in Normandy, including Panthers, that they recorded no good account of this action on 9 June. The 2nd Canadian Armoured Brigade summary from 26 June 1944 gives it one line: "One of the Sherman V tks succeeded in knocking out five Panthers." It was, it seems, just another bloody day. Later in June Henry's remarkable accomplishment was the subject of several—short—articles in Canadian papers. By the time the Canadian Press carried a story by Ross Munro on 21 June, Henry and his tank the "Comtesse de Feu" were credited with three more Panthers, bringing their score to eight. Typically, Munro identified the twenty-six-year-old Montrealer to his readership by noting Henry's hockey career with the Montreal Junior Royals. Munro claimed that Henry, his gunner Archie Chapman, loader Lloyd Seaman, and driver Tom Reeves were known in the 1st Hussars as the "Panther Killers."[18] In the incident of 9 June they were credited with four kills on their own and a share of a fifth, all apparently in just a few minutes.

But no detailed account of what happened between Canadian and German tanks outside Norrey on 9 June was even attempted, and citations for awards followed long after: Henry's was not written until December. Brigadier Bob Wyman, commander of 2nd Canadian Armoured Brigade, was notorious for his reluctance to award recognition for feats on the battlefield. Wyman seems to have believed that killing enemy tanks was his regiments' job, and no one should be singled out for simply doing that. Henry eventually received the French Croix de Guerre in 1945, while the man and his action on 9 June simply disappeared into obscurity.

The "Comtesse de Feu" was a Firefly, with a 17-pounder high-velocity gun. At least three other tanks in Henry's ersatz squadron, including Captain Tweedale's from the Fort Garrys, were also Fireflys. Their 76.2mm (3-inch) APCBS traveled at 1,204 meters per second and could cut through 131 millimeters of plate armor at 900 meters. The thickest armor on a Panther, the front glacis, was 80 millimeters thick, although the angle of the glacis's slope virtually doubled that on the horizontal plain. The rest of the Panther's armor, 40 to 50 millimeters on the sides of the hull and turret, was not nearly enough to stop a 17-pounder APCBS. The best that Panther crews could hope for was that the round went through one side of the tank and out the other without hitting anything or anyone inside.

Given that what transpired was an exceptional feat of gunnery, it is important to emphasize that Henry and his crew had very little experience—if any—with their own 17-pounder gun. All we know with certainty is that they had trained with another gun on a range tank at Warcop for a day and a half two months earlier, in early April. They then waited eight weeks before having an opportunity (on 6 June) to fire their own 17-pounder for the first time. It is likely they did, if only to make sure it worked. By 9 June everything depended on brief training received two months earlier in another Firefly.

On this day, everything worked fine. Henry and his troop, plus the six Shermans of the Fort Garry Horse under Captain Tweedale, had barely settled into their position north of the rail line outside Bretteville when the Panther attack on Norrey began. As Anglo-Canadian artillery poured a murderous fire into the valley of the Mue, what finally emerged from the smoke were a dozen Panther tanks crawling along open ground right in front of the Canadians at a distance of 850 to 1,050 yards.[19]

Typically, we know more about this action from the German side, the result of meticulous interviews conducted on survivors by their comrades and by amateur historians infatuated with the history of German panzer units. We know that the first 17-pounder shell reached SS Sergeant Alois Morawetz's Panther in less than a second. Morawetz was on the right flank of the German formation, just a few yards from the rail line. The APCBS shell hit the front of Morawetz's tank, seriously wounding the gunner and bringing the tank to a halt. Morawetz thought they had struck a mine.

By the time Morawetz composed himself and glanced out through his hatch periscope to see if anyone else from his section had struck a mine, the turret of the Panther to his left—probably the section leader Stagge—flew off in a shattering explosion. Clearly this was no minefield. Morawetz scrambled out and collapsed on the Panther's engine compartment. He awoke moments later with flame shooting out of the hatch of his turret like a blowtorch. He then noticed that a third Panther was burning.

Less than a 1,000 meters away, across the rail line, Canadian tank crews were going through their drills like they were on a range. "17-pounder! Traverse left! Steady," Henry barked through his microphone. The tank's turret moved slightly as his gunner, Trooper Archie Chapman, acquired the target. Chapman then repeated the orders, aligning his sights on a tank 900 yards away: "ON! 900. Tank!" Once the target and range were confirmed, Henry ordered "Fire!" and Chapman squeezed the trigger on the 17-pounder's electronic firing mechanism. Nearby, Tweedale and his gunner, Trooper W. L. Bennett, went through the same routine. Who fired first we will never know.

At 1,204 meters per second the round reached its target in less than a second. The first kill—Morawitz—seems to have come from Tweedale's tank. Munro claimed in his Canadian Press story that Henry's first hit blew the turret off a Panther, which would make it Stagg's tank (the second to be struck). Henry and his gunners lit up the third Panther, and from here on it was largely their show. The third Panther struck was commanded by Willi Fischer. Henry's first round stopped Fischer's tank, and the second went through the turret, right under Fischer's seat. He scrambled out as the tank began to blaze. Henry had already switched his attention to Sergeant Hermanni's tank, which Chapman hit with his first round and set alight. Two more lethal hits on SS Panthers followed in quick succession. In just a few minutes Henry and his crew destroyed four Panthers with five shots, but they were not quite finished.

Most of the twelve Shermans banging away at the Panthers had the standard 75mm gun. Reliable, fast, and accurate, the 75mm guns peppered the Germans with a barrage of shells that could not kill but stunned crews, sheared off track, or—as they soon learned—shattered the Panther's vulnerable hydraulic system and set it on fire.

By the time Henry and Chapman settled on a fifth Panther, probably the leader of 3rd Company's 2nd Section farther back in the field, moving targets were harder to see. As a result, the shell from Henry's 17-pounder struck his fifth Panther just as one from another Firefly hit the same tank. No matter, Henry was already searching for another target, and Trooper Chapman was just laying on a sixth when it was destroyed by the 17-pounder of Henry's troop sergeant, Art Boyle.

In the end, Henry and his crew were credited—generously as it turned out—with killing five Panthers, Tweedale with two, and the other Garrys with one. Sergeant Boyle's kill seems to have been lost in the scramble for credit. The math was wrong, in any event: seven Panthers were destroyed, not eight. But the outcome was unquestionable. The attack on Norrey by the Panthers of 12th SS was broken in a matter of minutes.[20] No Canadian casualties were reported.

It seems, however, that more than just 3rd Company of 12th SS Panzer Regiment was broken in the attack on Norrey; the Germans' faith in their own invulnerability was shattered by Canadian tank fire. Survivors from the blazing Panthers scurried back to the shelter of the railway underpass at la Villeneuve under a torrent of Anglo-Canadian artillery fire. Wunsche, his head bandaged from a wound the night before, had hurried forward to watch the attack of his 3rd Company. He was utterly dismayed by the results. "I could have screamed from rage and grief," Wunsche said in the aftermath. The 3rd Company commander, Captain Ludemann, a Wehrmacht officer who had temporarily replaced the wounded SS captain Rudolf von Ribbentrop (son of the Nazi foreign minister), suffered a nervous breakdown and had to be relieved. Von Ribbentrop resumed command despite his wounds.[21]

Having failed by both night and day, the Panthers of 12th SS Panzer Division displayed reluctance to expose themselves to Anglo-Canadian antitank fire afterward.

Historians speculate on why the infantry of 3rd Company, 1st Battalion, 26th PGR, dug in south of Norrey, never left their trenches to support this attack. The rout of the Panthers may account for that, and perhaps artillery fire kept the Hitler Youth in their trenches again. However, it is just as likely that Kurt Meyer once again failed to coordinate his actions. Eventually, 1st Battalion did stir into action. Later in the afternoon, 2nd Company rose from its trenches west of Norrey and attacked the Reginas' D Company (once again reinforced, this time it seems by men from the support platoon) at Cardonville. Captain A. K. Pousette, Gordon Brown's new FOO, was forced to defend his observation post with hand grenades. And then, what was left of the

Reginas' B Company on the eastern edge of Bretteville also came under attack. Its FOO, Lieutenant O'Brennan, was due to be relieved, but an attempt to do so failed when Captain Steele's Sherman OP tank was hit by German tank fire and driven back. O'Brennan stayed on and the next day was still there, 200 yards out in front of B Company's position on the crest of the rise east of the village, when he was overrun by tanks and called a Mike target on his own position.[22]

So the 12th SS continued to probe and push, all along the line. In the afternoon of 9 June the gun position at Bray finally became untenable when an 88mm shell burst over the 22nd Battery command post, killing or wounding most of the men in it. That proved to be the last straw. The entire 12th Field Group, RCA—12th and 13th RCA and 2nd RMAS—decamped for a new gun position west of Camilly on the road to Secqueville. By one estimate, the regiments at Bray had fired more than 1,500 rounds per gun from 7 to 9 June 1944: 72,000 105mm shells.[23] That works out to some 36,000 two-round 120-pound crates of ammunition lugged from the beach. At a weight of 33 pounds per shell, that also means that just short of 1,200 tons of steel and high explosive were fired at the enemy from the gun position at Bray in three days of intense fighting.

The fact that the guns were never short of ammunition speaks volumes for the organization and effort behind the front. Gunner Geoffrey Hall, a driver for 44th Battery, arrived on the evening of 6 June with the ammunition trucks of 13th RCA. It was close to midnight before they got ashore, and their guns were already running low on ammunition, so work started immediately. "We went straight for two days and nights driving, and without sleep," Hall recalled in 2004. The ammunition came off the beaches onto the back of his three-ton Canadian-built Ford truck, traveled inland by convoy, and was dumped right behind the guns. Hall had two helpers to handle the ammunition because the "gunners were too busy."[24]

None of the attacks on 9 June unsettled the Canadians in their fortress positions at Putot, Norrey, and Bretteville. That day Rommel finally admitted defeat when he ordered a temporary halt to all plans for a corps-level panzer counterattack. Without the key ground astride the Mue there could be no grand-sweeping panzer assault to crush the Allied landings. Moreover, by 9 June the British and the Americans were gradually and inexorably seeping into the Normandy countryside from Bayeux westward. It was time to forget about trying to drive the Allies back into the sea and time to focus on simply stopping them from advancing any farther.

The suspension of the panzer corps plan did not stop 12th SS from trying to capture Norrey. The final major assault on this part of 7th Brigade's fortress came in the early hours of 10 June. Having tried every conceivable combination of tank, infantry, daylight, and nighttime attack, 12th SS now resolved to take Norrey by surprise in the dark, using its last available infantry, 12th Pioneer Battalion. At 0300 hours its three companies (of unknown strength) moved through the positions of 1st Battalion, 26th PGR, in silence, without supporting artillery or mortar fire, and crept up the southern open slope toward the village. First Company, in the center, got to within 100 meters of the Canadian trenches before they were stopped by a fusillade of small arms fire and forced to ground. So too were 2nd Company on the right and 3rd Company on the left. Once the Canadians opened fire, SS mortars and guns of 2nd Battalion of 12th SS Artillery Battalion began to strike the Reginas' defenses, while Canadian artillery pounded the Pioneers.

As Canadian small arms fire slackened, the commander of 1st Company, Oberleutenant Otto Toll, organized a frontal assault on Norrey in an attempt to rush the Canadian defenses. Helmut Schuck, who survived the attack, later observed with a hint of melancholy, "The enemy seemed to have expected this."[25] Within minutes, most of 1st Company's noncommissioned officers were dead or wounded, and Toll himself was struck down by a machine gun burst and died half an hour later. The survivors retreated to a small gully that was already packed with seriously wounded. Attacks by 2nd and 3rd Companies on the flanks fared no better.

The only account of this attack from the Canadian side is an interview with John Swityk, in command of one of the 6-pounders on the southeast corner of Norrey, done by Walter Keith in February 2008; there is no mention of it in any other source, not even the Reginas' war diary. Swityk recalled that the attack lasted all day, with "wave after wave of Germans coming at them through the wheat fields to the south of Norrey." The Germans got close but never penetrated the C Company positions, which were defended "by rifle and MG fire."

Swityk's recollection is confirmed by German survivors' accounts. Certainly Helmut Schuck stayed in the gulley until 1600 hours, when the remnants of 12th SS Pioneer Battalion were ordered to withdraw (the Canadians had already allowed German medical teams to remove the wounded).[26] The Germans admitted to "significant" losses: eighty men killed, wounded, or missing. Canadian losses appear to have been negligible.

Hubert Meyer's conclusion to this, and the previous three days' actions, bears repeating in full:

> Four attempts [Canadians count eight] to capture Norrey, one of the Cornerstones of the Canadian defensive position, had failed. The village, together with Bretteville, formed a strong barrier, blocking the attack plans of the Panzerkorps. For this reason, repeated attempts were made to take these positions through a number of attacks. They failed because of insufficient forces, partly because of rushed planning caused by real or imagined time pressures. Last but not least, they failed because of the courage of the defenders which was not any less than that of the attackers. It was effectively supported by well constructed positions, strong artillery, anti-tank weapons and by tanks.[27]

The beachhead battles were not over, but the initial attempt to sweep the Allies back into the sea by a panzer assault was. The Overlord operational plan had worked: the Canadians had stopped the panzers.

CONCLUSION

> The Canadian defence of Norrey and Bretteville over the
> period 8th to 10th June must surely go down as one of the
> finest small unit actions of WW II.
>
> Michael Reynolds,
> *Steel Inferno: 1 SS Panzer Corps in Normandy*

IN THE AFTERMATH of the successful Canadian defense of the beachhead, there was a denouement that demonstrated the problem of hasty
attacks over open ground in Normandy, already so amply revealed in
the failed German assaults. On 11 June the British pushed south of
Bayeux, toward Cristot and Villers Bocage, in an attempt to outflank
Caen from the west. Third Canadian Division mounted a hasty attack
toward le Mesnil-Patry in support, with the intent of capturing the high
ground south of Cheux. The force consisted of B Squadron from the
1st Hussars, now up to strength courtesy of a British tank delivery unit,
and D Company of the Queen's Own Rifles with some 106 men. No
preliminary reconnaissance of the ground was done, and no supporting
fire was arranged. Brigadier Wyman, who organized the attack, clearly
thought the German positions could be "bounced." The attack went
forward despite the strong protests of the commanders of the units involved. Major Tubb of the Reginas' C Company learned of the attack
when the tanks, with the Queen's Own on the back, squeezed their
way through Norrey and out the western road toward le Mesnil-Patry.
Tubb thought it a poorly conceived operation and found it curious that
no one had asked him who and what was out there.

There were plenty of 12th SS in the fields west of Norrey, including
tanks of the 2nd Battalion of 12th SS PR. The Canadian force was
virtually annihilated. Only two tanks returned: 99 of the 106 men of
the Queen's Own who participated in the attack were listed as missing
in action. In the end, 114 Canadians died, again some of them while
POWs. If anything, the disaster at le Mesnil-Patry proved what the

Germans already knew well: the hardest thing to do in the open fields around Caen was to attack an enemy who was prepared and waiting.

The abortive advance to le Mesnil-Patry is typically portrayed as further evidence of Canadian (and of course Allied) tactical incompetence. After all, the vanguard of 9th Brigade had been sent packing on 7 June, in the Canadian official histories' words, "by a force roughly its own size." And as all those familiar with the Normandy campaign know—especially Anglo-American historians—the Canadians had "stalled" outside of Caen through their own lack of initiative or, as Anthony Beevor recently observed, were prevented from getting forward by powerful German counterattacks.

It is now clear that this "understanding" of events from D-Day to 10 June is seriously flawed. As demonstrated in chapters 4 and 5, the vanguard of 9th Brigade did battle with a much larger force on 7 June than historians have imagined. It will be recalled that the North Nova Scotia's battle group consisted of a single infantry battalion of reduced strength for the assault (fewer than 900 men) and fifty tanks from the Sherbrookes, supported (eventually) by twenty-one 105mm guns, a few M10s, and some mortars and Vickers machine guns from the Cameron Highlanders. In the morning they attacked and defeated a force roughly their own size: an ersatz battalion from 716th Division and Kampfgruppe Rauch from 21st Panzer, supported by both artillery and powerful antitank guns. The presence of 25th PGR of 12th SS dramatically tipped the odds in favor of the Germans in the afternoon, and did so in a number of crucial ways. The 25th PGR was well supported by the heavy battalion of the 12th SS Division's artillery, which brought the number of German field artillery pieces engaged in the battle for the road to Carpiquet on 7 June to more than fifty. They fired with impunity throughout the afternoon while Canadian artillery and the vanguard's counterbattery resources, the cruisers HMS *Belfast* and HMS *Diadem*, remained "off-line." Powerful Pak 43/41 88mm antitank guns raked the Canadian advance from great distances, often so far away that their locations could only be surmised. Meanwhile, the tanks of 12th SS roamed the battlefield almost unhindered because the antitank guns that were supposed to support the Canadians were delayed getting ashore. Finally, 12th SS committed two over-strength PG battalions to their attack: perhaps as many as 2,000 infantry. When combined with the infantry of 716th Division and troops of 21st Panzer already on the battlefield, the Novas were outnumbered at least three or four to one. Only in tanks were the two forces roughly equal in numbers and quality. The Germans, however, were vastly superior in the quality and quantity of antitank guns deployed, at least until the panzers of 12th SS tried to push north of Buron and ran into prepared Canadian positions at les Buissons.

So the Canadian official history's quip that the vanguard was defeated by a force "roughly its own size" is a gross misrepresentation of the facts. It also needs to be emphasized that, in the absence of British forces to the east and any discernible "alternate position" on the eighty-meter contour between Buron and Authie, the decision to establish 9th Brigade's forward position at les Buissons was the only viable option. Anyone who has seen the ground will understand why the line was held there.

The great defensive battle was of course that of 7th Brigade from 8 to 10 June. It fought 26th PGR and elements of Panzer Lehr to a standstill, and killed or damaged a large portion of 12th SS Panther Battalion. And it did so with companies weakened by the D-Day assault and, in several cases, hastily rebuilt on 7 June. More important, the defense of Putot-Bretteville-Norrey by 7th Brigade (and the 9th Brigade fortress at les Buissons) was not an accidental victory: it was no chance encounter between Canadians surging south only to be stopped by German counterattacks. Seventh Brigade was where it was supposed to be, on the division "covering position." It fought its battle in accordance with the Overlord operational plan, and it achieved its objective of stopping "the probable counter attack"—not simply the probable counterattack on the Canadian sector, but the probable counterattack on the whole Overlord operation.

The unsuccessful attack on le Mesnil-Patry on 11 June is typically portrayed as the last in a series of "failures" that marked the first week ashore for the Canadians, explicable as yet another example of the tactical incompetence of the Anglo-Canadians. This book suggests quite a different paradigm for understanding that event. Perhaps it was so cavalierly conceived and executed because up to this point so much of what 3rd Canadian Division had to do had gone well: the equipment, training, organization, and doctrine all seemed to work. Through it all

A Sherman Firefly of the 2nd Canadian Armoured Brigade, probably from the 1st Hussars judging by the cap badges, in Normandy in early June 1944. (LAC PA-131391)

the urge of 2nd Canadian Armoured Brigade to—in Monty's famous phrase—"crack about in tanks" had never abated. It got its chance on 11 June, and it was a bloody fiasco. Third Canadian Division never did it like that again.

The attack by 12th SS Pioneer Battalion on Norrey on 10 June marked the end of the German plans to clear the start line and send 1st SS Panzer Corps down either side of the Mue River to destroy the Allied landings. This area had long been identified by both COSSAC and 21st Army Group planners as the key ground. Planning estimates, war games, and "German" staff studies in the fall of 1943 all identified the ground west and north of Caen as the key to any German attempt to destroy a landing north of Bayeux. Although some concern was expressed about the Sommervieu-Bazenville ridge, it was clear to Freddie Morgan and his staff, and to later Allied planners, that the crucial ground was around Caen. Even the final Overlord plan recognized this with its intent to capture Caen on the first day, thereby denying the enemy the good tank country north of the city. In the event, 3rd British Division lacked the combat power to take Caen in the initial strike, not least because the Germans had already moved a panzer division into the area.

Freddie Morgan was probably correct in wanting to seize Caen on D-Day with paratroopers, but in retrospect the events probably worked out better for the Allies (and especially the Canadians) in the long run. Had paratroopers captured Caen on D-Day, 21st Panzer would never have been able to get its tanks through the city to attack the 3rd British Division. In that case, the capture of Caen would have fulfilled the Overlord plan to use the city and its river and canal system as impenetrable tank obstacles. Had that happened, however, it may well have freed the tanks of 21st Panzer to join in a corps-level counterattack west of Caen in the days that followed. In that scenario, a three-division corps-level attack astride the Mue was a real possibility by 8 June (if the Germans were able to overcome their own muddled command structure). Both Panzer Lehr and 12th SS Panzer were in line and ready to go immediately west of Caen on that day. Had the armor of 21st Panzer been concentrated and ready to support them, events astride the Mue River from 8 to 10 June would have unfolded rather differently. This was the scenario feared by Overlord planners, and what 3rd Canadian Division came prepared to meet. Whether the panzer divisions could have pushed their attack to Courseulles, and what they might have achieved by doing so, we will never know. What we do know is that the German decision to hold the line north and east of Caen with forces already in place, including the armor of 21st Panzer Division, proved costly to them and beneficial to the Allies—and it was certainly good news for the Canadians.

If there remains any doubt about the central importance of the ground on either side of the Mue River, one need only look closely at the Germans' own plans and actions. They, too, knew that the landing could not be defeated by horse-drawn infantry divisions. The infantry

and guns of 352nd Division—the only first-rate German infantry division in the landing area—were a danger at Omaha Beach, to be sure.
But they had to succeed on the beach. The tale of the counterattack
by 352nd Division's Kampfgruppe Meyer on 50th British Division on
D-Day speaks volumes about that division's inability to conduct mobile operations. The only counterattack that mattered was armored,
and the only place that could happen on a scale large enough to matter
was west of Caen, where there was sufficient ground to echelon panzer
divisions in depth and avenues for a rapid assault to the sea. If Rommel
had had his way, three panzer divisions at a minimum would already
have been on that ground in May 1944, ready to strike up either side
of the Mue River: 21st Panzer (which he moved into place), 12th SS,
and Panzer Lehr. We have the German high command and Operation
Fortitude South to thank that Rommel failed in his bid to concentrate
in such forces near Caen.

Once the invasion started, at least three attempts were made to
launch a decisive panzer counterattack to the sea astride the Mue: by
84th Corps on D-Day, 1st SS Panzer Corps on 7–9 June, and Panzer
Group West on 10 June. It is true, in the end, that a corps-level panzer
attack never actually developed, but that was not for want of trying.
German focus on this key ground lingered. When Field Marshal Gun-
ther von Kluge took over command in the west from von Rundstedt
in early July, the first thing he planned was a major panzer offensive
astride the Mue River pointed at the sea. The COSSAC planners had
been right all along.

The panzer corps attack failed for many reasons. The fairly rapid
movement of the British divisions on either flank forced the Germans
to commit their panzer formations piecemeal. This is the standard explanation for the failed German plans, and it is partly true. The 3rd
British Division's drive on Caen, for example, was blunted on D-Day
by 21st Panzer Division, and that division was not able to extricate
itself from the fighting to concentrate and become a viable component
of a corps-level attack. Similarly, the Canadian drive for Carpiquet—
never toward Caen—forced the leading elements of 12th SS Panzer
into a holding action on 7 June as well. The battalion commanders
of 25th PGR were so anxious about stopping another attempt by 9th
Canadian Brigade to advance to Carpiquet that they prevented Meyer

No longer "Frisch and Frolic" after a month on the front lines: Hitler Youth of the 12th SS behind the wire of a Canadian POW holding area in early July. (LAC PA-131397)

from drawing their troops into his hasty and ill-fated attacks on Bretteville and Norrey. Finally, the rapid advance of 50th British Division profoundly shaped the battle in the middle of the Allied landing zone. It forced the commitment and destruction of 84th Corps' only strategic reserve on D-Day, Kampfgruppe Meyer of 352nd Division, and its capture of Bayeux and steady movement inland greatly eased the American exit from Omaha Beach on 7 June. Indeed, so quickly did Rommel's "Old Friends" from North Africa move that late on 8 June he was forced to redirect Panzer Lehr away from the Canadians to stop the British drive south of Bayeux. Panzer Lehr was ultimately successful but only at enormous cost to both sides in the rolling and wooded "Bessin" countryside around Tilley-sur-seulles.[1]

That said, there was a brief opportunity on 8–9 June—as Schweppenburg lamented after the war—when both 12th SS and Panzer Lehr were concentrated in front of the Canadians and might well have acted in concert. That they did not do so was primarily the result of the muddle in German command and control, which was nothing short of catastrophic. As tedious and self-serving as Schweppenburg's postwar complaints appear, he was right: the failure to grip the battle west of Caen in the first days after the landings was a "self-inflicted wound" for the Germans. The natural tendency for the Germans, and historians alike, is to blame Hitler. In fact, General Fritz Halder, when preparing the postwar historical summaries of German military actions for the US Army, ordered his colleagues to ensure that Hitler bore the blame for German military failure, not the generals.[2] It is clear that explaining away failure as someone else's fault dominates much of the German writing, and that historians have accepted their assertions uncritically. The facile comparison of Canadian casualties on 7 June with those suffered by 12th SS alone is a glaring example of this. Moreover, the consistently low casualties reported by historians of the SS suggest either that they did not push their attacks vigorously at all or that the reported casualties were much lower than the reality. In contrast, Canadian accounts insist that the Hitler Youth attacked with intensity, and that the body counts of dead Germans in front of their positions attest to it. As Helmut Ritgen indicated in his comment about the inflated figures for losses to Panzer Lehr during its approach march on 7 June, such things need to be taken with a large grain of salt.

The fact was, by 1944 the Germans did not know how to fight the Western Allies. The "old tactics of shock and surprise employed in Russia" no longer worked. If the Germans, who were masters of chaos on the battlefield, could not get the battle to tumble and become fluid, they did not know what to do. Their doctrine, organization, and equipment, especially their devolution of command, control, and firepower to a low level, were structured for mobile battle. Even the counterattack doctrine was based on the tempo of the battle and was deeply ingrained in the Wehrmacht.[3] In that sense Rommel was correct: German generals in command in the west in 1944 did not understand that if the Allies got ashore, and got their guns up and their airpower on line, it would be nearly impossible to move them. He knew that the Anglo-Canadians, who had learned only too well from two world wars how to fight Germans, would hide under their guns and kill German counterattacks. This was not an elegant form of warfare, it was not the blitzkrieg that everyone strived for after 1939–1940, and historians do not like it, but it worked. And it worked well on either side of the Mue River between 7 and 10 June 1944.

The third reason the corps-level attack failed west of Caen is that 12th SS was not a very effective military formation: brainwashed Hitler Youth led by thugs from the Nazi Party were a recipe for ferocity, not efficiency.[4] No one ever said that they were not brave and dedicated, and by all accounts they fought stubbornly and with a will. But we do know that 12th SS was unable—or unwilling—to properly coordinate its own activities and to work well with the Wehrmacht formations around it. The Canadian official historian C. P. Stacey came to this conclusion decades ago. Hubert Meyer admits it in his history of 12th SS, and Michael Reynolds comes to the same conclusion in his work on 1st SS Panzer Corps, *Steel Inferno*. Canadian soldiers, whom Anglo-American historians seldom talked to, would have told them as much. Gordon Brown could never figure out what 12th SS thought it was doing on the night of 8–9 June: nothing conformed to the basics of sound tactics as he understood them. As Colonel Freddie Clifford said in 2002, "The Germans did dumb things and we killed those bastards in large numbers." It may well be that Rommel, Dollman, Bayerlein, Marcks, and Schweppenburg were content to let the Hitler Youth break themselves on Canadian guns. At best they might achieve something worthwhile; at worst they were fighting and inflicting casualties and damage on the enemies of the Reich.

It is true, as well, that the Allies controlled the skies. This created an unfamiliar and clearly unpleasant operational environment for the Germans, and they complained about it incessantly. In the early stages of the campaign the impact of Allied air superiority on ground operations was threefold. First, most of the work done by fighter-bombers was flying interdiction missions, not tactical air support for troops at the front. There is ample evidence in German accounts of delays trying to get to Normandy as a result of these operations, but much of this is overstated for this early stage of the battle. In general German formations arrived in the battle zone more complete for the initial beachhead battles than did 3rd Canadian Division, which was plagued by delays in getting vital units ashore. The weather remained poor for the first week of the campaign. The war diary of the Cameron Highlanders of Ottawa records 7 June as cool and partly cloudy, 8 June as cool with showers, 9 June as heavy rain that cleared at noon, 10 June as rain, and 11 June as overcast. Allied air strikes on German columns moving to Normandy, although spectacular, neither inflicted decisive losses to the combat power of the panzer units moving to the Caen sector nor seriously delayed their arrival. Twenty-First Panzer was already in position. The arrival of 12th SS was delayed primarily by the initial misdirection of its concentration area to the north, a victory for Allied deception operations. It is true the Panther battalion of 12th SS was stalled on the road for a day because of fuel shortages occasioned by the destruction of tanker trucks by Allied air strikes. This might not have happened had the SS simply asked 21st Panzer for fuel: they did not. And Panzer Lehr was assembled, less its Panther battalion (which was on railcars in Germany), in front of the Canadians by noon on 8 June—again with less fuel they it would have liked, but still ready to attack and less than twenty kilometers from the sea. Perhaps the greatest impact of airpower on panzer operations in the immediate aftermath of the landings was the panic engendered in 21st Panzer Division by the glider overflight late on D-Day. This led to the retreat of its armor from the coast around Lyon-sur-mer. Historians would never have forgiven an Allied formation for such a thing.

Of greater importance was the impact of Allied air superiority on German command and control. It was simply too dangerous for senior German officers to fly, so all of them—as in the example of Rommel coming back from leave on 6 June—were forced to use French highways and often more sheltered but longer secondary roads. As a result, the movements of key officers, staffs, and orders were delayed and the trips were often perilous, as Allied fighter-bombers patrolled the French interior. Rommel's experience on 10 June speaks volumes: he was forced to dive into the ditch thirty times during his arduous trip from Roch Guyon back to Normandy to confer with Schweppenburg.

One of the seven 12th SS Panthers killed by Lieutenant Gordon Henry's force of 1st Hussars and Fort Garry Horse on 9 June. This photo was taken on 8 July, and the Panther shows clear signs of its month spent as a target for Canadian gunners. (LAC PA-130338)

Fritz Bayerlein, commander of Panzer Lehr, was nearly killed on 8 June while trying to find his own advanced headquarters.

The utter destruction of Panzer Group West's headquarters shortly after Rommel's departure on 10 June highlights the final crucial component of Allied air superiority: decapitation attacks on headquarters revealed by either Ultra or simple direction finding. In short, it was just really hard for the Germans to command and control effectively in the presence of overwhelming Allied airpower. And it was not just airpower that posed this threat: Fritz Witt, commander of 12th SS, was killed on 14 June when his headquarters was targeted by naval gunfire.

The final reason the longed-for panzer corps counterattack never took place is simply that the Canadians fought exceptionally well. By accepting blithely that the panzer corps attack failed to materialize, the Canadian official history did a dreadful disservice to the men whose story it was supposed to tell. Much of what 12th SS did on 8–10 June 1944 was an attempt to capture the start line for the corps attack, and it failed miserably to do so. Panzer forces could assemble on the plain east of the Mue River, which was occupied by the 25th PGR on 7 June, but nothing could sweep north with any effect west of the river until the villages of Norrey, Bretteville, and Putot were cleared. The villages and the road and rail lines, if defended, formed a powerful check on any armor movement. The one attempt to push north, west of Putot on the morning of 8 June, was canalized into a killing ground and largely destroyed by antitank fire, while the only Panzer Lehr unit in the area was virtually annihilated by Anglo-Canadian naval and artillery fire.

To get to Courseulles-sur-mer and onto the Sommervieu-Bazenville ridge east of Bayeux, the villages held by 7th Brigade had to be taken. Behind them the power of armored divisions could be properly echeloned, guns sited, and supplies mustered. If Fritz Bayerlein is to be believed, Panzer Lehr was poised for a thrust to the sea on 8 June and was simply waiting for the 12th SS to clear the way. The stout defense of Putot by the Royal Winnipeg Rifles and the tenacity of the Reginas denied Bayerlein that chance. The 12th SS, despite its fanaticism, overstrength units, and Panther tanks, simply could not shake the Canadians from their positions.

The decision on 8 June to redirect Panzer Lehr west, to stop 50th British Division, therefore came after it was clear that the Canadians could not be moved—at least not quickly and with acceptable losses. So, hard fighting on the key ground and the refusal to yield the start line at a critical moment had a great deal to do with the failure to launch 1st SS Panzer Corps toward the beach, or to keep the idea in play after 10 June. That, perhaps more than anything else, was the single most important Canadian contribution to the success of Overlord: just about as the operational plan anticipated.

By 10 June all of Schweppenburg's dreams of a panzer corps thrust down either side of the Mue River were gone, and by the end of the day so was he. Improved weather on the afternoon of 10 June finally gave full rein to Allied airpower. That afternoon Rommel made a harrowing trip to Panzer Group West's headquarters, established in an orchard at La Caine twenty kilometers southwest of Caen, to discuss the employment of the panzer divisions. At issue was probably von Rundstedt's order of 0730 hours that morning. "As a consequence of certain information," Hesketh writes in his confidential history of Allied deception, "CinC West has declared 'a state of alarm II' for Fifteenth Army in Belgium and Northern France."[5] This meant that the armor released to Rommel barely thirty-six hours earlier, both 1st SS Panzer Division and the panzer regiment of 116th Panzer Division, was being diverted to the Pas de Calais.

The reason for this diversion was a transmission from agent Garbo, the main conduit for the Fortitude South deception, just after midnight. Garbo's detailed two-hour-long report focused on three things. The first was that the landings in Normandy were clearly a diversion designed to "draw the maximum of our reserves to the area of operation and to retain them there so as to be able to strike a blow somewhere else with assured success." Second, the Allies still had some fifty operational divisions available to strike that blow. And third, the forces of FUSAG mustered in the southeast of England "are now inactive," which means "that they must be held in reserve to be employed in the other large scale operations." He went on to suggest that the recent heavy bombing in the Pas de Calais area "give reason to suspect an attack in that region of France."[6] When asked after the war about that fateful decision to redirect the panzer reinforcements from Rommel to the Pas de Calais region on 10 June, Field Marshal Wilhelm Keitel, chief of the German armed forces, confirmed that Garbo's message was the reason.[7] The main threat was not Normandy; it was the Pas de Calais.

Perhaps the Germans were anxious about the rumor that General George S. Patton was now in command of FUSAG, but that rumor was not confirmed by Garbo for another three days. In the meantime, the imminent threat of a landing in the Pas de Calais was crucial in preserving the Normandy beachhead. Michael Howard concluded that

Garbo's warning on 9 June "continued to pin down nineteen infantry and two armoured divisions of the Fifteenth Army—units whose intervention in the Normandy battle really might have tipped the scales."[8] If that was so, then the rump of "McNaughton's Dagger," First Canadian Army, which was concentrated in Kent as a key component of Fortitude South, deserves some credit. It also helped stop the panzers.

How much of this information on FUSAG passed between Rommel and Schweppenburg under the shade of those apple trees in the grounds of the Château La Caine on the afternoon of 10 June we will never know. What we do know is that after much heated discussion they agreed that the attack by 1st SS Panzer Corps was no longer possible. It was finally called off. The immediate threat to the beachhead was over: plain hard fighting remained. The tanks necessary to launch a decisive counterstroke on the Allies would have to come from much farther east. On 12 June, 2nd SS Panzer Corps, fighting on the Russian front, received orders for Normandy.

The collapse of German hopes for a quick panzer thrust against the Allied landing in lower Normandy was punctuated on 10 June by the catastrophic destruction of the headquarters of Panzer Group West. It had been found through Ultra intercepts the day before. About an hour after Rommel left Schweppenburg's headquarters, it was swarmed by Allied aircraft. The attack lasted about ten minutes. It started with rocketing and strafing from some forty RAF Typhoons, followed by waves of US Army Air Force Mitchells, which dropped 436 500-pound bombs. The results were devastating. As Luther wrote, "The entire operations staff was wiped-out." Thirty-two men were killed, including Schweppenburg's chief of staff. Schweppenburg escaped, badly shaken, with minor injuries, but his headquarters was destroyed.[9] The dead were buried in a bomb crater, and three days later what was left of the command element of Panzer Group West retreated to Paris to rebuild itself.

This event, perhaps more than the ill-fated attack on Norrey by the 12th SS Pioneer Battalion, signaled the end of the initial beachhead battles. All German attempts to either mount a serious panzer counterattack or drive the Canadians off the start line for such an operation had been utter failures. When it was over, the Canadians were—as the American critics of the Anglo-Canadians claim—sitting on their asses outside Caen. They were exhausted and seriously weakened, but they were unbroken. Over the course of the first six days ashore, 3rd Canadian Division, 2nd Canadian Armoured Brigade, and their supporting arms had suffered some 2,831 causalities, more than 1,000 of these dead.[10] The figures for the dead are, of course, inflated—but not in the way Ritgen suggests for German losses, and not because Canadians were tactically inept. Rather, they include some 159 POWs shot while under the care of the 12th SS. Howard Margolian estimates that one in five Canadian dead between 7 and 10 June (156 out of 677 who died in the initial beachhead battles) were murdered while prisoners of war.

The intensity and murderous nature of these early Canadian battles have been largely overlooked in the general Normandy literature. In part this is because it was primarily the Canadians who fought the 12th SS, and consequently non-Canadian historians have shown little curiosity about them. It did not help the Canadian case in the larger Normandy literature that the SS war crimes went largely unpunished. The British, who commanded the higher-echelon formations normally charged with investigating such things, refused to prosecute. Only when General Eisenhower heard of the mass shooting of Royal Winnipeg Rifles prisoners on the side of the road by Mohnke's troops on the night of 8 June did SHAEF intervene and begin an investigation. That case was pursued until the Malmedy Massacre of January 1945, when eighty American POWs were murdered during the Battle of the Bulge. At that point, SHAEF dropped the Canadian case and switched to the more politically important American one. As a result, only Kurt Meyer was ever brought to trial for his murder of Canadians. The court was convened in Aurich, Germany, in December 1945 by First Canadian Army. Six combat-experienced officers presided, with now Major General Harry Foster as president of the court. Meyer was found responsible for the murder of twenty POWs in his headquarters at the Abbey d'Ardennes on 7–8 June 1944 and sentenced to be shot. British intervention resulted in commutation of his sentence to life in prison. Meyer was released in 1954 in the general amnesty granted former German officers as part of West Germany's integration into NATO. He spent his last few years selling beer to the Canadian army in Germany. Mohnke escaped justice entirely. He was repatriated to West Germany in 1955 after a decade in a Russian camp, and all subsequent attempts to prosecute him failed. He died in 2001 at the ripe old age of ninety. Of the others, only Seibken was brought to justice by the British and hanged.

The Canadians largely disappear from the Normandy story for a month after 10 June. For the remainder of June, 3rd Canadian Division rebuilt itself while holding the line. In fact, 3rd Canadian Division stayed in the line for the whole of the Normandy campaign and paid dearly for that privilege. By the time the campaign was finished, it had the highest casualty rate of any Allied formation. It also stayed almost consistently in contact with 1st SS Panzer Corps. By the time the Canadians reappear in the Normandy narrative in early July, the lone Canadian division is a very small part of a greatly expanded Allied force. That division did take Caen (at least that portion north of the Orne River) from the west as part of a I British Corps operation. It is a much-celebrated victory and may explain in part why historians think Caen was a Canadian objective from the outset. As part of that battle, Operation Charnwood, the North Nova Scotia Highlanders had the privilege of recapturing Authie.[11] The Reginas then captured the shattered remains of the abbey, but the evidence of the murdered POWs did not come to light until the next spring.[12] A few days after Caen fell, 2nd Canadian Division came into the line and II Canadian Corps became operational. Finally, on 23 July, First Canadian Army—the designated Overlord "follow-on" army—under General Harry Crerar assumed control of operations around Caen and to the east. When 4th Canadian Armoured Division entered the fray at the end of July, Canada's contribution to the Normandy campaign was complete.

The army Crerar commanded in Normandy was not the army of Andy McNaughton's dreams. It was, in fact, the "Anglo-Canadian" army rejected the previous December, composed of II Canadian and I British Corps, and under a commander whom Montgomery could barely tolerate. This coalition force, which included the Polish Armoured Division, pushed south of Caen toward Falaise. In no small way the drive down the Caen-Falaise highway, across a plain and through the heart of the toughest German defenses in the dying days of a major war, had echoes of the glorious Hundred Days campaign of 1918. In that earlier campaign, fought along the Arras-Cambria highway across a great plain, the Canadian Corps had earned accolades from friend and foe alike for its skill and success. Crerar even invoked that earlier campaign in his orders. In contrast, the drive to Falaise in 1944 by First Canadian Army was a stuttering series of apparent missteps and missed opportunities: failure to employ mobility effectively, failure to deal decisively with a weakened enemy, and failure to close the Falaise gap promptly. Perhaps. But that is a subject best left to another time.

Although Crerar's army did an important job in the drive south of Caen in July and August, not least making the American breakout at St. Lô possible, it is likely that Canada's greatest contribution to Allied victory in Normandy was secured in the first four days ashore. Third Canadian Division did not simply advance into the space between Caen and Bayeux on D+1 to provide a continuous front between these high-profile British objectives. Nor was its task simply to cut the lateral highway and rail line between the two cities and then sit on them. It landed as perhaps the single most powerful Allied unit in the whole Overlord plan, and it had a specific and critical mission. It was never supposed to take Caen from the west, and it did not miss an opportunity to bounce the Odon and seize the high ground around Point 112—made famous in late June by the futile attempts of VIII British Corps to take it. The Canadians' Overlord task was clear: they were to capture and hold the ground over which the only serious threat to the overall success of the whole Normandy operation could come. Over the course of four days of intense fighting, they did just that.

They stopped the panzers.

See notes on fly leaves !

NOTES

Introduction

1. As quoted in Hubert Meyer, *The 12th SS: The History of the Hitler Youth Panzer Division*, vol. 1 (Mechanicsburg, PA: Stackpole Books, 2005), 191.

2. Stephen Badsey, "Culture, Controversy, Caen and Cherbourg: The First Week of the Battle," in John Buckley, ed., *The Normandy Campaign 1944: Sixty Years On* (London: Routledge, 2006), 48–63, especially 59.

3. In Toronto a special screening for Canadian veterans was punctuated by derisive cheering when, on two occasions during a three-hour film, the Canadians were mentioned en passant. Thanks to Dr. Stephen Harris, acting director, Directorate of History and Heritage, National Defence Headquarters, Ottawa, for this information.

4. The "Tunnel King" in the POW camp was a Canadian named Wally Flood. Flood acted as the technical adviser for the film, but his character, played by Charles Bronson, was turned into an RAF officer of uncertain east European extraction.

5. Colonel C. P. Stacey, *Canada's Battle in Normandy: The Canadian Army's Share in the Operations, 6 June – 1 September 1944*, Canadian Army at War series (Ottawa: King's Printer, 1946).

6. Colonel C. P. Stacey, *The Canadian Army 1939–1945: An Official Historical Summary* (Ottawa: King's Printer, 1948).

7. Stacey, *Canada's Battle in Normandy*, 24.

8. Ibid., 170.

9. Stacey, *The Canadian Army*, 46.

10. Ibid., 174.

11. See the copy in the Directorate of History and Heritage (DHH), National Defence Headquarters, Ottawa, DHH 010.013 (D5). Hunter's "many discussions" with Pollock are referred to in footnote 391 of the report, which is available online through the DHH website.

12. Ross Munro, *From Gauntlet to Overlord: The Story of the Canadian Army* (Toronto: Macmillan, 1946), 49.

13. Milton Shulman, *Defeat in the West* (London: Secker and Warburg, 1947).

14. Ibid., 108.

15. See the Wilmot Papers, Liddell Hart Centre for Military History, Kings College, London.

16. Chester Wilmot, *The Struggle for Europe* (London: Collins, 1952), 296.

17. Ibid., 299–300.

18. Gordon Harrison, *Cross-Channel Attack: United States Army in World War II: The European Theatre of Operations* (Washington, DC: Office of the Chief of Military History, US Army, 1951), 348.

19. Martin Blumenson, the author of *Breakout and Pursuit* and the historian of Third US Army, was a frequent visitor to my graduate program at the University of New Brunswick, and seminar discussions often focused on the process of historical writing and the perils of writing official history. Blumenson visited shortly after I heard that I would soon be going to Ottawa as an official historian, and there was much good-natured banter about joining the fraternity, and so forth. I later had the "pleasure" of telling him that one of my first acts as an official historian was to destroy the Canadian copies of his drafts of *Breakout and Pursuit*. For the record, there was virtually no marginalia or commentary penciled on the drafts.

20. See Stacey's request to his German historian, A. G. Steiger, 18 December 1951: "Have you found any contemporary documentary evidence whether any part of 21 Pz Div actually reached the coast?" Stacey Papers, University of Toronto Archive, SGR II file 18. AHQ and CMHQ reports are available online at www.cmp-cpm.forces.gc.ca/dhh-dhp. Click "Histories" and then "Reports."

21. See especially Army Headquarters, Historical Section (GS), Report No 50, "The Campaign in North-West Europe: Information from German Sources—Part I: German Defence Preparations in the West," by Captain A. G. Steiger, 30 April 1951.

22. The works were published in 1979 in twenty-four volumes as *World War II German Military Studies* by Garland Publishing of New York. A compilation of these studies focused on the Normandy campaign was edited and published by David Isby and Greenhill Books of London in three volumes as *Fighting the Invasion* (2000), *Fighting in Normandy* (2001), and *Fighting the Breakout* (2004).

23. In addition to correspondence with Steiger in Stacey's personal papers at the University of Toronto Archives, there is extensive correspondence between the two in the DHH Stacey Papers. See LAC RG 24, vol. 20524 for a copy of the questions posed to Fritz Kramer, chief of staff 1st SS Panzer Corps, by the US Army in Munich in 1951 concerning the preliminary moves of panzer forces.

24. C. P. Stacey, *The Victory Campaign: The Operations in North-West Europe, 1944–1945*, vol. 3, *The Official History of the Canadian Army in the Second World War* (Ottawa: Queen's Printer, 1960), 118–119.

25. Ibid., 133.

26. Ibid.

27. Ibid. The paragraph straddles pp. 131–132, quotation on 131.

28. See ibid., 38–41.

29. Ibid., 137.

30. Major L. F. Ellis, *Victory in the West*, vol. 1, *The Battle of Normandy* (London: HMSO, 1962), 206.

31. Ibid., 228.

32. See the discussion of British anxiety about the disintegration of their power and the urge to keep it together in John Darwin, *The Empire Project: The Rise and Fall of the British World System, 1830–1970* (Cambridge: Cambridge University Press, 2009), chap. 12, "The Price of Survival."

33. Ellis, *Victory in the West*, xviii.

34. C. P. Stacey, *Arms, Men and Governments: The War Policies of Canada 1939–1945* (Ottawa: Department of National Defence, 1970).

35. Ibid., 237.

36. Reginald Roy, *1944: The Canadians in Normandy* (Ottawa and Toronto: The Canadian War Museum and Macmillan of Canada, 1984). Roy was a veteran infantry officer with combat experience in Italy, and a former member of Stacey's postwar staff. I am grateful to Dr. Steve Harris, acting director, DHH Ottawa, for the information on Reg Roy's role.

37. Max Hastings, *Overlord: D-Day and the Battle for Normandy 1944* (New York: Simon & Schuster, 1984), 53–54, quotation on 124–125.

38. John A. English, *The Canadian Army and the Normandy Campaign: A Study of Failure in High Command* (New York: Praeger, 1991), 136.

39. Badsey, "Culture, Controversy, Caen and Cherbourg," 48–63, especially 59.

40. Russell A. Hart, *Clash of Arms: How the Allies Won in Normandy* (Boulder, CO: Lynne Rienner, 2001), 248.

41. Ibid., 187.

42. See, for example, Robin Neillands, *The Battle of Normandy 1944* (London: Cassell, 2002), which mentions that the Canadians had "plenty of trouble," ultimately losing 3,000 men in five days fighting against the Hitler Youth, "which disputed every meter of ground" (100).

43. See Stacey's memoir, *A Date with History: Memoirs of a Canadian Historian* (Ottawa: Deneau, 1983), for a discussion of his postwar relationship with senior officers.

44. As it turns out, these were also the basic assumptions of my training as a historian at the University of New Brunswick in the 1970s under Professor Dominick Graham. Shortly after joining the Directorate of History in 1983, I asked the assembled historians at coffee break when we were going to start rewriting Stacey. My suggestion met with a stony silence, followed by the comment that Stacey's was the best army official history of the Second World War and did not need redoing.

45. Mark Zuehlke, *Holding Juno: Canada's Heroic Defence of the D-Day Beaches: June 7–12, 1944* (Toronto: Douglas and MacIntyre, 2005).

46. Michael Reynolds, *Steel Inferno: 1 SS Panzer Corps in Normandy* (New York: Sarpedon, 1997), 85.

Chapter 1: All Roads Lead to Courseulles

1. As quoted in Doug Delaney, *Corps Commanders: Five British and Canadian Generals at War, 1939–45* (Vancouver: University of British Columbia Press, 2011), 260.

2. David W. Hogan Jr., *A Command Post at War: First Army Headquarters in Europe, 1943–45* (Washington, DC: Center of Military History, 2000), 45–46.

3. Quoted in John A. English, *The Canadian Army and the Normandy Campaign: A Study of Failure in High Command* (New York: Praeger, 1991), 189.

4. Lt. W. W. Barrett, *The History of 13 Canadian Field Regiment, Royal Canadian Artillery 1940–1945* (n.p., n.d.), 23.

5. Norman Scarfe, *Assault Division: A History of the 3rd Division from the Invasion of Normandy to the Surrender of Germany* (London: Collins, 1947), 93.

6. Operation Overlord General Part I, July 43–Feb 44, "Preliminary Note on 'Overlord,'" ca. 15 July 1943, The National Archives (TNA), Kew, England, WO 205/643.

7. Stacey, *Victory Campaign*, 18.

8. Editorial, "World Battlefronts: The Second Front," *Time*, 10 August 1942, 29–31.

9. See John Swettenham, *McNaughton*, vol. 2, *1939–1943* (Toronto: Ryerson, 1969), especially chap. 9.

10. Quoted in "The Preliminary Planning for Operation 'OVERLORD': Some Aspects of the Preparations for an Allied Re-entry to North-West Europe, 1940–1944," Report No. 42, Historical Section (GS) Army Headquarters, 5 March 1952, para. 244.

11. Jean Portugal, *We Were There: The Army*, vol. 4 (Toronto: Royal Canadian Military Institute Heritage Society, 1998), 1803. See also Canadian Military Headquarters, Report No. 182, "The Strategic Role of First Canadian Army, 1942–1944," by Capt. J. M. Hitsman, 23 May 1949.

12. Portugal, *We Were There*, 1801.

13. Gen. Sir Charles Loewen, *Memoirs*, vol. 1 (Toronto: privately published, 1985), 251.

14. "Tactical Problems of an Invasion of North West Europe," HF G Staff (training) memo, May 1943, TNA, WO 232/15.

15. Weekly Training Report, 27 November 1943, Library and Archives of Canada (LAC) RG 24, microfilm reel T-1769.

16. Portugal, *We Were There*, 1805–1806.

17. "Overlord Planning Notes for Meeting of Branch Heads—21 Army Group," 5 August 1943, LAC RG 24, vol. 10540, file 215A21.014 (D5).

18. "Study of Tasks of 'Overlord' Assault Divisions," 1 September 1943, LAC RG 24, vol. 10540, file 214A21.014 (D6).

19. "Operation Overlord: Disposition of Enemy Forces, appreciation of possible reactions . . . ," TNA WO 219/1837.

20. "COSSAC War Game September 1943," TNA WO 219/1836.

21. See "New D-Day Scenario," no date but clearly early October 1943, TNA WO 219/1837

22. "Op 'Overlord' Tasks of Assault Divisions," 14 September 1943, LAC RG 24, vol. 10540, file 215A21.014 (D4).

23. "Re-examination of Rate of Reinforcement–NEPTUNE," G2 Int COSSAC to HQ 1st US Army, 22 October 1943, TNA WO 219/1837.

24. "Comparison to Italian Campaign esp. Salerno," Maj. Gen. P. G. Whiteford, ACOS, G-2 Int, COSSAC, 13 January 1944. Salerno was seen as "entirely different to NEPTUNE," with "practically no coastal defences and no static troops holding the coastline," a conclusion that Americans who landed there would find hard to accept. TNA WO 219/1837.

25. Report No. 42, Historical Section (GS), Army Headquarters, "The Preliminary Planning for Operation 'OVERLORD,'" 77.

26. John N. Rickard, *The Politics of Command: Lieutenant-General A. G. L. McNaughton and the Canadian Army 1939–1943* (Toronto: University of Toronto Press, 2010), 128.

27. Col. C. P. Stacey, *Six Years of War: Official History of the Canadian Army in the Second World War*, vol. 1, *The Army in Canada, Britain and the Pacific* (Ottawa: Queen's Printer, 1957), 250.

28. Rickard, *Politics of Command*, 149.

29. For the best analysis of Exercise Spartan and McNaughton's performance, see ibid., chaps. 9 and 10.

30. Ibid., 166.

31. Lester Pearson diary, 11–25 June 1944, LAC MG 26 N8, vol. 1.

32. Angus L. Macdonald diary, 23 December 1943, Public Archives of Nova Scotia.

33. For an excellent discussion of this period, see Swettenham, *McNaughton*, chap. 10.

34. See the Minutes of the Publicity Coordination Committee, 20 July 1943, LAC RG 26/31, vol. 10.

35. See Marc Milner, "The Royal Canadian Navy and 1943: A Year Best Forgotten?" in Paul D. Dickson, ed., *1943: The End of the Beginning* (Water-

loo, ON: Laurier University Centre for Military Strategic and Disarmament Studies, 1995), for a discussion of King's repeated attempts in 1943 to find Canadian military victories to use in his speeches.

36. Report No. 42, Historical Section (GS), Army Headquarters, "The Preliminary Planning for Operation 'OVERLORD,'"235.

37. Sir John Dill to Alan Brooke, 16 October 1943, Liddell Hart Centre for Military History, Alanbrooke Papers 6/2/2.

38. Michael Howard, *British Intelligence in the Second World War*, vol. 5, *Strategic Deception* (New York: Cambridge University Press, 1990), 114.

39. Operation "OVERLORD" Plan, 21 A Grp/oo/74/Ops, 20 December 1943, TNA WO 205/643, Operation Overlord: General Plans.

40. Ralston to Stuart, telegram GS 2437, 9 February 1944, Ralston Papers, LAC MG27 BIII v52.

41. Loewen, *Memoirs*, 251.

42. For a good account of Crerar's awkward relationship with Montgomery in Italy, see Richard S. Malone, *A Portrait of War 1939–1943* (Toronto: Collins, 1983), 196–200.

43. McNaughton to Ralston, telegram, 25 December 1944, Ralston Papers, LAC MG27 BII v52.

44. Broadcast monitored in Ottawa at 1530 GMT, 29 December 1943, Ralston Papers, LAC MG 27 BII v52.

45. Operation "OVERLORD" Plan, 21 A Grp/oo/74/Ops, 29 December 1943, TNA WO 205/643, Operation Overlord: General Plans.

46. Nigel Hamilton, *Montgomery: Master of the Battlefield* (New York: McGraw-Hill, 1983), 530.

47. "COSSAC Int Estimate of 31 January 1944," TNA WO 219/1837.

48. Brereton Greenhous et al., *Crucible of War 1939–1945: The Official History of the Royal Canadian Air Force*, vol. 3 (Toronto: University of Toronto Press, 1994), 272.

49. Hamilton, *Montgomery*, 498.

50. 21st Army Group (AG) estimation, ca. 17 February 1944, TNA WO 219/1837.

51. Maj. Gen. N. R. Bull, memo on "Enemy Reinforcement," 24 February 1944, TNA WO 219/1837.

52. Weekly Neptune Reviews, GSI 21st AG, No. 15, 21 May 1944, speculated that the Germans were moving to seal off the Cotentin, and also that 21st Panzer had moved to south of Caen. TNA WO 205/532.

53. Meeting of Chiefs of Staff, 21st AG, St. Paul's School, 20 March 1944, TNA WO 232/15.

54. LAC RG 24, reel T-7620, 939, my emphasis.

55. LAC RG 24, reel T-7620, 1031.

56. Ellis, *Victory in the West*, 228.

Chapter 2: Prelude to Battle

1. Information based on copies in the Richard Kennedy Papers, National World War II Museum, New Orleans, file 2002-510.

2. Hamilton, *Montgomery*, chap. 9.

3. "21st AG Organization of Artillery," TNA WO 205/22.

4. Landing tables for Second British Army are attached to its war diary, 2 July 1944, TNA WO 171/234.

5. War diary, 3rd Anti-Tank Regiment, RCA, LAC RG 24 C-3, vol. 14562.

6. Recollections of Brigadier P. S. A. Todd in Portugal, *We Were There*, 1808.

7. Ibid.

8. Michael R. McNorgan, *The Gallant Hussars: A History of the 1st Hussars Regiment, 1856–2004* (Aylmer, ON: The 1st Hussars Cavalry Fund/The Aylmer Express, 2004), 104.

9. Sherbrooke Fusiliers' war diary, 7 April 1944, report on the Warcop exercises in the war diary appendixes, LAC microfilm reel T-12758.

10. McNorgan, *Gallant Hussars*, 104.

11. Sherbrooke war diary, 13–14 April 1944, Operation Pedal II orders in the appendixes, LAC microfilm reel T-12758.

12. Portugal, *We Were There*, 1807.

13. 7th Brigade's operational order is dated 18 May 1944.

14. See Anthony Beevor, *D-Day: The Battle for Normandy* (New York: Viking, 2009), 3.

15. Carlo D'Este, *Patton: A Genius for War* (New York: HarperCollins, 1995), 593.

16. Howard, *British Intelligence in the Second World War*, 120.

17. D'Este, *Patton*, 593.

18. Roger Hesketh, *Fortitude: The D-Day Deception Campaign* (New York: Overlook Press, 2000), 172.

19. Ibid., 175.

20. Ibid., 172 and 128.

21. Stacey, *Victory Campaign*, 75. The Canadian files for Exercise Quicksilver are thin, virtually useless, but LAC RG 24, vol. 10550, 215A21.033 (D3) contains a list of US Army communications teams and their locations as part of the exercise.

22. "Historical Record of Deception in the War Against Germany and Italy," TNA CAB 154/101.

23. 2nd Canadian Corps war diary, May–June 1944, LAC microfilm reel T-1866.

24. Hesketh, *Fortitude*, 97–98.

25. Stacey, *Victory Campaign*, 46.

26. As quoted in D'Este, *Patton*, 586.

27. Hesketh, *Fortitude*, 181.

28. 21st Army Group letter, 20 February 1944, TNA WO 205/1837.

29. By early April the Allies grouped German divisions into panzer/panzer grenadier, mobile, static, and limited employment categories. F. H. Hinsley, *British Intelligence in the Second World War*, abridged edition (Cambridge: Cambridge University Press, 1993), 455. Volume 2, part 2 of Hinsley's multi-volume version contains a separate appendix (no. 14) on intelligence concerning the location of both 352nd Division and 21st Panzer.

30. *World War II German Military Studies*, vol. 12, pt. 5, *The Western Theatre* (New York: Garland, 1979), MS B-720, 17.

31. Meyer, *12th SS*, 47–49.

32. Assessments taken from "Periodic Review of Conditions in Europe and the Scale of Opposition to 'Overlord,'" Joint Intelligence Sub-Committee report, 25 May 1944, updated to 26 May, TNA, PREM 3/342/9. See also Hamilton, *Montgomery*, 584; Hinsley, *British Intelligence in the Second World War*, abridged edition, 455.

33. Hinsley, *British Intelligence in the Second World War*, abridged edition, 456.

34. "Enemy Reaction to Overlord: Land Forces," 6 May 1944, TNA WO 219/1837.

35. Horst Boog et al., *Germany and the Second World War*, vol. 3, *The Strategic Air War in Europe and the War in the West and East Asia 1943–1944/45* (Oxford: Clarendon Press, 2006), see especially pt. 2, chap. 3, sec. 5, "Behaviour and Morale of German Troops in the West," 544.

36. Russell Hart, "Osthärte im Westheer: The 'Easternization' of the German Army in the West, 1944," paper presented at the conference "1944: Seventy Years On," Royal Military Academy, Sandhurst, England, 14–18 April 2014.

37. Boog et al., *Germany and the Second World War*, 519.

38. Quoted in Matthew Cooper, *The German Army 1933–1945* (Chelsea, MI: Scarborough House, 1990), 497–498.

39. Boog et al., *Germany and the Second World War*, 519.

40. Hinsley, *British Intelligence in the Second World War*, abridged edition, 457.

41. JIC estimates, 25 May 1944, TNA, PREM 3/342/9.

42. Hinsley, *British Intelligence in the Second World War*, abridged edition, 458.

43. Harrison, *Cross-Channel Attack*, 260.

44. With updates to 26 May 1944, TNA PREM 3/342/9.

45. Hinsley, *British Intelligence in the Second World War*, abridged edition, 458.

46. See F. H. Hinsley, *British Intelligence in the Second World War: Its Influence on Strategy and Operations*, vol. 3, pt. 2 (New York: Cambridge University Press, 1988), appendix 14.

47. Weekly Neptune Review, GSI 21st Army Group, No. 16, 28 May 1944, TNA WO 205/532.

48. Hinsley, *British Intelligence in the Second World War*, abridged edition, 460.

49. According to Hinsley, I British Corps appeared to take no notice of this warning and operated on the assumption that 21st Panzer was twenty to thirty miles inland and would not be a factor on D-Day. See his vol. 3, pt. 2, appendix 14. Surviving documents in the National Archives in Britain (checked against Hinsley's claims) support his contention: the presence of 21st Panzer in the Caen area is very clear in the intelligence summaries of all formations prior to D-Day.

50. Eric Larabee, *Commander in Chief: Franklin Delano Roosevelt, His Lieutenants and Their War* (Annapolis, MD: US Naval Institute Press, 1987), 455.

Chapter 3: The Assault, 6 June

1. Boog et al., *Germany and the Second World War*, 581.

2. Marlis G. Steinart, *Hitler's War and the Germans: Public Mood and Attitude during the Second World War* (Athens: Ohio University Press, 1977), 258.

3. See drafts of "Time Out for a War," typescript, retype 3/4, chaps. 1–8, Ingersoll Papers, Gottlieb Archives, Boston University, box 17, file 7.

4. Stacey, *Victory Campaign*, 39–41.

5. See "Operation Fortitude Deception Plan," vol. 2, 1155; the quotation is from a plan dated 5 November 1943, emphasis in the original, TNA WO 219/308.

6. Canadian AHQ Narrative No. 42, 131.

7. Lt.-Col. G. W. L. Nicholson, *The Canadians in Italy 1943–1945: Official History of the Canadian Army in the Second World War*, vol. 2 (Ottawa: Queen's Printer and Controller of Stationery, 1956), 391.

8. The most recent scholarly assessment of Operation Fortitude, Mary Kathryn Barbier's *D-Day Deception: Operation Fortitude and the Normandy Invasion* (Westport, CT: Praeger Security International, 2007), is unaware (as indeed are all studies of Operation Fortitude) that it was widely assumed prior to 1944 that First Canadian Army would lead the attack on France. The Canadian army's value in FUSAG and the Fortitude deception was therefore probably more significant than Anglo-American historians have assumed. In fairness, it needs to be said that the Operation Fortitude deception records at

the TNA, the WO 219 series, are typically focused on the general threat, not specific formations.

9. Howard, *British Intelligence in the Second World War*, 115.

10. Larabee, *Commander in Chief*, 453.

11. William F. Buckingham, *D-Day: The First 72 Hours* (Stroud, Gloucestershire: Tempus, 2004), 115.

12. Boog et al., *Germany and the Second World War*, 585.

13. Buckingham, *D-Day*, 153.

14. Ibid., 152.

15. See the extracts from 352nd Division's radio log published in David Isby, ed., *Fighting the Invasion: The German Army at D-Day* (London: Greenhill Books, 2000), 205–206.

16. Buckingham, *D-Day*, 154.

17. Ibid., 157.

18. Harrison, *Cross-Channel Attack*, 304.

19. Hogan, *Command Post at War*, 40.

20. For a landing table, see *V Corps Operations in the E.T.O., 6 Jan. 1942–9 May 1945*, G-3 Historical Section, V Corps (n.p., n.d.), 33–34. For information on the artillery units and the division organization, see Shelby Stanton, *World War II Order of Battle* (New York: Galahad Books, 1984).

21. 16th Regiment Combat Team was supported by 7th FA and 62nd Armoured FA; 116th RCT was supported by 111th FA and 58th Armoured FA.

22. *V Corps Operations in the E.T.O.*, 63.

23. Harrison, *Cross-Channel Attack*, 313.

24. Samuel Eliot Morison, *History of United States Naval Operations in World War II*, vol. 11, *The Invasion of France and Germany* (Boston: Little, Brown, 1968); for a description of the destroyer actions, see 142–149, quotation on 147.

25. Cable 90024, 8 June 1944, in *The Papers of Dwight David Eisenhower: The War Years III*, ed. Alfred D. Chandler (Baltimore: Johns Hopkins University Press, 1970), emphasis added.

26. See the telephone diary of 352nd Division, Isby, 2000, 207. 915th GR set off to search for parachutists at 0420 hours (German time; 0320 hours British time) and expected to take three to four hours to arrive.

27. Ethan Rawls Williams, LCDR USN, "50 Div in Normandy: A Critical Analysis of the British 50th (Northumbrian) Division on D-Day and in the Battle of Normandy" (MA thesis, US Army Command and General Staff College, 2007), 61.

28. Ken Ford, *Battle Zone Normandy: Sword Beach* (Stroud, Gloucestershire: Sutton, 2004), 32.

29. For a discussion of the naval fire support issue, see Daniel P. Malone,

"Breaking Down the Wall: Bombarding Force E and Naval Fire Support on June Beach" (MA thesis, University of New Brunswick, 2005).

30. Stacey, *Victory Campaign*, 109.

31. Lt. G. M. Ruffie and L./Bdr. J. B. Dickie, *The History of the 14 Field Regiment 1940–1945* (Amsterdam: Wereldbibliothek, 1945), 26–27.

32. Information on tides, etc., from *ISIS Report on France*, vol. 2, *Normandy West of the Seine*, pt. V(B), *Ports*, Kennedy Papers, World War II Museum, New Orleans, file 2002-510.

33. Will R. Bird, *No Retreating Footsteps: The Story of the North Nova Scotia Highlanders* (Amherst, NS: Furlong's Rapid Print & Digital Design, 2007), 63.

34. Stacey, *Victory Campaign*, 109.

35. The German plan of deployments in the Caen sector prior to D-Day shows no antitank guns in the Tailleville area; TNA WO 205/532. This plan is reproduced in Jean-Claude Perrigault, *21.Panzerdivision* (Bayeux, France: Heimdal, 2002). Stacey's map of "German Forces and Defences" on 6 June 1944 (opposite page 50 in Stacey 1960) shows two antitank guns.

36. Ian V. Hogg, *German Artillery of World War Two* (London: Greenhill Books, 1997), 214–218.

37. The Canadian official history never explains the delay; see Stacey, *Victory Campaign*, 109.

38. Bill Lee's testimony in Stan Medland, "Confrontation in Normandy: The 3rd Canadian Anti-Tank Regiment on D-Day," *Canadian Military History* 3 (1994): 60.

39. Ibid., 55.

40. Brigadier A. L. Pemberton, MC, *The Development of Artillery Tactics and Equipment* (part of Second World War 1939–1945 Army in-house series), (London: War Office, 1950), 223.

41. Terry Copp, *Fields of Fire: The Canadians in Normandy* (Toronto: University of Toronto Press, 2003), 53.

42. Ibid., 55.

43. Buckingham, *D-Day*, 223.

44. Ibid., 228.

45. Boog et al., *Germany and the Second World War*, 595.

46. Ibid., 594.

47. Reynolds, *Steel Inferno*, 54–55.

48. Milton Shulman, *Defeat in the West* (London: Secker and Warburg, 1947), 103–104.

49. Reynolds, *Steel Inferno*, 57.

50. Buckingham, *D-Day*, 233.

51. Feuchtinger's testimony in P. Whitney Lackenbauer and Chris Madsen,

eds., *Kurt Meyer on Trial [A Documentary Record]* (Kingston, ON: Canadian Defence Academy Press, 2007). Shulman's *Defeat in the West* puts the fuel issue a day later.

52. Shulman, *Defeat in the West*, 105.

53. Reynolds, *Steel Inferno*, 60.

Chapter 4: 9th Brigade Advances

1. Copp, *Fields of Fire*, 62.

2. Stacey, *Victory Campaign*, 77. See also "Overlord Operational Order, HQ RCA, 3rd Canadian Division, 15 May 1944," LAC microfilm reel T-15455.

3. Perrigault, *21.Panzerdivison*, 232.

4. Hinsley, *British Intelligence in the Second World War*, abridged edition, 475.

5. Stacey, *Victory Campaign*, 126–127.

6. Copp, *Fields of Fire*, 65.

7. Stacey, *Victory Campaign*, 126.

8. Ibid., 133.

9. Testimony of Lt. Col. Charles Petch, "Report of the Court of Enquiry re: Shooting of Allied Prisoners of War . . . ," DHH 90/168.

10. Lt. Col. Richard M. Ross, OBE, *The History of the 1st Battalion Cameron Highlanders of Ottawa (MG)* (privately published, n.d.), 42.

11. Telephone interview with Don Learment by Doug Hope, ca. 2003.

12. Operational order, RCA, 3rd Canadian Division, LAC microfilm reel T-15455.

13. Lackenbauer and Madsen, *Kurt Meyer on Trial*, 483; the court's summary of evidence is more emphatic about this than the published version of Meitzel's testimony, see 440. Copp notes that they, and elements of 21st Panzer, were there, but he does not attempt to assess their dispositions and strength; see *Fields of Fire*, 65.

14. Lackenbauer and Madsen, *Kurt Meyer on Trial*, 440. Meitzel's claim is supported by Perrigault, *21.Panzerdivision*, 505.

15. Perrigault (*21.Panzerdivision*, 261) says that elements of the 716th Division held Buron, and Meitzel put them in Franqueville and Authie; Lackenbauer and Madsen, *Kurt Meyer on Trial*, 440.

16. Lackenbauer and Madsen, *Kurt Meyer on Trial*, 449.

17. I am grateful to Dr. Andrew Wheale, Royal Military College, Sandhurst, United Kingdom, for sharing his research on 21st Panzer with me.

18. This description of the battlefield is based on more than a decade of leading battlefield study tours in the area.

19. War diary, Sherbrooke Fusiliers, LAC microfilm reel T-12758.

20. Perrigault, *21.Panzerdivision*, 219, lists this unit as equipped with 8.14cm Granatwerfers. Lt. N. Davies of the Sherbrookes' B Squadron claimed the rocket-equipped half-track was on the left side of the road. See the report of B Squadron's action by Lt. Davies in LAC microfilm reel T-12758.

21. See Lt. L. N. Davies's account, war diary of the Sherbrookes, LAC microfilm reel T-12758.

22. Bird, *No Retreating Footsteps*, 77.

23. The Stormont, Dundas, and Glengarry Highlanders arrived at les Buissons about 1000 hours and had to clear it of snipers. See Lt. Col. W. Boss and Brig. Gen. W. J. Patterson, *Up the Glens: Stormont, Dundas and Glengarry Highlanders 1783–1994* (Cornwall, ON: The Old Book Store, 1995), 102.

24. Bird, *No Retreating Footsteps*, 75.

25. Account Recce Squadron and No. 2 Troop, C Sqn Sherbrooke Fusiliers, by Sgt. T. C. Reid, LAC microfilm reel T-12758.

26. Bird, *No Retreating Footsteps*, 77.

27. Zuehlke, *Holding Juno*, 90.

28. Bird, *No Retreating Footsteps*, 77.

29. Ibid.

30. Lt. N. Davies, account of B Squadron on 7 June 1944, LAC microfilm reel T-12758.

31. Gun positions described in Craig W. H. Luther, *Blood and Honor: The History of the 12th SS Panzer Division "Hitler Youth," 1943–1945* (San Jose, CA: James Bender, 1987), 129; and Meyer, *12th SS*, 139.

32. See Sherbrookes' reports in LAC microfilm reel T-12785.

33. Lackenbauer and Madsen, *Kurt Meyer on Trial*, 141–142.

34. Zuehlke, *Holding Juno*, 90.

35. Stacey, *Victory Campaign*, 128.

36. War diary, 14th RCA, 7 June 1944, LAC RG 24, vol. 14, 471. See also Lt. G. E. M. Ruffee and L./Bdr. J. B. Dickie, *The History of the 14 Field Regiment Royal Canadian Artillery 1940–1945* (Amsterdam: Wereldbibliotheek NV, 1945), 28.

37. Copp, *Fields of Fire*, 66.

38. Telephone interviews with Struther and Alkenbrack by Doug Hope, n.d.

39. Rev. R. Myles Hickey, *The Scarlet Dawn* (Fredericton, NB: Unipress, 1949), 172.

40. For an account of the NSR attempt to take the Douvres radar station, see Marc Milner, *D-Day to Carpiquet: The North Shore Regiment and the Liberation of Europe* (Fredericton, NB: Goose Lane Editions/NB Military Heritage Project, 2006), chap. 4.

41. Zuehlke, *Holding Juno*, 90. The account of the Sherbrookes' reconnaissance troop for 7 June 1944 notes that at 1230 hours they were fighting near St. Contest. LAC microfilm reel T-12758.

42. Bird, *No Retreating Footsteps*, 78.

43. 12th SS artillery was not ordered to open fire until sometime after 1300 hours.

44. Sherbrookes' C Squadron reports, LAC microfilm reel T-12758.

45. Zuehlke, *Holding Juno*, 92.

46. This account is drawn from the interviews of Capt. J. A. Wilson and Capt. E. S. Gray, both NNSH, in late June 1944 by a historical officer. It remains the most cogent short account of events. Directorate of History and Heritage (DHH), NDHQ, Ottawa, 145.2N2011 (D3).

47. Bird, *No Retreating Footsteps*, 80.

48. Account of B Squadron by Lt. N. Davies, LAC microfilm reel T-12758.

49. LAC microfilm reel T-12758.

50. Lt. Col. H. M. Jackson, MBE, ED, *The Sherbrooke Regiment (12th Armoured Regiment)* (privately published, 1958), 124.

51. In his testimony at the Kurt Meyer trial, Lt. Col. Petch recalled that he ordered the advance from Buron to Authie at "about one o'clock"; Lackenbauer and Madsen, *Kurt Meyer on Trial*, 441. The NNSH war diary reported that the leading elements of the battalion reached Authie at 1230 hours; see the verbatim version reprinted in Terry Copp and Robert Vogel, *Maple Leaf Route: Caen* (Alma, ON: Maple Leaf Route, 1983), 70–72. The Novas' history says Authie was secure at 1330 hours; Bird, *No Retreating Footsteps*, 80.

52. Jackson, *Sherbrooke Regiment*, 124.

Chapter 5: Death in the Afternoon

1. Bird, *No Retreating Footsteps*, 51.

2. Meyer, *12th SS*, 134. Kurt Meyer claimed in 1945 that the division had 214 tanks in service and 22 Mk IV Jagdpanzers, and that the division was at full personnel strength on 6 June 1944; Lackenbauer and Madsen, *Kurt Meyer on Trial*, 68. For the most comprehensive assessment of the strength of 12th SS during this period, see Arthur Gulachsen, "The Defeat and Attrition of the 12th SS Panzer Division 'Hitlerjugend': A Case Study, June 6th–July 12th, 1944" (MA thesis, University of New Brunswick, 2005).

3. Hastings, *Overlord*, 118.

4. 12th SS had an operational strength on 6 June 1944 of roughly 17,000, since not all of its units were complete. Buckingham, *D-Day*, 44.

5. I am grateful to Chris Kretschzmar for tracking down this information. The size of the companies of 12th SS is confirmed in the notes taken by Walter

Keith in the fall of 1944 when he joined the Regina Rifles as a subaltern. These list the companies as 210 men.

6. Details from Gulachsen, "Defeat and Attrition of the 12th SS Panzer Division 'Hitlerjugend.'" The camouflage uniforms confused Canadians in the first few days ashore; they often reported parachutists in their war diaries. It turns out that 21st Panzer troops also wore their camouflaged shelter half as a smock, so that it was not always easy to distinguish 21st Panzer from 12th SS.

7. Hogg, *German Artillery of World War Two*, 214–217, 197–200.

8. Buckingham, *D-Day*, 259.

9. Shulman, *Defeat in the West*, 105.

10. Lackenbauer and Madsen, *Kurt Meyer on Trial*, 141–142.

11. Meyer, *12th SS*, 138. See also Niklas Zetterling, *Normandy 1944: German Military Organization, Combat Power and Organizational Effectiveness* (Winnipeg: Fedorowicz, 2000), for a discussion of 12th SS organization and equipment.

12. Howard Margolian, *Conduct Unbecoming: The Story of the Murder of Canadian Prisoners of War in Normandy* (Toronto: University of Toronto Press, 1998), 45–46.

13. Testimony of Lt. Col. Petch, in Lackenbauer and Madsen, *Kurt Meyer on Trial*, 141.

14. Testimony of Maj. Don Learment, ibid., 161.

15. Davies account is in Sherbrookes' war diary, LAC microfilm reel T-12758.

16. Copp, *Fields of Fire*, 66.

17. Lawrence James Zapporzan, "Rad's War: A Biographical Study of Sydney Radley-Walters from Mobilization to the End of the Normandy Campaign 1944" (MA thesis, University of New Brunswick, 2001), 149.

18. Interview with Capt. J. A. Wilson and Capt. E. S. Gray, Directorate of History and Heritage, National Defence Headquarters, Ottawa, file 145.2N2011 (D3).

19. Stacey, *Victory Campaign*, 79.

20. The rise at St. Contest is slight but important. At its southwestern edge, near the highway, it provides a superb view of the battlefield and is often used by Canadian tours as a stand to discuss this battle.

21. Bird, *No Retreating Footsteps*, 85.

22. I am grateful to Marcus Faulkner, Kings College, University of London, whose research on naval fire support is the basis for this information. The log of HMS *Belfast* at the National Archives records nothing of this failed attempt on 7 June. Doug Hope did an extensive evaluation of fire support from both *Belfast* and *Diadem* on 6–8 June 1944, and I am grateful to him for sharing his work.

23. War diary, 14th RCA, 7 June 1944, LAC RG 24, vol. 14471; Ellis, *Victory in the West,* 229.

24. Malcolm Langille, interview with Doug Hope, ca. 2003.

25. Boss and Patterson, *Up the Glens,* 103.

26. Bird, *No Retreating Footsteps,* 73.

27. "History of HQ RCA 3 Cdn Inf Div," no date but clearly compiled in the summer of 1945. DHH 142.33 (D1); see 6.

28. Portugal, *We Were There,* 1811–1812. When asked about this by the author in 2006, Garth Webb, a troop commander with 66th Battery of 14th Field, was totally dismissive of the idea that the guns had failed on D+1.

29. Lackenbauer and Madsen, *Kurt Meyer on Trial,* 141.

30. Ross, *History of the 1st Battalion Cameron Highlanders of Ottawa (MG),* 42; Bird, *No Retreating Footsteps,* 84.

31. Zapporzan, "Rad's War," 151.

32. Five of the eight British 17-pounders engaged were lost in the action. Copp, *Fields of Fire,* 104.

33. Lackenbauer and Madsen, *Kurt Meyer on Trial,* 142.

34. Ibid.; Bird, *No Retreating Footsteps,* 87.

35. Testimony by Lt. Col. Petch, in Lackenbauer and Madsen, *Kurt Meyer on Trial,* 142.

36. War diary, Sherbrooke Fusiliers, 7 June 1944, LAC microfilm reel T-12758. Fitzpatrick was killed nearby a month later, on 8 July, during the final assault on Caen.

37. Bird, *No Retreating Footsteps,* 89.

38. Ibid., 90.

39. See Margolian, *Conduct Unbecoming,* chap. 5, "The Milius Murders."

40. Ibid., 59–61; Lackenbauer and Madsen, *Kurt Meyer on Trial,* 162. Lieutenants Jack Veness and Jack Fairweather survived the ordeal of initial capture and later escaped from a POW train, fought with the French resistance, and rejoined the Canadian army later in the campaign. For their remarkable story, see Will R. Bird, *The Two Jacks: The Amazing Adventures of Major Jack M. Veness and Major Jack L. Fairweather* (Philadelphia: Macrae Smith, 1955).

41. Bird, *No Retreating Footsteps,* 87.

42. Ibid., 95.

43. Ibid.

44. Ibid., 97.

45. Meyer, *12th SS,* 141–142.

46. Bird, *No Retreating Footsteps,* 97.

47. Zapporzan, "Rad's War," 147.

48. Meyer, *12th SS,* 144.

49. Bird, *No Retreating Footsteps,* 98; Lackenbauer and Madsen, *Kurt Meyer on Trial,* 162.

50. Lackenbauer and Madsen, *Kurt Meyer on Trial*, 163–164.

51. Margolian, *Conduct Unbecoming*, 63–64.

52. Zapporzan, "Rad's War," 149.

53. Doug Hope, "The Battle at Buron and Authie June 7th 1944" (unpublished manuscript, 2008).

54. Interview with Col. D. Struther by Doug Hope, n.d.

55. Bird, *No Retreating Footsteps*, 98.

56. The Novas' history claims that it happened after 1930 hours; see ibid., 100. 14th RCA war diary records firing about that time.

57. Bird, *No Retreating Footsteps*, 100–101.

58. The Novas' war diary in Copp and Vogel, *Maple Leaf Route*, 72–74.

59. Buckingham, *D-Day*, 258.

60. Ibid., 259.

61. Canadian figures from Copp, *Fields of Fire*, 66; 12th SS figures from Buckingham, *D-Day*, 259. I have found no accounting of 21st Panzer or 716th Division losses in this battle.

62. War diary for 7 June 1944, LAC microfilm reel T-12785.

63. Buckingham, *D-Day*, 259.

64. Ibid.

65. Bird, *No Retreating Footsteps*, 97

66. Shulman, *Defeat in the West*, 105.

67. Reynolds, *Steel Inferno*, 69.

68. During the trial of Meyer, the defense claimed that forty-one POWs were murdered, while the prosecution alleged that the number could be as high as forty-six (these figures include the murders at the abbey, for which Meyer was held responsible); Lackenbauer and Madsen, *Kurt Meyer on Trial*, 485, 507. Margolian claims that thirty-seven died in the fields around Authie, a claim supported by the people of the village.

69. Hastings, *Overlord*, 125.

70. Dempsey diary, 8 June 1944, TNA, WO 285/9.

Chapter 6: According to Plan

1. Testimony of John Swityk to Walter Keith. Landing tables for the Reginas provided by Walter Keith.

2. For details, see Portugal, *We Were There*, 1772–1773; and Gordon Brown and Terry Copp, *Look to Your Front: Regina Rifles, A Regiment at War: 1944–45*, Laurier Centre for Military Strategic and Disarmament Studies (Kitchener-Waterloo, ON: Wilfrid Laurier University Press, 2001), chap. 2.

3. It appears that the citizens of Courseulles held no grudge against Gariepy. He returned to the town after the war, eventually became mayor, and was re-

sponsible for the recovery of 1st Hussars DD tank that now graces the town center.

4. McNorgan, *Gallant Hussars*, 121–122.

5. Brown and Copp, *Look to Your Front*, 27.

6. Bruce Tascona and Eric Wells, *Little Black Devils: A History of the Royal Winnipeg Rifles* (Winnipeg: Frye, 1983), 147. I once timed a student, wearing only shorts, a T-shirt, and running shoes, in a sprint from the low-water mark to the wrack line: it took him forty seconds.

7. McNorgan, *Gallant Hussars*, 121–122.

8. Reginald Roy, *Ready for the Fray: The History of the Canadian Scottish Regiment (Princess Mary's) 1920–2002* (Calgary, AB: Bunker to Bunker, 2002), 228.

9. *Into Action with the 12th Field* (n.p., n.d.), 45.

10. Barrett, *History of 13 Canadian Field Regiment*, does not specify the time, nor does the history of 12th RCA, but since both began to move off the beach around 1530 to 1550 hours, this seems about right.

11. Interview with Lt. Col. Webb, 23 June 1944, DHH 142.4F12013 (D1).

12. Tom Greenlees, the regiment survey officer, recalled no losses to the reconnaissance party when coming ashore. Letter to the author, 11 April 2002.

13. Interview with Maj. R. Mackenzie, Toronto, 29 April 2004.

14. Interview with Col. F. le P. T. Clifford, Ottawa, 25 April 2002.

15. Medland, "Confrontation in Normandy," 55.

16. Ibid., 56.

17. "Memorandum of Interview with Lt Col F. M. Matheson, OC Regina Rif," Army Historical Officer, 24 June 1944, DHH 145.2R11011 (D4).

18. Tony Foster, *Meeting of Generals* (Toronto: Metheun, 1986), 30.

19. Ibid.

20. Stacey, *Victory Campaign*, 125.

21. War diary/battle log, 7 June 1944, 0735, LAC microfilm reel T-12015.

22. McNorgan, *Gallant Hussars*, 125.

23. Stacey, *Victory Campaign*, 126.

24. Information courtesy of Walter Keith.

25. 13th RCA, war diary, 7 June 1944.

26. Barrett, *History of 13 Canadian Field Regiment*, 37.

27. Harold Merrick to the author, 11 April 2002.

28. "Memorandum on DF and DF (SOS) Tasks," n/d, North Shore Regiment Archives, Bathurst, NB.

29. Tony Foulds, "In Support of the Canadians: A British Anti-Tank Regiment's First Five Weeks in Normandy," *Canadian Military History* 7 (1998): 73.

30. There is uncertainty in the existing literature about the locale of B Company. Walter Keith's research, based on a thorough examination of the

published material, including interviews, as well as research into citations for valor, demonstrates conclusively that B Company was in the field northeast of Norrey, stretching to the road running east out of Bretteville. See, for example, John Treleaven's citation for the Croix de Guerre and grid references in the Reginas' war diary.

31. Major Lockie Fulton interview, in Portugal, *We Were There*, 2918. Fulton claims the M10s were from 3rd Anti-Tank, RCA, but the evidence in the regiment's unpublished history, "3rd Canadian Anti-Tank Regiment, R.C.A.," compiled by Dick Willows, claims that all the M10s were with 8th and 9th Brigades.

32. Copp, *Fields of Fire*, 68.

33. 7th Brigade war diary, 7 June 44, LAC microfilm reel T-12758.

34. Fulton interview, in Portugal, *We Were There*, 2918.

35. *Little Black Devils*, 150.

Chapter 7: Putot, 8 June

1. "COSSAC Int Estimate of 31 January 1944," TNA WO 219/1837.

2. Harrison, *Cross-Channel Attack*, 337–339.

3. *ISIS Report on France: Volume 2: Normandy West of the Seine: Part I, Geography*, Inter-Service Topographic Department, May 1943, BR 876 J (11), 19, copy in the Richard Kennedy Papers, MS 2002-510-02, National World War II Museum, New Orleans.

4. See the diary of Sir Miles Dempsey, entries for June 1944, TNA WO 285/9.

5. Meyer, *12th SS*, 162–163.

6. As quoted in Isby, *Fighting the Invasion*, 48.

7. "Operation Overlord: Disposition of Enemy Forces, appreciation of possible reactions . . . ," TNA WO 219/1837.

8. Isby, *Fighting the Invasion*, 42.

9. Ibid., 47.

10. Franz Kurowski, *Elite Panzer Strike Force: Germany's Panzer Lehr Division in World War II* (Mechanicsburg, PA: Stackpole Books, 2011), 22.

11. Ibid., 26.

12. Ibid., 27.

13. Beevor, *D-Day*, 176.

14. Figures from Buckingham, *D-Day*, 233.

15. Beevor, *D-Day*, 176.

16. Kurowski, *Elite Panzer Strike Force*, 32.

17. Helmut Ritgen, *The Western Front: Memoirs of a Panzer Lehr Officer* (Winnipeg: J. J. Fedorowicz, 1995), 40.

18. Ritgen says "near Cheux" (ibid., 39), while Kurowski says le Mesnil-Patry (*Elite Panzer Strike Force*, 35).

19. Ritgen, *Western Front*, 40.

20. Margolian, *Conduct Unbecoming*, 76–77, 87, 101.

21. Meyer, *12th SS*, 162.

22. Tubb, in Portugal, *We Were There*, 912; Barrett, *History of 13 Canadian Field Regiment*, 38.

23. Citation for Mention in Despatches, for Sgt. Archibald Herbert John James "for gallant and outstanding action during the assault across the Leopold Canal 6–10 Oct 44."; copy provided by Walter Keith.

24. Mel Clark, letter to John Raulston Saul, 24 April 2001; copy provided by Walter Keith.

25. Report of the 2nd Canadian Armoured Brigade on fighting in the first two weeks ashore, dated 26 June 1944, author's copy, original source unknown, para 14.

26. Quotations from the 2nd Armoured Brigade report of 26 June. No other source mentions this incident, perhaps because—in the end—no serious action occurred.

27. As quoted in Meyer, *12th SS*, 165.

28. See ibid., 50. For the best account of the Reginas' battle, see Brown and Copp, *Look to Your Front*.

29. Barrett, *History of 13 Canadian Field Regiment*, 37.

30. Interview with Clifford, 25 April 2002.

31. Mel Clark's letter to John Ralston Saul, 24 April 2001.

32. 7th Brigade war diary, entries for 7 and 8 June, LAC microfilm reel T-12758.

33. Ritgen, *Western Front*, 38.

34. Tascona and Wells, *Little Black Devils*, 151.

35. Ibid.

36. Margolian, *Conduct Unbecoming*, 79.

37. Brian A. Reid, *Named by the Enemy: A History of the Royal Winnipeg Rifles* (Altona, MB: Robin Brass/The Royal Winnipeg Rifles, 2010), 173.

38. Meldram, in Portugal, *We Were There*, 3115.

39. *3rd Canadian Anti-Tank Regiment, R.C.A.*, 29.

40. Mike Bechthold, "Defending the Normandy Bridgehead: The Battles for Putot-en-Bessin, 7–9 June 1944," in Geoffrey Hayes, Mike Bechthold, and Matt Symes, eds., *Canada and the Second World War: Essays in Honour of Terry Copp* (Waterloo, ON: Wilfrid Laurier University Press, 2012), 375.

41. Portugal, *We Were There*, 3055.

42. Bechthold, "Defending the Normandy Bridgehead," 378.

43. Tascona and Wells, *Little Black Devils*, 152.

44. Portugal, *We Were There*, 3045.

45. See Bechthold, "Defending the Normandy Bridgehead," nn. 27, 28.

46. Foulds, "In Support of the Canadians," 74; Roy, *Ready for the Fray*, 240.

47. Kurowski, *Elite Panzer Strike Force*, 35.

48. Bechthold, "Defending the Normandy Bridgehead," 376; Meyer, *12th SS*, 167.

49. Meyer, *12th SS*, 173.

50. Oliver Haller, "Defeat of the 12th SS: 7–10 June 1944," *Canadian Military History* 3 (1994): 15.

51. Margolian, *Conduct Unbecoming*, 84–85.

52. Meyer, *12th SS*, 175.

53. Kurowski, *Elite Panzer Strike Force*, 36.

54. Hesketh, *Fortitude*, 202.

55. Isby, *Fighting the Invasion*, 48.

56. A brief description of the fire plan is in the radio log of 7th Canadian Infantry Brigade, TNA WO 179/2879.

57. Quoted in Bechthold, "Defending the Normandy Bridgehead," 380.

58. Ibid., 381–382.

Chapter 8: Bretteville and Cardonville, 8 June

1. Hesketh, *Fortitude*, 202.

2. Meyer, *12th SS*, 177.

3. Ibid.

4. *Vanguard: The Fort Garry Horse in the Second World War* (n.p., n.d.), 21.

5. War diary, 3rd Anti-Tank Regiment, RCA, 10 June 1944, LAC RG 24 C-3, vol. 14562.

6. The extract from C Squadron's diary is appended to the regimental history, *Vanguard*, 136. McAleese was killed in action on 18 July 1944.

7. 21st Army Group Daily Intelligence Summary, No. 124, 8 June 1944, War Diary GSO 1, HQ, 21 Army Group, TNA WO 171/129.

8. See 3rd Canadian Division Intelligence Summary, No. 2, 9 June 1944, LAC microfilm reel T-12758.

9. Portugal, *We Were There*, 834.

10. See Brown's sketch of Cardonville farm, ibid., 846. It is not an entirely accurate map, but the detail is fascinating.

11. War diary, 2nd RMAS, 8 June 1944, TNA ADM 202/306.

12. The war diary, 79th Medium RA, for 8 June 1944 records being "in action" at 1730 hours and later "engaged tanks to the front." TNA WO 171/1065.

13. War diary, 6th RA, TNA WO 171/967; war diary, 191st RA, TNA WO 171/1004.

14. Margolian, *Conduct Unbecoming*, 71.

15. Quoted in Reynolds, *Steel Inferno*, 78.

16. Margolian, *Conduct Unbecoming*, 104.

17. Quoted in Reynolds, *Steel Inferno*, 79.

18. 94th Battery of 3rd Anti-Tank, RCA, was a composite battery for the Overlord Operation, with two of its own 6-pounder troops, G and H, and K Troop of 105th Battery. H Troop was in support of the Winnipegs at Putot, so by simple elimination the two troops at the east end of Bretteville were G and K. *3rd Canadian Anti-Tank Regiment R.C.A.*, 24.

19. G. W. L. Nicholson, *The Gunners of Canada: The History of the Royal Regiment of Canadian Artillery*, vol. 2 (Toronto: McClelland and Stewart, 1972), 282.

20. Information provided by Walter Keith.

21. See Robert Engen, *Canadians under Fire: Infantry Effectiveness in the Second World War* (Montreal-Kingston: McGill-Queen's University Press, 2009).

22. HQ 7th Brigade battle log, 9 June, serial 391, 0615 hours, TNA WO 179/2879.

23. Information provided to Walter Keith by J. McNinch.

24. 7th Brigade battle log, 9 June, 0045 hours, observes that the DF and SOS fires had been arranged. TNA WO 179/2879.

25. Meyer, *12th SS*, 181–183.

26. Brown and Copp, *Look to Your Front*, 68.

27. Account of John Swityk as told to Walter Keith, 15 February 2008.

28. Tom Greenlees to the author, 16 February 2002. For the most detailed account of this action, see Brown and Copp, *Look to Your Front*, 78.

29. Luther, *Blood and Honor*, 165.

30. Rifleman Wolfe's recommendation for a decoration was provided by Walter Keith.

31. Gunner Milner remained deeply impressed with Clifford's professionalism. On one occasion when Milner and others from the headquarters of 13th RCA were sheltering in a basement in Carpiquet during a heavy bombardment, the walkout door suddenly burst open, and a small figure tumbled down the steps and landed in a heap on the floor: it was Clifford. He was disheveled and covered in red dust from shattered roofing tiles, but tightly gripped in his hands were a compass and a field service notepad filled with bearings to the offending guns.

32. Col. Clifford, who claimed to witness the incident, says it happened at noon on 8 June, but the Reginas' accounts all place it the following night in the midst of the Panther attack. See Brown's account in Portugal, *We Were There*, 852; interview with Clifford, 25 April 2002; and Reynolds, *Steel Inferno*, 79.

33. Barrett, *History of 13 Canadian Field Regiment*, 39.

34. *Into Action with the 12th Field*, 48–49.

35. Interview with Sergeant James O. Moffat, 21 April 2004, author's collection, provided by Tom Greenless.

36. 13th RCA Intelligence Log, 0145/09.

37. Reynolds, *Steel Inferno*, 78.

38. Margolian, *Conduct Unbecoming*, 91.

39. For a detailed account of Mohnke's murders, and indeed all those by 12th SS in Normandy, see ibid.

40. Zuehlke, *Holding Juno*, 201.

41. Portugal, *We Were There*, 839.

42. Ibid., 840.

43. 7th Brigade battle log, TNA WO 179/2879.

44. Portugal, *We Were There*, 842.

45. Ibid., 843.

46. Ibid., 848.

47. See Gordon Brown's remarkable account of his company's defense of Cardonville in ibid., 833–845. A short version is also available in Brown and Copp, *Look to Your Front*, 79–84.

48. Telephone conversation with Walter Keith, 2012. Hubert Meyer lists this attack as made by the II/26th but is otherwise strangely silent on it; see Meyer, *12th SS*, 57.

49. "Record of Enemy Casualties," Gordon Brown Papers, Saskatchewan Archives; copy courtesy of Walter Keith.

50. Luther, *Blood and Honor*, 166.

51. Stacey, *Victory Campaign*, 137.

52. Meyer, *12th SS*, 184.

53. Foster, *Meeting of Generals*, 324.

54. Meyer, *12th SS*, 186.

Chapter 9: Norrey, 9–10 June

1. Luther, *Blood and Honor*, 169.

2. Quoted in ibid., 170.

3. Zuehlke, *Holding Juno*, 239.

4. Ibid., 240.

5. Margolian, *Conduct Unbecoming*, 107.

6. Luther, *Blood and Honor*, 171.

7. Meyer, *12th SS*, 189.

8. For a discussion of this, see David Wilson, "The Development of Tank-Infantry Co-operation Doctrine in the Canadian Army for the Normandy Campaign of 1944" (MA thesis, University of New Brunswick, 1992).

9. Report of 2nd Canadian Armoured Brigade, 26 June 1944, author's copy, claims that the brigade's delivery regiment brought these forward on 8 June; see paragraph 13. John Marteinson and Michael R. McNorgan, *The Royal Canadian Armoured Corps: An Illustrated History* (Ottawa and Kitchener, ON: Canadian War Museum and Robin Brass Studio, 2000), 244, claim that heavy seas in the Channel meant that the brigade's tank delivery unit, the Elgin Regiment, was not yet ashore.

10. Dempsey's diary of 11 June 1944 mentioned his instructions that 4th Armoured Brigade be retained in the Colomby area. TNA WO 285/9.

11. 4th Armoured Brigade war diary, 1–30 June 1944, TNA WO 171/601.

12. 2nd RMAS remained in the Bray area, supporting the capture of Rots by the Royal Marines and the Chaudieres. On 18 June it redeployed to the airborne bridgehead east of the Orne, and four days later, after the Centaurs were handed over to the Royal Artillery, the Royal Marine gunners started going home on leave. 2nd RMAS war diary, TNA ADM 202/306.

13. *Into Action with the 12th Field*, 49–50.

14. Stacey, *Victory Campaign*, 138.

15. Meyer, *12th SS*, 58.

16. Barrett, *History of 13 Canadian Field Regiment*, 40.

17. Brown and Copp, *Look to Your Front*, 69–70.

18. "Five Shot, Five Tanks . . . ," filed by the Canadian Press on 21 June 1944 by Ross Munro, clipping from unknown newspaper, courtesy of Mike Bechthold.

19. Maj. C. D. A. Tweedale, "First Reinforcements," in *Vanguard*, 126.

20. Marteinson and McNorgan, *Royal Canadian Armoured Corps*, 244.

21. Luther, *Blood and Honor*, 175.

22. Barrett, *History of 13 Canadian Field Regiment*, 41.

23. *Into Action with the 12th Field*, 47

24. Interview with Gunner Geoffrey Hall, 20 April 2004, courtesy of Tom Greenless.

25. Meyer, *12th SS*, 195.

26. Ibid.

27. Ibid., 197.

Conclusion

1. The "Bessin" is the transition zone between the open "Campagne" around Caen and the more familiar bocage to the west of Bayeux (hence Port-en-Bessin north of Bayeux). It is characterized by rolling farmland with large fields divided (generally) by tree lines rather than hedgerows. See the discussion of Norman geography in *ISIS Report on France: volume 2: Normandy*

West of the Seine: Part I, Geography, Inter-Service Topographic Department, May 1943, BR 876 J (11), 19; copy in the Richard Kennedy Papers, MS 2002-510-02, National World War II Museum, New Orleans.

2. See Wolfgang Wette, *The Wehrmacht: History, Myth and Reality* (Cambridge, MA: Harvard University Press, 2006), chap. 5. Former German officers working on Halder's project for the US Army Historical Division in the decade and a half after the war had to agree to his vision that the Wehrmacht was completely innocent of complicity in Hitler's war of genocide, and blame "all the tactical and strategic defeats not on their own mistakes, but rather on a combination of difficult terrain and climatic conditions on the one hand, and Hitler's dilettantism and stubbornness on the other." See 231–232.

3. See Robert M. Citino, *The German Way of War: From the Thirty Years' War to the Third Reich* (Lawrence: University Press of Kansas, 2005).

4. For an excellent discussion of the problems that ideology imparted on 12th SS Division's combat capability, see Mike Sullivan, "Hitler's Teenage Zealots: Fanatics, Combat Motivation and the 12th SS Panzer Division *Hitler-jugend*" (MA thesis, University of New Brunswick, 1997).

5. Hesketh, *Fortitude,* 202.

6. Ibid., 209.

7. Ibid., 210.

8. Howard, *British Intelligence in the Second World War,* 189.

9. Luther, *Blood and Honor,* 180.

10. Stacey, *Victory Campaign,* 140.

11. The regiment's historian, Will R. Bird, lost his only son, Captain Stephen Bird, in the second battle for Authie.

12. The Canadians murdered in the Abbey d'Ardennes garden remained on the missing list until the spring of 1945. Jacques Vico, whose family ran the abbey as a farm, recalled going out to the garden that spring and finding his mother's flowers blooming in a random pattern in disturbed soil. Bodies were discovered, and war crimes investigators soon identified them as the men missing from 7–8 June 1944.

SELECTED BIBLIOGRAPHY

ARCHIVES

Canada

Directorate of History and Heritage, National Defence HQ, Ottawa, Ontario
Library and Archives of Canada, Ottawa, Ontario
Public Archives of Nova Scotia, Halifax, Nova Scotia
University of Toronto Archives, Toronto, Ontario

Great Britain

BBC Archives, Reading
Bodleian Library, Oxford
Churchill College Archives, Cambridge
Imperial War Museum, London
Liddell Hart Centre for Military History, London
The National Archives of Britain, Kew

United States

George Marshall Research Library, Lexington, Virginia
Howard Gottlieb Archives, Boston University, Boston, Massachusetts
The National World War II Museum, New Orleans, Louisiana
Roosevelt Presidential Library, Hyde Park, New York
US 1st Division Archives, Cantigny, Illinois

PUBLISHED AND OTHER SOURCES

Army Headquarters, Historical Section (General Staff). Report No. 42. "The Preliminary Planning for Operation 'OVERLORD': Some Aspects of the Preparations for an Allied Re-entry to North-West Europe, 1940–1944." By Maj. T. M. Hunter, 5 March 1952.
———. Report No. 50. "The Campaign in North-West Europe: Information from German Sources—Part I: German Defence Preparations in the West." By Capt. A. G. Steiger, 30 April 1951.

———. Report No. 50. "The Campaign in North-West Europe: Information from German Sources—Part II: Invasion and the Battle of Normandy, 6 Jun–22 Aug 44." By A. G. Steiger, 14 October 1952.

Atkinson, Rick. *The Guns at Last Light: The War in Western Europe, 1944–1945*. New York: Henry Holt, 2013.

Barbier, Mary Kathryn, *D-Day Deception: Operation Fortitude and the Normandy Invasion*. Westport, CT: Praeger Security International, 2007.

Barrett, Lt. W. W. *The History of 13 Canadian Field Regiment, Royal Canadian Artillery 1940–1945*. N.d., n.p.

"The Battle of the 716. Division in Normandy (6 June to 23 June 1944)." Headquarters, European Command, Office of the Chief Historian, Operational History (German) Branch, MS B-621. N.d.

Bechthold, Mike. "Defending the Normandy Bridgehead: The Battles for Putot-en-Bessin, 7–9 June 1944." In Geoffrey Hayes, Mike Bechthold, and Matt Symes. eds., *Canada and the Second World War: Essays in Honour of Terry Copp*, 367–390. Waterloo, ON: Wilfrid Laurier University Press, 2012.

Beevor, Anthony. *D-Day: The Battle for Normandy*. New York: Viking, 2009.

Bernage, Georges. *Historica, No. 23. Les Canadiens Face a la Hitler Jugend (7–11 Juin 1944): Un Voyage au Bout d l'Enfer*. Bayeux, France: Editions Heimdal, 1991.

———. *The Panzers and the Battle of Normandy, 5 June to 20 July 1944*. Bayeux, France: Editions Heimdal, 2000.

Bird, Will R. *No Retreating Footsteps: The Story of the North Nova Scotia Highlanders*. Amherst, NS: Furlong's Rapid Print and Digital Design, 2007.

Boog, Horst, et al. *Germany and the Second World War*. Vol. 7, *The Strategic Air War in Europe and the War in the West and East Asia 1943–1944/45*. Oxford: Clarendon Press, 2006.

Boss, Lt. Col. W., and Brig. Gen. W. J. Patterson. *Up the Glens: Stormont, Dundas and Glengarry Highlanders 1783–1994*. Cornwall, ON: The Old Book Store, 1995.

Brown, Gordon, and Terry Copp. *Look to Your Front: Regina Rifles, a Regiment at War: 1944–45*. Laurier Centre for Military Strategic and Disarmament Studies. Kitchener-Waterloo, ON: Wilfrid Laurier University Press, 2001.

Buckingham, William F. *D-Day: The First 72 Hours*. Stroud, Gloucestershire: Tempus, 2004.

Buckley, John. *British Armour in the Normandy Campaign 1944*. London: Frank Cass, 2004.

———, ed. *The Normandy Campaign 1944: Sixty Years On*. London: Routledge, 2006.

Canadian Military Headquarters. Report No. 147. "Canadian Participation in the Operations in North-West Europe, 1944, Part I: The Assault and Subsequent Operations of 3 Cdn Inf Div and 2 Cdn Armd Bde, 6–30 June 44." By Major J. R. Martin. N.d.

———. Report No. 167. "The Participation of First Canadian Army in Strategic Planning, 1942." By Maj. G. W. L. Nicholson. 3 December 1946.

———. Report No. 182. "The Strategic Role of First Canadian Army, 1942–1944." By Capt. J. M. Hitsman. 23 May 1949.

Cooper, Matthew. *The German Army 1933–1945*. Chelsea, MI: Scarborough House, 1990.

Copp, Terry. *Fields of Fire: The Canadians in Normandy*. Toronto: University of Toronto Press, 2003.

Copp, Terry, and Robert Vogel. *Maple Leaf Route: Caen*. Alma, ON: Maple Leaf Route, 1983.

Danchev, Alex, and Daniel Todman, eds. *War Diaries 1939–1945: Field Marshall Lord Alanbrooke*. London: Weidenfeld and Nicholson, 2001.

D'Este, Carlo. *Patton: A Genius for War*. New York: HarperCollins, 1995.

Delaney, Doug. *Corps Commanders: Five British and Canadian Generals at War, 1939–45*. Vancouver: University of British Columbia Press, 2011.

Ellis, Maj. L. F. *Victory in the West*. Vol. 1, *The Battle of Normandy*. London: HMSO, 1962.

Engen, Robert. *Canadians under Fire: Infantry Effectiveness in the Second World War*. Montreal-Kingston: McGill-Queen's University Press, 2009.

English, John A. *The Canadian Army and the Normandy Campaign: A Study of Failure in High Command*. New York: Praeger, 1991.

Ferrell, Robert H., ed. *The Eisenhower Diaries*. New York: Norton, 1981.

V Corps Operations in the E.T.O., 6 Jan. 1942–9 May 1945. G-3 Historical Section, V Corps. N.p., n.d.

Ford, Ken. *Battle Zone Normandy: Sword Beach*. Stroud, Gloucestershire: Sutton, 2004.

Foster, Tony. *Meeting of Generals*. Toronto: Metheun, 1986.

Foulds, Tony. "In Support of the Canadians: A British Anti-tank Regiment's First Five Weeks in Normandy." *Canadian Military History* 7, no. 2 (1998): 71–78.

Greenhous, Brereton, et al. *Crucible of War 1939–1945: The Official History of the Royal Canadian Air Force*. Vol. 3. Toronto: University of Toronto Press, 1994.

Gulachsen, Arthur. "The Defeat and Attrition of the 12th SS Panzer Division 'Hitlerjugend': A Case Study, June 6th–July 12th, 1944." MA thesis, University of New Brunswick, 2005.

Hamilton, Nigel. *Montgomery: Master of the Battlefield*. New York: McGraw-Hill, 1983.

Harrison, Gordon. *Cross-Channel Attack: United States Army in World War II: The European Theatre of Operations*. Washington, DC: Office of the Chief of Military History, US Army, 1951.

Hart, Russell A. *Clash of Arms: How the Allies Won in Normandy*. Boulder, CO: Lynne Rienner, 2001.

Hastings, Max. *Overlord: D-Day and the Battle for Normandy 1944*. New York: Simon and Schuster, 1984.

Hayes, Geoffrey, Mike Bechthold, and Matt Symes, eds. *Canada and the Second World War: Essays in Honour of Terry Copp*. Waterloo, ON: Wilfrid Laurier University Press, 2012.

Hesketh, Roger. *Fortitude: The D-Day Deception Campaign*. New York: Overlook Press, 2000.

Hickey, Rev. R. Myles. *The Scarlet Dawn*. Fredericton, NB: Unipress, 1949.

Hinsley, F. H. *British Intelligence in the Second World War*. Abridged edition. Cambridge: Cambridge University Press, 1993.

———. *British Intelligence in the Second World War: Its Influence on Strategy and Operations*. Vol. 3, pt. 2. New York: Cambridge University Press, 1988.

"History of the 21st Panzer Division from Time of Its Formation until the Beginning of the Invasion." Headquarters, European Command, Office of the Chief Historian, Operational History (German) Branch, MS B-441. By Generalleutenant Edgar Feuchtinger. 18 February 1947.

Hogan, David W., Jr. *A Command Post at War: First Army Headquarters in Europe, 1943–45*. Washington, DC: Center of Military History, 2000.

Hogg, Ian V. *German Artillery of World War Two*. London: Greenhill Books, 1997.

Howard, Michael. *British Intelligence in the Second World War*. Vol. 5, *Strategic Deception*. New York: Cambridge University Press, 1990.

Into Action with the 12th Field. N.p., n.d.

Isby, David, ed. *Fighting the Invasion: The German Army at D-Day*. London: Greenhill Books, 2000.

ISIS, Inter-Service Topographical Department. "Report on France, volume 2: Normandy West of the Seine: Part I, Geography." BR 876 J (Restricted). May 1943. National World War II Museum.

———. "Report on France, volume 2: Normandy West of the Seine: Part V(B) Ports." BR 876 J (Restricted). March 1943. National World War II Museum.

Jackson, Lt. Col. H. M., MBE, ED. *The Sherbrooke Regiment (12th Armoured Regiment)*. Privately published, 1958.

Jarymowycz, Roman Johann. *Tank Tactics from Normandy to Lorraine*. Boulder, CO: Lynne Rienner, 2001.

Kurowski, Franz. *Elite Panzer Strike Force: Germany's Panzer Lehr Division in World War II*. Mechanicsburg, PA: Stackpole Books, 2011.

Lackenbauer, P. Whitney, and Chris Madsen, eds. *Kurt Meyer on Trial [A Documentary Record]*. Kingston, ON: Canadian Defence Academy Press, 2007.

Larabee, Eric. *Commander in Chief: Franklin Delano Roosevelt, His Lieutenants and Their War*. Annapolis, MD: US Naval Institute Press, 1987.

Little Black Devils: A History of the Royal Winnipeg Rifles. Winnipeg: Frye, 1983.

Loewen, Gen. Sir Charles. *Memoirs*. Vol. 1. Toronto: Privately published, 1985.

Luther, Craig W. H. *Blood and Honor: The History of the 12th SS Panzer Division "Hitler Youth," 1943–1945*. San Jose, CA: James Bender, 1987.

Malone, Daniel P. "Breaking Down the Wall: Bombarding Force E and Naval Fire Support on Juno Beach." MA thesis, University of New Brunswick, 2005.

Malone, Richard S. *A Portrait of War 1939–1943*. Toronto: Collins, 1983.

Margolian, Howard. *Conduct Unbecoming: The Story of the Murder of Canadian Prisoners of War in Normandy*. Toronto: University of Toronto Press, 1998.

Marteinson, John, and Michael R. McNorgan. *The Royal Canadian Armoured Corps: An Illustrated History*. Ottawa and Kitchener, ON: Canadian War Museum and Robin Brass Studio, 2000.

McNorgan, Michael R. *The Gallant Hussars: A History of the 1st Hussars Regiment, 1856–2004*. Aylmer, ON: The 1st Hussars Cavalry Fund/The Aylmer Express, 2004.

Medland, Stan. "Confrontation in Normandy: The 3rd Canadian Anti-tank Regiment on D-Day." *Canadian Military History* 3, no. 1 (1994): 55–60.

Meyer, Hubert. *The 12th SS: The History of the Hitler Youth Panzer Division*. Vol. 1. Mechanicsburg, PA: Stackpole Books, 2005.

Milner, Marc. *D-Day to Carpiquet: The North Shore Regiment and the Liberation of Europe*. Fredericton, NB: Goose Lane Editions/NB Military Heritage Project, 2006.

———. "The Guns of Bretteville: 13th Field Regiment, RCA, and the Defence of Bretteville-l'Orgueilleuse, 7–10 June 1944." *Canadian Military History* 16, no. 4 (2007): 5–24.

———. "No Ambush, No Defeat: The Advance of the 9th Canadian Infantry Brigade on D+1." In Geoffrey Hayes, Mike Bechthold, and Matt Symes, eds., *Canada and the Second World War: Essays in Honour of Terry Copp*, 335–366. Waterloo, ON: Wilfrid Laurier University Press, 2012.

———. "Reflections on Caen, Bocage and the Gap: A Naval Historian's Critique of the Normandy Campaign." *Canadian Military History* 7, no. 2 (1998): 7–17.

———. "Stopping the Panzers: Reassessing the Role of 3rd Canadian Infantry Division in Normandy, 7–10 June 1944." *Journal of Military History* 74 (2010): 491–522.

Montgomery, Field Marshal, The Viscount Montgomery of Alamein. *Normandy to the Baltic*. London: Hutchinson, 1947.

Nicholson, G. W. L. *The Gunners of Canada: The History of the Royal Regiment of Canadian Artillery*. Vol. 2. Toronto: McClelland and Stewart, 1972.

North-West Europe 1944–45: The Achievement of 21st Army Group. London: HMSO, 1953.

"Operation 'Neptune': Eastern Task Force Naval Operation Orders." 8 May 1944. The National Archives, Kew.

"Operation 'Neptune': Force 'J' Naval Operation Orders." 19 May 1944. The National Archives, Kew.

"OVERLORD: 1 Corps Operation Order No. 1." 5 May 1944. The National Archives, Kew.

"OVERLORD: Royal Canadian Artillery 3 Canadian Infantry Division, Operation Order No. 1." 15 May 1944. The National Archives, Kew.

"OVERLORD: 7th Canadian Infantry Brigade Group Operation Order No. 1." 18 May 1944. The National Archives, Kew.

"OVERLORD: 3 Canadian Infantry Division Operation Order No. 1." 13 May 1944. The National Archives, Kew.

The Papers of Dwight David Eisenhower: The War Years III. Ed. Alfred D. Chandler. Baltimore: Johns Hopkins University Press, 1970.

Pemberton, Brig. A. L., MC. *The Development of Artillery Tactics and Equipment*. London: War Office, 1950.

Perrigault, Jean-Claude. *21.Panzerdivision*. Bayeux, France: Heimdal, 2002.

Portugal, Jean. *We Were There: The Army*. Vol. 4. Toronto: Royal Canadian Military Institute Heritage Society, 1998.

Reid, Brian A. *Named by the Enemy: A History of the Royal Winnipeg Rifles*. Altona, MB: Robin Brass/The Royal Winnipeg Rifles, 2010.

"Report of the Court of Enquiry re: Shooting of Allied Prisoners of War by the Germans Armed Forces in the Vicinity of Le Mesnil-Patry, Les Saullets, Buron and Authie Normandy, 7–11 June 1944." Directorate of History and Heritage, NDHQ, Ottawa.

Reuth, Ralf Georg. *Rommel: The End of a Legend*. London: Haus Books, 2008.

Reynolds, Michael. *Eagles and Bulldogs in Normandy 1944: The American 29th Infantry Division from Omaha to St Lo and the British 3rd Infantry Division from Sword to Caen*. Havertown, PA: Casemate, 2003.

———. *Steel Inferno: 1 SS Panzer Corps in Normandy*. New York: Sarpedon, 1997.

Rickard, John N. *The Politics of Command: Lieutenant-General A. G. L. McNaughton and the Canadian Army, 1939–1943*. Toronto: University of Toronto Press, 2010.

Ritgen, Helmut. *The Western Front: Memoirs of a Panzer Lehr Officer.* Winnipeg: J. J. Fedorowicz, 1995.

Ross, Lt. Col. Richard M., OBE. *The History of the 1st Battalion Cameron Highlanders of Ottawa (MG).* Privately published, n.d.

Roy, Reginald. *Ready for the Fray: The History of the Canadian Scottish Regiment (Princess Mary's) 1920–2002.* Calgary, AB: Bunker to Bunker Publishing, 2002.

Ruffee, Lt. G. E. M., and L./Bdr. J. B. Dickie. *The History of the 14 Field Regiment Royal Canadian Artillery 1940–1945.* Amsterdam: Wereldbibliotheek NV, 1945.

Scarfe, Norman. *Assault Division: A History of the 3rd Division from the Invasion of Normandy to the Surrender of Germany.* London: Collins, 1947.

Shulman, Milton. *Defeat in the West.* London: Secker and Warburg, 1947.

Speidel, Hans. *Invasion 1944: Rommel and the Normandy Campaign.* Chicago: Henry Regnery, 1950.

Stacey, Colonel C. P. *Six Years of War: Official History of the Canadian Army in the Second World War.* Vol. 1, *The Army in Canada, Britain and the Pacific.* Ottawa: Queen's Printer, 1957.

———. *The Victory Campaign: The Operations in North-West Europe, 1944–1945.* Vol. 3, *The Official History of the Canadian Army in the Second World War.* Ottawa: Queen's Printer, 1960.

Stanton, Shelby. *World War II Order of Battle.* New York: Galahad Books, 1984.

Steinart, Marlis G. *Hitler's War and the Germans: Public Mood and Attitude during the Second World War.* Athens: Ohio University Press, 1977.

Sullivan, Mike. "Hitler's Teenage Zealots: Fanatics, Combat Motivation and the 12th SS Panzer Division *Hitlerjugend*." MA thesis, University of New Brunswick, 1997.

Swettenham, John. *McNaughton.* Vol. 2, *1939–1943.* Toronto: Ryerson Press, 1969.

Szamveber, Norbert. *Waffen-SS Armour in Normandy: The Combat History of SS-Panzer Regiment 12 and SS-Panzerjäger Abteilung 12 Normandy 1944, Based on Their Original War Diaries.* Solihull, England: Helion, 2012.

"12th SS Panzer Division 'Hitlerjugend,' June to September 1944." Headquarters, European Command, Office of the Chief Historian, Operational History (German) Branch, MS P-164. Lt. Col. Hubert Meyer, June 1954.

Vanguard: The Fort Garry Horse in the Second World War. N.p., n.d.

Wette, Wolfgang. *The Wehrmacht: History, Myth and Reality.* Cambridge, MA: Harvard University Press, 2006.

Williams, Ethan Rawls, LCDR USN. "50 Div in Normandy: A Critical Analysis of the British 50th (Northumbrian) Division on D-Day and in the Battle of Normandy." MA thesis, US Army Command and General Staff College, 2007.

Wilmot, Chester. *The Struggle for Europe*. London: Collins, 1952.

Wilson, David. "The Development of Tank-Infantry Co-operation Doctrine in the Canadian Army for the Normandy Campaign of 1944." MA thesis, University of New Brunswick, 1992.

World War II German Military Studies. Vol. 10, pt. 4, *The OKW War Diary Series*. New York: Garland, 1979.

World War II German Military Studies. Vol. 12, pt. 5, *The Western Theatre*. New York: Garland, 1979.

Zapporzan, Lawrence James. "Rad's War: A Biographical Study of Sydney Radley-Walters from Mobilization to the End of the Normandy Campaign 1944." MA thesis, University of New Brunswick, 2001.

Zetterling, Niklas. *Normandy 1944: German Military Organization, Combat Power and Organizational Effectiveness*. Winnipeg: J. J. Fedorowicz, 2000.

Zuehlke, Mark. *Holding Juno: Canada's Heroic Defence of the D-Day Beaches: June 7–12, 1944*. Toronto: Douglas and MacIntyre, 2005.

INDEX

He has fallen into the same trap and pushed to regiments
under the carpet

5th and 6th Royal Berkshire regiments.
Interviewed at 40th reunion. names withheld

1 Our joint Task. Lead the canadians up the beach
on D day
   Take or kill bead defences. Become directors
   of traffic to get canadians off the beach and on
   their way.

   5th Landed ahead at Courseulles-ser-mer
        We had been practicing to take a gun position
        that looked over the harbour entrance
        Late photo's showed French work; mussel beds.
        That was our way in
        We went up the beach very little resistance
        walked across the mussel beds to the door
        Kocked it opened   Handy Hoc object taken
        no shots fired
        Other had similar stories
        They all asked where are the canadians?
        They were slow moving up the beach and
        took a number of casualties as a result

   6th Landed at Bernieres-sur-mer.
        On approach noted germans firing on fixed line
        Told pilot not to drop ramp. and chaps to go over
        the side and watch the sounds
        They all got to sea wall. Grenades sew end of that one
        Canadians slow getting up the beach
        We got some tanks off the beach they then stopped
        until some of our unit stopped the german
        anti Tank gun outside of village
        They then stoped for tea à rum lot

   Visit Bernieres and find Rue du Royal Berkshires